# social attitudes

*The fifth report 1995-1996*

in Northern Ireland

# social attitudes

*The fifth report 1995-1996*

## in Northern Ireland

*Edited by*

RICHARD BREEN

PAULA DEVINE

LIZANNE DOWDS

**APPLETREE PRESS**

First published by
The Appletree Press Ltd
19–21 Alfred Street
Belfast BT2 8DL
1996

© The contributors, 1996

Index compiled by Helen Litton

All rights reserved. No part of this
publication may be reproduced or
transmitted in any form or by any means,
electronic or mechanical, photocopying,
recording or in any information or retrieval
system, without prior permission, in
writing, from the publisher.

A catalogue record for this book is available from the British Library.

ISBN 0-86281-593-2

Printed in Ireland

# Contents

The contributors 7

Introduction 9
Richard Breen, Paula Devine and Lizanne Dowds

1. Public support for democratic values in Northern Ireland 13
   Bernadette C. Hayes and Ian McAllister

2. Who wants a United Ireland? Constitutional preferences among Catholics and Protestants 33
   Richard Breen

3. Informal care in Northern Ireland 49
   Eileen Evason and Gillian Robinson

4. Women and work 70
   Janet Trewsdale and John Kremer

5. Race, ethnicity and prejudice in Northern Ireland 94
   John D. Brewer and Lizanne Dowds

6. Satisfaction with health services in Northern Ireland 112
   Ann Largey and Ciaran O'Neill

7. National identity 140
   Karen Trew

8. Gender discrimination among married full-time employees in Northern Ireland: some initial findings 153
   John Spencer, Mary Trainor and Boyd Black

9. Community relations, equality and the future 178
   Tony Gallagher

Appendix 1: Technical details of the survey 193
Alan McClelland

Appendix 2: Using NISA data 209

Appendix 3: The questionnaires 211

Index 279

# The Contributors

Richard Breen
Professor of Sociology and Director of the Centre for Social Research, The Queen's University of Belfast

John D. Brewer
Professor of Sociology, The Queen's University of Belfast

Paula Devine
Research Fellow, Centre for Social Research, The Queen's University of Belfast

Lizanne Dowds
Research Fellow, Centre for Social Research, The Queen's University of Belfast

Boyd Black
Senior Lecturer, Department of Economics, The Queen's University of Belfast

Eileen Evason
Professor, Department of Social Administration and Policy, University of Ulster

Tony Gallagher
Reader in Education, The Queen's University of Belfast

Bernadette C. Hayes
Reader, Department of Sociology and Social Policy, The Queen's University of Belfast

John Kremer
Senior Lecturer, School of Psychology, The Queen's University of Belfast

Ann Largey
Lecturer, Department of Economics, The Queen's University of Belfast

Ian McAllister
Professor, Department of Government, University of Manchester

Alan McClelland
Survey Manager, Central Survey Unit, Policy Planning and Research Unit

Ciaran O'Neill
Lecturer, Department of Economics, The Queen's University of Belfast

Gillian Robinson
Lecturer, Department of Social Administration and Policy, University of Ulster

John Spencer
Professor of Economics and Director of the School of Social Sciences, The Queen's University of Belfast

Mary Trainor
Senior Research Officer, Department of Economics, The Queen's University of Belfast

Karen Trew
Senior Lecturer, School of Psychology, The Queen's University of Belfast

Janet Trewsdale
Senior Lecturer, Department of Economics, The Queen's University of Belfast

# Introduction

Richard Breen, Paula Devine and Lizanne Dowds

This is the fifth volume of *Social Attitudes in Northern Ireland*, reporting some of the findings of the Northern Ireland Social Attitudes (NISA) survey carried out in 1994. The NISA survey has now been fielded on six occasions – annually from 1989 to 1991 and again from 1992 to 1995. Preparations are underway both for the 1996 survey and for the sixth volume of *Social Attitudes*, which will draw on the data collected in 1995.

The main use to which the NISA survey has so far been put is in the reporting and analysis of the attitudes held by the people of Northern Ireland to a range of issues, and most of the contributors to this volume follow in that tradition. However, the survey provides increasing scope for comparative analysis. In particular, because the survey has been running for several years now, it is becoming ever more valuable in revealing changes in attitudes over time. In the present volume Tony Gallagher's chapter on community relations, equality and the future makes use of such time-series data. However, the potential for charting the evolution of social attitudes has never been exploited to anything like its maximum extent. Meanwhile, recent political events in Northern Ireland make the case for such analysis even more compelling. For example, the 1994 survey on which we report in this volume was undertaken some six months before the paramilitary groups announced their cease-fires; the 1995 survey was carried out some seven or eight months after these events. When we come to analyse the latter data it will be interesting indeed to see what impact these developments might have had on issues relating to community relations or on such things as people's constitutional preferences.

One difficulty faced by researchers who might wish to undertake time-series analyses using the NISA data is that all topics cannot be included every year. The NISA survey has a modular format: groups of questions relating to a specific issue are included in the survey in some years but not in others. One consequence of this is that, although we may not have data from the survey on a given topic in every year, there is a very wide range of issues that have been included in, say, two or three years. In the present volume we have added an appendix (Appendix 2) that summarises the modules fielded in each year. We hope that this will help anyone who might want to carry out their own time-series analyses. The data themselves are publicly available from the Economic and Social Research Council's Data Archive at the University of Essex.

As well as the potential for time-series analyses, the NISA survey can also be used to make comparisons with Great Britain (GB) – something that a number of our contributors do. This is possible because NISA began life as an extension of the British Social Attitudes (BSA) survey, which was started in 1983 by Social and Community Planning Research (SCPR). NISA remains an SCPR survey, ensuring continuing strict comparability between the Northern Ireland and the GB survey, as well as maintaining the independence of the survey – SCPR continues to have final responsibility for the questionnaires. With the exception of the module of questions dealing with community relations in Northern Ireland, all the modules on the NISA survey are also included in the BSA survey. Comparisons are therefore possible and, because they are based on identical questions, somewhat less problematic than is often the case. Scope for comparative research is extended by the inclusion of a module that is fielded simultaneously in over 20 countries across four continents. This is done under the auspices of the International Social Survey Programme (ISSP). In 1993 the module dealt with the environment; in 1994 it explored changing gender roles and in 1995 it covered beliefs about national identity.

As is now usual in these collections the various authors were approached by the editors and asked to write a chapter on a broadly defined topic. How they did this and what specific issues they chose to examine was left up to them. Our major task as editors was to ensure that the volume was as stylistically coherent as we could make it. The analysis, interpretation and reporting of the results are solely the responsibility of the authors themselves.

There can be no doubt that there is remarkable diversity in the views of the adult population of Northern Ireland, some entirely unexpected, some less so. Richard Breen looks at preferences concerning the long-term constitutional future of Northern Ireland. He finds that although around 90 per cent of Protestants favour retention of the Union with Great Britain, among Catholics there is much more uncertainty with a substantial minority (about a quarter in 1994) saying that they too wish to retain the Union. Karen Trew focuses on the way in which people describe their national identity: overwhelmingly, Protestants choose the labels 'British' or 'Ulster' while Catholics prefer 'Irish'. However, a not insignificant proportion of both communities pick 'Northern Irish'. Who are these people – do they differ in significant ways from the other members of their community group? John Brewer and Lizanne Dowds examine the link between national identity and attitudes towards ethnic minority groups and point out that those with the closest identification with Britain are those who have most absorbed its racist popular culture. In the final chapter of this collection, Tony Gallagher reviews the state of community relations in Northern Ireland and comments that the 1994 survey results are consistent with a sense that Northern Ireland was on a knife-edge at that time. Bernadette Hayes and Ian McAllister highlight the dramatically low levels of political trust among Catholics in Northern Ireland and contrast this with the fact that Protestants have some of the highest levels of political trust and efficacy in the United Kingdom. The implications that this has for maintaining a sustainable democracy in Northern Ireland are discussed frankly by the authors. Gender issues are touched on in several chapters. Has the scope for caring for elderly relatives reached saturation point among middle-aged women in Northern Ireland? What are the accommodations that working mothers must make to remain in paid employment? Is it possible to compare the earnings of men and women on an equal basis? Finally, just who is happy with health services (and why) is explored and discussed by Ann Largey and Ciaran O'Neill in the context of the Patient's Charter.

**Acknowledgements**

The first three years of the NISA survey were made possible by financial support from the Central Community Relations Unit (CCRU) and the Nuffield Foundation. The securing of funding from Northern Ireland government departments has made possible the survey's continuation and this has been due in no small part to the efforts of CCRU and the Policy Planning and Research Unit (PPRU).

The survey fieldwork is carried out by the Central Survey Unit and particular thanks are due to Kevin Sweeney and Alan McClelland. Final responsibility for the form and content of the survey rests with SCPR who also undertake the coding and data preparation required to make the survey accessible to researchers.

At the Centre for Social Research, Queen's University, Lois McCammond did an excellent job of putting the draft chapters into a common layout. We would also like to express our appreciation of the efforts made by the chapter authors, all of whom produced their drafts in the face of unreasonable deadlines and cheerfully tolerated our interference with their texts. Finally we would like to thank the people of Northern Ireland without whose help there would be no NISA data to analyse.

# 1

# Public Support for Democratic Values in Northern Ireland

Bernadette C. Hayes and Ian McAllister

**Introduction**

The Northern Ireland conflict has traditionally been characterised as a sectarian conflict between two religious communities, Protestant and Catholic. Although this view has often been disputed over the past quarter of a century, mainly by Marxists, few social scientists question the basic proposition that the major divide, or the principal source of political identity in Northern Ireland, is religious affiliation. Although religion may be related to other social cleavages, such as class, and although it may act as a surrogate for the territorial aspirations of particular groups in Northern Ireland (Ruane and Todd, 1992; O'Dowd, 1991; Moxon-Browne, 1983, 1991; Fulton, 1988; Bruce, 1986; Rose, 1971), religious affiliation still constitutes the core division and the primary determinant of electoral choice and political opinion (Hayes and McAllister, 1995; Coulter, 1994; Curtice and Gallagher, 1990).

While religion may determine electoral choice, it is not clear how religion influences democratic values. Popular support for the central tenets of democracy – regular, competitive and free elections – is a prerequisite for the successful operation of the democratic process. Although Northern Ireland maintained formal democratic institutions from 1921 to 1972, the province was not a competitive democracy in the conventional sense, since there was no possibility that the Protestant and unionist majority would ever lose an election, nor that the Catholic and nationalist opposition could ever win. It was a hegemonic state in which one community enjoyed permanent government, while the other community was consigned to permanent political opposition (O'Leary and Arthur, 1990). Since the introduction of direct rule in 1972, even limited local democracy has been withdrawn from the province, with the partial (and short-lived) exceptions of the 1973 Assembly, the 1975 Constitutional Convention and the 1982 Assembly, all of which failed in their goal of re-establishing devolution.

This chapter examines the prevalence among ordinary citizens of democratic values in Northern Ireland, using the 1994 NISA Survey. We examine how popular support for democratic values in Northern Ireland differs from other parts of the United Kingdom, and the extent to which these values vary between Protestants and Catholics. Based on Northern Ireland's limited experience of democracy in the twentieth century and the levels of political violence that have occurred since 1968, we might expect popular support for democratic values to be significantly lower in the province than elsewhere in the United Kingdom. We then examine which socio-economic groups within the two communities are most likely to exhibit democratic values. Finally, we assess the influence of support for democratic values on constitutional preferences and party political support, questions of major current importance as the British and Irish governments seek to initiate discussions between all the political parties on the constitutional future of Northern Ireland.

## Values and the Democratic Process

Widespread popular support for democratic values lies at the core of any democratic system. In line with their importance for the survival and legitimacy of democratic systems, researchers have sought to identify a single, underlying set of values about which there is a general, popular consensus. To the extent that these values are prevalent within the society and form an integral part of the political culture, democratic procedures will be maintained; to the extent that they are distributed unevenly between social groups, the democratic system may be placed under threat. Despite many opinion surveys, dispersed in time and space, there is as yet no agreement on what constitutes a core set of democratic values. However, the two major dimensions about which there is most agreement assess citizens' feelings of political efficacy towards the political system and their trust in government (see McAllister, 1992, p. 42). These two dimensions form the basis for the analysis below.

*Political efficacy* is defined as the belief that a citizen can influence the political process and that public officials and political leaders are both responsive and responsible to the electorate. Angus Campbell and his collaborators identified the concept over 40 years ago when they defined political efficacy as 'the feeling that individual political action does have, or can have, an impact on the political process ... the feeling that political and social change is possible, and that the individual citizen can play a part in bringing about this change' (Campbell et al., 1954, p. 187). Although political efficacy has been measured by a variety of survey items (for reviews, see Hayes and Bean, 1993; Abramson, 1983), all focus on the underlying view that citizens believe that governments will act in their best interests and remain responsive to the demands that they make upon them.

The second dimension of support for democratic values concerns popular feelings of *political trust*. Although political efficacy is highly correlated with feelings of trust in government, the two are conceptually distinct (see Craig et al., 1990). As Lane (1959) has pointed out, whereas efficacy assesses feelings of personal instrumentation, or how individuals perceive their treatment if approached by an elected representative or an official, trust assesses more broadly based values about how government and its representatives act within the society as a whole. Moreover, while feelings of efficacy have shown a gradual decline in the United States since the end of the Second World War, there has been a much more dramatic decrease in levels of political trust (Dalton, 1988; Abramson, 1983). Like efficacy, political trust has also been measured in a variety of ways in survey research; however, all of these measures assess the degree to which respondents consider that elected officials and governments act in the interests of the society as a whole.

In summary, political efficacy and trust are two central concepts in contemporary theories of political participation and democratic politics. In fact, political efficacy and trust are considered to be the two key measures which indicate the overall health of a democratic system. When it was discovered that most Americans felt relatively efficacious towards government in the 1950s and early 1960s, this finding was seen as evidence of stability and the government's effectiveness in responding to popular concerns. But when feelings of powerlessness and a mistrust of government became widespread during the late 1960s and throughout the 1970s – following the turmoil of the Vietnam War and the scandal of Watergate – there was concern that these developments might ultimately pose a threat to the legitimacy of the established democratic order. Consonant with their theoretical status, this chapter investigates the nature and prevalence of both these concepts within Northern Ireland.

**Religious and National Differences in Democratic Values**
The different political experiences of the four nations within the United Kingdom (England, Wales, Scotland and Northern Ireland) would suggest that there should be significant variations in democratic values between the citizens of each nation. Although the United Kingdom is constitutionally a unitary state, in practice each of the four nations retains its own national identity and, in some cases, the major

attributes of self-government. Although Wales lost its status as a separate principality in 1536, it did not lose its national identity, which is underpinned by the Welsh language. Scotland existed as a separate kingdom under its own monarch for a century before the union of 1707 abolished the Scottish parliament. Even today, Scotland retains its own legal and educational systems, which coexist with their English counterparts. Although Southern Ireland ceded from the United Kingdom in 1921, Northern Ireland has remained as an integral part of the United Kingdom, albeit with a radically different party system from that found elsewhere in the United Kingdom, as well as the operation of devolved self-government until 1972. These very different historical experiences might lead us to expect that public support for democratic values would differ considerably across the four nations of the United Kingdom.

Arguing against this hypothesis are the forces of political socialisation and modernisation. The roots of fundamental political values are often linked to political socialisation, to everyday political experiences and to contacts between citizens and politicians or bureaucrats. In a unitary political system based on equal representation for all parts of the United Kingdom in the Westminster parliament, these are aspects of the political process which should be experienced and perceived in a similar way by most voters, regardless of where they live. The political experiences or perceptions of a voter living in Inverness should not, in this view, differ from the experiences of a voter living in Ipswich or Ilfracombe. Similarly, perceptions and images of politics are conveyed by a predominantly national mass media; this might be expected to create a uniformity of political views, suppressing whatever historical and regional differences remain in the political culture. The combined influence of political socialisation and modernisation should ensure that support for democratic values differs little across the four nations of the United Kingdom.

To test these two contrasting hypotheses, we compare support for political efficacy and trust in England, Scotland, Wales and Northern Ireland, with the Northern Ireland estimates being disaggregated for the two religious communities. Political efficacy and trust are usually assessed by a battery of items, all designed to capture the respondent's sense of political competence and his or her sense of trust in the major political institutions and actors. The 1994 NISA survey contained ten items measuring popular attitudes towards these two dimensions of political beliefs. The questions were asked in Britain as well as in Northern Ireland; support for each of them is shown in Table 1. A factor analysis, the results of which are reported in the appendix to this chapter (see Table A1, page 31), showed that each group of items formed a single factor under the respective headings of efficacy and trust.

Popular support for political efficacy in Northern Ireland is, by any standards, low, and the levels differ little between Protestants and Catholics. A clear majority

## Table 1
### Support for political efficacy and trust by nation

|  | Northern Ireland |  |  | Great Britain |  |  |
|---|---|---|---|---|---|---|
|  | Prot | Cath | All | Eng | Wales | Scot |
| *Political efficacy* |  |  | (% disagree) |  |  |  |
| 1. People like me have no say in what the government does. | 14 | 14 | 14 | 24 | 10 | 23 |
| 2. Sometimes politics and government seem so complicated that a person like me cannot really understand what is going on. | 17 | 18 | 18 | 20 | 26 | 11 |
| 3. Those we elect as MPs lose touch with people pretty quickly. | 12 | 10 | 11 | 13 | 17 | 23 |
| 4. It doesn't really matter which party is in power, in the end things go on much the same. | 26 | 17 | 22 | 35 | 24 | 37 |
| 5. Parties are only interested in people's votes, not their opinions. | 13 | 15 | 14 | 16 | 8 | 25 |
| *Political trust* |  |  |  |  |  |  |
| How much do you trust... | (% say 'almost always' or 'most of the time') |  |  |  |  |  |
| 6. A UK government of <u>any</u> party to place the needs of the nation above the interests of their own party? | 29 | 13 | 22 | 25 | 15 | 32 |
| 7. Politicians of <u>any</u> party in the UK to tell the truth when they are in a tight corner? | 12 | 7 | 10 | 9 | 13 | 14 |
| 8. Local councillors of <u>any</u> party to place the needs of their area above the interests of their political party? | 38 | 27 | 34 | 33 | 43 | 19 |
| 9. Top civil servants to stand firm against a minister who wants to provide false information to parliament? | 41 | 23 | 33 | 31 | 31 | 34 |
| 10. Police not to bend the rules in trying to get a conviction? | 64 | 27 | 48 | 50 | 52 | 43 |
| (*n*) | (381) | (278) | (659) | (973) | (62) | 105) |

of the respondents agree with each of the five statements, reflecting a degree of alienation and a sense of powerlessness about how the political system operates. For example, only 14 per cent of the respondents disagree with the statement that 'people like me have no say in what the government does', and there is no difference in this view between the two religious communities. The only item on which there is a significant difference in Protestant–Catholic views is whether the party in power is unable to change things; in this case 26 per cent of Protestants disagree with the statement compared to 17 per cent of Catholics. This presumably reflects the Protestant community's greater experience with government, and as the majority community, their guaranteed role in any future system of devolved government.

Although public support for political efficacy is stronger in Britain than in Northern Ireland, comparatively high levels of alienation are still apparent in Britain. In Wales, for example, the average proportion saying that they disagreed with the five items on this topic in Table 1 is 17 per cent, compared to 16 per cent for the Northern Ireland respondents. In England, support for efficacy is higher, with an average of 22 per cent disagreeing, and Scotland has the highest figure in the United Kingdom, at 24 per cent. There are particularly significant variations between the various parts of the United Kingdom: the Welsh believe that they have the least say in what government does, while the Scots exhibit the greatest levels of powerlessness. However, the Scots are also the group who are most likely to believe that they can keep in touch with their MPs. The Welsh are most likely to be fatalistic about what parties can accomplish while in power, as well as being the most likely to be cynical about the role of parties.

In contrast to political efficacy, significant differences emerge consistently among Protestants and Catholics in relation to political trust. In all cases, Protestants are clearly the more trusting of the two groups. Not only do Protestants rank ahead of Catholics on all five items, but this is particularly the case in relation to their views on the trustworthiness of government, the practices of top civil servants, and most significant of all, the operation of the police force. For example, 29 per cent of Protestants believe that UK governments place the needs of the nation above the interests of their own political party, over twice the proportion of Catholics who agree with this statement. About two-fifths of Protestants trust senior civil servants to ensure that politicians tell the truth, compared to less than one quarter of Catholics. And nearly two-thirds of Protestants believe that the police would not bend the rules to secure a conviction, while only just over one quarter of Catholics share this view.

The differences in the levels of political trust between the other parts of the United Kingdom are much less dramatic, although major differences remain in relation to trust in the United Kingdom government and trust in local councillors. For example, the Welsh are particularly distrustful of the government placing the needs of the nation above the interests of their own party, while the Scots are particularly cynical about the role of local councillors. Nevertheless, the average level of trust in England is 30 per cent, in Wales 31 per cent, and in Scotland, 28 per cent. This compares with an average level of trust of 37 per cent among Northern Ireland Protestants, but only 19 per cent among Catholics.

The differing experiences of the two religious communities have obviously had a major impact on their feelings towards the political system, their beliefs about how it operates and who it benefits. In the rest of the United Kingdom, the aggregate differences do not emerge as very large, suggesting that the twin forces of modernisation and political socialisation have overcome traditional, historically-based variations – albeit with some variations on single items, which reflect different views of particular regional institutions, such as local government. In Northern Ireland, however, direct experiences with the political system over the past century, and more specifically since the start of the Troubles in 1968, are likely to have created the major differences in political trust observed above. Since widespread trust in the basic institutions of the state is a principal prerequisite for the successful operation of the democratic process, the low levels of Catholic trust shown here will obviously impact on the success of any future devolved government in Northern Ireland.

## Democratic Types in Theory and Practice

Research on public opinion and democratic politics has argued that the persistence and health of democratic systems depends on having citizens with different democratic outlooks (Bachrach, 1967). Democratic systems require citizens who are politically involved, who will join political parties, debate the merits of different policies, and who will provide the personnel that makes the political process work. But too many activists and too high a level of political involvement in a political system may result in instability. For example, the collapse of democracy in many South American countries in the 1960s and 1970s came about because there was too much political interest within the population, rather than too little (Higley and Gunther, 1992). But equally, extensive political apathy will contribute to corruption and a lack of turnover within the political elite, and ultimately undermine the notion of accountability that is at the heart of democratic politics. Political apathy was a major contributing factor to the collapse of democracy in Lebanon in the 1970s (Mackey, 1989).

Four democratic types, based on responses to the efficacy and trust questions, can be identified (Figure 1). Citizens who have low scores on both of the sets of

### Figure 1
### A typology of democratic types

|  | Efficacy Low | Efficacy High |
|---|---|---|
| **Trust** Low | Weak democrat | Skeptic |
| **Trust** High | Optimist | Strong democrat |

questions are obviously weak democrats; they have little trust in the political process, or belief that it will serve them well. In most cases, weak democrats also have very low levels of political interest. Their weak sense of democracy is therefore offset by a general sense of political apathy, so that their weak commitment to democratic norms does not provide any motivation to remedy the problem. At the other extreme, strong democrats are those who have high scores on the two scales; they have both interest in and commitment to the democratic process. The two intermediate categories may be termed optimists and skeptics. Optimists are characterised by high trust but a low degree of efficacy: they have faith in political institutions and individuals in the abstract, but little sense that they themselves would receive fair treatment. Skeptics take a contrary view: they believe that they would be treated well, but have little trust in politics.

Estimating the distribution of these four ideal types across the United Kingdom shows that in each of the four nations, weak democrats are by far the largest of the four groups (Table 2). They are most numerous in Wales, making up 53 per cent of the population, least numerous in England, at 43 per cent, and constitute just under half of all citizens in Northern Ireland and Scotland. Optimists are the

## Table 2
### Democratic types in the United Kingdom (%)

|  | Northern Ireland | England | Wales | Scotland |
|---|---|---|---|---|
| Weak democrats | 49 | 43 | 53 | 49 |
| Skeptics | 9 | 15 | 4 | 15 |
| Optimists | 31 | 23 | 24 | 14 |
| Strong democrats | 11 | 18 | 19 | 21 |
| Total | 100 | 100 | 100 | 100 |
| (n) | (689) | (812) | (50) | (92) |

Note: For the purposes of this analysis, only individuals who responded favourably to at least three of the five statements have been classified as individuals expressing either high levels of political efficacy or trust.

second largest group in three of the four nations, the exception being Scotland where strong democrats are more numerous. Indeed, in Northern Ireland, no less than 31 per cent of citizens are optimists. The distribution of skeptics also varies substantially, from a low of 4 per cent in Wales to 15 per cent in England and Scotland. Finally, strong democrats, the pool from whom most political activists are drawn, make up just 11 per cent of the citizens in Northern Ireland, compared to twice that number in Scotland and slightly less in England and Wales.

Although popular support for democratic ideals is somewhat lower in Northern Ireland than in Great Britain, it is important to note, however, that there are also significant variations between the two religious communities within Northern Ireland in relation to this issue. For example, although weak democrats are again by far the largest of the four groups, they are more numerous among Catholics (60 per cent), than Protestants (40 per cent). A similar, though converse, pattern emerges in relation to the religious distribution of strong democrats. Here, it is Protestants (13 per cent) who significantly outnumber Catholics (8 per cent) in terms of both their belief in and commitment to the democratic process. Furthermore, this relationship holds regardless of levels of political interest. Even among individuals who express high levels of political interest, Protestants again outnumber Catholics by a substantial margin; 24 per cent as compared to only 16 per cent.

In principle, then, the prerequisites for popular support for democratic norms appear to exist in Northern Ireland in much the same way as they do in other parts of the United Kingdom. Two points support this interpretation. First, weak democrats exist in approximately equal proportions compared to the rest of Britain. Second, there are substantially more optimists in the province than elsewhere in Britain. Against this, however, is the comparative paucity of strong democrats, particularly among Catholics in Northern Ireland. Moreover, this relationship remains regardless of level of political interest; a crucial factor given the undoubtedly higher levels of political activism in Northern Ireland than in other parts of the United Kingdom.

**Identifying Democratic Citizens**
Although levels of public support for democratic values are significantly lower among Catholics than Protestants, to what extent can these differences be explained by other factors, such as gender, age or education? In other words, what roles, if any, do differences in age, education, or socio-economic status play in accounting for the religiously divided views of Northern Ireland citizens in relation to their support for democratic values? To examine this question, Figure 2 presents the results from a series of multiple regression analyses of political efficacy and trust (our two dependent variables) on respondent's religious affiliation as well as eight other socio-demographic characteristics, including gender, marital status, age, education, and employment status (the independent variables). However, to facilitate parsimony in presentation, only variables with a statistically significant, or differential, influence are shown. The variables, their coding and their means and standard deviations are presented in the appendix to this chapter, Table A2, page 32. For the multiple regression analyses, two figures are depicted: partial regression coefficients ($b$s), which show the unit change in the dependent variable by a unit change in the independent variable, and standardised coefficients (betas), which show the overall impact of the independent variable in question.

The results in Figure 2 are consistent with the conclusions of our earlier analyses. Even allowing for the influence of a range of other background characteristics, such as age, occupation or gender (included in the models but not shown as the results were not statistically significant), whereas religious affiliation is a key factor in distinguishing levels of political trust among the Northern Irish population as a whole, it has no impact in relation to political efficacy. Rather, only in relation to political trust is religious background a divisive predictor of attitudes within this society. Net of all other factors, Protestants are notably more likely to express a more trusting opinion in relation to their political representatives than Catholics.

## Figure 2
### The influence of socio-demographic factors on political efficacy and trust*

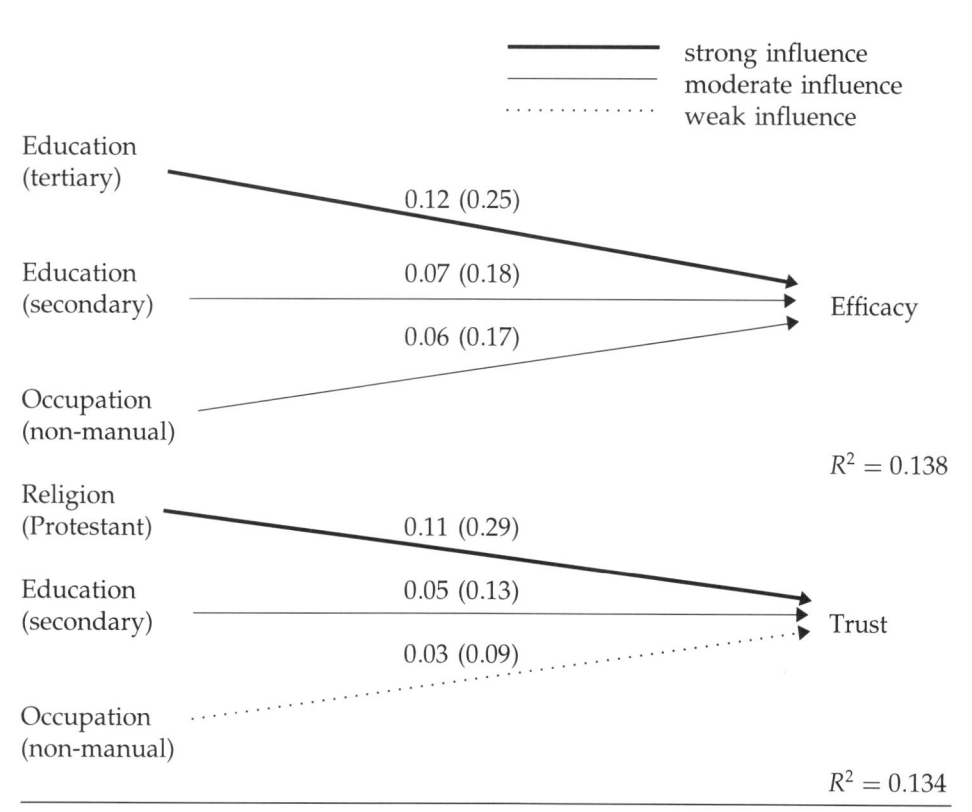

——— strong influence
——— moderate influence
·········· weak influence

Education (tertiary) —— 0.12 (0.25) —→ Efficacy
Education (secondary) —— 0.07 (0.18) —→
Occupation (non-manual) —— 0.06 (0.17) —→

$R^2 = 0.138$

Religion (Protestant) —— 0.11 (0.29) —→ Trust
Education (secondary) —— 0.05 (0.13) —→
Occupation (non-manual) ········ 0.03 (0.09) ········→

$R^2 = 0.134$

* Figures are unstandardized (bs) and standardized (betas) partial regression coefficients that measure the independent impact of each predictor when controlling for the effects of all other variables in the model. Standardized regression coefficients are given in parentheses. Only variables with a statistically significant influence are shown

More specifically, as the unstandardised regression coefficient shows ($b = 0.11$), levels of trust are in fact 11 per cent higher among Protestants than Catholics. A similar, though weaker pattern, is echoed in relation to the non-manually employed and school-educated. Of these three characteristics, however, religious affiliation is by far the strongest predictor of political attitudes in this instance. As the standardised regression coefficients suggest, the differential influence of religious affiliation is twice as strong as that among the school-educated (0.29 as compared to 0.13) and over treble the impact of holding a non-manual occupation (0.29 as compared to 0.09).

Religious affiliation, however, is not a significant predictor of political efficacy. Even when a range of other social background characteristics are taken into account, Protestants are neither more or less efficacious than Catholics. Rather the key distinguishing characteristics in this instance are education and occupational background. It is these two factors, and not differences in religious affiliation, which divide the Northern Irish population in terms of their attitudes towards this issue. Of these two factors, however, attaining a third level educational qualification stands out as having, by far, the strongest influence; approximately double that of having obtained either a secondary level educational qualification or having a non-manual occupation. Thus, as is also the case in previous international research (see Hayes and Bean, 1993), even in Northern Ireland, differing levels of political efficacy remain fundamentally a question of educational and occupational differences.

## Constitutional Options and Party Support

Democratic values are not simply abstract concepts: they have practical political consequences. Values underpin much of our thinking about everyday political issues and events and they offer a shorthand method of interpreting and evaluating the mass of political information that deluges citizens every day of their lives. When values interact with the situations in which individuals find themselves, the result is a particular form of conduct, or a set of preferences which may result in some specific type of behaviour. As Rokeach (1973, p. 169) suggests in the *The Nature of Human Values*, much of the data about any beliefs – social, economic, political or cultural – are 'fundamentally reducible, when stripped to their barest essence, to opposing value orientations'. Democratic values, then, are a shorthand method of enabling a person to make swift judgements about political phenomena, without the need to spend time acquiring objective information or knowledge.

In this section we outline the role of democratic values in shaping what people think about the practical political choices that face them in Northern Ireland: the constitutional options that exist for the province, and the political parties they choose to support. In each case, the range of choices has diversified immeasurably since the start of the conflict in 1968. Previously, the only two constitutional options that existed in the public mind were continued union with Britain or Irish reunification. Since the failure of the 1973–74 Assembly and the 1974 powersharing Executive, other options, such as negotiated or unilateral independence, repartition and confederation, have all been widely canvassed (for a review see, for example, McGarry and O'Leary, 1990). Although none of these options have been seriously considered by the British or Irish governments, they underline the extent to which some groups have sought to break the logjam by proposing more radical solutions.

But perhaps even more important than these constitutional alternatives is the question of who has the right to take decisions concerning Northern Ireland's future: the people of Northern Ireland alone, in conjunction with the people of Britain, or in conjunction with the people of the Irish Republic. Opinion surveys have shown that there is a significant minority within each religious community who are prepared to move away from the dominant constitutional view of their community (Moxon-Browne, 1983; Rose, 1971). For example, there has always been a significant minority of Catholics who have supported continued union with Britain in order to preserve the political and economic status quo. The 1985 Anglo-Irish Agreement further complicated the constitutional alternatives, when the British government explicitly permitted the Irish Republic to have a role in the affairs of Northern Ireland for the first time.

Party support has become equally complex over the past quarter of a century (for a review, see O'Leary, 1990). The split among unionists in how to deal with the post-1968 conflict led to the emergence of two rivals to the once dominant Ulster Unionist Party (UUP): the Democratic Unionist Party (DUP), led by Ian Paisley, and an amorphous collection of parties, the most electorally important of which was the Vanguard Unionist Party, which was active in the mid-1970s. There have been equally major shifts in nationalist support. In 1970, the old Nationalist Party, the northern descendant of the party defeated by Sinn Fein in the 1918 general election, was supplanted by the Social Democratic and Labour Party (SDLP) (McAllister, 1977). The SDLP remained the dominant nationalist party until the early 1980s, when the Provisional IRA's entry into electoral politics through its political wing, Sinn Fein, divided the nationalist vote. Within the biconfessional, or religiously integrated, centre of the political spectrum, the Alliance Party replaced the Northern Ireland Labour Party in the early 1970s (McAllister and Wilson, 1978).

To examine the role of democratic values in shaping constitutional options, Table 3 shows the mean scores on the political efficacy and political trust scales, for Protestants and Catholics who support a variety of alternatives for Northern Ireland. These alternatives are divided into the two main constitutional options, views on whether or not British troops should be withdrawn, and who should decide Northern Ireland's constitutional future. Political efficacy plays compara-

## Table 3

### Democratic values, constitutional opinions and religion (mean percentage scores)

|  | Efficacy | | Trust | |
| --- | --- | --- | --- | --- |
|  | Prot | Cath | Prot | Cath |
| Total | 17 | 15 | 36* | 19 |
| *Constitutional future* | | | | |
| Union with Britain | 16 | 12 | 37* | 25 |
| Irish reunification | 25 | 16 | #31* | 17 |
| *British troop withdrawal* | | | | |
| Support | 16 | 14 | 32* | 12 |
| Oppose | 17 | 17 | 37* | 28 |
| *Decision on constitution* | | | | |
| Northern Ireland | 17 | 17 | 36* | 24 |
| Britain and Northern Ireland | 12 | 17 | 36 | 33 |
| Ireland, North and South | #18 | 12 | #51* | 14 |
| (n) | (381) | (278) | (381) | (278) |

# Less than 20 cases.
An asterisk denotes difference between religions is statistically significant at $p < 0.05$.

tively little role in shaping constitutional options, with one exception. Protestants who favour Irish reunification – a small minority (6 per cent) – are significantly more likely to believe in government responsiveness compared to those who opt for the status quo. For example, Protestants who choose union with Britain score 16 on the scale, compared to 25 for those who opt for Irish reunification. There is a similar, though less marked, trend among Catholics who choose the same option. Clearly, preferences for such a change, which would overturn the current constitutional arrangement, have to be underpinned by a belief in the effectiveness of government to bring it about, regardless of religion.

There are much more significant variations in political trust. First, Catholics who choose the unionist alternative (25 per cent) are more likely to be trustful of the institutions of the state than their coreligionists who choose Irish reunification. Equally, Catholics who choose the status quo – British troops remaining in the province and Britain and Northern Ireland deciding the constitutional future – are more trustful than those who opt for other alternatives. There are also significant variations among Protestants, with the small numbers of Protestants who want Irish reunification (6 per cent) being less trustful and those who want the Irish people to decide on the constitutional alternatives (5 per cent) being more trustful. The presence or absence of political trust therefore plays a major role in

Table 4

**Democratic values and party identification (mean percentage scores)**

|  | Efficacy | Trust |
|---|---|---|
| Ulster Unionist Party | 13 | 41 |
| Democratic Unionist Party | 21 | 31 |
| Alliance Party | 23 | 37 |
| (Alliance, Protestant) | (19) | (37) |
| (Alliance, Catholic) | #(33) | #(37) |
| SDLP | 16 | 21 |
| Sinn Fein | 16 | 5 |
| (n) | (443) | (409) |

# Less than 20 cases.

underpinning constitutional opinions, particularly within the Catholic community.

In assessing the importance of democratic values in determining party support, the main point of comparison is between the supporters of each of the parties within the three major blocks, unionist, nationalist and biconfessional. Within the unionist block, Table 4 shows that supporters of the DUP are, perhaps surprisingly, more likely to demonstrate significantly greater political efficacy than their UUP counterparts, but are much less trustful. Among the two nationalist parties, supporters of the SDLP and Sinn Fein share a common scepticism about the responsiveness of government, but differ dramatically in their levels of political trust, with Sinn Fein supporters scoring 5, compared to 21 for supporters of the SDLP. Finally, separating out Protestant and Catholic supporters of the Alliance Party shows that they differ only on efficacy, with Alliance supporters who are Catholic scoring more highly than their Protestant counterparts.

These results are consistent with the differing historical origins of the parties and the differing experiences of their supporters. The greater levels of efficacy among DUP supporters may rest at least partly on their presence in local government, where DUP councillors have made significant changes over the past two decades, while the high levels of trust among UUP supporters probably reflect the party's historic identification with the institutions of the state, even though this identification effectively ceased in 1972 with the introduction of direct rule from Westminster. Similarly, both the SDLP and Sinn Fein have no experience of government (with the exception of the SDLP's four-month role in the ill-fated power-sharing Executive in 1974) and so their supporters have the same levels of political efficacy. However, SDLP supporters, with their commitment to constitutional methods of achieving political change, have much higher levels of trust compared to their Sinn Fein competitors, who have traditionally combined both constitutional and extra-constitutional methods of achieving their goals.

## Conclusion

Democratic systems can exist only where they have widespread popular support. In turn, popular support for democratic values must combine a range of different characteristics, as well as different levels of support. Support for feelings of political trust or political efficacy alone will not sustain a democratic system: both are required, as is a generally held sense of obedience towards political laws. Similarly, democracy cannot flourish if too many citizens are active or too many are passive; what is required is a delicate balance between the two extremes. As Bernard Berelson (quoted in Bachrach, 1967) put it three decades ago: 'what seems to be required of the electorate as a whole is a distribution of qualities along important dimensions. We need some people who are active in a certain respect, others in the middle, and still others passive.'. Given the delicate popular base upon which democratic institutions rest, it is perhaps not surprising that democracy has proved to be the most fragile of political institutions. It cannot simply be established within a country: it requires widespread support and a functioning system which regularly satisfies popular demands in order to nurture and build the popular values that sustain it. The legacy of distrust towards political institutions that exists in Russia and the former communist states of Eastern Europe is, for example, a major inhibition to the establishment of democracy in those countries (Rose, 1995). Even within countries that have a democratic tradition, Putnam's work on Italy shows that democracy works in very different ways at the regional level, depending on the values of the local citizens (Putnam, 1993).

In this chapter we have examined the extent of support for democratic values among Protestants and Catholics in Northern Ireland, and also more broadly comparing Northern Ireland with the rest of the United Kingdom. The legacy of political violence in Northern Ireland is evident in the low levels of trust in political institutions which are apparent among the province's Catholics. By contrast, Protestants have much higher levels of democratic values; indeed, they display some of the highest levels of political efficacy and trust in the whole of the United Kingdom. The lack of trust among Catholics is one of the reasons why the province has the lowest proportion of strong democrats found anywhere in the United Kingdom and it also helps to elucidate their views on constitutional options as well as their patterns of party support.

Democracy is so fragile because of the time that it takes to establish the values that underpin it. As the post-1991 Russian experience demonstrates, these popular values cannot be generated in the short-term; they can only come about through citizens' experiences with democratic politics, and their belief that it operates to their benefit, and to the benefit of the society as a whole. In Northern Ireland, the history of democracy has not served to enhance the Catholic citizen's view of democracy: the Stormont parliament operated to exclude them from political office for half a century; and the 1973–74 powersharing Executive, which included the SDLP, collapsed after a loyalist strike and the failure of the British government to support it. Building up a Catholic sense of political trust must be one of the major priorities for the British and Irish governments. Without it, the long-term survival of any democratic institutions that may be established in Northern Ireland must be in doubt.

## References

ABRAMSON, P.R. 1983. *Political Attitudes in America*, Freeman, New York.

BACHRACH, P. 1967. *The Theory of Democratic Elitism*, Little Brown, Boston.

BRUCE, S. 1986. *God Save Ulster: The Religion and Politics of Paisleyism*, Clarendon Press, Oxford.

CAMPBELL, A., GURIN, G. and MILLER, W.E. 1954. *The Voter Decides*, John Wiley & Sons, New York.

COULTER, C. 1994. 'Class, Ethnicity and Political Identity in Northern Ireland', *Irish Journal of Sociology*, **4**, 1–26.

CRAIG, S.C., NIEMI, R.G. and SILVER, G.E. 1990. 'Political Efficacy and Trust: A Report on the NES Pilot Study Items', *Political Behavior*, **12**, 289–314.

CURTICE, J. and GALLAGHER, A.M. 1990. 'The Northern Irish Dimension', in R. Jowell, S. Witherspoon and L. Brook (eds), *British Social Attitudes: the Seventh Report*, Gower, Aldershot.

DALTON, R.J. 1988. *Citizen Politics in Western Democracies*, Chatham House, New Jersey.

FULTON, J. 1988. 'Sociology, Religion and "The Troubles" in Northern Ireland: A Critical Approach', *Economic and Social Review*, **20**, 5–24.

HAYES, B.C. and MCALLISTER, I. 1995. 'Social Class, Class Awareness and Political Beliefs in Northern Ireland and the Irish Republic', *Economic and Social Review*, **26**, 349–368.

HAYES, B.C. and BEAN, C.S. 1993. 'Political Efficacy: A Comparative Study of the United States, West Germany, Great Britain and Australia', *European Journal of Political Research*, **23**, 261–280.

HIGLEY, J. and GUNTHER, R. (EDS) 1992. *Elites and Democratic Consolidation in Latin America and Southern Europe*, Cambridge University Press, Cambridge.

LANE, R.E. 1959. *Political Life*, Free Press, Glencoe, Illinois.

MACKEY, S. 1989. *Lebanon: Death of a Nation*, Contemporary Books, New York.

MCALLISTER, I. 1977. *The Northern Ireland Social Democratic and Labour Party: Political Opposition in a Divided Society*, Macmillan, London.

MCALLISTER, I. 1992. *Political Behaviour*, Longman, Melbourne.

MCALLISTER, I. and WILSON, B. 1978. 'Bi-Confessionalism in a Confessional Party System: The Northern Ireland Alliance Party', *Economic and Social Review*, **9**, 207–25.

MCGARRY, J. and O' LEARY, B. (EDS) 1990. *The Future of Northern Ireland*, Clarendon Press, Oxford.

MOXON-BROWNE, E. 1991. 'National Identity', in P. Stringer and G. Robinson (eds), *Social Attitudes in Northern Ireland: The First Report*, Blackstaff Press, Belfast.

MOXON-BROWNE, E. 1983. *Nation, Class and Creed in Northern Ireland*, Gower, London.

O'DOWD, L. 1991. 'Social Class', in P. Stringer and G. Robinson (eds), *Social Attitudes in Northern Ireland: The First Report*, Blackstaff Press, Belfast.

O'LEARY, B. 1990. 'Party Support in Northern Ireland, 1969-89', in J. McGarry and B. O'Leary (eds), *The Future of Northern Ireland*, Clarendon Press, Oxford.

O'LEARY, B. and ARTHUR, P. 1990. 'Northern Ireland as a Site of State and National-Building Failures', in J. McGarry and B. O'Leary (eds), *The Future of Northern Ireland*, Clarendon Press, Oxford.

PUTNAM, R.D. 1993. *Making Democracy Work*, Princeton University Press, New Jersey.

ROKEACH, M. 1973. *The Nature of Human Values*, Free Press, New York.

ROSE, R. 1971. *Governing Without Consensus: An Irish Perspective*, Faber, London.

ROSE, R. 1995. 'Mobilizing Demobilized Voters in Postcommunist Societies', *Party Politics*, **1**, 549–563.

RUANE, J. and TODD, J. 1992. 'Diversity, Division and the Middle Ground in Northern Ireland', *Irish Political Studies*, **7**, 73–98.

## Appendix A

### Table A1

### Varimax rotated factor loadings showing dimensions of political efficacy and trust by nation

| Items | Great Britain | | Northern Ireland | |
|---|---|---|---|---|
| | Factor I | Factor II | Factor I | Factor II |
| | Efficacy | Trust | Efficacy | Trust |
| 1. Say in government | 0.57 | 0.24 | 0.55 | 0.16 |
| 2. Understand government | 0.66 | −0.11 | 0.52 | 0.02 |
| 3. MPs in touch with their public | 0.57 | 0.35 | 0.80 | 0.02 |
| 4. Relevant which political party is in power | 0.75 | 0.01 | 0.64 | 0.14 |
| 5. Party interest extends beyond votes | 0.69 | 0.34 | 0.82 | 0.08 |
| 6. Trust the government to put the nation above party | 0.23 | 0.67 | 0.10 | 0.75 |
| 7. Trust politicians to tell the truth | 0.07 | 0.71 | 0.06 | 0.69 |
| 8. Trust councillors to put area above party | 0.23 | 0.54 | 0.18 | 0.67 |
| 9. Trust civil servants to stand up to ministers | 0.01 | 0.75 | 0.05 | 0.75 |
| 10. Trust the police not to bend the rules | 0.05 | 0.55 | 0.05 | 0.64 |
| Alpha reliability coefficient | 0.706 | 0.700 | 0.711 | 0.753 |

*Note:* These results are based on factor analysis. This is a statistical technique which identifies the underlying structure from a set of correlated and conceptually related measures. The results reinforce the distinction between political efficacy and trust as identified in Table 1. Whereas the first four items load strongly on Factor I (all are above 0.5), which we can interpret straight-forwardly as political efficacy, they have weak loadings on Factor II (around 0.2 or less). In contrast, items 6–9 have high loadings on Factor II, which we can interpret as political trust, while their loadings on Factor I are small. These two dimensions also have extremely good reliabilities, as measured by a Cronbach's alpha value of 0.7 or above in all cases.

## Table A2

### Definition, means and standard deviations for variables used in the analysis

| Variable | Scoring | Mean | Standard deviation |
|---|---|---|---|
| Religion | 1 = Protestant; 0 = Catholic | 0.58 | 0.49 |
| Gender | 1 = male; 0 = female | 0.50 | 0.50 |
| Marital status | 1 = married; 0 = other | 0.62 | 0.49 |
| Age | Years | 44.75 | 18.18 |
| *Education* | | | |
| Tertiary | 1 = yes; 0 = no | 0.16 | 0.37 |
| Secondary | 1 = yes; 0 = no | 0.44 | 0.50 |
| No qualifications | Omitted category | 0.40 | 0.49 |
| Union membership | 1 = member; 0 = non-member | 0.26 | 0.44 |
| Subjective class | 1 = middle; 0 = working | 0.20 | 0.40 |
| Occupation | 1 = non-manual; 0 = manual | 0.49 | 0.50 |
| Employment status | 1 = labour active; 0 = other | 0.58 | 0.49 |
| Efficacy | From a low of 0 to a high of 1 | 0.31 | 0.18 |
| Trust | From a low of 0 to a high of 1 | 0.35 | 0.18 |

# 2

# Who Wants a United Ireland? Constitutional Preferences among Catholics and Protestants

Richard Breen

**Introduction**

Since the partition of Ireland under the terms of the 1921 Anglo-Irish Treaty, the constitutional position of Northern Ireland has been a central source of political and social division within the province. Individual preferences about the future of Northern Ireland not only differ sharply between the Unionist and Nationalist poles, but these preferences themselves have now come to take on an unusually central role in determining what this position shall be. The UK government has maintained that the constitutional position of Northern Ireland is a matter to be decided by the people of Northern Ireland. As a consequence the importance of understanding exactly what constitutional preferences people hold and why they hold them has received a new impetus. In this chapter we use the Northern Ireland Social Attitudes (NISA) survey data to examine a number of questions concerning the constitutional preferences held by people in Northern Ireland.

We begin by looking at how these preferences have changed since the NISA surveys began in 1989. Then we examine the results of the 1994 survey in greater detail in order to say something about what distinguishes those who hold different constitutional preferences. Clearly the most important characteristic that distinguishes those who favour the retention of the Union with Britain from those who favour a united Ireland is religion. However, we also examine differences within each of the two major religious groups. How much variation is there in constitutional preferences among Catholics and among Protestants, and how might such variation as exists be explained? In regard to this latter question there are two hypotheses that we will seek to test. The first is that variation in constitutional preferences is due to differences in the socio-economic and demographic characteristics of individuals. So we might expect, for example, that middle class or better educated Protestants will be less unionist than working class

Protestants and that middle class Catholics will be less nationalist than their working class counterparts. The second hypothesis is that, particularly among Catholics, variation in constitutional preferences has less to do with the individual's own socio-economic position and is more strongly linked to his or her perceptions of the position of the Catholic community *vis-a-vis* the Protestant community. In other words, strength of Nationalist feeling depends less on whether a Catholic is well-educated, middle class and so on and more on the degree to which he or she thinks that Catholics are discriminated against in Northern Ireland.

### Constitutional Preferences: Change over Time

The data we use come from all of the NISA surveys from 1989 through to 1994. In each of these years – with the exception of 1992 when there was no NISA survey – respondents have been asked the following question about their constitutional preferences:

*'Do you think the long-term policy for Northern Ireland should be for it to remain part of the United Kingdom or to reunify with the rest of Ireland?'*

### Table 1
### Preferred long-term policy for Northern Ireland (%)

|  | 1989 | 1990 | 1991 | 1993 | 1994 |
| --- | --- | --- | --- | --- | --- |
| Remain part of UK | 69 | 68 | 71 | 70 | 63 |
| Reunify Ireland | 24 | 25 | 22 | 20 | 27 |
| Other option | 3 | 3 | 2 | 5 | 6 |
| Don't know | 4 | 4 | 4 | 5 | 4 |
| Not answered | 0 | 1 | 2 | 0 | 1 |

*Note: totals may not add up to exactly 100 because of rounding.*

Other possible responses are not provided in the question format but are recorded. Table 1 shows the responses to this question in each NISA survey since 1989. Every year the great majority of people – around 70 per cent in the period 1989–1993 and somewhat less in 1994 – chose the response 'Remain part of the UK' while between a fifth and a quarter favoured the reunification of Ireland. The numbers expressing support for any other option were very small. The option of an independent Northern Irish state received the support of no more than one per cent of respondents in each survey. Around five per cent of respondents each year said that they did not know which long-term policy they would prefer but hardly anyone refused to answer the question.

Our most recent information comes from the survey carried out in the spring of 1994. This was after the Downing Street Declaration of 1993 but before the cease-fires of autumn 1994 and it is perfectly possible that constitutional preferences might have shifted in some way in response to these later events that will not be known until the 1995 survey results become available. What the data do show, however, is stability or a very slight increase over the 1989–1993 period in the percentage favouring Northern Ireland's remaining within the UK (though this change is not statistically significant) and thus a decrease in the popularity of the united Ireland option. But, in the 1994 data, we see something of a reversal with a considerable increase (from 20 to 27 per cent) in the number preferring a united Ireland and a drop in the percentage wishing to retain the Union.

Table 2

Preferred long-term policy for Northern Ireland by religion (%)

|  | 1989 | 1990 | 1991 | 1993 | 1994 |
|---|---|---|---|---|---|
| *Protestants* | | | | | |
| Remain part of UK | 93 | 93 | 92 | 90 | 90 |
| Reunify Ireland | 3 | 5 | 4 | 56 | |
| Other option | 2 | 1 | 1 | 4 | 3 |
| Don't know | 2 | 1 | 1 | 1 | 1 |
| Not answered | 0 | 0 | 1 | 0 | 0 |
| *Catholics* | | | | | |
| Remain part of UK | 32 | 33 | 35 | 36 | 24 |
| Reunify Ireland | 56 | 55 | 53 | 49 | 60 |
| Other option | 4 | 5 | 2 | 5 | 7 |
| Don't know | 7 | 6 | 7 | 10 | 8 |
| Not answered | 1 | 1 | 2 | 1 | 1 |
| *Others* | | | | | |
| Remain part of UK | 81 | 72 | 79 | 74 | 66 |
| Reunify Ireland | 13 | 19 | 13 | 13 | 15 |
| Other option | 4 | 5 | 4 | 6 | 14 |
| Don't know | 3 | 2 | 4 | 7 | 5 |
| Not answered | 0 | 2 | 0 | 0 | 0 |

## Community Background and Constitutional Preferences

As we might expect, the major factor that explains variation in constitutional preferences is community background or religion, distinguishing Catholics from Protestants. Table 2 shows the preferred long-term policy for Northern Ireland for each of three groups. These are Catholics, Protestants and those who are of another religion (neither Catholic nor Protestant) or who have no religion or who refuse to state their religion (this group is labelled 'Others').

Table 2 shows that in excess of 90 per cent of Protestants wish to see the Union retained, and there has been little change in the position over the five years. No more than six per cent of Protestants favour a united Ireland. Similarly, the 'Others' who cannot be placed in either of the main religious groups are overwhelmingly in favour of retaining the Union, although their support has fluctuated over time. As we might expect, this group is relatively small, making up, at most, 14 per cent of the sample.

The major change over the period 1989–1994 is found among Catholics. Up to 1993 the trend here was towards a decline in nationalism and an increase from 32 to 36 in the percentage favouring the retention of the Union. However, the latter fell to 24 per cent in 1994 and the percentage favouring Irish unification increased from 49 in 1993 to 60 in 1994. This is a substantial change and is responsible for the overall increase in the percentages preferring a united Ireland shown in Table 1. In summary: over the period Protestant preferences have not changed but among Catholics the gradual drift towards the Union was sharply reversed in 1994.

## National and Constitutional Identity

Apart from the direct question that asks people about their preferences for long-term policy in Northern Ireland there are three other items in the questionnaire that give a less direct insight into individual constitutional preferences. The first of these is what we term 'national identity'. This is captured by the following question:

*Which of these best describes the way you usually think of yourself?*

and the possible responses are 'British', 'Irish', 'Ulster', 'Northern Irish', 'Sometimes British, sometimes Irish' and 'Other'. As very few people (less than half of one per cent) choose the 'Other' response, we omit them from our analysis. In other research (Breen, 1994) it has been shown that, as far as constitutional and political preferences are concerned, there is no difference in the responses of those who claim to be 'British' or 'Ulster'. Similarly there is no difference in the responses of those who claim to be 'Northern Irish' or 'Sometimes British, sometimes Irish'.

Accordingly, in Table 3 we show, for the four surveys for which this information is available, the percentage distribution of Protestant and Catholic respondents across three categories: (a) 'British' or 'Ulster', (b) 'Northern Irish' or 'Sometimes British, sometimes Irish', and (c) 'Irish'.

### Table 3
#### Responses to national identity question by religion and year (%)

|  | 1989 P | 1989 C | 1991 P | 1991 C | 1993 P | 1993 C | 1994 P | 1994 C |
|---|---|---|---|---|---|---|---|---|
| British/Ulster | 79 | 12 | 82 | 12 | 85 | 13 | 82 | 10 |
| N.Irish/Sometimes | 18 | 29 | 16 | 27 | 13 | 26 | 15 | 28 |
| Irish | 3 | 60 | 2 | 62 | 2 | 61 | 3 | 62 |

P = Protestant; C = Catholic

In contrast to the direct measure of constitutional preferences reported in the previous table, Table 3 shows remarkable stability over time. Around four-fifths of Protestants consider themselves to be 'British' or 'Ulster', with the great majority of the remainder picking either the label 'Northern Irish' or the 'Sometimes British, sometimes Irish' option. Three per cent or less choose the description 'Irish'. Among Catholics just over 60 per cent regard themselves as 'Irish', just under 30 per cent as 'Northern Irish' or 'Sometimes British, sometimes Irish', with around 12 per cent considering themselves 'British' or 'Ulster'.

### Table 4
#### Responses to constitutional identity question by religion and year (%)

|  | 1989 P | 1989 C | 1991 P | 1991 C | 1993 P | 1993 C | 1994 P | 1994 C |
|---|---|---|---|---|---|---|---|---|
| Unionist | 71 | 0 | 73 | 0 | 75 | 0 | 76 | 0 |
| Neither | 29 | 59 | 27 | 48 | 25 | 59 | 24 | 45 |
| Nationalist | 0 | 40 | 0 | 51 | 0 | 40 | 0 | 54 |

P = Protestant; C = Catholic

Table 4 reports another measure of identity, which we call 'constitutional identity'. This is the response to the question:

*Generally speaking, do you think of yourself as a Unionist, a Nationalist or neither?*
and the possible replies are 'Unionist', 'Nationalist' or 'Neither'. Table 4 shows that among Protestants around three-quarters pick 'Unionist' with the rest responding

'Neither'. Catholics differ from Protestants in this respect in two ways. First, Catholics are almost equally split between the labels 'Neither' and 'Nationalist'. Secondly, in contrast to the stability over time evident in the Protestant replies, the balance of responses between these two alternatives shifts substantially from one year to the next. So, for example, in 1993 40 per cent claimed to be Nationalists, while in 1994, 54 per cent did so. What is perhaps most striking – though unsurprising – about the responses shown in Table 4 is that no Protestants call themselves Nationalists and no Catholics call themselves Unionists.

## Party Support

Patterns of political party support are primarily structured by the position of the party on the constitutional issue. This means that community background or religion is a very strong predictor of party support. However, within the main Unionist and Nationalist political blocs there is party competition within the Protestant and Catholic communities, respectively. This takes place on the basis of different policy approaches to the constitutional issue but also on the basis of conventional left/right support. Thus, Sinn Fein and the DUP receive a greater share of their support from the working class than do the SDLP, Alliance or the Ulster Unionists (Evans and Duffy, in press).

Table 5

**Support for Unionist and Nationalist parties and Alliance according to religion (%)**

|  | 1989 | 1990 | 1991 | 1993 | 1994 |
|---|---|---|---|---|---|
| *Protestants* | | | | | |
| Unionist | 88 | 90 | 87 | 88 | 86 |
| Alliance | 12 | 10 | 12 | 11 | 14 |
| Nationalist | 0 | 0 | 1 | 1 | 0 |
| *Catholics* | | | | | |
| Unionist | 3 | 1 | 1 | 2 | 0 |
| Alliance | 11 | 14 | 13 | 13 | 11 |
| Nationalist | 86 | 85 | 86 | 86 | 89 |
| *Others* | | | | | |
| Unionist | 50 | 67 | 65 | 58 | 51 |
| Alliance | 34 | 26 | 29 | 24 | 25 |
| Nationalist | 16 | 7 | 6 | 19 | 24 |

Table 5 shows the extent of the religious divide in patterns of party support by reporting the percentages of Catholics, Protestants and Others who support Unionist parties (Democratic Unionist Party (DUP), Ulster Unionist Party (UUP) and Other Unionist Parties), the Alliance party, and Nationalist parties (Social Democratic and Labour Party (SDLP) and Sinn Fein). (A small percentage of respondents support other parties or support no party but they are excluded from Table 5). Here there is remarkable stability over time, with Protestants and Catholics presenting almost a mirror image of each other. Just under 90 per cent of Catholics support Nationalist parties while just under 90 per cent of Protestants support Unionist parties. Within each community support for the Alliance party runs at about 12 per cent.

Thus far then, we have looked at the position, over the 1989–1994 period, of Catholics and Protestants on four variables – their preferred long-term option for Northern Ireland, their national and constitutional identity and their party support. There are several points to note about the responses to these questions. First is the consistency over time in the pattern of responses, particularly among Protestants. However on two issues – long-term policy for Northern Ireland and constitutional identity – this stability contrasts with the relatively high degree of change among Catholics. Second, not only does the Catholic community display somewhat more year to year variation, but there is also clearly much more variation among the Catholic community within each year. So, in Table 2, we see that whereas virtually all Protestants favour the retention of the Union there is a substantial minority of Catholics – as high as 36 per cent in 1993 and as low as 24 per cent in 1994 – who also favour this option over that of a united Ireland. In addition, while very small percentages of Protestants favour any option for Northern Ireland other than retention of the Union or reunification, and very few of them say that they do not know what option they prefer, as many as 15 per cent of Catholics favour some other option or say they do not know. Similarly, while 80 per cent of Protestants choose the national identity label 'British' or 'Ulster', Catholic responses are a little more evenly divided with almost 40 per cent seeing themselves as something other than 'Irish'. In Table 4 we see that while only one quarter of Protestants claim not to be Unionists, as many as 60 per cent of Catholics (in 1989 and 1993) claim not to be Nationalists. However, this variation among Catholics is not evident in party support. Despite their apparently greater degree of heterogeneity on the other items we have examined, Catholics, to the same extent as Protestants, do not stray beyond the traditional boundaries of sectarian politics.

## Constitutional Preferences, Identity and Party Support

In the remainder of this chapter we confine our attention to the 1994 NISA data with three aims in mind. First, to look at the relationships between the direct measure of constitutional preferences and the three less direct measures – namely the two identity items and party support. Second, we examine the degree to which socio-economic and demographic factors such as age, level of education and social class, might be related to constitutional preferences. Finally we look at the relationship between the constitutional preferences people hold and their perceptions of the standing of the Catholic community relative to that of the Protestant community in Northern Ireland – or, for short, perceptions of Catholic disadvantage. The purpose of these analyses is, as noted in the introduction, to assess the extent to which individual socio-economic position shapes constitutional preferences and the extent to which the latter are shaped by perceptions of the position of the Catholic community as a whole, *vis-a-vis* the Protestant community.

### Table 6
### Constitutional preferences by national identity, personal identity and party preference

| | % preferring: | |
|---|---|---|
| | Union with Britain | United Ireland |
| *National identity* | | |
| British/Ulster | 94 | 6 |
| Northern Irish/Sometimes British... | 60 | 40 |
| Irish | 24 | 76 |
| *Constitutional identity* | | |
| Unionist | 97 | 3 |
| Neither | 65 | 35 |
| Nationalist | 13 | 87 |
| *Party preference* | | |
| DUP | 98 | 2 |
| UUP | 98 | 2 |
| Alliance | 80 | 20 |
| SDLP | 24 | 76 |
| Sinn Fein | 4 | 96 |

Table 6 shows the relationship between constitutional preferences, our two measures of identity and party preference. So, for example, we see that 94 per cent of those who describe their national identity as 'British' or 'Ulster' favour retention of the Union with Britain. The figures in this table are as we might have expected, though some features are worth drawing attention to. It is notable that all those responses to the two identity questions and party preference item that fall on the unionist side (that is, national identity 'British' or 'Ulster', constitutional identity unionist and preference for one of the two unionist parties) are associated with very high levels of support for the Union – indeed virtually everyone who gives one of the unionist replies is in favour of the Union. This might seem like a tautology, until we consider the nationalist replies. So, for example, people who consider themselves 'Irish', far from all being in favour of Irish unity, are divided in a ratio of three to one between preferring a united Ireland and preferring retention of the Union. Similarly, while it is true that almost all Sinn Fein supporters favour a united Ireland, the balance among those who prefer the SDLP is once again three to one in favour of a United Ireland. Indeed, far from the pattern of SDLP support being the mirror image of support for, say, the Ulster Unionist party, it actually mirrors that of the Alliance party. On the evidence presented here, support for the Alliance party might be characterised as unionist with a substantial minority of nationalists, while support for the SDLP might be characterised as nationalist but with a substantial minority of unionist supporters.

The picture that Table 6 presents in many ways replicates our earlier findings. The Protestant community is very homogenous in its constitutional preferences, the way its members view their national and constitutional identity, and in their support for Unionist parties. In other words, Protestants tend to cluster very tightly around a characteristic 'unionist' position. The Catholic community, on the other hand, is more heterogenous. While it is clearly the case that the great majority of Catholics consider themselves Irish and support Nationalist parties, there is, nevertheless between 25 and 40 per cent of their number (depending on the item in question) who depart from the characteristic 'nationalist' position.

**Socio-economic and Demographic Influences on Constitutional Preferences**

Table 7 shows the percentage of all respondents and of Protestants and Catholics who prefer the retention of the Union, according to a number of socio-demographic variables. These are gender, age, educational qualifications and social class. Our measure of social class is the Goldthorpe schema (Goldthorpe, 1980) in which the 'Salariat' comprises managers, professionals and those in higher

### Table 7
#### Percentage who wish to retain Union with Britain (1994 data)

|  | All | Protestants | Catholics |
|---|---|---|---|
| *Gender* | | | |
| Men | 69 | 94 | 21 |
| Women | 71 | 94 | 36 |
| *Age* | | | |
| 18–25 | 64 | 97 | 14 |
| 26–35 | 70 | 98 | 30 |
| 36–45 | 65 | 88 | 37 |
| 46–55 | 71 | 97 | 32 |
| 56+ | 77 | 93 | 30 |
| *Social class* | | | |
| Salariat | 70 | 93 | 28 |
| Routine non-manual | 74 | 94 | 33 |
| Petty bourgeoisie | 68 | 88 | 24 |
| Foremen and technical workers | 83 | 96 | 23 |
| Working class | 68 | 96 | 31 |
| *Education* | | | |
| None | 69 | 93 | 32 |
| CSE < grade 1 | 71 | 97 | 25 |
| O-level or CSE grade 1 | 77 | 98 | 28 |
| A-level | 70 | 98 | 25 |
| Higher education but less than degree | 75 | 98 | 26 |
| Degree or higher | 48 | 67 | 23 |

Base: All Protestants and Catholics who prefer retention of the Union or a united Ireland (excludes those who give any other reply to constitutional preference question and excludes those not recorded as either Protestant or Catholic).

white collar occupations, while the 'Routine non-manual' class includes all other white collar workers. The 'Petty bourgeoisie' is made up of all employers and the self-employed (see Erikson and Goldthorpe, 1992, Chapter 1 for a fuller description).

What is most evident in Table 7 is the absence of any very clear relationships between these socio-economic or demographic factors and people's constitutional preferences. The exceptions to this are gender (Catholic men are significantly more likely to favour a united Ireland than are Catholic women) and education where, for all respondents, possession of a degree is associated with lower levels of support for maintenance of the Union. Young Catholics also emerge as less supportive of the Union. However, it is very obvious that there are no substantive or statistically significant differences among people at the other levels of education nor is variation in constitutional preferences linked in any consistent way to social class or age differences (with the single exception noted above). We also examined the relationship between constitutional preferences and household income and here we found a significant relationship among Protestants such that those with a higher income tend to be less likely to want to see the Union retained. However, among Catholics there was no relationship.

In general terms, we have to conclude that socio-economic and demographic factors play little part in explaining why people of either religious group have particular constitutional preferences. If anything, these factors play a more significant role among Protestants than Catholics, but one might well be more impressed by the weakness of their effect rather than their strength. Analyses of NISA data for 1989, 1990 and 1993 (Breen, 1994) also found that socioeconomic and demographic factors explained more of the variation in preferences among Protestants than Catholics.

**Perceptions of Disadvantage and Constitutional Preferences**

The NISA data contain two items that yield direct measures of respondents' views as to the extent of disadvantage suffered by Catholics relative to Protestants in Northern Ireland. The first of these is a question that asks:

*Thinking of Catholics – do you think there is a lot of prejudice against them in Northern Ireland nowadays, a little, or hardly any?*

In our analysis we score the responses 0 = hardly any, 1 = a little and 2 = a lot.

The second is a set of questions that allows us to allocate respondents to one of five categories – Catholics have a much better chance of getting a job than Protestants; Catholics have a somewhat better chance; members of both communities have the same chance; Protestants have a somewhat better chance of getting a job than Catholics; Protestants have a much better chance of getting a job. Scores on this measure run from 0 = Catholics have a much better chance to 4 = Protestants have a much better chance.

Thus the first item measures the respondent's belief in whether prejudice against Catholics exists and the second focuses more directly on inequality in the labour market. Table 8 shows the correlation between these two measures and

### Table 8
### Correlations between perceptions of Catholic disadvantage and constitutional preferences

|  | All | Catholics | Protestants |
|---|---|---|---|
| Prejudice against Catholics? | 0.204 | 0.1758 | 0.0868 |
| Protestant better chance of job? | 0.407 | 0.299 | -0.062 |

*Note: a positive correlation means that a higher score on the disadvantage measure is associated with a preference for a United Ireland.*

constitutional preferences. A correlation between two variables can take an absolute value between zero and one. A value near zero shows that there is no relationship between the two variables, whereas the closer the correlation is to one the stronger the relationship between them. In this case we see that our overall measure of prejudice and our measure of labour market disadvantage are both significantly related to constitutional preferences, with the latter being rather more strongly related. The direction of the relationship is as we would expect: people who believe that there is prejudice against Catholics and those who believe that Protestants have a better chance of getting a job are more likely to prefer a united Ireland. If we then look at these correlations within each religion, we find that the relationships are weaker. However, among Catholics the relationships with beliefs about labour market disadvantage and with beliefs about anti-Catholic prejudice are still significant. In other words, those who believe that Protestants have a better chance of getting a job and/or that prejudice against Catholics exists are more likely to prefer Irish unity than those who believe that both communities have similar chances of getting a job or who believe that there is little or no anti-Catholic prejudice.

These results suggest that, among Catholics, variation in constitutional preferences is not sensitive to variation in individuals' socioeconomic and demographic position but it is sensitive to individuals' perceptions of how Catholics fare, relative to Protestants. Breen (1995) shows also that constitutional preferences are related to people's beliefs about the impartiality or otherwise of the security forces. Those Catholics who prefer a united Ireland are more likely to believe that the security forces favour Protestants. Unfortunately we do not have measures of this in the 1994 NISA survey.

The fact that individual position is of so little importance considerably weakens the thesis that upward mobility on the part of individual Catholics will tend to make them less nationalist in their preferences. Rather, our results (and those of

Breen, 1994) suggest that what is important is how Catholics perceive the position of their own community rather than themselves individually. In this sense, then, a weakening of nationalist sentiment is more likely to be found where there is a perception of a general improvement in the position of the Catholic community. This may, of course, involve a degree of upward social mobility, but this is perhaps less important than a perception of equality of treatment and of condition between the two communities.

## Catholic Unionists

The Protestant community is strikingly homogenous in its constitutional preferences. This suggests that internal diversity among Protestants should not be overemphasised. Although there is some variation among Protestants in their national identity, between those who see themselves as 'British' and those who consider themselves 'Ulster', this seems to have little significance for constitutional

### Table 9
### Identity and party preference among Protestants, Catholics who favour Irish unity and Catholics who favour Union with Britain (%)

|  | Protestants | Catholics preferring United Ireland | Catholics preferring Union with Britain |
|---|---|---|---|
| *National identity* | | | |
| British/Ulster | 82 | 3 | 22 |
| N. Irish/Sometimes British... | 15 | 28 | 38 |
| Irish | 3 | 69 | 40 |
| *Constitutional identity* | | | |
| Unionist | 76 | 0 | 3 |
| Neither | 24 | 36 | 75 |
| Nationalist | 0 | 64 | 22 |
| *Party preference* | | | |
| DUP | 27 | 0 | 0 |
| UUP/Other Unionist | 59 | 0 | 0 |
| Alliance | 14 | 224 | |
| SDLP | 0 | 82 | 74 |
| Sinn Fein | 0 | 16 | 2 |

preferences. Among those who consider themselves 'Ulster' exactly the same distribution across the constitutional preference categories exists as among those who consider themselves 'British'. Similarly, the often heard view that a substantial body of middle class Protestants are more likely to accept a united Ireland, or some compromise that weakens the Union, receives little support from our analysis. It is certainly the case that those Protestants who express a preference for a united Ireland are predominantly well educated and have higher incomes, but they are very few in number. Around 90 per cent of Protestants support the Union.

Table 9 looks at the national identity, constitutional identity and party support among three groups – Protestants, Catholics who favour a united Ireland and Catholics who favour retention of the Union. The consistency of Protestants in their responses to the four items is once again evident. There is also a high level of consistency in the responses of those Catholics who favour a united Ireland. However, among the third group – which we might call 'Catholic unionists' – national identity, constitutional identity and party support are sometimes in conflict with the preference for retention of the Union with Britain. They are much more evenly divided across the three national identity categories than are Protestants or Catholics who favour a united Ireland, and three-quarters of them profess to being neither a Unionist nor a Nationalist. Perhaps the most striking difference is to be observed in political party support. Whereas the two Unionist parties are supported exclusively by supporters of the Union, of the two Nationalist parties by far the larger (the SDLP) is supported by a high percentage of Catholics whose preferred long-term constitutional preference is for the retaining of the Union with Great Britain. As Table 6 shows, they account for roughly one quarter of SDLP supporters.

**Conclusion**

At present it appears that around two out of three adults in Northern Ireland favour a long-term policy of retaining the Union with Britain. Among Protestants about six per cent favour a united Ireland in the long term, while among Catholics, around one quarter say they want to see the Union preserved.

Forecasting is a notoriously unreliable business, but this has not deterred much speculation surrounding the issue of a future Catholic majority in Northern Ireland. Extrapolating from the results of the 1991 census, it has been suggested that Catholics may form the majority in Northern Ireland some time in the next century. However, even putting aside the uncertainties attached to purely demographic forecasts, the constitutional and political implications of a Catholic majority are quite unknown. Given the current pattern of Catholic constitutional preferences, a Catholic majority is far from being the same thing as a majority in favour of Irish unity. Indeed, assuming 70 per cent of Catholics supported Irish unity (and that no Protestants did) a majority in favour of unification would require that the adult Catholic population be more than *two and a half* times larger than the Protestant population. But, of course, it is unlikely that the current pattern of constitutional preferences among Catholics (and possibly among Protestants) will be maintained. The evidence we have suggests some shift among Catholics (and no change among Protestants) between 1989 and 1993 towards greater support for the Union, though this trend is not statistically significant. However, in 1994 this trend was dramatically reversed with a very marked decline in the percentage of Catholics in favour of the Union. More generally, changing, but unpredictable, economic or political circumstances may lead to further change in constitutional preferences, but the direction of such changes cannot be predicted.

In a recent paper, Ruane and Todd (1992) have warned against overemphasis on the potential for middle-ground politics in Northern Ireland. Our results reinforce this, at least in respect of the Protestant community where relatively little variation in constitutional preferences can be seen. Among Catholics there is greater variation and here, of course, we would point particularly to the group we labelled 'Catholic unionists'. On the one hand this might be seen as indicative of greater potential for some kind of middle-ground politics, but (and as the corollary to this) it can also be seen as an indicator of a possible volatility in constitutional preferences that makes predictions particularly unreliable.

**References**

BREEN, R. 1994. 'Constitutional preferences, socio-economic status and perceptions of disadvantage among Catholics and Protestants in Northern Ireland', unpublished report to the Central Community Relations Unit.

BREEN, R. 1995. 'Beliefs about the Treatment of Catholics and Protestants by the Security Forces' in Breen, R., Robinson, G. and Devine, P. (eds), *Social Attitudes in Northern Ireland: The Fourth Report*, Appletree Press, Belfast.

ERIKSON, R. and GOLDTHORPE, J.H. 1992. *The Constant Flux*, Clarendon Press, Oxford.

EVANS, G. and DUFFY, M. 1996. 'Beyond the sectarian divide: the social bases and political consequences of Nationalist and Unionist Party competition in Northern Ireland', *British Journal of Political Science*, in press.

GOLDTHORPE, J. H. with LLEWELLYN, C. and PAYNE, C. 1980. *Social Mobility in Modern Britain*, Clarendon Press, Oxford.

RUANE, J. and TODD, J. 1992. 'Diversity, Division and the Middle Ground in Northern Ireland', *Irish Political Studies*, **7**: 73–98.

# 3

# Informal Care in Northern Ireland

Eileen Evason and Gillian Robinson

## Introduction

Over the past 15 years in Great Britain and Northern Ireland there has been a growing interest in the needs and circumstances of carers – persons who provide assistance on an unpaid basis for elderly persons and persons with disabilities living in the community (see, for example, Finch and Groves, 1983; Joshi, 1987; Ungerson,1987; Parker,1990; Carers National Association,1994; Twigg and Atkin, 1994; Evason, Whittington and Knowles, 1992; Evason and Whittington, 1995). Indeed, as Parker and Lawton (1994, p. 1) note 'it has become increasingly difficult to keep up with the wealth of research and writing on informal care and carers'.

This increase in interest was the result of a number of trends and developments. First and foremost, during the 1980s there was a growing awareness of the way in which the need for care was expanding in the United Kingdom and, indeed, in all industrialised societies. The issue here is not simply the increase in the number of persons of pensionable age. The great majority of this total age group are fit and able to lead independent active lives. For policy makers, concern has focused on the increase in the number of very elderly persons who are likely to need substantial support from health and welfare services. In 1985, 34 per cent of retired persons in Britain were aged 75–85 and eight per cent were aged 85 or over. At that point, projections suggested that by the year 2025 the total number of persons aged 65 or over would increase to 11 million with 12 per cent of this age group being 85 or over (OPCS, 1987). The need for care is not, of course, confined to the very elderly: medical advances have also meant increased longevity for persons born with disabilities or disabled in later life.

A second element in the debate has related to the willingness and capacity of the family generally, and women in particular, to provide care and support. Here it is important to note that all of the evidence (Parker, 1990) indicates that, far from withdrawing from caring in favour of an all pervasive welfare state, the family remains the most important source of support for elderly persons and persons with disabilities. Thus, the proportion of elderly persons in institutional care of some form in the 1980s was no greater than at the turn of the century. Nevertheless, although relatives are continuing to care, they are doing so in a very new context and references to some past golden age of duty and responsibility are not helpful. To begin with, whilst the notion of family care conveys a picture of the young and fit helping elderly persons, in practice where those requiring care are aged 80 or over then their children will themselves be of, or approaching, pensionable age and care by siblings and spouses will obviously mean care of the elderly by the elderly. Moreover, greater longevity may mean that, whereas at the turn of the century the care of an elderly parent was unlikely to last more than a few years, now there is the possibility that the years for which care is required may approach those devoted to the care of dependent children. Turning to the family itself, there have been substantial changes. Smaller families mean fewer children to provide support. The traditional source of family care – the never married daughter – is now a rarity and married daughters are now much more likely to be in employment. On top of all of this, account must be taken of the impact of rising separation and divorce rates which may confuse once clear cut chains of responsibilities and patterns of relationships.

The issue of caring therefore relates to the emergence of a very new set of problems requiring new thinking and fresh perspectives. During the 1980s, however, there was some concern (Finch and Groves, 1983) that the new policies and concepts being developed in fact consisted of 'old wine in new bottles'. In 1981, the White Paper *'Growing Older'* asserted that 'care in the community must increasingly mean care by the community' (DHSS, 1981, p. 3). There was, subsequently, much discussion of the need to recognise and develop informal networks of care (Barclay, 1982; Cumberlege Report, 1986; Griffiths Report, 1988) and, put briefly, it appeared that the tension between a growing need for care and a government committed to reducing the role of the state would be resolved through greater reliance on informal care. It also appeared that the implications of this strategy would be obscured by the use of broad, gender neutral concepts which implied that persons needing support could, and did, call on an array of helpers – relatives, friends, neighbours and the local community. In short, the terms used appeared to gloss over the gender of carers, the role of main carers and the costs of caring.

Much research has therefore addressed the reality of informal care. Researchers have found it difficult to locate the networks to which policy documents refer and have concluded that there is little scope for their development (Abrams et al., 1989). Friends and neighbours do not appear to play any significant role (Martin, White and Meltzer, 1989; Evason and Whittington, 1995). Informal care appears from the research to mean family care with the larger part of the task of caring falling on women (Millar, 1990; Parker, 1990; Evason and Whittington, 1995).

As there is no obvious sampling frame for carers, however, much of what has been published has been based on work relating to relatively small groups of carers, often at the heavy end of caring, and it has thus been difficult to extrapolate from these to the population of carers as a whole. In Great Britain this difficulty has been mitigated to some extent by detailed and secondary analysis of data obtained as part of the General Household Survey (GHS) of 1985 (Green, 1988; Parker and Lawton,1994). In Northern Ireland, whilst the same questions were included in the 1985 Continuous Household Survey (CHS), nothing beyond the most basic data has been produced. One option for researchers interested in this area would have been to investigate the possibility of further analysis of the 1985 data. Such an exercise would be of limited value. The problem relating to the Northern Ireland and, indeed, British data is not simply its age, but the fact that its collection preceded the very deep changes in policy and provision that have occurred over the past decade.

The reorganisation of community care in April 1993 was part of a broader pattern of change involving the withdrawal of the National Health Service from the provision of long-term and continuing care. This process of tightening access to hospital care has been spelt out most clearly in the guidance issued recently to health authorities in England on the circumstances in which such care is appropriate. These developments have rearranged responsibility for the provision of care and also significantly altered the way in which the costs of care are met. Put at its simplest, much of the care required has been diverted from the free National Health Service (NHS) into means-tested residential and domiciliary services. In consequence, there is a growing debate at the time of writing on the prospect of the benefits of wider home ownership cascading sideways to pay for care rather than down through the generations.

In the light of these changes, the module on informal care included in the 1994 Northern Ireland Social Attitudes (NISA) survey was designed therefore not only to provide us with up to date information on carers in Northern Ireland but also to examine the extent to which these broad policy developments on meeting the costs of care are in tune with the attitudes of the general population. The data therefore have considerable significance. Before turning to the analysis, two general observations should be made. First, it is perhaps easy in dealing with this kind of data to conceptualise caring as a burden imposed on those who care and it needs to be remembered that the great majority of those who care wish to do so (Evason and Whittington, 1995). Second, any perception of a conflict of interest between women who care and those requiring aid is unsatisfactory as women receive, as well as give, the bulk of care. The perspective of Walker (1983) which emphasises the structured dependence of women as carers and cared for is therefore more helpful.

## The Volume of Informal Welfare in Northern Ireland

Table 1 is of considerable interest as it indicates that in 1994 22 per cent of males

### Table 1
#### Percentage of adults who are/were carers by gender

|  | 1985 GB[1] male | 1985 GB[1] female | 1985 NI[2] male | 1985 NI[2] female | 1994 NI male | 1994 NI female |
|---|---|---|---|---|---|---|
| Cares for someone in same household | 4 | 4 | 4 | 6 | 4 | 6 |
| Cares for someone in another household | 8 | 11 | 5 | 8 | 18 | 23 |
| Cares for someone in same household and for someone in another household |  |  |  |  | * | 1 |
| Total | 12 | 15 | 9 | 14 | 22 | 29 |

* Less than 1 per cent
[1] Green, 1988, Table 2.1
[2] Policy Planning and Research Unit, 1986, Tables 16 and 17

and 29 per cent of females in Northern Ireland report that they are providing assistance to persons who are sick, handicapped or elderly. These informal carers account for 26 per cent of the adult population. The majority (57 per cent) of informal carers are female. The table also indicates that the proportion of the population stating that they provide informal care in Northern Ireland in 1994 is significantly higher than the levels of informal caring identified in Great Britain and Northern Ireland in 1985. The substantial increase noted, however, is a consequence of a much higher proportion of adults in Northern Ireland in 1994 reporting that they care for persons in another household. The proportion of adults in 1994 caring for someone in the same household is almost identical to that found in 1985.

As the questions used in the 1994 NISA and 1985 CHS surveys were identical, two possible explanations for these differences may be suggested. First, the attention given in the media to carers over the past decade may have produced a bandwagon effect with respondents wishing to identify themselves with a group that has been a focus of concern. Second, there is the possibility that our module has picked up the consequences of policies which limit statutory support within the broader context of a growing need for care. In other words, more people are caring on an informal basis to fill a widening gap between need and state provision. Looking at these two explanations we have no way of determining exactly which is of the greater significance. We are inclined to place emphasis on the second, however, noting the indications from other research (see Evason and Whittington, 1995, for a fuller discussion) that the new community care arrangements put in place in 1993 may be resulting in less rather than more statutory support for those in need. Whatever the explanation, and even though, as we indicate below, much of this activity is not at the heavy end of caring, the level of support reported is substantial. For policy makers and practitioners therefore the data raise the question of how much room there really is for any increase in the contribution of this sector to the care of elderly persons and persons with disabilities over the coming decade.

Table 2 details the age of carers by gender in Northern Ireland in 1994. The

### Table 2
#### Percentage of adults who are carers by gender and age

|  | Male | Female |
| --- | --- | --- |
| 18–24 | 19 | 25 |
| 25–44 | 21 | 31 |
| 45–59 | 22 | 43 |
| 60 or over | 26 | 15 |
| Total | 22 | 29 |

volume of support reported by those in younger age groups is perhaps surprising. Nevertheless, the group most likely to be providing informal care is women aged between 45 and 59. This is a predictable concentration given that women do more caring generally and the significance of elderly parents in the total need for care. Nevertheless, it is still important to note that our data suggest that as many as 43 per cent of women in the 45–59 age group in Northern Ireland are already providing informal care and account may need to be taken therefore of the capacity of this key grouping to do more.

Table 3 indicates that half of these carers had been providing assistance for five years or more and underlines the point made in the introduction that undertaking

## Table 3
### Duration of caring by gender (%)

|  | Male | Female | Total |
|---|---|---|---|
| Less than 3 years | 31 | 37 | 34 |
| 3 years – less than 5 years | 20 | 13 | 16 |
| 5 years or more | 49 | 50 | 50 |
| $n$ | 82 | 110 | 192 |

caring responsibilities today can have quite different implications for carers in comparison with, for example, the turn of the century.

A good deal of the literature focuses on the impact of caring on the health of carers (see, for example, Evason, Whittington and Knowles, 1992). Table 4 indicates the percentage of carers by age reporting significant health problems. The module did not include a question on whether carers thought their health

## Table 4
### Carers reporting significant health problems by age and gender (%)

|  | 18–24 | 25–44 | 45–59 | 60 or over | Total |
|---|---|---|---|---|---|
| Male | 22 | 6 | 30 | 37 | 20 |
| Female | 7 | 11 | 41 | 33 | 23 |

problems were to any extent a consequence of caring but, bearing in mind the small numbers, it is noteworthy that four in ten female carers in the 45–59 years age group reported significant health problems themselves.

Tables 5 and 6 examine the social class and marital status of carers and all respondents. There is no evidence of non-manual classes playing less of a role in informal welfare as a result, for example, of an enhanced capacity to purchase care. With regard to marital status, male carers seem more likely to be single but the numbers are small.

Table 7 shows little difference between men and women who are carers and the general population. Male carers are most likely to be in full-time employment or retired while female carers are split between those who are home makers, in part-time or full-time employment.

### Table 5
### Social class of carers and all respondents by gender (%)

|  | Male Carers | Male All | Female Carers | Female All |
|---|---|---|---|---|
| I and II | 31 | 29 | 14 | 17 |
| III non-manual | 14 | 13 | 29 | 31 |
| III manual | 33 | 34 | 16 | 11 |
| IV and V | 15 | 20 | 31 | 31 |
| Never had a job/not classifiable | 7 | 4 | 10 | 10 |

### Table 6
### Marital status of carers and all respondents by gender (%)

|  | Male Carers | Male All | Female Carers | Female All |
|---|---|---|---|---|
| Married/cohabiting | 66 | 70 | 59 | 53 |
| Single | 29 | 22 | 23 | 26 |
| Widowed/divorced/separated | 5 | 8 | 18 | 21 |

### Table 7
### Employment status of carers and all respondents by gender (%)

|  | Male Carers | Male All | Female Carers | Female All |
|---|---|---|---|---|
| Full-time employee/self-employed | 63 | 60 | 24 | 26 |
| Part-time employee/self-employed | 3 | 3 | 19 | 14 |
| Homemaker | 0 | 1 | 35 | 30 |
| Retired | 16 | 16 | 7 | 14 |
| Other# | 19 | 20 | 16 | 16 |

# Other includes those in full-time education and the unemployed.

## Variations in Caring Responsibilities

Whilst this general data is of interest, it has long been apparent that informal care can cover widely differing circumstances extending from the person who does a small amount of shopping for an elderly neighbour to the daughter who cares 24 hours a day for a parent with severe dementia. Thus, as Parker and Lawton (1994, p. 2) note, whilst the overall figure of six million carers based on the GHS data for Great Britain has been widely used, many of these carers are not engaged in the intensive and difficult sort of support which is the focus of many small-scale surveys or, indeed, the examples presented as typical in the media.

One way of addressing this problem, although it is less than satisfactory, is to distinguish between carers on the basis of the number of hours of caring provided each week and the number of days each week on which care is given. Green's (1988) analysis of the 1985 data for Great Britain used a cut off point of 20 hours per week and Table 8 indicates that when this is applied to the 1994 data for Northern Ireland the outcome is surprisingly similar.

Table 9 extends the analysis of hours devoted to caring and indicates a very

### Table 8
### Number of hours per week spent caring (%)

| Hours per week | GB 1985* | NI 1994 |
| --- | --- | --- |
| Less than 10 | 57 | 57 |
| 10–19 | 19 | 23 |
| 20 or more | 24 | 20 |

*Green, 1988

### Table 9
### Number of hours per week spent caring by gender (%)

| Hours per week | Male | Female | All |
| --- | --- | --- | --- |
| Less than 10 | 71 | 47 | 57 |
| 10–19 | 17 | 28 | 23 |
| 20–39 | 6 | 8 | 7 |
| 40–59 | 1 | 2 | 2 |
| 60 or more | 5 | 14 | 10 |
| n | 82 | 110 | 192 |

sharp gender differential. This data allows us to address a matter that has puzzled researchers in Northern Ireland for some time: the high proportion of males identifying themselves as carers in the CHS data and their low profile in small-scale studies. The table indicates that for the majority of male carers (71 per cent) their caring input is for under 10 hours a week, whilst the reverse is the case for female carers. Only 23 per cent of those providing care of 40 hours a week or more are male. In short, women are more likely to be informal carers and their caring input is significantly higher. In consequence, Table 10 indicates that the majority of male carers are involved in providing support for under four days each week whilst the greatest concentration of female carers is to be found amongst those caring for seven days a week.

### Table 10
#### Number of days each week care is provided by gender (%)

| Number of days | Male | Female | All |
| --- | --- | --- | --- |
| 1 | 27 | 18 | 22 |
| 2 | 15 | 13 | 14 |
| 3 | 17 | 15 | 15 |
| 4 | 4 | 7 | 6 |
| 5 | 10 | 4 | 7 |
| 6 | 4 | 2 | 3 |
| 7 | 23 | 41 | 33 |
| $n$ | 82 | 110 | 192 |

### Table 11
#### Age group of carers and those who care for 10 hours a week or more (%)

| Age group | All carers | Carers who care for 10 hours a week or more |
| --- | --- | --- |
| 18–24 | 12 | 9 |
| 25–44 | 42 | 35 |
| 45–59 | 29 | 34 |
| 60 or over | 17 | 22 |
| $n$ | 192 | 83 |

The relatively high incidence of persons in the younger age groups reporting that they provide informal care was noted above. As Table 11 indicates, however, confining attention to those caring for 10 hours a week or more produces a slightly different pattern with the majority of those caring for over 10 hours a week being aged 45 or over.

**The Need for Care**

The data from this module tell us a good deal about carers and also, of course, about those who require support. We cannot, however, simply extrapolate from this, or any other, data on carers, and assume that so many carers equals so many people requiring care for a number of reasons. First, a small number of carers may be assisting more than one person. Second, and running in the reverse direction, there may be an element of double counting where, for example, an elderly person receives varying degrees of support from a number of family members. Nevertheless, our data do provide some indication of the very substantial need for assistance in Northern Ireland and this is in keeping with data showing particularly high levels of disability amongst adults in this part of the United Kingdom (McCoy and Smith, 1992).

Tables 12 and 13 indicate that the majority (67 per cent) of those assisted are aged 65 and over and the most commonly reported reason for needing help is old age/frailty. Twenty nine per cent of respondents reported more than one reason. Of particular interest is the fact that 16 per cent of those assisted are aged 85 or over.

## Table 12

### Age of person cared for*

| Age group | % |
| --- | --- |
| Under 18 | 12 |
| 18–49 | 9 |
| 50–64 | 13 |
| 65–74 | 22 |
| 75–84 | 29 |
| 85 or over | 16 |
| $n$ | 192 |

*Where more than one person is cared for, the tables in this section refer to the main person cared for.*

## Table 13
### Reasons for needing help

|  | % |
|---|---|
| Old age/frailty | 49 |
| Physical disability | 40 |
| Physical illness | 29 |
| Mental handicap | 8 |
| Mental illness | 4 |

*Note: percentages add up to more than 100 as respondents could list several reasons why the person needed help.*

### The Direction and Nature of Care

Table 14 details the relationship between those providing support and those

## Table 14
### Relationship to person cared for (%)

| Relationship | All carers | Carers who care for 10 hours a week or more |
|---|---|---|
| Spouse | 5 | 11 |
| Child/stepchild | 8 | 14 |
| Parent | 35 | 43 |
| Parent-in-law | 8 | 5 |
| Another relation | 34 | 20 |
| Friend/neighbour | 10 | 6 |
| $n$ | 192 | 82 |

assisted in Northern Ireland in 1994 by all carers and those providing care for 10 hours or more each week. The data confirm earlier findings (1985 GHS and CHS) to the effect that informal care means, by and large, family care. Only 10 per cent of all informal carers are assisting persons to whom they are not related and those caring for 10 hours a week or more are even more tightly focused on their immediate relatives.

Tables 15 and 16 indicate the extent and types of help provided. Female carers are more heavily engaged than male carers in all tasks apart from gardening and

## Table 15
### Type of help provided (%)

|  | All carers | Male carers | Female carers | Carers who care for 10 hours a week or more |
|---|---|---|---|---|
| Personal care, washing, dressing | 32 | 18 | 42 | 50 |
| Physical help, bed, chair, stairs | 24 | 8 | 35 | 35 |
| Paperwork/financial matters | 34 | 25 | 41 | 37 |
| Shopping and housework | 68 | 55 | 77 | 81 |
| Gardening and decorating | 37 | 46 | 29 | 40 |
| Companionship | 59 | 54 | 63 | 65 |
| Takes him/her out | 48 | 40 | 54 | 53 |
| Gives medicine | 16 | 6 | 24 | 31 |
| Supervision | 21 | 12 | 28 | 30 |

## Table 16
### Number of types of help provided (%)

|  | All carers | Male carers | Female carers | Carers who care for 10 hours a week or more |
|---|---|---|---|---|
| 1 or 2 | 39 | 53 | 28 | 25 |
| 3 or 4 | 34 | 34 | 34 | 33 |
| 5 or more | 27 | 13 | 38 | 42 |
| *n* | 192 | 82 | 110 | 82 |

decorating and 38 per cent of female carers provide five or more kinds of help compared with 13 per cent of male carers. It is also noticeable that personal care figures more prominently in the support given by those providing help for 10 or more hours a week.

**Other Sources of Support**

Tables 17 and 18 detail the care and support provided to those cared for apart from that given by carers. Table 17 confirms the narrowness in practice of informal welfare: other relatives are far and away the most commonly mentioned sources of additional support. Taking the two tables together it is difficult to see any evidence of a mixed economy of welfare with voluntary, private, statutory and informal

### Table 17
### Other non-statutory help given by gender of carer (%)

|  | Male | Female |
|---|---|---|
| Other relative | 64 | 71 |
| Voluntary worker | 4 | 12 |
| Friend | 4 | 4 |
| Paid help | – | 4 |

### Table 18
### Receipt of statutory services by gender of carer (%)

|  | Male | Female |
|---|---|---|
| Regular GP visits | 28 | 13 |
| Community/district nurse | 40 | 25 |
| Health visitor | 21 | 13 |
| Social worker | 9 | 13 |
| Home help | 21 | 19 |
| Meals on wheels | 4 | 1 |
| Other | 6 | 8 |

sectors working together. Statutory and family provision are dominant. Finally, at a number of points female carers report rather lower levels of statutory support for those they assist than male carers; for example, only 25 per cent of female carers compared with 40 per cent of male carers appeared to have the help of a community or district nurse. However, the work of Parker and Lawton (1994) suggests a need for caution in interpreting this data. A number of variables apart from gender may be at work here. Nevertheless, the data raise an issue which at the very least merits further research.

**Attitudes to Caring**
The second half of the module was designed to examine the general public's attitudes towards, and beliefs about, caring. Additionally, the objective was to determine the level of support for recent directions in community care policy. Table 19 details responses on the first eight attitudinal items. To a large extent the findings are unequivocal with the majority of respondents considering that carers

## Table 19
### Attitudes to caring (%)

|  | Strongly agree/agree | Neither agree nor disagree | Strongly disagree/disagree |
|---|---|---|---|
| 1 ...these days people who need care get most of their help from relatives | 78 | 7 | 14 |
| 2 ...carers are too often taken for granted by the authorities | 93 | 3 | 3 |
| 3 ...looking after family members is a duty and carers should not be paid by the authorities | 15 | 11 | 73 |
| 4 ...relatives are much less willing than they used to be to look after other members of the family | 66 | 8 | 24 |
| 5 ...all carers should be entitled to a state benefit which recognises their work | 89 | 6 | 4 |
| 6 ...nowadays, government provides most of the help for people needing care | 28 | 10 | 61 |
| 7 ...women should be prepared to give up their jobs to care for family members who are sick, disabled or elderly | 14 | 15 | 69 |
| 8 ...men should be prepared to give up their jobs to care for family members who are sick, disabled or elderly | 9 | 12 | 78 |

are taken for granted, that there should be payment in recognition of the work they do and that women should not be expected to give up their jobs to care. There is, however, some contradiction between the responses to items 1 and 4. On the one hand people believe relatives provide most of the help that is needed, but the majority of respondents also consider relatives to be less willing to help than they used to be. It may be that people are drawing on their own experience at one point and broader popular stereotypes of declining family and community life at another. Leaving this aside, the data shows a good deal of awareness of the existence of informal carers and support for them.

*Variations by Gender, Age and Class*

Despite the greater involvement of women in caring, there are hardly any significant variations in the attitudes of men and women towards the role of the

Table 20

## Attitudes to caring by age group

|  | 18–34 years | 35–54 years | 55 years or over |
|---|---|---|---|
| % who strongly agree/agree that: | | | |
| 1 ...these days people who need care get most of their help from relatives | 82 | 81 | 69 |
| 2 ...carers are too often taken for granted by the authorities | 93 | 96 | 88 |
| 4 ...relatives are much less willing than they used to be to look after other members of the family | 57 | 67 | 75 |
| 5 ...all carers should be entitled to a state benefit which recognises their work | 88 | 90 | 92 |
| % who strongly disagree/disagree that: | | | |
| 3 ...looking after family members is a duty and carers should not be paid by the authorities | 73 | 78 | 66 |
| 6 ...nowadays, government provides most of the help for people needing care | 65 | 66 | 50 |
| 7 ...women should be prepared to give up their jobs to care for family members who are sick, disabled or elderly | 79 | 71 | 56 |
| 8 ...men should be prepared to give up their jobs to care for family members who are sick, disabled or elderly | 81 | 79 | 73 |

## Table 21

### Attitudes to caring by social class

|  | I and II | IIINM* | IIIM* | IV and V |
|---|---|---|---|---|
| *% who strongly agree/agree that:* | | | | |
| 1 ...these days people who need care get most of their help from relatives | 74 | 78 | 4 | 77 |
| 2 ...carers are too often taken for granted by the authorities | 96 | 94 | 93 | 89 |
| 4 ...relatives are much less willing than they used to be to look after other members of the family | 71 | 60 | 67 | 65 |
| 5 ...all carers should be entitled to a state benefit which recognises their work | 88 | 90 | 89 | 92 |
| *% who strongly disagree/disagree that:* | | | | |
| 3 ...looking after family members is a duty and carers should not be paid by the authorities | 78 | 74 | 74 | 66 |
| 6 ...nowadays, government provides most of the help for people needing care | 71 | 67 | 56 | 55 |
| 7 ...women should be prepared to give up their jobs to care for family members who are sick, disabled or elderly | 73 | 70 | 71 | 66 |
| 8 ...men should be prepared to give up their jobs to care for family members who are sick, disabled or elderly | 81 | 78 | 76 | 77 |

* IIINM = III Non-manual; IIIM = III Manual

family and the state in caring. In fact, the differences are slight for all but three of the items. The most marked difference is noted in responses to '...all carers should be entitled to a state benefit which recognises their work': 45 per cent of women strongly agree with this statement compared to 33 per cent of men. Also in their responses to the statement '...carers are too often taken for granted by the authorities', some 56 per cent of women strongly agree with this compared to 50 per cent of men. The final item which demonstrated these stronger views by women is '...these days people who need care get most of their help from relatives'; 35 per cent of women strongly agree with this compared to 29 per cent of men.

Table 20 indicates a strong consensus across age groups on items 2 and 5. Beyond these, however, there is less agreement. The variations on items 3 and 7 are probably attributable to the prevalence of more traditional attitudes towards women and the family amongst older respondents. The causes of the remaining variations are less clear. Older respondents have a much more positive view of the contribution of the state and are considerably less positive about the role of the family in caring today. This may be a consequence of actual experience or responses coloured by a, perhaps, idealised view of the past. Additionally there may be a complex interaction occurring here between age, gender and provision and receipt of informal care. This is one of the issues to be addressed by the researchers in further analysis of the data.

Table 21 details attitudes by social class. Whilst there is some variation, the most obvious aspect of the data is the consistency of opinion across social classes on most of these items.

**The Future**

It was noted in our introduction that during the 1980s a number of policy documents argued for more reliance on informal care in meeting the need over the coming years. Table 22 indicates that the majority of respondents consider that providing the bulk of care required by the elderly over the next few years is a matter for government. There is minority support for the family taking responsibility. Interestingly, the voluntary sector is not seen as having a significant role to play nor are friends and neighbours.

In the 1990s there has been a significant rearrangement of the financing of care with costs being transferred to the individual and family. The reduction of the role of the NHS means more people coming within the scope of the means test. For example, where residential or nursing home care is required and the person in need of care has savings/assets of £8,000 or more (to be increased to £10,000 in April 1996) including the family home (unless this is occupied by a spouse or elderly/disabled relative), then there is liability for the full cost of care. Frequently this can only be met through the sale of the home and the fact that, for example, the person has made a will leaving the house to his or her children is irrelevant. Thus modest assets acquired over a lifetime will be absorbed by the cost of care and the payment over decades of tax and national insurance contributions is of no significance. The implication of this policy is that individuals need to consider

## Table 22
### Who should provide the bulk of care for elderly people?

|  | All respondents (%) |
|---|---|
| *Should it be...* |  |
| Relatives/spouse | 28 |
| The government | 61 |
| Friends/neighbours | 2 |
| Voluntary organisation | 3 |
| Government + relatives | 1 |
| Mixture of all | 3 |
| Don't know/not answered | 2 |
| $n$ | 754 |

## Table 23
### Responsibilities for care of the elderly (%)

|  | Strongly agree/agree | Neither agree nor disagree | Strongly disagree/disagree |
|---|---|---|---|
| ... it should be everyone's responsibility to make their own provision so that they can pay for their own care when they are old | 21 | 11 | 67 |
| ... people who have paid tax all their lives should **not** be expected to pay for any care they may need when they are old | 81 | 5 | 12 |
| ... relatives should be made to care for close family members who need help | 19 | 12 | 68 |
| ... if necessary, elderly people should sell their own home to meet the cost of living in an old person's home | 16 | 9 | 74 |

taking out private insurance to cover such costs should they require such care in the future. A further option would be for the State to require a greater contribution from the family.

Table 23 indicates limited support in Northern Ireland for current policy directions. There is little support for people having to make their own provision; strong support for help which is free at the point of need; very modest support for compelling relatives to assist and the majority of respondents are opposed to elderly people having to sell their assets to pay for care.

**Conclusion**

This chapter has presented the main results of the module on caring included in the 1994 NISA survey. The module has yielded a substantial volume of data that should be of considerable interest to practitioners and policy makers. Most importantly, the module gives us an up-to-date picture of the volume of informal care currently being provided in Northern Ireland and the views of the general public on both caring and the very radical changes in policy that have occurred in recent years.

The main conclusions we would draw from the data are as follows. First, the proportion of the population engaged in providing support on an informal basis to elderly persons and persons with disabilities is at such a level that consideration must be given to whether it is realistic to expect this sector to do even more as the need for care increases over the coming years. A commitment at the lower end of the spectrum of say 5–10 hours a week can still be a significant contribution for persons responsible for running a home and/or in paid employment. Moreover, caring is not evenly distributed across the population and the contribution of the key grouping – women in the 45–59 year age group – is already very substantial.

Second, the data indicates yet again that informal care means care given by relatives – there is little evidence here of the existence of broader helping networks. This highlights the importance of a more integrated perspective. If informal care means family care, then the capacity of this sector to cope must be assessed within a broader framework taking account of changes in, and pressures on, the family. For example, there is a need to consider the extent to which creation of a flexible labour force with greater insecurity and stress and longer, less predictable working hours may impair the capacity of family members to care. Indeed, this would be an interesting topic for future research.

Third, it is clear that there is very little support amongst the general population for the new approaches to meeting the costs of care which have developed over the past 10 years. The costs of care must be met in one way or another but it would appear desirable that the mechanisms for doing so enjoy some measure of public support. This will require a much more intensive and comprehensive public debate than has so far occurred.

## References

ABRAMS, P. et al. 1989. *Neighbourhood Care and Social Policy*, HMSO, London.

BARCLAY, P. 1982. *Social Workers, Their Roles and Tasks. Report of the Barclay Committee*, Bedford Square Press, London.

CARERS NATIONAL ASSOCIATION 1994. *Community Care: Just a Fairy Tale?*, C.N.A., London.

CUMBERLEGE REPORT 1986. *Neighbourhood Nursing – a Focus for Care*, HMSO, London.

DEPT OF HEALTH 1995. *NHS Responsibilities for Meeting Continuing Health Care Needs*, HMSO, London.

DHSS 1981. *Growing Older*, HMSO, London.

EVASON, E., WHITTINGTON, D. and KNOWLES, L. 1992. *Quality and Caring*, Centre for Health and Social Research, University of Ulster, Coleraine.

EVASON, E. and WHITTINGTON, D. 1995. *The Cost of Caring – Final Report of a Longitudinal Study into the Circumstances of Carers in Northern Ireland*, Northern Ireland Equal Opportunities Commission, Belfast.

FINCH, J. and GROVES, D. (EDS) 1983. *A Labour of Love: Women, Work and Caring*, Routledge and Kegan Paul, London.

GREEN, H. 1988. *1985 General Household Survey Informal Care Report*, HMSO, London.

GRIFFITHS REPORT 1988. *Community Care: Agenda for Action*, HMSO, London.

JOSHI, H. 1987. 'The Cost of Caring', in Glendinning, C. and Millar, J. (eds), *Women and Poverty*, Wheatsheaf Books, Brighton.

MARTIN, J., WHITE, A. and MELTZER, H. 1989. *Disabled Adults: Services, Transport and Employment*, HMSO, London.

McCOY, D. and SMITH, S. M. 1992. *The Prevalence of Disability among Adults in Northern Ireland*, Policy, Planning and Research Unit, Belfast.

MILLAR, J. 1990. *The Social Economic Situation of Solo Women in Europe*, Centre for the Analysis of Social Policy, University of Bath, Bath.

OPCS 1987. *Population Projections 1985–2025*, HMSO, London.

PARKER G. 1990. *With Due Care and Attention*, Family Policy Studies Centre, London.

PARKER, G. and LAWTON, D. 1994. *Different Types of Care, Different Types of Carer: Evidence from the General Household Survey*, HMSO, London.

POLICY PLANNING AND RESEARCH UNIT 1986. *Continuous Household Survey.* PPRU, Belfast.

TWIGG, J. and ATKIN, K. 1994. *Carers Perceived*, Open University Press, Buckingham.

UNGERSON, C. 1987. *Policy is Personal: Sex, Gender and Informal Care*, Tavistock, London.

WALKER, A. 1983. 'Care for Elderly People: A Conflict Between Women and the State', in Finch, J. and Groves, D. (eds), *A Labour of Love: Women, Work and Caring*, Routledge and Kegan Paul, London.

# 4

# Women and Work

J.M. Trewsdale and J. Kremer

**Introduction**

Despite the considerable increase in interest in women's issues over recent years, across the United Kingdom as a whole, hard empirical data on women and employment remain scarce. For example, the last large-scale survey devoted exclusively to women and work in Great Britain was carried out over 15 years ago by Martin and Roberts (1984), and yet it is still regarded as the definitive survey in this field, and has spawned a number of secondary analyses which continue to inform current debate (for example, Dex, 1988).

During the 1990s, government statistics, including the now quarterly Labour Force Survey (LFS) and the annual Continuous Household Survey (CHS), have yielded more up-to-date information, and this has been supplemented at regular intervals by material derived from the British Social Attitudes Survey (BSA) (Witherspoon, 1985; 1988; Witherspoon & Prior, 1991; Thomson, 1995). However, as anyone involved with employment statistics will appreciate, times are changing very quickly and the role played by gender in this labour market dynamic cannot be overestimated. The decline in employment in the traditional manufacturing industries and the accompanying rise in employment in the service sector which has occurred over the last 20 years has represented a fundamental change in the employment structure of the United Kingdom (Johnes and Taylor, 1989). As government itself has recognised through Operation 2000, there is now a need to attract women back into paid employment in order to meet shortfalls in particular sectors of the economy. Accordingly it is also necessary to constantly monitor and evaluate the changing profile of women in the labour market but, at the present time, it is unlikely that the available data in Great Britain enable this task to be performed adequately (see Brannen et al., 1994).

In comparison with information available on Great Britain, the research picture in Northern Ireland is somewhat healthier. Apart from data which are available directly through government in Northern Ireland, including the Northern Ireland LFS and CHS, the Equal Opportunities Commission for Northern Ireland, together with locally based research projects, has ensured a healthy flow of information on gender and employment (see Montgomery and Davies, 1990; Trewsdale, 1990; Kremer and Montgomery 1993). The picture which this research presents is of a huge rise in the number of women working and especially working part time, but set against a backcloth of organisations which have been slow to respond to the new demands created by the changed workforce (Kremer et al., 1996).

The purpose of this chapter is to continue to fuel this programme of local research by exploring the responses of employees to the changing labour market in the 1990s, and in particular the role of women, who comprise the largest part of the 'flexible workforce' as it has come to be known. It has been argued that the emergence of 'the flexible workforce' is both demand and supply led. In part it is said to reflect industry's desire to increase flexibility by employing in response to fluctuating market demands; in part it may reflect employees' willingness to work part-time (Anderton and Mayhew, 1994; Curtice, 1993). The Northern Ireland Social Attitudes (NISA) results offer an opportunity to consider which thesis is most tenable. If, by and large, women are happy with the structure and characteristics of the new order then one may conclude that their wishes and preferences are dominant; dissatisfaction, on the other hand, may suggest that although they wish to take up employment, the structure of that employment primarily reflects not their needs but the needs and wishes of the employers. In addition, and with this theme very much in mind, the NISA data allow us to consider the structural and attitudinal impediments which stand in the way of women's advancement in the labour market, and ultimately impact on the achievement of equality of opportunity for women and men at work.

To address these related concerns and at the same time to tell the story of gender and employment in Northern Ireland in the 1990s, this chapter has been divided into a number of sections. To begin, a profile of the changing labour market is offered, highlighting the role played by part-time women workers. This is followed by a consideration of attitudes to work, including the reasons why women and men work, and their satisfaction with work itself, their hours, their mobility and their pay. Third is a consideration of the perceptions and realities of equality of opportunity in employment, including the availability of childcare services, family friendly working arrangements and trade union activism. Finally, these themes are used to draw conclusions as to where women currently stand and where they are likely to stand as we approach the millennium.

## Gender and the Labour Market: Stability and Change

It may be useful to begin by presenting the basic facts on structural change. In Northern Ireland in 1971 there were just under 500,000 employees of whom 38 per cent (188,300) were female; by 1995 the total had risen to 566,000 with women accounting for 50 per cent (283,000) (Census of Employment, Department of Economic Development) The net increase of 76,100 employees over the 24 year period was the result of an 18,800 decrease in male employees offset by a 95,000 increase in female employees in employment. The majority of the increase was attributable to an explosion in female part-time employment. A full-time/part-time breakdown of the data shows that whereas in 1971, 19 per cent of the female employees in employment were part-time, by June 1995 the percentage had risen to 43 (Department of Economic Development Press Notice, September 1995; data are provisional).

Against this backcloth of structural change the broad results of the NISA survey reflect those presented in the Labour Force Survey (LFS) for 1994. As can be seen from Table 1, 93 per cent of women in employment in the NISA survey were

### Table 1
### Women in work: NISA and Labour Force Survey data (%)

|  | NISA | LFS |
|---|---|---|
| Employees | 93 | 92 |
| Full-time | 63 | 57 |
| Part-time | 30 | 35 |
| Self-employed | 5 | 4 |
| Government training schemes | 2 | 3 |

Note: NISA data: age 18–59 years; LFS data age 16–59 years
Source: LFS, 1994

working as employees, and 30 per cent were working part-time. The self-employed account for just over 5 per cent of the total. This compares with 92 per cent, 38 per cent and 5 per cent, respectively, for the LFS. The percentage difference in the figures for the part-time proportion may be due to the fact that the LFS refers to all persons aged 16 and over whereas the NISA data are for those aged 18 and over.

## Occupation and Industrial Segregation

Overall, the structures of occupational and industrial segregation which emerge from the survey do not show any significant departures from the patterns which have developed during the past quarter of a century (Trewsdale, 1987; Ruggie, 1988). A high proportion of women work in the service sector (see Table 2). This is

**Table 2**

**Persons in employment* by industry (SIC80)***

|  | Full-time | | Part-time | |
|---|---|---|---|---|
|  | Male (%) | Female (%) | Male (%) | Female (%) |
| Agriculture | 5 | 1 | 33 | 1 |
| Energy and Water | 3 | 1 | 0 | 0 |
| Metal extrac. | 2 | 0 | 0 | 1 |
| Metal goods/eng. | 8 | 3 | 7 | 2 |
| Other manf. | 13 | 13 | 9 | 5 |
| Construction | 12 | 1 | 0 | 1 |
| *Service Sector:* | | | | |
| Distribution and Hotels | 18 | 20 | 5 | 22 |
| Transport and Communication | 7 | 3 | 12 | 2 |
| Banking and Finance | 7 | 9 | 14 | 4 |
| Other Services | 20 | 48 | 21 | 62 |
| Not Classified | 3 | 2 | 0 | 1 |

* includes the self-employed.
** Standard Industrial Classification

particularly true of part-time workers – 90 per cent of all part-time female workers in the survey are in services compared with 80 per cent of females working full-time. These percentages are in contrast to the results for males which showed just under 53 per cent of male full-time workers employed in the services. The service sector covers a wide area of industries including Distribution and Hotels, Transport and Communication, Banking and Finance and the sector known as 'Other services', the sector in which the highest proportion of female workers is found. 'Other services' includes personal services (e.g. hairdressers), education (schools, universities and colleges) medical and other health services (hospitals, dental practices, nursing homes), and other public sector services such as the police, the justice system and social security offices. Also included in this extensive division are recreational services and other cultural services which cover things as diverse as sports facilities and the arts.

## Table 3
### Persons in employment* by occupation (SOC)**

| Occupation | Full-time Male (%) | Full-time Female (%) | Part-time Male (%) | Part-time Female (%) |
|---|---|---|---|---|
| Managers and Administrators | 17 | 8 | 28 | 3 |
| Professional | 10 | 10 | 16 | 2 |
| Associated Professional and Technical | 7 | 9 | 0 | 12 |
| Clerical and Related | 7 | 29 | 0 | 20 |
| Craft and Related | 26 | 4 | 12 | 3 |
| Personal and Protective Services | 3 | 16 | 5 | 26 |
| Sales | 7 | 12 | 7 | 14 |
| Plant and Machine Operators | 15 | 7 | 0 | 2 |
| Other | 8 | 5 | 33 | 20 |

* includes the self-employed.
** Standard Occupational Classification.

Similar distinctions are apparent in the results for occupations (see Table 3) Women workers are to be found in the traditional female occupations, 'clerical and related', 'personal and protective services' and 'sales'. These occupations account for almost 60 per cent of both full-time and part-time female jobs.

There are, however, significant differences between female occupations in Northern Ireland and Great Britain. Only 27 per cent of full-time female workers in Northern Ireland are in the most prestigious groups: 'managers and administrators', 'professional' (which includes teachers), and 'associated professional and technical' occupations, which includes nurses. The corresponding figure for Great Britain in 1991 was around 36 per cent. On the other hand 16 per cent of full-time and 26 per cent of part-time females were in 'personal and protective' services in Northern Ireland compared with figures for Great Britain of 11 per cent and 17 per cent respectively in 1991 (BSA). This result should, however, be treated with some caution for the overall NISA survey figure of 20 per cent of all female workers in this category compares with a 1991 Census of Population figure of 13 per cent and a Women's Working Lives Survey of 15 per cent. Some of the inconsistency might be explained by a two-year difference in the lower age limit; 16 in the case of the Census of Population and 18 for the NISA survey.

It is clear that women have a well-established position in certain sectors and occupations in the economy. The picture of industrial segration is reinforced by the results of two further questions asked of male respondents in the survey:

*Where you work, are there any women doing the same sort of work as you?*

*Do you think of your work as ...*

*... mainly men's work*

*... mainly women's work*

*... or, work that either men or women do?*

As Table 4 shows, well over half of the male employees (58%) reported that there were no women employees doing the same sort of work that they themselves were doing, and over one third thought of their work as 'mainly men's work'.

Table 4

**Segregation in the workplace: response from males (%)**

| | |
|---|---|
| Are there any women doing the same sort of work as you? | yes: 42 |
| | no: 58 |
| Work is mainly men's work | 35 |
| Men's or women's work | 64 |

Given the increase in part-time jobs, the vast majority of which are considered 'women's work' (see Davies and Downey, 1993), this segregation of the labour force can be expected to increase for as long as the major expansion in jobs is to be found in the service sector and as long as those jobs are offered predominantly on a part-time basis. What evidence there is of an increase in male part-time employment is to be found in the agriculture industry where it is more likely to be a second job rather than the primary source of income (Trewsdale, 1992).

Finally, the survey shows that employment is relatively stable, with just over one half of workers having been with the same employer for over five years and 76 per cent for two years or more. As Table 5 shows, male employees are less mobile than female employees, 55 per cent compared with 45 per cent having been with the same employer for over five years. As would be expected, full-time employees (54 per cent) are more likely to have over five years service with the same employer than part-time workers (32 per cent). The full-time/part-time breakdown of the female workforce reflects this difference with 51 per cent of full-time workers having more than five years with the same employer compared with just 32 per cent of part-timers. It appears, therefore that the female part-time worker is

### Table 5
### Length of time with current employer (%)

|  | Under 2 years | 2–5 years | Over 5 years |
|---|---|---|---|
| Male | 23 | 22 | 55 |
| Female | 25 | 30 | 45 |
| *Female:* | | | |
| Full-time | 22 | 27 | 51 |
| Part-time | 32 | 36 | 32 |

either more vulnerable to dismissal or alternatively more mobile than her full-time counterpart.

## Women's Attitudes to Work
### Why do Women Work?

A common misconception is that full-time and part-time workers differ fundamentally in the reasons why they work and what they expect from work, and that men differ from women in this respect (Hakim, 1991). The reality is that these differences are marginal, and the NISA results confirm this. When asked why they work, two-thirds of the women stated that work meant more to them than earning a living. On this question, full-time workers returned only a marginally higher figure than part-timers: 67 per cent compared with 65 per cent. The remaining one-third appear to have a simple approach to their employment; they work solely to earn a living (see Table 6).

### Table 6
### Why an employee works (%)

|  | Male | Female | Female Full-time | Part-time |
|---|---|---|---|---|
| Just a means of earning a living | 39 | 34 | 33 | 36 |
| More than a means of earning a living | 61 | 66 | 67 | 65 |

Respondents who gave this answer were asked why they stayed in their present job. Table 7 shows that among female full-time workers, two in five believed that there were no better jobs available, just over one in five that they did not possess the right skills to move on and just less than two in five that they would feel the same in any job. Similar factors affected the part-time worker's decisions although

## Table 7
### Reasons why employees stay in current job if 'only earning a living' (%)

|  | Male | Female | Female Full-time | Female Part-time |
|---|---|---|---|---|
| No better job available | 46 | 39 | 40 | 36 |
| Not the right skills to move on | 27 | 25 | 24 | 33 |
| Feel the same in any job | 28 | 31 | 37 | 30 |

*Note: percentages may not add up to 100 due to rounding.*

more of them – one-third – felt that they did not possess the requisite skills to make a move possible (see Appendix A).

Respondents were asked whether they would still want a paid job, even if they had enough money to live on (see Table 8). Over 77 per cent said they would, with

## Table 8
### Would employee prefer a paid job if had enough to live on? (%)

|  | Male | Female | Female Full-time | Female Part-time |
|---|---|---|---|---|
| Prefer paid job | 77 | 77 | 82 | 69 |
| Wouldn't bother to work | 23 | 21 | 16 | 30 |
| Don't know | 1 | 2 | 2 | 0 |

*Note: percentages may not add up to 100 due to rounding.*

the full-time female workers some 12 percentage points in excess of part-time workers (82 per cent and 69 per cent, respectively).

At first sight there appears to be some inconsistency between the results reported in Tables 6 and 8. Around 33 per cent of full-time workers said that they work only to earn a living (Table 6); but only 16 per cent of full-time workers said they would not bother to work if they had enough money to live on (Table 8). The differences are not too surprising: full-time workers are likely to give a more carefully considered response to the proposition that they need not have a job at all, than to a general question about why they work. But it is the differences in the full-time and part-time workers' responses to the results reported in Table 8 that is more interesting. A much larger proportion of the part-time workers clearly would not work if they did not have to. This reflects the findings for Great Britain of

Hakim (1991). The part-time female worker may be on the margin of the labour force but the thrust of the evidence suggests that she is more likely to work out of financial necessity than her full-time counterpart.

In line with previous research (Kremer and Montgomery, 1993; Curtice, 1993), the part-time workers appear to be happier with their hours of work than their full-time counterparts. Only one fifth expressed a preference for longer or shorter hours compared with nearly one third of full-time workers who would have

Table 9

Preference for hours worked per week (%)

|  | Male | Female | Female Full-time | Female Part-time |
|---|---|---|---|---|
| More hours | 3 | 4 | 1 | 10 |
| Fewer hours | 29 | 24 | 31 | 10 |
| Happy with hours | 68 | 72 | 68 | 81 |

preferred shorter hours, see Table 9. These data are derived from all working women in the sample; however, when the results to this question are analysed taking into account childcare facilities for dependent children, the picture changes somewhat (as can be seen later in this chapter).

The answers to these questions suggest that the new employment patterns have tapped a rich vein of labour supply. Employers may have wanted a more flexible labour force but it is unlikely that their efforts would have succeeded if there had not been large numbers of women who felt they had to work because of financial necessity but who preferred a part-time rather than a full-time commitment.

On the other hand, women workers' attitudes to their general working conditions suggest that full-time workers may experience less role conflict than part-time workers. As can be seen from Table 10, just over one half of women workers said they did 'the best work they could even if sometimes it interfered with the rest of their life'. But the female full-time worker demonstrated a relatively higher level of dedication by returning a figure of just under 55 per cent compared with 42 per cent for the female part-time worker. In contrast 51 per cent of female part-time workers stated they worked 'hard, but, not so as to interfere with the rest of their life' compared with just under 38 per cent of the full-time female workers. The remaining percentage represented the group who stated that they 'worked only as hard as they had to'.

## Table 10
### How hard does the employee work? (%)

|  | Only as hard as I have to | Hard, but so as not to interfere with the rest of my life | The best I can, even if it sometimes interferes with the rest of my life |
|---|---|---|---|
| Male | 18 | 36 | 46 |
| Female | 7 | 42 | 51 |
| *Female:* | | | |
| Full-time | 8 | 38 | 55 |
| Part-time | 8 | 51 | 42 |

### Pay and Relative Pay

As well as being relatively happy with the hours she works, the female part-time worker seems to be reasonably content with her earnings. Of the full-time female workers who answered the question, 60 per cent were of the opinion that their wages were 'reasonable' but 23 per cent stated that they were 'a bit low' and a further 13 per cent were under the impression that their wages were 'very low'. On the other hand the part-time female workers seemed relatively more satisfied with their current earnings, with 69 per cent thinking them 'reasonable', 21 per cent considering them 'a bit low' and 6 per cent stating that they were 'very low'. When asked how they viewed the pay gap between the highest and lowest paid people at their place of work (Table 11), over one half (55 per cent) of full-time female workers were of the opinion that the pay gap was either 'too big' or 'much too big' and 38 per cent stated that the pay gap was 'about right'. The proportion of part-time female workers who thought the pay gap either 'too big' or 'much too big'

## Table 11
### Attitudes of female employees to paygap at place of work (%)

|  | Full-time | Part-time |
|---|---|---|
| Much too big | 25 | 28 |
| Too big | 30 | 27 |
| About right | 38 | 30 |
| Too small | 3 | 11 |
| Much too small | 0 | 1 |
| Don't know | 4 | 3 |

was exactly the same as the full-time proportion, namely 55 per cent, but only 30 per cent thought it about right, with a further 11 per cent under the impression that it was too small.

It would seem that the female part-time worker is reasonably content with her pay packet and that there is no marked difference between the attitudes of female full-time and part-time workers on the question of the distribution of pay within the workplace.

**Unemployment and the Future**
When the women were asked to speculate on the future, over 50 per cent of both full-time and part-time women workers said it was 'not at all likely' that they would be leaving their present job, with a further 30 per cent saying that it was 'not very likely'. This is in keeping with the relative lack of mobility demonstrated earlier by the length of time employees had been with the same employer. Their opinion was also sought on the length of time they thought it would take them to find a job should they become unemployed. The women tended to have what could be regarded as a slightly more pessimistic view of the economic climate with only 31 per cent under the impression that it would take less than 6 months to find a job, compared with 39 per cent of men. The answers to this question must, however, be treated with some caution for it should be noted that 80 per cent of the sample had not experienced unemployment in the previous five years. This may explain why the 'don't knows' featured highly in the answers , with 18 per cent of females and 20 per cent of males not having any clear view on their job prospects.

**Equality of Opportunity: The Myths and The Realities**
The remainder of the chapter will focus on the practice and perception of equality of opportunity, as defined by men and women. Two themes in particular will be identified. The first is childcare, an issue which has been shown to impact above all others on women's working lives (Martin and Roberts, 1984; Kremer and Montgomery, 1993). The second is a more general consideration of conditions of employment including the availability of family-friendly working arrangements and also trade union involvement among women and men. Above all else, this analysis should help to identify the structural impediments which continue to act as a brake on progress towards equality of opportunity, and also how these structural factors may interact with attitudinal concerns.

As a backcloth to this analysis, it may be interesting to begin by considering the general attitudes towards equality of opportunity. Anyone who has been involved in personnel and human resource management in Northern Ireland will not need reminding of the significance of equal opportunities legislation in the province, whether in relation to community background or gender. With this in mind, the series of questions in the NISA survey dealing with perceptions of equal opportunities issues are of great interest. Anecdotal evidence accumulated through equal opportunities training would suggest there is a feeling abroad that 'things may have gone too far', and the NISA survey provides a good opportunity to examine this speculation.

A series of questions asked respondents how far they felt attempts to deliver equal opportunities had gone specifically for women, for blacks and Asians, for gays and lesbians, and for the provision of sites for gypsies and travellers. The questions concerned the United Kingdom as a whole but nevertheless replies are likely to reveal general perceptions of local campaigns which have aimed to encourage equality of opportunity. Table 12 shows the pattern of responses for all men and women surveyed.

### Table 12
#### Perceived progress of equality of opportunity (%)

|  | Women Male | Women Female | Blacks and Asians Male | Blacks and Asians Female | Gays and lesbians Male | Gays and lesbians Female | Gypsies and travellers Male | Gypsies and travellers Female |
|---|---|---|---|---|---|---|---|---|
| Gone much too far | 3 | 1 | 4 | 1 | 30 | 30 | 5 | 6 |
| Gone too far | 9 | 6 | 11 | 7 | 31 | 28 | 12 | 14 |
| About right | 58 | 46 | 46 | 44 | 26 | 29 | 36 | 34 |
| Not gone far enough | 27 | 40 | 30 | 38 | 8 | 8 | 36 | 37 |
| Not gone nearly far enough | 2 | 4 | 2 | 3 | 2 | 1 | 5 | 4 |
| Don't know | 1 | 3 | 6 | 7 | 3 | 4 | 4 | 5 |

Considering gender first, the table would suggest that there is a large number of both men and women who feel that gender equality is still some distance away. As anticipated this feeling is at its strongest among women, 44 per cent of whom responded that equal opportunities had not gone far enough. Ethnic discrimination would also appear to be seen as more of a problem by women than men but it is striking that this pattern does not hold for attitudes towards rights for gays and lesbians, where there appears to be little sympathy for such rights across the sample as a whole. Previous research has indicated that homophobia is a significant problem in Northern Ireland (Sneddon and Kremer, 1991) and these results would tend to confirm that this prejudice remains.

Attitudes towards women's equality might be expected to vary according to respondent's age. However, this was not found to be generally true, although younger women were somewhat more likely to feel that women's equality had not gone far enough. Those women employed in clerical and related jobs were most likely to say that attempts had not gone far enough (55 per cent), while, of all occupational groupings, women managers were most inclined to say that things had 'gone too far' (22 per cent) (see Appendix A). For the delivery of equality of opportunity in the workplace, support from management is vital in order to encourage a culture change (Kremer et al., 1996). For women managers, that is those who have climbed highest in the system, to feel the least need for further progress on the one hand may be understandable but on the other hand is also regrettable and may be significant in terms of the advancement of equal opportunities in the province as a whole and also within particular organisations.

Taken as a whole, these results would suggest that there is not a feeling abroad that 'things have gone too far' in terms of the delivery of equality of opportunity for men and women. This finding has to be encouraging in relation to the further advancement of equal opportunities' policies and procedures in the workplace.

**Childcare**

Recent years have witnessed dramatic changes in social attitudes towards women's rights and roles in society and most especially with regard to employment issues. As the labour market has witnessed an increase in female participation so recent surveys in Northern Ireland and elsewhere have witnessed a growing trend towards liberalisation most especially among the young but also among the older population (Kremer, 1993). At the same time, the research indicates that there are bounds to the trend of liberalisation and these bounds are often defined with reference to perceived childcare obligations, and particularly when children are under five years old (Turner, 1993). For example, the Women's Working Lives Survey revealed that over 90 per cent of women agreed that a woman should have the right to decide herself if she should work when her children had left home but this figure fell to 68 per cent when thinking of women with school age children and 40 per cent with children under school age (Kremer, 1993).

Such attitudes are likely to be associated with considerations of childcare arrangements and the availability of childcare services. In Northern Ireland, provision of adequate childcare services remains high on the equal opportunities agenda. A recent survey of provision and needs (Turner et al., 1994) confirmed the widely held view that childcare services in Northern Ireland are poor, with state provision and formal types of care uncommon for those with children under five. By way of example, it was found that 31 per cent of parents with children under five used grandparents to look after pre-school children and, with the exception of playgroups (18 per cent), no other form of childcare was mentioned by more than 10 per cent of the sample. Nurseries and creches, whether state, in or out of the workplace, were particularly notable by their absence.

The NISA survey contained a series of questions relating to childcare arrangements and preferences for childcare. Initially a more general question was asked concerning the sharing of all domestic duties. Among married men, 21 per cent felt that duties were shared equally and 72 per cent said 'someone else' took primary responsibility, presumably most often their partner. In contrast, only 12 per cent of wives felt that duties were shared and 83 per cent said domestic duties were primarily their responsibility. Hence if the 'new man' resides anywhere he is probably most at home in the minds of men themselves! It was noteworthy that this figure was not influenced significantly by a woman's part-time or full-time employment status, nor by the presence or absence of children, confirming the view that a woman's family status and economic activity has little bearing on the extent of her domestic responsibilities.

As regards current childcare arrangements, Table 13 identifies the services used by employed mothers with children aged under five and between five and 12 years, and also includes comparative data drawn from the 1994 BSA survey. Although respondents were given the opportunity to list all types of childcare used, the table lists arrangements in a prioritised form. That is, those who used a particular service were counted only in that category, beginning with nurseries and working sequentially down the list. In this way, the incidence of formal means of childcare can be disentangled from multiple response sets.

Comparing Northern Ireland with Great Britain, one very notable statistic is the smaller percentage of day or workplace nursery users in Northern Ireland. Only 2 per cent of those with children under five were using nurseries in Northern Ireland, in comparison with 16 per cent in Great Britain. This shortfall is met, most notably, by the greater incidence of replies in the category 'mother's help/nanny', a category which previous research would suggest encompasses unregistered childminders who look after children in the child's own home (Turner et al., 1994). Concurrent with poor formal childcare provision, the use of unpaid or poorly paid

## Table 13
### Prioritised childcare arrangements (%)*

|  | Under 5 years |  | 5–12 years |  |
| --- | --- | --- | --- | --- |
|  | NI | GB | NI | GB |
| Nursery (day or workplace) | 2 | 16 | – | 1 |
| Childminder | 22 | 22 | 1 | 7 |
| Mother's help/nanny | 18 | 7 | 2 | 3 |
| Work while children at school | 4 | 6 | 40 | 34 |
| Work from home | 2 | – | – | 4 |
| Look after themselves until mother returns | 1 | – | 3 | 8 |
| Friend/neighbour | 12 | 2 | 7 | 8 |
| Relative | 32 | 30 | 35 | 20 |
| Partner/husband | 4 | 16 | 11 | 11 |
| Other | 2 | 1 | – | 4 |

*Arrangements were prioritised in the order as presented above. (That is, partner/husband was only coded if no other arrangement was cited.)

carers, including relatives and grandparents, is thought to remain relatively high in Northern Ireland (Hinds, 1989; Turner et al., 1994). At first glance these statistics would suggest that the use of relatives, if not friends and neighbours, in reality may not be significantly greater in Northern Ireland. However, given geographical issues such as journey times to work and proximity of relatives in Northern Ireland and Great Britain then it may be important to look further at the nature of the care which is provided, for example taking into account the length of time which is involved and the interaction between this form of care and other arrangements.

Previous research has suggested that questions concerning satisfaction with childcare arrangements may reveal little as the majority of parents say that they are happy with present arrangements (indeed to argue otherwise could be a tacit admission of child neglect). When asked how convenient existing childcare arrangements were, among working parents of those with children under five, 73 per cent maintained arrangements were 'very convenient' and a further 19 per cent said 'fairly convenient'. Similarly, 74 per cent said they were 'very satisfied' with current childcare arrangements and 21 per cent said 'fairly satisfied'. Few variables appeared to impact on these responses, although it is noteworthy that 76 per cent of men with children under five thought their childcare arrangements were 'very convenient' (and 77 per cent were 'very satisfied') but only 67 per cent of women replied 'very convenient' and 69 per cent 'very satisfied', respectively. Once more, these statistics reveal interesting, if predictable, sex differences in the perception of domestic life.

When asked if they would change the hours they worked, given a free choice of childcare arrangements, 86 per cent of men said they were happy with their current hours but for women there was a more powerful indication that paid work had to accommodate childcare. Given a choice of childcare arrangements, 20 per cent of working mothers with children under five would like to work more hours (including 38 per cent of part-time women workers). What is more, a further 21 per cent would prefer to work fewer hours, presumably to care for children themselves. Among those with children aged 5–12 years, 25 per cent would prefer more hours but only 9 per cent would opt for fewer hours.

The NISA survey also asked working parents with young children what their preference would be for childcare arrangements, given a free choice. Among men with children under five, the most popular choice was for their partner to look after the children (55 per cent), followed by a mother's help or nanny (11 per cent). Hence, men's preference was for childcare to be based within the home, with a strong bias towards the mother as the primary carer. The pattern for working women was quite different: 24 per cent would prefer to work school hours only, 19 per cent would prefer childcare to be provided by a relative, 15 per cent by a childminder and 10 per cent a friend or neighbour.

Looking at women who were not in paid work at the time of survey, their reasons for not working may be revealing of both the structural and attitudinal constraints which mothers feel may serve to keep them at home. When presented with a list of reasons which parents of young children could give for not working or not working many hours, those women not in paid work were asked which were important to them personally (see Table 14).

The table indicates that these mothers are more likely to cite personal preference or choice for remaining at home, either because they feel it is better for the children (73 per cent) or because they enjoy looking after their children full-time (69 per cent). At the same time, a substantial minority do mention structural or financial reasons, with cost being mentioned by 43 per cent of those with children aged under five years. The total number of responses, averaging at over three per respondent, also indicates that there is often a combination of personal preferences

## Table 14
### Mothers not in paid work: reasons for not working (%)

|  | With children: Under 5 years | 5–12 years |
|---|---|---|
| It's better for the children if I am home to look after them | 73 | 89 |
| I enjoy spending time with my children more than working | 69 | 83 |
| It would cost too much to find suitable childcare | 43 | 36 |
| I cannot find the kind of childcare I would like | 35 | 24 |
| I cannot find the kind of work I want with suitable hours | 30 | 29 |
| My life would be too difficult if I had to combine childcare and paid work | 29 | 38 |
| I cannot find the kind of work I want near my home | 25 | 35 |
| My partner would not want me to work | 17 | 18 |

*Note: several reasons could be chosen.*

and structural constraints which act in concert. The salience of each, and the source of each attitude, must remain a matter for conjecture, although it may be noteworthy that partner's preferences were mentioned least often.

Taken as a whole, the NISA survey highlights the dominant role which childcare continues to play in the lives of working women in Northern Ireland, the accommodations which working mothers must make to remain in paid employment, the different perceptions and priorities of men and women in relation to childcare, and the variance between existing practice and women's stated preferences. Comparisons with Great Britain reveal that although the Irish Sea may often conjure differences which are more imagined than real, the provision of formal and institutional childcare services in Northern Ireland remains low and for the majority of working women, childcare arrangements proceed with the assumption that state support is not and will not be available. To genuinely progress equality of opportunity for men and women at work, this assumption must continue to be challenged.

### Working Arrangements

The reality of equal opportunities was next explored by considering the range of family-friendly and flexible working arrangements which were available for women and men at work. Those in paid employment were asked to indicate which

## Table 15
### Availability of flexible and family-friendly working arrangements (%)

| Arrangement | Men (all) | Women (full-time) | Women (part-time) |
| --- | --- | --- | --- |
| Part-time working | 22 | 41 | n/a |
| Flexible hours | 20 | 24 | 28 |
| Job sharing | 12 | 24 | 19 |
| Some work from home | 15 | 9 | 6 |
| Term-time contracts | 3 | 9 | 20 |
| Workplace nursery | 4 | 6 | 1 |
| School holidays care | 2 | 5 | 2 |
| Childcare allowance | 1 | 2 | 1 |
| Career breaks | n/a | 31 | 21 |
| Paternity leave | 24 | n/a | n/a |
| Time off to care for sick child | 25 | 35 | 34 |

*Note: column percentages do not add up to 100 as multiple responses were possible.*

arrangements were currently available for them at their place of employment. Table 15 shows the availability of these arrangements for all men (*n* = 483, 22 working part-time), women working full-time (that is more than 30 hours per week; *n* = 200) and women working part-time (between 10 and 29 hours per week; *n* = 99).

Immediately it is clear that the availability of flexible and family-friendly arrangements for employees in Northern Ireland is limited, and women in part-time employment appear to be the least privileged. At the same time, it is encouraging to note that approximately one fifth of working women were able to job share and one quarter could work flexible hours and take career breaks; these were predominantly women working in clerical and related posts. While not directly comparable, these findings generally accord with the picture presented in the United Kingdom from the late 1980s (Brannen et al., 1994), although the availability of career break schemes would appear to be more widespread in the present sample.

In addition to general availability, a further set of questions tapped supply and demand. That is, those who did not have a particular arrangement available at present were asked if they would avail themselves of that service should it be made available and those who had an arrangement already in place at work were asked if they actually used the service. The percentages who would like to use (if available) and presently do use (when available) various arrangements are shown in Table 16.

## Table 16
### Use of and demand for family-friendly working arrangements (%)

| Arrangement | Men (all) Currently use | Men (all) Would use | Women (full-time) Currently use | Women (full-time) Would use | Women (part-time) Currently use | Women (part-time) Would use |
|---|---|---|---|---|---|---|
| Part-time working | 19 | 22 | 6 | 58 | n/a | n/a |
| Flexible hours | 67 | 64 | 82 | 78 | 81 | 61 |
| Job sharing | 2 | 12 | 4 | 37 | 50 | 52 |
| Some work from home | 84 | 29 | 72 | 40 | * | 44 |
| Term-time contracts | * | 27 | 65 | 43 | 95 | 56 |
| Workplace nursery | 13 | 26 | * | 34 | * | 37 |
| School holidays care | * | 26 | * | 37 | * | 47 |
| Childcare allowance | * | 40 | * | 43 | * | 53 |
| Career breaks | n/a | n/a | 17 | 48 | 20 | 58 |
| Paternity leave | 49 | 43 | n/a | n/a | n/a | n/a |
| Time off to care for sick child | 51 | 46 | 27 | 50 | 66 | 65 |

* Where the cell size was smaller than 15, the percentage figure has not been presented.

Although the prevalence of many family-friendly arrangements is so low that statistical inference cannot be drawn, it would appear that the profile of supply and demand is highly specific to each type of arrangement. For example, although over three quarters of those who are able to work at home avail themselves of this opportunity, those who do not have this facility do not seem as keen (although this interpretation ignores the lack of potential for home working in certain occupations). In contrast, flexible working hours appear both to be used widely at present and recognised as useful among those without this arrangement. There is also a high demand for workplace nurseries and school holidays care, a demand which the overwhelming majority of employers have failed to recognise. Clearly, there is considerable scope for more imaginative and sensitive responses to women and family-friendly working arrangements among a great many employers in Northern Ireland.

**Trade Union Membership**
In efforts to achieve gender equality at work, the trade union movement

remains a potentially powerful agent for change. At the same time, over recent years a great many trade unions have come to acknowledge that the movement has been singularly unsuccessful in either attracting women members or supporting women workers, whether in Northern Ireland or elsewhere (Clancy and MacKeogh, 1987; Miller and McDade, 1993). By way of explanation it has been argued that many structural factors conspire to make trade union activism more difficult for women than for men. These factors include the preponderance of women in part-time employment and in sectors of the economy where union organisation is most difficult to organise, down to nuts and bolts issues such as the timing of union meetings and the ubiquitous and non-family-friendly residential conference.

A series of questions in the NISA survey were directed specifically towards trade union membership and availability of membership. Looking first at membership, 43 per cent of all women in paid employment and 37 per cent of all men (including the self-employed, 83 per cent of whom were men) were currently members of either trade unions or staff associations. Part-time working women were notable for being least likely to belong to a trade union; 31 per cent of those working fewer than 30 hours per week were members at the time of survey. Once more this was a particular group of workers which the trade union movement has been keen to embrace but there is little evidence of substantial involvement to date.

Of those in the sample who had ever been in paid employment, 45 per cent of men and 52 per cent of women had never been a trade union member, and among current members the pattern of membership across sectors of the labour market was extremely variable. By way of example, only 15 per cent of women currently employed in sales had ever belonged to a union, in comparison with 71 per cent of professional women. Fifty nine per cent of all working men and 46 per cent of all working women had trade unions available at their place of work. However, this was true for 59 per cent of full-time women workers but only 42 per cent of part-timers. Considering membership figures alongside those of trade union availability, for men, 30 per cent of those working in organisations where unions were available had chosen, for whatever reason, not to belong to a trade union or staff association. For women, the equivalent figure was lower, at 25 per cent. This finding may suggest that lack of availability rather than lack of motivation remains the most important obstacle to increasing women's involvement in the trade union movement and that the 1990s have certainly not witnessed a rise in female union membership in Northern Ireland.

## Conclusion

One of the most important features of the development of the labour market in Northern Ireland and in other western European countries has been the change in the structure of the workforce. The emergence of the 'flexible workforce' has been in essence the growth of female part-time employment as male employment has tended to remain static or, as in the case of Northern Ireland, to decline. This development has presented the female worker with a series of decisions which have to be made in the context of her economic activity and her domestic responsibilities. While the problems in themselves are not necessarily new, the NISA survey does provide an insight into the current opinions of working women on their working conditions. Women and men recognise that gender inequality continues to form an important part of the working environment, but at the same time it would seem that the working woman in Northern Ireland remains relatively content with her basic working conditions. A high proportion of these women look on work as more than simply earning a living; they are reasonably content with both their hours and their pay; and in their opinion they are stable, hardworking employees. The high proportion of female part-time workers in the service sector (more than 90 per cent), working in what are still considered 'women's jobs' continues to exacerbate segregation in the workplace; only two in five men were working alongside women in 1994, and over a third considered they were engaged in 'mainly men's work'. When one moves beyond the workplace itself to the infrastructure which supports the working woman, the picture changes. The provision of formal childcare services, especially for the under fives, remains extremely low. Availability of family-friendly working arrangements is likewise poor, and despite the best efforts of the trade unionists over recent years, trade union availability does not yet meet demand among working women. Large numbers of men and women alike feel that equality of opportunity between the sexes has not been achieved, and evidence presented here would suggest that this perception is valid and that employers still have some ground to cover in order to make the target of equality of opportunity more attainable.

## References

ANDERTON, B. and MAYHEW, K. 1994. 'A comparative analysis of the UK labour market', in Barrell, R. (ed), *The UK Labour Market. Comparative aspects and institutional developments*, Cambridge University Press, Cambridge.

BRANNEN, J., MESZAROS, G., MOSS, P. and POLAND, G. 1994. *Employment and Family Life: A Review of Research in the UK*, Employment Department, Sheffield.

CLANCY, P. and MACKEOGH, K. 1987. 'Gender and Trade union participation', in Curtin, C., Jackson, P. and O'Connor, B. (eds.), *Gender in Irish Society*, Galway University Press, Galway.

CURTICE, J. 1993. 'Satisfying work – if you can get it'. In Jowell, R., Brook, L. and Dowds, L. (eds), *British Social Attitudes: international report – 10th edition*, Dartmouth, Aldershot.

DAVIES, C. and DOWNEY, A. 1993. 'Women's rights or responsibilities? Reconciling the demands of home and work', in Stringer, P. and Robinson, G. (eds), *Social Attitudes in Northern Ireland: the Third Report*, Blackstaff Press, Belfast.

DEX, S. 1988. *Women's Attitudes Towards Work*, Macmillan Press, Basingstoke.

HAKIM, C. 1991. 'Grateful slaves and self-made women: Fact and fantasy in women's work orientations', *European Sociological Review*, **7**, 101–121.

HINDS, B. 1989. *Women and Social Policy in Northern Ireland: Childcare Provision and Employment*, Gingerbread (Northern Ireland), Belfast.

JOHNES, G. and TAYLOR, J. 1989. 'Labour', in Artis, M.J. (ed.), *The UK Economy*, Weidenfeld and Nicholson, London.

KREMER, J. 1993. 'Attitudes and motivations', in Kremer, J. and Montgomery, P. (eds), (op. cit.).

KREMER, J., HALLMARK, A., BERWICK, S., CLELLAND, J., DUNCAN, J., LINDSAY, W. and ROSS, V. 1996. 'Gender and equality of opportunity in public sector organizations', *Journal of Occupational and Organizational Psychology*, in press.

KREMER, J. and MONTGOMERY, P. 1993. *Women's Working Lives*, HMSO, Belfast.

MARTIN, J. and ROBERTS, C. 1984. *Women and Employment: A Lifetime Perspective*, HMSO, London.

MILLER, R. and McDADE, D. 1993. 'Trade Union Involvement', in Kremer, J. and Montgomery, P. (eds), (op. cit.).

MONTGOMERY, P. and DAVIES, C. 1990. *Women's Lives in Northern Ireland Today: A Guide to Reading*, Centre for Research on Women, University of Ulster, Coleraine.

MONTGOMERY, P. and DAVIES, C. 1991. 'A woman's place in Northern Ireland', in Stringer, P. and Robinson, G. (eds), *Social Attitudes in Northern Ireland: the First Report*, Blackstaff Press, Belfast.

RUGGIE, M. 1988. 'Gender, Work and Social Progress', in Jenson, J., Hagen, E. and Reddy, C. (eds), *Feminization of the Labour Force: Paradoxes and Promises*, Polity Press, Cambridge.

SNEDDON, J. and KREMER, J. 1991. 'AIDS and the moral climate', in Stringer, P. and Robinson, G. (eds), *Social Attitudes in Northern Ireland: the First Report*, Blackstaff Press, Belfast.

THOMSON, K. 1995. 'Working mothers: Choice or circumstance?', in Jowell, R., Curtice, J., Park, A., Brook, L.and Ahrendt, D. (eds), *British Social Attitudes: The Twelfth Report*, Gower, Aldershot.

TREWSDALE, J. M. 1987. *The aftermath of recession: changing patterns of female employment and unemployment in Northern Ireland. Womanpower No. 4*, Equal Opportunities Commission Northern Ireland (EOCNI), Belfast.

TREWSDALE, J. M. 1990. 'Labour force characteristics', in Harris, R., Jefferson, C. and Spencer, J. (eds), *The Northern Ireland Economy: a Comparative Study in the Economic Development of a Peripheral Region*, Longman, London.

TREWSDALE, J. M. 1992. *Part-time employment in Northern Ireland. Report 98*, Northern Ireland Economic Council (NIEC), Belfast.

TURNER, I. 1993. 'Childcare', in Kremer, J. and Montgomery, P. (eds), (op. cit.).

TURNER, I., KREMER, J. and WARD, P. 1994. *The Use of and Demand for Childcare Services for the Under Fives in Northern Ireland*, Planning and Policy Research Unit (PPRU), Belfast.

WITHERSPOON, S. 1985. 'Sex roles and gender issues', in Jowell, R. and Witherspoon, S. (eds), *British Social Attitudes: The 1985 Report*, Gower, Aldershot.

WITHERSPOON, S. 1988. 'Interim report: A woman's work', in Jowell, R., Witherspoon, S. and Brook, L. (eds), *British Social Attitudes: The Fifth Report*, Gower, Aldershot.

WITHERSPOON, S. and PRIOR, G. 1991. 'Working mothers: free to choose?', in Jowell, R., Brook, L. and Taylor, B. (eds), *British Social Attitudes: The Eighth Report*, Dartmouth, Aldershot.

# Appendix A

## Table A1
### Highest qualification by age: full-time female employees (%)

|  | 18–24 | 25–34 | 35–44 | 45–54 | 55+ | Total |
|---|---|---|---|---|---|---|
| Degree | 1 | 2 | 4 | 2 | 1 | 10 |
| Higher ed. below degree | 3 | 6 | 3 | 3 | 1 | 16 |
| 'A' level or equivalent | 5 | 6 | 3 | 3 | 1 | 18 |
| 'O' level or equivalent | 11 | 9 | 5 | 3 | 0 | 28 |
| CSE or equivalent | 1 | 3 | 3 | 1 | 1 | 8 |
| No qualifications | 0 | 1 | 5 | 8 | 6 | 20 |
| Total | 22 | 26 | 22 | 22 | 10 | 100 |

## Table A2
### Highest qualification by age: part-time female employees (%)

|  | 18–24 | 25–34 | 35–44 | 45–54 | 55+ | Total |
|---|---|---|---|---|---|---|
| Degree | 0 | 1 | 0 | 1 | 1 | 2 |
| Higher ed. below degree | 0 | 6 | 3 | 1 | 4 | 13 |
| 'A' level or equivalent | 0 | 3 | 6 | 0 | 0 | 9 |
| 'O' level or equivalent | 2 | 11 | 5 | 6 | 1 | 25 |
| CSE or equivalent | 1 | 4 | 6 | 3 | 0 | 14 |
| No qualification | 0 | 5 | 17 | 10 | 4 | 36 |
| Total | 3 | 30 | 37 | 22 | 9 | 100 |

## Table A3
### Perceived progress of equality of opportunity for women by major occupational grouping

|  | Gone much too far/ gone too far | About right | Not gone far enough/ not nearly far enough |
|---|---|---|---|
| Managerial | 22 | 58 | 19 |
| Professional | 0 | 61 | 40 |
| Prof. & technical | 8 | 40 | 53 |
| Clerical | 5 | 38 | 57 |
| Craft | 2 | 36 | 63 |
| Personal & protective | 3 | 47 | 50 |
| Sales | 1 | 49 | 50 |
| Plant & machinery | 13 | 56 | 31 |
| Other | 17 | 33 | 51 |

5

# Race, Ethnicity and Prejudice in Northern Ireland

John D. Brewer and Lizanne Dowds

**Introduction**

Race is one of those concepts where there is a common sense definition as well as a scientific one; and to add further confusion, most folk models of race are based on out-dated and old fashioned nineteenth-century scientific ideas. As it is understood today by contemporary biological science, race refers to categories of people who share the same gene pool. This is referred to as a genotype. Nineteenth-century biology understood race to describe outward physical appearance, described today as phenotype. Banton (1977) refers to these nineteenth-century scientific ideas as the doctrine of racial typology, in which people were categorised into races, so called, on the basis of physical characteristics, usually skin colour but also other facial and body features. Integral to this typology was the belief that cultural and mental capabilities were linked to outward physical appearance, so that it was the fate of groups of people with certain physical characteristics to be forever culturally and mentally inferior. Not surprisingly, therefore, these ideas are also referred to as 'scientific racism' (for an excellent discussion of the idea of race in science see Stepan, 1982).

Modern scientists have long since abandoned the doctrine of racial typology and do not understand race to describe phenotype. However, common sense ideas sometimes have greater durability than scientific ones, and these out-moded nineteenth-century scientific ideas are still influential because folk models of race have appropriated them. The lay person by common sense understands race today to mean outward physical appearance, usually skin colour, associating with it mental and cultural capabilities, and accords these notions a spurious scientific validity. However, these notions are social and cultural rather than scientific, which is why many social scientists advocate abandoning the use of the term race (or enclosing it in quotation marks to signify its contested nature) and suggest alternatives, usually the concept of ethnicity but also such terms as 'racial categorisation' (see Miles, 1982). Banton (1979) describes race as a folk concept in order to emphasise that the groups categorised as races reflect social learning and taste rather than some objective, scientific classification. It is because race is a social rather than a scientific notion, that the categorisation of people into races reflects contingent social processes and thus the classification of the races changes over time or across cultures.

This is not to deny that there are real physical differences between people, but to describe these differences as racial is a matter of social convention and cultural learning. Nor is this to deny that racialisation, or what Miles calls 'racial categorisation', is a common process. Groups of people are frequently racially categorised (that is, portrayed as physically different). These physical differences, however, can be real or imagined. In the latter case, the process of racial categorisation involves the attribution of physical differences to what are in effect cultural or ethnic differences. In this instance, ethnic markers (features of cultural difference such as national origin, language, custom and tradition) are perceived and presented as being racial markers (some feature of outward physical appearance). The process of racialising cultural difference is more likely to occur in societies where 'race' has currency in popular culture and in national heritage and tradition, such as former colonial societies, like Great Britain, or countries with large multi-racial populations, such as South Africa and the United States of America. In such circumstances, however, deployment of terms like 'race' and 'racial difference' becomes meaningless scientifically; the logic in using this terminology is simply that it reproduces folk models or common sense understandings of what the terms mean.

### Race, Ethnicity and the Irish

The case of the Irish illustrates these processes very well. Perceptions in Britain of the nature of the social markers distinguishing the Irish have to be located in the context of Irish–British colonial relations. Lebow (1976, p. 78) has suggested that a feature of all colonial relationships is that the colonised are attributed various cultural and mental traits, such as indolence, stupidity, cowardliness and violence, in order to establish the privileges of the colonisers or colonial settlers. In some colonial relationships, the social markers between the two groups are phenotypical, but even where the differences are ethnic (as in the case of the Irish) a process of racial categorisation can occur in order to present the differences as physical rather than cultural. Thus, in Victorian Britain, for example, the Irish were caricatured in cartoons (see Darby, 1983), jokes (see Davies, 1987) and in media and political discourse (see Curtis, 1971) as phenotypically different. Curtis shows how the caricature evolved into a distinctly ape-like presentation, with the Irish being seen as 'the off-spring of a liaison between a gorilla father and a prognathous mother' (1971, p. 37), so that the Irish comprised the missing link in Darwin's theory between apes and humankind.

The racialisation of the Irish occurred at the high-point of Irish immigration in the nineteenth century and when the popularity of the doctrine of racial typology or scientific racism was at its zenith. The Irish were conceived as a separate physical type and attributed a whole range of negative mental and cultural characteristics. Miles (1982, pp. 121–150) links this racialisation of the Irish to Irish–British economic relations, and the ideological, economic and political functions it served in supporting British capital. But however we cast the social processes lying behind racialisation, cultural and ethnic differences with the Irish were presented as phenotypical ones and while the physical variations themselves were more imagined than real, a racial discourse was selected to present them because of the validity accorded to scientific racism and the resonance of this racist doctrine in British popular culture.

A legacy of this racialisation of the Irish is the description of Catholic–Protestant relations in Northern Ireland as a form of race relations. In 1970, de Paor asserted that 'in Northern Ireland, Catholics are blacks who happen to have white skins'. McKernan referred to the groups in Northern Ireland as 'racial groups defined by religious affiliation' (1982, p. 170). This involves loose terminology without defining what is meant by race or identifying the phenotypical features that constitute the supposed racial difference (other examples of this loose use of the word race to describe the Northern Ireland conflict include Fraser, 1973 and Lijphart, 1975). Barritt and Carter (1962), however, have suggested that the phenotypical variations between Catholics and Protestants are seen in body build and facial appearance.

A more reasonable application of racial discourse to Northern Ireland was Moore's argument (1972) that the conflict comprised a 'race relations situation'. This applied Rex's earlier definition of race relations situations (1970; for an updated version of this definition see Rex, 1986, p. 20). According to this view, three elements are involved in such situations. First there is severe conflict, discrimination, exploitation and oppression, going beyond that which is normal in a free labour market. Secondly a process of categorisation is involved, whereby the people affected are treated as forming a collectivity or group of some kind. Finally, justification of this is sought by powerful groups on the basis of some deterministic theory. Rex now realises that this is a 'deliberately perverse' definition of the field of race relations (1986, p. 20) because it gives no recognition to the differences between situations in which phenotypical features are the social marker and those where the markers are cultural. He also now admits that it is an abnormal usage of the term race to apply it to Catholics and Protestants. The most appropriate conceptual vocabulary for understanding Catholic–Protestant relations is drawn from ethnic relations or the theorisation of sectarianism (see Brewer, 1992).

## Racial and Ethnic Minority Groups in Northern Ireland

In support of the previous discussion, the treatment of race and ethnicity in this chapter does not address Catholic-Protestant relations, but relations with and perceptions of Northern Ireland's racial and ethnic minority groups. It is also important to note that these minority groups are mostly socially marked by cultural difference rather than physical variation, despite the lay person's understanding of them as 'racial' differences. However, because attitude surveys which address these relations tap into people's folk models of race and since some of the minority groups are phenotypically different, we do use the phrase 'racial and ethnic minority group', but accord the concept 'race' no scientific validity.

Northern Ireland, in fact, has an exceedingly low number of such minority groups. A recent report on racism and poverty in Northern Ireland estimated that they comprised less than 1 per cent of Northern Ireland's total population, and 1.5 per cent only if travellers were included as a minority group, which seems appropriate (The Northern Ireland Anti-Poverty Network, 1994, p. 1). This fact, however, makes a consideration of social attitudes in Northern Ireland towards racial and ethnic minorities interesting on two counts. By comparing the profile of these attitudes with those in Great Britain it is possible to isolate better the effect on such attitudes of experiential contact with minority group members, and to assess the extent to which Britain's more racist popular culture has been disseminated to Ireland, despite the different colonial experiences of the two countries.

## Perceptions of Prejudice

Perceptions of prejudice against ethnic minorities are markedly different in Northern Ireland compared to those in Great Britain (see Table 1). For example, six times as many people in Great Britain than in Northern Ireland think that there is a lot of prejudice against Asians. Only 7 per cent of Northern Ireland respondents think that there is a lot of prejudice against Chinese and only fractionally more (10 per cent) perceive a lot of prejudice against Asians. In Britain, by comparison, 59

## Table 1
### Perceived prejudice against ethnic minorities (%)

|  | Chinese | Black people |  | Asians |  | Travellers |
|---|---|---|---|---|---|---|
|  | NI | GB | NI | NI | GB | NI |
| A lot | 7 | 47 | 10 | 59 | | 45 |
| A little | 34 | 44 | 36 | 34 | | 37 |
| Hardly any | 54 | 8 | 49 | 5 | | 14 |
| Don't know | 5 | 2 | 5 | 2 | | 3 |

per cent felt that there was a lot of prejudice against Asians, and 47 per cent that there was a lot of prejudice against black people. Of course the answers to this question must be affected by respondents' own attitudes towards racial and ethnic minorities: some of those who are hostile themselves may refuse to acknowledge prejudice as a 'problem' at all, others may seek to reinforce their own views by maintaining that many others feel as they do and that there is therefore a great deal of 'prejudice'. However, the differences in the pattern of responses to these questions are too great to be explained by anything other than an ecological factor. The Chinese and Asian populations within Northern Ireland are so small and everyday contact so rare, that many white respondents (who are the great majority of respondents in both surveys) see little or no prejudice because they see little or nothing of racial and ethnic minorities. It is not that the risk of prejudice against any Chinese or Asian person is low, but the overall problem is perceived as small (if there is one at all) because the numbers of people affected are so small.

When Northern Ireland respondents are asked this question about the population of travellers (with whom respondents will be more familiar and have greater experiential contact), the pattern of responses is quite close to that of respondents in Great Britain in relation to black people. (Travellers are defined in the questionnaire as 'people who have no permanent home but travel from site to site'. This definition also covers New Age travellers but this particular group is not referred to in this chapter as they were thought to be relatively rare in Northern Ireland in comparison with other groups of travellers.)

But although the perceptions of prejudice against racial and ethnic minorities in Northern Ireland are dramatically lower than those in Great Britain, attitudes among population sub-groups vary in similar ways in both regions, which illustrates how these attitudes can be successfully located in a sociological profile

## Table 2

### Percentage, by sub-groups, perceiving 'a lot' of prejudice against Asians

|  | GB | NI |
|---|---|---|
| *Gender* | | |
| Men | 60 | 10 |
| Women | 58 | 9 |
| | | |
| *Age* | | |
| 18–34 | 65 | 15 |
| 35–59 | 60 | 8 |
| 60+ | 51 | 5 |
| | | |
| *Education* | | |
| Degree | 66 | 20 |
| Higher ed. or 'A' level | 64 | 12 |
| 'O' level/CSE | 61 | 10 |
| No qualifications | 52 | 7 |
| | | |
| *Social class* | | |
| I and II | 62 | 9 |
| III non-manual | 56 | 8 |
| III manual | 58 | 12 |
| IV and V | 59 | 11 |
| | | |
| All | 59 | 10 |

which transcends region (see Table 2). For example, in both Great Britain and Northern Ireland it is the elderly who are least likely to say that there is 'a lot' of prejudice against Asians, and the most highly educated who are most likely to perceive a problem. There are no systematic differences in the two cases according to social class or between the views of men and women.

The Northern Ireland population is similarly sanguine when asked about the amount of prejudice compared with five years previously and compared with five years into the future (Table 3). About two thirds of the sample thought that things

## Table 3
### Prejudice now compared with:

|  | Five years ago | | In five years time | |
|---|---|---|---|---|
|  | NI (%) | GB (%) | NI (%) | GB (%) |
| More | 12 | 34 | 11 | 39 |
| Less | 19 | 22 | 18 | 20 |
| About the same | 63 | 42 | 66 | 35 |
| Don't know | 4 | 2 | 4 | 3 |

had not changed much over the last five years and that things would not have changed much five years from now. Only just over 10 per cent thought that there was more prejudice now and about the same proportion thought that there would be more in the future.

Asking respondents about their views on the amount of prejudice and whether they think this has changed over time offers an interesting insight into the differences between living in Northern Ireland and Great Britain that arise from the varying experiences of prejudice towards racial and ethnic minority groups. But it would be wrong to try and draw conclusions indirectly about respondents' own prejudices on the basis of answers to these questions. However, the survey included other questions which confronted Northern Irish respondents with the possibility of increased contact with people from racial and ethnic minorities, and these are discussed below.

### Anti-immigration Feeling

Respondents to both the British and Northern Ireland surveys were asked whether they thought there should be more, less or about the same amount of settlement allowed for different groups of people. Of course, attitudes towards immigration may reflect many pragmatic considerations, but they are also likely to reflect some aspects of prejudice against outsiders. Respondents living in Northern Ireland were much less opposed to immigration than were their counterparts in Britain (Table 4). For example, only 39 per cent thought that there should be less settlement allowed for people from China and Hong Kong while over half of British respondents were in favour of cutting immigration for this group.

The contrast with Great Britain does not, however, affect two fundamental

### Table 4
#### Percentage saying the UK should allow less settlement for:

|  | GB | NI |
|---|---|---|
| Indians and Pakistanis | 60 | 37 |
| West Indians | 54 | 34 |
| People from China and Hong Kong | 52 | 39 |
| People from EC countries | 40 | 23 |
| Australians and New Zealanders | 30 | 19 |

considerations that the data highlight. The first is that the numbers of Northern Irish respondents opposing immigration is still very high; the second is that attitudes to the *type* of potential immigrant are identical to those of the British sample. Opposition is least to those immigrants likely to be English speaking and white, and greatest to men and women of colour, who are thus phenotypically different. Phenotypical variation therefore has some effect on attitudes to race and ethnicity in Northern Ireland.

Despite the overall difference in the level of opposition to immigration, the patterns across sub-groups in Great Britain and Northern Ireland show some interesting similarities and differences. Taking attitudes to Indian and Pakistani settlement as an example (Table 5), lower middle class respondents in both Great Britain and Northern Ireland were less likely to favour immigration – perhaps perceiving a potential competition for jobs, while women and young people were slightly more in favour. In Great Britain (but not in Northern Ireland) graduates stood out as particularly tolerant in this respect.

**Integration at Work and at Home**

Attitudes in Northern Ireland towards immigration, however, are likely to be heavily contextualised by people's realisation that there is a low prospect of there ever being a great deal of settlement. In order to directly address people's attitudes to contact with racial and ethnic minority members, all white respondents to both the British and the Northern Irish surveys were asked a version of 'social distance' questions, including whether they would mind having a suitably qualified person of Asian (or Chinese) origin appointed as their boss and whether they would mind if one of their close relatives were to marry a person of Asian (or Chinese) origin (Table 6).

## Table 5
### Percentage, by sub-groups, saying the UK should allow less settlement for Indians and Pakistanis

|  | GB | NI |
|---|---|---|
| *Gender* | | |
| Men | 63 | 41 |
| Women | 58 | 33 |
| | | |
| *Age* | | |
| 18–34 | 52 | 34 |
| 35–59 | 59 | 38 |
| 60+ | 72 | 41 |
| | | |
| *Education* | | |
| Degree | 36 | 36 |
| Higher ed. or 'A' level | 60 | 38 |
| 'O' level/CSE | 63 | 37 |
| No qualifications | 66 | 37 |
| | | |
| *Social class* | | |
| I and II | 55 | 37 |
| III non-manual | 62 | 32 |
| III manual | 70 | 52 |
| IV and V | 57 | 30 |
| | | |
| All | 60 | 37 |

While respondents in Northern Ireland appear much less opposed to immigration than their counterparts in Great Britain, there is no difference in the reaction of the two groups to more personal contact at work or as part of the family. Almost a fifth of Northern Irish respondents admit that they would mind if they had an Asian person as their boss and over a third would mind if an Asian person were to marry into the family. Interestingly, attitudes seem slightly more tolerant towards a prospective Chinese boss or spouse, the ethnic minority group

### Table 6
**Percentage saying that they personally would mind 'a lot' or 'a little' if:**

|  | NI | GB |
|---|---|---|
| Given Asian boss | 18 | 15 |
| Close relative married Asian | 37 | 37 |
| Given W. Indian boss | – | 13 |
| Close relative married W. Indian | – | 37 |
| Given Chinese boss | 11 | – |
| Close relative married Chinese | 32 | – |

with whom respondents are likely to have had most contact but who also less phenotypically different than Asians. However, the results highlight overwhelmingly that there is little difference between attitudes in Northern Ireland and Great Britain with respect to integration in work or home. Within population subgroups (Table 7), the same kind of patterns prevail as was the case with the immigration questions. In Great Britain and Northern Ireland, it is the elderly who are the most opposed to integration and the young and highly educated who are the least resistant.

Of course, many people may be reluctant to admit to an unequivocal prejudice and these questions generally under-estimate levels of personal prejudice because of the reluctance of people to admit to it. The survey attempted to compensate for this by asking respondents what they thought that 'most white people' would feel about the same scenarios. While many people may choose not to voice their own feelings, they are quite willing to attribute those feelings to other people. The data bear this out (Table 8), by showing increased levels of resistance amongst Northern Irish respondents to contact with members of racial and ethnic minorities as employers or family members, although proportions are still lower than among respondents in Great Britain.

### Legislation

Thus far it is clear that social attitudes towards racial and ethnic minorities have much the same sociological profile in Northern Ireland and Great Britain, but that the level of tolerance shown is affected by the critical differences in experiential contact with racial and ethnic minority members. This also seems to affect attitudes towards aspects of the legislative framework governing race relations.

## Table 7
### Percentage, by sub-groups, saying they themselves would mind 'a lot' or 'a little' if a close relative were to marry an Asian

|  | GB | NI |
|---|---|---|
| *Gender* | | |
| Men | 38 | 41 |
| Women | 35 | 32 |
| | | |
| *Age* | | |
| 18–34 | 23 | 24 |
| 35–59 | 41 | 40 |
| 60+ | 49 | 51 |
| | | |
| *Education* | | |
| Degree | 23 | 22 |
| Higher ed. or 'A' level | 36 | 32 |
| 'O' level/CSE | 34 | 37 |
| No qualifications | 43 | 42 |
| | | |
| *Social class* | | |
| I and II | 36 | 22 |
| III non-manual | 33 | 32 |
| III manual | 42 | 37 |
| IV and V | 39 | 42 |
| | | |
| All | 37 | 37 |

With less experience of racial discrimination, Northern Irish respondents were slightly less likely than British respondents to support a law outlawing it (69 per cent compared to 73 per cent), although support for the idea is still strong in both societies, while higher levels of tolerance (and direct experiences with sectarian violence) may have influenced the much greater support for a special law against racial violence (51 per cent compared to 36 per cent).

## Table 8
### Percentage saying other people would mind 'a lot' or 'a little' if:

|  | NI | GB |
| --- | --- | --- |
| Given Asian boss | 43 | 56 |
| Close relative married Asian | 61 | 72 |
| Given W. Indian boss | – | 51 |
| Close relative married W. Indian | – | 73 |
| Given Chinese boss | 34 | – |
| Close relative married Chinese | 55 | – |

Respondents were also asked a number of questions relating to 'changes that have been happening in the UK over the years' and whether these changes have gone too far, including:
- *attempts to give equal opportunities to black people and Asians in Britain*
- *providing sites for gypsies and travellers to stay on.*

In the Northern Irish survey, only 11 per cent said that changes in equal opportunities for black people and Asians have 'gone much too far' or 'too far', compared to 25 per cent of British respondents, although the sociological profile of those believing so is similar in the two places (Table 9). Lower middle class respondents are markedly more opposed to the changes in equal opportunities and the age and education effects are as before.

Where experiential contact with the ethnic group in Northern Ireland is more likely (as in the case of gypsies and travellers), the pattern of responses compared to Great Britain is very close indeed (Table 10). In some ways this reinforces the argument that where contact is greater, prejudice is greater. On the other hand, contact with gypsies and travellers is likely to be a great deal higher in Northern Ireland than in Britain and it is interesting that negative attitudes are not correspondingly *higher* in Northern Ireland than in Britain.

### Colonial Relationships and Attitudes to Race and Ethnicity

In its origins Northern Ireland is a settler society, but unlike other such societies (notably Australia and the United States of America), its indigenous population has not been exterminated or socially demoralised. Through such methods as endogamy, residential segregation, distinct cultural associations and a segregated school system, the social organisation of the two communities ensures their effortless survival. However, this colonial background has left a legacy of

## Table 9

**Percentage, by sub-groups, saying that changes in equal opportunities for black people and Asians have 'gone much too far'/'gone too far'**

|  | GB | NI |
|---|---|---|
| *Gender* | | |
| Men | 26 | 15 |
| Women | 23 | 8 |
| | | |
| *Age* | | |
| 18–34 | 22 | 8 |
| 35–59 | 26 | 12 |
| 60+ | 26 | 14 |
| | | |
| *Education* | | |
| Degree | 6 | 5 |
| Higher ed. or 'A' level | 25 | 9 |
| 'O' level/CSE | 26 | 10 |
| No qualifications | 30 | 14 |
| | | |
| *Social class* | | |
| I and II | 21 | 12 |
| III non-manual | 23 | 7 |
| III manual | 34 | 20 |
| IV and V | 25 | 10 |
| | | |
| All | 25 | 11 |

inequality and conflict between the two communities in Northern Ireland, which may have resulted in different perceptions of the colonial experience and of the metropolitan core society of Britain. Attitudes towards racial and ethnic minority groups in Northern Ireland may be influenced by whether or not respondents feel some sort of empathy with racial and ethnic minorities because of shared experiences as the colonised or empathy and identification with the colonisers as a result of settler origins.

## Table 10
### Percentage, by sub-groups, saying that changes in the provision of sites for gypsies and travellers have 'gone much too far'/'gone too far'

|  | GB | NI |
|---|---|---|
| *Gender* | | |
| Men | 22 | 17 |
| Women | 19 | 20 |
| | | |
| *Age* | | |
| 18–34 | 17 | 14 |
| 35–59 | 18 | 19 |
| 60+ | 28 | 23 |
| | | |
| *Education* | | |
| Degree | 7 | 15 |
| Higher ed. or 'A' level | 17 | 16 |
| 'O' level/CSE | 22 | 14 |
| No qualifications | 26 | 23 |
| | | |
| *Social class* | | |
| I and II | 16 | 14 |
| III non-manual | 21 | 16 |
| III manual | 24 | 23 |
| IV and V | 23 | 20 |
| | | |
| All | 20 | 18 |

The contrast between Protestant and Catholics does not necessarily reflect differences in response to the colonial experience, but a self-identification of nationality goes some way to describing it. The Northern Ireland survey asked respondents what nationality they considered themselves, offering 'British', 'Irish', 'Ulster' and 'Northern Irish', as well as asking them their religious affiliation. By examining the attitude toward aspects of race relations among these sub-groups in the Northern Irish sample (Table 11), it is possible to address this issue to a limited extent.

## Table 11

### Percentage saying:

|  | Protestant | Catholic | British/Ulster | Northern Irish | Irish | All |
|---|---|---|---|---|---|---|
| Less Asian immigration | 45 | 24 | 44 | 29 | 26 | 37 |
| Would mind a lot or a little if close relative married Asian | 46 | 29 | 44 | 35 | 26 | 37 |
| Most white people would mind a lot or a little if close relative married Asian | 63 | 58 | 63 | 60 | 59 | 61 |
| Equal opportunities for blacks and Asians has gone too far or much too far | 15 | 7 | 15 | 10 | 6 | 11 |
| Providing sites for gypsies and travellers has gone too far or much too far | 23 | 12 | 24 | 14 | 11 | 18 |

We find that some significant differences emerge. Those who are most tolerant are respondents who describe themselves as 'Catholic', 'Irish' or 'Northern Irish', who also might be characterised as having shared, or who identify with, the colonial experience of racial and ethnic minorities from other former British colonies. These differences remain important even when the other variables are taken into consideration – that is, age or social class differences do not account for the effect (see Appendix A for details of logistic regression models). However, these differences are reduced considerably when people attribute attitudes to 'most white people' rather than themselves. It is impossible to say whether 'Catholics', 'Irish' or 'Northern Irish' simply have a greater unwillingess to admit to prejudice and intolerance within themselves but, because they are prejudiced, attribute it to others, or whether this finding is a comment on the higher levels of prejudice and intolerance they see around them in most white people. However, the results do seem to indicate that those with the closest identification with Britain, arising from their own colonial relationship with it, have absorbed to a greater extent its racist popular culture and discourse, which affects attitudes toward racial and ethnic minorities from Britain's other former colonies. The fact that the same effect is seen with regard to gypsies and travellers, where the history and context is entirely different, is interesting but too complicated to unravel with this data alone. Overall levels of prejudice towards travellers are greater than they are towards any other ethnic group – this is true for both Catholic and Protestant respondents. The higher levels of Catholic prejudice might be expected as it is to Catholic areas that travellers will gravitate and Catholics who have the greatest experiential contact. Nonetheless, Protestant attitudes may be complicated by the fact that travellers will inevitably be perceived as Catholic (in addition to whatever other attributes they may be thought to hold).

## Conclusion

Attitudes towards racial and ethnic minorites in Northern Ireland seem to have much the same sociological profile as they do in Great Britain, but contrasts emerge based on key differences in the experience of living in the two societies. People in Northern Ireland are much less likely to have experiential contact with members of racial and ethnic minority groups, which leads to some differences in attitudes towards social distance, immigration, the perceived levels of prejudice, and to legislation covering aspects of race relations. However, people in Northern Ireland display more prejudice and intolerance toward travellers, the one minority group they do have experiential contact with, which seems to suggest that the differences in attitude between the two societies are mainly grounded in the nature of race and ethnic relations in the two societies.

It is also apparent that Britain's racist popular culture, which is rooted in its experiences as a colonial society and mass immigration from former colonies, has been disseminated to neighbouring Northern Ireland, despite its different colonial experience. This cultural diffusion is not surprising given the proximity of the two societies and Northern Ireland's position within the United Kingdom. But it is also the case that these racist notions have been absorbed to a greater extent by those with a closer identification with Britain. Some respondents in Northern Ireland have resisted to some extent Britain's racist popular culture and display more tolerant attitudes in matters of race and ethnic relations. Those respondents who seem to identify with or share similar experiences as the racial and ethnic minorities from Britain's other former colonies are more tolerant than those with experiences as settlers or identification with the colonial core society.

## References

BANTON, M. 1977. *The Idea of Race*, Tavistock, London.

BANTON, M. 1979. 'Analytical and folk concepts of race and ethnicity', *Ethnic and Racial Relations*, **2**: 127–138.

BARRIT, D. and CARTER, C. 1962. *The Northern Ireland Problem*, Oxford University Press, Oxford.

BREWER, J. 1992. 'Sectarianism and racism, and their parallels and differences', *Ethnic and Racial Relations*, **15**: 352–364.

CURTIS, L.P. 1971. *Apes and Angels: The Irishman in Victorian Caricature*, Smithsonian Institution Press, Washington.

DARBY, J. 1983. *Dressed to Kill*, Appletree Press, Belfast.

DAVIES, C. 1987. 'Language, identity and ethnic jokes about stupidity', *International Journal of the Sociology of Language*, **65**: 29–44.

DE PAOR, L. 1970. *Divided Ulster*, Penguin, Harmondsworth.

FRASER, M. 1973. *Children in Conflict*, Secker and Warburg, London.

LEBOW, R. N. 1976. *White Britain and Black Ireland*, Institute for the Study of Human Issues, Philadelphia.

LIJPHART, A. 1975. 'The Northern Ireland problem', *British Journal of Political Science*, **5**: 83–106.

McKERNAN, J. 1982. 'Value systems and race relations in Northern Ireland and America', *Ethnic and Racial Studies*, **5**: 156–174.

MILES, R. 1982. *Racism and Migrant Labour*, Routledge, London.

MOORE, R. 1972. 'Race relations in the six counties', *Race*, **14**: 21–42.

REX, J. 1970. *Race Relations in Sociological Theory*, Weidenfeld and Nicolson, London.

REX, J. 1986. *Race and Ethnicity*, Open University Press, Milton Keynes.

STEPAN, N. 1982. *The Idea of Race in Science*. Macmillan, London.

THE NORTHERN IRELAND ANTI-POVERTY NETWORK 1994. *Racism and Poverty Seminar Report*, The Northern Ireland Anti-Poverty Network, Belfast.

## Appendix A: Results of Logistic Regressions

### Table A1

**Factors associated with wanting less Asian immigration**

|  | B | Sig | R |
| --- | --- | --- | --- |
| Being Protestant | −0.9137 | 0.0000 | −0.1658 |
| Being social class IIIm | 0.8106 | 0.0001 | 0.1283 |

*Chi-squared = 41.60 with 2 degrees of freedom.*

### Table A2
**Factors associated with minding a lot or little if close relative were to marry an Asian**

|  | B | Sig | R |
|---|---|---|---|
| Being male | −0.5178 | 0.0013 | −0.0927 |
| Being older | 0.5267 | 0.0000 | 0.1458 |
| Less highly educated | 0.1746 | 0.0545 | 0.0419 |
| Having a British national identity | −0.3329 | 0.0006 | −0.1011 |

*Chi-squared = 61.17 with 4 degrees of freedom.*

### Table A3
**Factors associated with saying that changes in equal opportunities for black people and Asians have gone too far or much too far**

|  | B | Sig | R |
|---|---|---|---|
| Being male | −0.5752 | 0.0283 | −0.0741 |
| Less highly educated | 0.3941 | 0.0073 | 0.1009 |
| Having a British national identity | −0.5087 | 0.0283 | −0.0741 |
| Being social class IIIm | 0.5767 | 0.0313 | 0.0718 |

*Chi-squared = 33.01 with 4 degrees of freedom.*

### Table A4
**Factors associated with saying that changes in providing sites for gypsies and travellers have gone too far or much too far**

|  | B | Sig | R |
|---|---|---|---|
| Being older | 0.3408 | 0.0119 | 0.0818 |
| Having a British national identity | −0.4359 | 0.0008 | −0.1198 |
| Lower social class | 0.1912 | 0.0315 | 0.0637 |

*Chi-squared = 24.34 with 3 degrees of freedom.*

# 6

# Satisfaction with Health Services in Northern Ireland

Ann Largey and Ciaran O'Neill

**Introduction**

Public health care input rates per capita have traditionally been higher in Northern Ireland than in other regions of the UK. This in part reflects a greater need in Northern Ireland for health services (Northern Ireland Economic Council (NIEC), 1994) and in part the legacy of a previous overspend by government (HM Treasury, Needs Assessment Study, 1979). The reassessment of needs together with the narrowing, in recent years of some aspects of need (for example, the reduction in infant mortality rates and a drop in the percentage of people with long standing illnesses) has seen a diminution of Northern Ireland's favoured position. In many respects, however, Northern Ireland remains a relatively disadvantaged region and indeed in some respects its needs relative to those of other UK regions have increased. Tables A1 and A2 in Appendix A give details of health service staff per capita, the percentage of persons who reported having a limiting long standing illness, infant mortality rates, the percentage of those over sixteen who smoke and changes in all of these over time.

The organisational structure of the NHS in Northern Ireland differs from that elsewhere in the UK. The nature of these differences includes the separation of responsibility for health and personal social services in Great Britain, while these are integrated under the board structure in the province. Both systems have been in a state of transition following the 1991 reforms which attempted to open up the health service to a more market-orientated ethos and system of allocation. A fuller discussion of the differences between the systems of delivery and the changes to these resulting from the reforms is beyond the scope of this chapter (see Ham, 1994, NIEC op cit. and Drummond, 1991).

This chapter examines variations in satisfaction with health services across health board areas in Northern Ireland and uses multivariate analysis to examine the relationship between satisfaction and various factors which may be important in explaining it. The chapter concludes with a discussion of the results and the policy implications of the findings.

### Table 1a
### Satisfaction with NHS services – Northern Ireland 1994 (%)

|  | Very Satisfied | Quite Satisfied | Neither | Quite Dissatisfied | Very Dissatisfied |
|---|---|---|---|---|---|
| Dentist | 25 | 49 | 15 | 8 | 4 |
| GP | 38 | 48 | 6 | 6 | 3 |
| Inpatient | 30 | 44 | 13 | 10 | 3 |
| Outpatient | 18 | 47 | 13 | 16 | 6 |
| Overall | 10 | 41 | 17 | 20 | 13 |

### Table 1b
### Satisfaction with NHS services – Eastern Health and Social Services Board 1994 (%)

|  | Very Satisfied | Quite Satisfied | Neither | Quite Dissatisfied | Very Dissatisfied |
|---|---|---|---|---|---|
| Dentist | 23 | 49 | 17 | 8 | 3 |
| GP | 32 | 51 | 7 | 7 | 4 |
| Inpatient | 25 | 46 | 14 | 11 | 4 |
| Outpatient | 16 | 45 | 15 | 17 | 7 |
| Overall | 9 | 43 | 18 | 19 | 11 |

### Table 1c
### Satisfaction with NHS services – Northern Health and Social Services Board 1994 (%)

|  | Very Satisfied | Quite Satisfied | Neither | Quite Dissatisfied | Very Dissatisfied |
|---|---|---|---|---|---|
| Dentist | 22 | 51 | 14 | 8 | 5 |
| GP | 37 | 49 | 5 | 6 | 4 |
| Inpatient | 32 | 42 | 12 | 12 | 1 |
| Outpatient | 16 | 46 | 14 | 20 | 5 |
| Overall | 9 | 35 | 16 | 26 | 14 |

### Table 1d
### Satisfaction with NHS services – Southern Health and Social Services Board 1994 (%)

|  | Very Satisfied | Quite Satisfied | Neither | Quite Disssatisfied | Very Dissatisfied |
|---|---|---|---|---|---|
| Dentist | 29 | 45 | 12 | 9 | 4 |
| GP | 48 | 43 | 4 | 4 | 1 |
| Inpatient | 36 | 40 | 13 | 7 | 4 |
| Outpatient | 27 | 48 | 10 | 10 | 6 |
| Overall | 10 | 41 | 18 | 15 | 17 |

### Table 1e
### Satisfaction with NHS services – Western Health and Social Services Board 1994 (%)

|  | Very Satisfied | Quite Satisfied | Neither | Quite Dissatisfied | Very Dissatisfied |
|---|---|---|---|---|---|
| Dentist | 31 | 50 | 12 | 5 | 3 |
| GP | 44 | 42 | 6 | 4 | 3 |
| Inpatient | 32 | 46 | 13 | 6 | 3 |
| Outpatient | 21 | 55 | 9 | 11 | 5 |
| Overall | 12 | 45 | 13 | 17 | 12 |

### Level of Satisfaction with Health Services

In Table 1a the percentages expressing levels of satisfaction with various aspects of services are presented and a breakdown of these figures for the four health board areas in the province is given in Tables 1b to 1e. Respondents who did not express an opinion are not included in the analysis. Table 2 provides a comparison of results in 1994 with those in previous years. (As individual percentages are rounded to the nearest whole number in these tables, the figures given may not add up to 100.)

As can be seen from the tables, a majority of respondents in all cases were satisfied with the health services they received. Of the specific aspects of service referred to, respondents would appear to be most pleased with GP services and least pleased with outpatient services. While caution is warranted in interpreting results from just four years, the degree of satisfaction expressed with the various

## Table 2
## Changes in levels of satisfaction 1989–1994 (%)

| Satisfaction with: | 1989 | 1991 | 1993 | 1994 |
|---|---|---|---|---|
| *NHS overall* | | | | |
| Very/quite satisfied | 45 | 45 | * | 51 |
| Neither (dis)/satisfied | 17 | 20 | * | 16 |
| Quite/very dissatisfied | 38 | 35 | * | 33 |
| *Dentists* | | | | |
| Very/quite satisfied | 76 | 76 | 74 | 74 |
| Neither (dis)/satisfied | 12 | 16 | 14 | 15 |
| Quite/very dissatisfied | 12 | 8 | 11 | 11 |
| *General Practitioners* | | | | |
| Very/quite satisfied | 82 | 85 | 86 | 85 |
| Neither (dis)/satisfied | 8 | 6 | 6 | 6 |
| Quite/very dissatisfied | 10 | 8 | 7 | 9 |
| *Inpatient Services* | | | | |
| Very/quite satisfied | 77 | 73 | 75 | 74 |
| Neither (dis)/satisfied | 13 | 15 | 13 | 13 |
| Quite/very dissatisfied | 10 | 12 | 12 | 13 |
| *Outpatient Services* | | | | |
| Very/quite satisfied | 65 | 60 | 63 | 65 |
| Neither (dis)/satisfied | 11 | 16 | 14 | 13 |
| Quite/very dissatisfied | 23 | 25 | 23 | 22 |

\* indicates figures are unavailable.

components and the ranking of the various components appear to have remained fairly stable through time. The exception to this is satisfaction with the overall level of service which increased between 1991 and 1994.

Satisfaction with the NHS as a whole remains lower than that for its component parts (such as GP services). However, as overall services comprise parts other than those referred to (for example, ambulance and paramedical services as well as home helps etc.), this should not be surprising. The result could be interpreted as indicating a lower degree of satisfaction with the elements of NHS that the respondents were not directly questioned about. The exact level of satisfaction with these omitted elements either collectively or individually is impossible to determine from the information available.

**Explaining Satisfaction through Multivariate Analysis**

Table 1 suggests that the people living within the Southern Health and Social Services Board (SHSSB) are more satisfied with certain components of the NHS than are respondents living in the Northern Health and Social Services Board (NHSSB), Western Health and Social Services Board (WHSSB) and Eastern Health and Social Services Board (EHSSB) areas. However, this does not necessarily mean that the Southern Board's delivery of these services is actually superior to that elsewhere in Northern Ireland as other factors affecting satisfaction have to be taken into account. For example, Campbell and Robinson (1993) note that satisfaction is associated with the age, sex and religion of the respondent. Older people express higher satisfaction with services, so if for instance a higher proportion of older people were surveyed in the SHSSB area, this alone may account for the higher level of satisfaction expressed. Two-way classification tables of the type above, while interesting, are therefore of limited use in understanding respondents' satisfaction with health services or in advising policy makers on how best to raise that satisfaction. To explain variations in satisfaction fully we must turn to multivariate analysis.

**The Data**

Data used in the analysis fell into three categories: respondents' subjective measures of satisfaction with services, personal characteristics of respondents and objective measures of availability of services. (Appendix B lists and briefly describes all the variables used in the analysis.)

Satisfaction levels for the NHS as a whole and for some of its various components were available from the NISA survey. The components for which satisfaction was measured were GPs/local doctors, dentists, inpatient care and outpatient care. In the latter two categories expectations or beliefs about specific elements of care, for example, waiting times for an appointment and for treatment after arriving for an appointment (some of which correspond directly to the rights of patients and standards for health authorities set out in the Patient's Charter (Northern Ireland Health and Personal Social Services, 1992)) were also investigated. Given the link between questions and the Patient's Charter, it may be possible to draw some inferences about the success and relevance of government policies towards the NHS. Specifically, we may ascertain whether the emphasis the government places on certain standards and targets for the NHS is shared by the general population in terms of adding to their satisfaction with services.

Personal characteristics of respondents, which may affect their expressed satisfaction, include their age, sex, religion, household income and level of education. These details were also available from the survey. Of course, not all individuals will have equal experience of services provided by the NHS, so we attempted to construct a variable which would identify individuals who have a higher probability of contact with NHS services. Individuals with disabilities or who were caring for elderly or disabled people were included in a 'risk' category, as were respondents living with a child under 5 or an adult over 75. These older and younger age groups were chosen since health care expenditure figures for the UK in 1991 show that per capita expenditure is much higher for the over 75 age group and for the under 5s (Newchurch Health Briefings, 1993). The inclusion of 'risk' in our analysis will allow us to tell if an increased probability of contact with NHS services adds to or diminishes satisfaction compared to 'non-risk' individuals.

Information on the availability of, and expenditure on, services at a board level was gathered from various public agencies. Figures were collected on expenditure per capita for GPs and dentists, number of GPs and dentists per capita, and expenditure on prescriptions per capita. In the case of inpatient and outpatient services, many specialities are not catered for in every area. Out of a total of 43 inpatient specialties available in Northern Ireland as a whole in 1993, only 12 were available in all four boards, for example. The average number of available beds per head of population for these 12 specialties was computed for each board. Also the proportion of the other 31 specialities catered for in each board was calculated, to give an indication of availability of services in the area. In outpatient care, the number of clinics per head of population held in the health board area was included, and again the proportion of 'non-core specialties' catered for in each area calculated. (By 'non-core' we mean those specialties not available everywhere which were available in the area in question.)

In carrying out our multivariate analysis of satisfaction with health care services we used a regression technique. This enables us to estimate how differences between people in their level of satisfaction are related to variations in their personal characteristics and to objective measures of service availability. But rather than simply allowing us to say, for example, that satisfaction with GP services is higher among older people, this method allows us to take into account the simultaneous relationship between all the personal characteristics and the objective measures on the one hand, and the level of satisfaction on the other. The technique used is called 'ordered probit analysis' and is explained in detail in Appendix C.

We carried out separate analyses of the level of satisfaction with (a) GP services; (b) outpatient services; (c) inpatient services and (d) dental services. In addition we investigated variations in overall satisfaction with the health service. Here we assumed that satisfaction was related not simply to the personal characteristics of the respondents and to the level of provision, but also to the degree of satisfaction expressed with each of the component parts of the service (GP service, outpatient service and so on). The idea here is that a person's view of how well the NHS is performing will be due to how he or she rates each of the services provided. But of course we have measured satisfaction with only four components of the service, which is hardly exhaustive. However, we hope that by also including in the analysis of overall satisfaction personal characteristics and variables that indicate which Health Board the respondent lives in, that this limitation will not prove too problematic.

From a policy perspective, we are particularly interested in the relationship between satisfaction and provision of services, and between satisfaction and beliefs about whether the criteria stressed in the Patient's Charter will be met. In order to obtain correct estimates of the relevant coefficients it is necessary to control for any influence of personal circumstances of the individual. Missing from our list of personal characteristics is a direct measure of the health-care needs of the respondent which will affect his or her demand for services and, for any level of provision, his or her satisfaction. This must be borne in mind when interpreting the coefficients on other personal characteristics. For example, the housing conditions of the respondent may affect need but information on this was not available. Other information such as the respondent's income or religion which may be correlated with housing conditions is however available. Thus variables such as income or religion may be acting as proxies for missing variables, and care is needed when interpreting results for these variables.

**Results**

Tables 3a to 3e summarise the results of the regressions (see the section on Regressions and Tests in Appendix C for a discussion of the tests implemented and the statistics quoted). For each part of Table 3 we have listed the number of individuals included in the regression (n), the log-likelihood figure with all variables included (L), the sets of variables tested, the corresponding likelihood

## Table 3a
### Summary of regression results: satisfaction with NHS overall

| Variable | Sign | LR | d.f. | Significant at: 10% | 5% | 1% |
|---|---|---|---|---|---|---|
| SAT1 | + | 48.7 | 4 | | | ✓ |
| SAT2 | + | 49.324 | 4 | | | ✓ |
| SAT3 | + | 37.594 | 4 | | | ✓ |
| SAT4 | + | 21.426 | 4 | | | ✓ |
| NHSPREJ | - | 4.242 | 1 | | ✓ | |
| PRIVMED | - | 0.42 | 1 | – | | |
| AGE | + | 7.458 | 3 | ✓ | | |
| SEX | - | 0.79 | 1 | – | | |
| INCOME | - | 15.838 | 3 | | | ✓ |
| HED | - | 6.634 | 3 | ✓ | | |
| CATH | - | 8.156 | 1 | | | ✓ |
| RISK | - | 2.474 | 1 | – | | |
| BOARD (N, E, W) | - | 14.112 | 3 | | | ✓ |

$n = 1039; L = -1324.710$

ratio statistics (LR), the number of degrees of freedom for testing (that is, d.f. = the number of variables in each set), and whether the variable is significant at the 10%, 5% and 1% levels of significance.

A positive sign on a significant variable indicates that an increase in the variable leads to an increase in satisfaction. For example, a positive sign corresponding to income indicates that those individuals in a higher income bracket are more satisfied with the service. Similarly a negative sign indicates that an increase in the variable will reduce satisfaction. In a case where no monotonic relationship of this nature exists, the sign is omitted from the table, but, where the variable is significant, the relationship is discussed in the text.

### Discussion

In order to explain variations in satisfaction with health services in Northern Ireland it is important to be clear about what we understand by the term 'satisfaction' in this context. Satisfaction with health services is not unidimen-

## Table 3b
### Summary of regression results: satisfaction with GPs/local doctors

| Variable | Sign | LR | d.f. | Significant at: 10% | 5% | 1% |
|---|---|---|---|---|---|---|
| GPCHANGE | + | 10.878 | 3 | | ✔ | |
| WCHHOSP | + | 24.64 | 3 | | | ✔ |
| NHSPREJ | – | 1.944 | 1 | – | | |
| PRIVMED | + | 0.334 | 1 | – | | |
| AGE | | 2.082 | 3 | – | | |
| SEX | – | 0.346 | 1 | – | | |
| INCOME | | 10.252 | 5 | ✔ | | |
| HED | – | 16.398 | 3 | | | ✔ |
| CATH | – | 0.562 | 1 | – | | |
| RISK | + | 2.162 | 1 | – | | |
| PRES | + | 13.746 | 1 | | | ✔ |
| GPPH | – | 15.326 | 1 | | | ✔ |
| GPEXPPH | + | 15.968 | 1 | | | ✔ |

$n = 1301; L = -1469.459$

sional; it relates to three separate and potentially competing benefits arising from those services. First, the service provided to the individual directly as a consumer or potential consumer of health services; second, the benefits provided to the individual by treating others and thus reducing risks to the individual of contracting a communicable disease from untreated others and; third, the benefits provided to the individual by treating other members of society through a positive externality based on philanthropy (for example, the benefit we derive from knowing children in need of health care receive that care, without ourselves being or having children, or being at risk of contracting (say) mumps from some child). The survey instrument does not distinguish between these in the wording of questions which could complicate our interpretation of results.

In interpreting coefficients on variables, it will be useful to bear the three components of satisfaction in mind, although not all components may be related to all variables. For example, theory suggests that the relationship between income (say) and the direct use element of satisfaction is likely to be negative. Thus, as income rises so too does the cost of the health service to the individual in terms of tax and national insurance payments. Similarly, the opportunity cost of time spent

## Table 3c
### Summary of regression results: satisfaction with inpatient services

| Variable | Sign | LR | d.f. | Significant at: 10% | 5% | 1% |
|---|---|---|---|---|---|---|
| INPAT1 | + | 10.57 | 3 | | ✔ | |
| INPAT2 | + | 0.212 | 3 | — | | |
| INPAT3 | + | 14.77 | 3 | | | ✔ |
| INPAT4 | + | 30.966 | 3 | | | ✔ |
| INPAT5 | + | 19.744 | 3 | | | ✔ |
| INPAT6 | + | 5.086 | 3 | — | | |
| INPAT7 | + | 15.288 | 3 | | | ✔ |
| WCHHOSP | + | 1.26 | 3 | — | | |
| NHSPREJ | — | 0.328 | 1 | — | | |
| PRIVMED | — | 0.83 | 1 | — | | |
| AGE | | 3.184 | 3 | — | | |
| SEX | — | 0.916 | 1 | — | | |
| INCOME | | 0.8 | 5 | — | | |
| HED | — | 30.868 | 3 | | | ✔ |
| CATH | — | 12.74 | 1 | | | ✔ |
| RISK | + | 3.638 | 1 | ✔ | | |
| HOSBEDPH | + | 0.99 | 1 | — | | |
| INSPEC | — | 1.958 | 1 | — | | |

$n = 1156; L = -1366.624$

waiting for or in treatment will rise. As costs rise, so too will expectations regarding the quantity and/or quality of care provided and, for any given quantity and/or quality of care provided, there is more likely to be a distinction between expectation and realisation and for satisfaction to fall as a result.

By exactly the same line of argument, as income rises so too does the cost to the patient of risk reduction. That is, the progressive tax structure will see the better off paying more relatively speaking than the less well off and their satisfaction being lower as a result. For these two aspects of satisfaction, it is possible to hypothesise a relationship between satisfaction and possible determinants. However, it is not evident that any relationship will exist between (say) income and those philanthropic benefits accruing to the individual from use of health services by

### Table 3d
### Summary of regression results: satisfaction with outpatient services

| Variable | Sign | LR | d.f. | Significant at: 10% | 5% | 1% |
|---|---|---|---|---|---|---|
| OUTPAT1 | + | 17.518 | 3 | | | ✔ |
| OUTPAT2 | + | 89.856 | 3 | | | ✔ |
| OUTPAT3 | + | 22.39 | 3 | | | ✔ |
| WCHHOSP | | 0.212 | 3 | – | | |
| NHSPREJ | – | 1.65 | 1 | – | | |
| PRIVMED | – | 3.372 | 1 | ✔ | | |
| AGE | | 176.364 | 3 | | | ✔ |
| SEX | – | 2.528 | 1 | – | | |
| INCOME | | 6.812 | 5 | – | | |
| HED | – | 17.524 | 3 | | | ✔ |
| CATH | – | 4.898 | 1 | | ✔ | |
| CLINICPH | + | 2.9 | 1 | ✔ | | |
| OUTSPEC | – | 5.234 | 1 | | ✔ | |

$n = 1213$; $L = -1530.458$

### Table 3e
### Summary of regression results: satisfaction with NHS dentists

| Variable | Sign | LR | d.f. | Significant at: 10% | 5% | 1% |
|---|---|---|---|---|---|---|
| NHSPREJ | – | 0.294 | 1 | – | | |
| PRIVMED | + | 2.484 | 1 | – | | |
| AGE | | 8.488 | 3 | | ✔ | |
| SEX | – | 12.134 | 1 | | | ✔ |
| INCOME | | 7.4 | 5 | – | | |
| HED | | 4.152 | 3 | – | | |
| CATH | + | 0.064 | 1 | – | | |
| DENTPH | – | 7.77 | 1 | | | ✔ |
| DENTEXPH | + | 5.614 | 1 | | ✔ | |

$n = 1402$; $L = -1781.739$

others. Such benefits will depend on the individual's own value set or moral code and are unlikely to be related in any way to education, income or religion.

For policy purposes, however, it may not be necessary to distinguish which motivation drives respondents' replies. It can be assumed that each respondent replies taking account (subconsciously) of the weights he or she attaches to each of the three motivations for satisfaction. If we believe that a measure of the health service authorities' (or government's) success in their health care policies is the overall satisfaction of individuals with them, we may assume that the underlying reasoning for the stated satisfaction of the respondents is not necessarily important. The satisfaction functions have been structured in such a way as to simply identify the relationship between the stated satisfaction of individuals with components of the NHS and those determinants over which policy makers have some control.

## Satisfaction with Overall NHS Services

As can be seen from Table 3a, the groups of variables which added to the explanation of overall satisfaction were: satisfaction with the various components of services referred to in the survey; the individual's income, religion, educational qualifications, belief as to whether one section of the community was treated more favourably than the other and the health board area in which the individual lived. Taking these variables in the order presented, as satisfaction with any of the component parts of service increased, so satisfaction with the overall service increased. Changes in log-likelihood values from the addition of different groups of variables are ranked in descending order of magnitude: inpatient, GP, outpatient and dentist services. This indicates their order of importance in explaining variations in satisfaction.

Of the remaining groups significant at the $\alpha = 0.01$ level, the variables may be listed in descending order of importance as income, board area and religion. That is, in terms of their impact upon satisfaction, these variables may be listed in this order. In terms of the nature of their impact, as income rose so satisfaction fell, individuals in the Southern Board were less satisfied than those in the other board areas and Catholics were less satisfied than non-Catholics. Views of preferential treatment were significant at the $\alpha = 0.05$ level. Education was significant at $\alpha = 0.1$ level. Care is warranted in the interpretation of these results. Functions for satisfaction with each measured component of the NHS contained respondent characteristics (such as income) as explanatory variables and their impact on satisfaction with those elements of the NHS have therefore been accounted for.

Recall that the inclusion of personal characteristics and dummy variables for the boards in the analysis of overall NHS satisfaction is in an attempt to capture the effects of missing variables – those components of the NHS for which individuals' satisfaction was not elicited. The coefficients on these variables capture their effect on components, such as community care, which are not mentioned in the survey. Based on the discrepancy between the levels of satisfaction with the NHS as a whole and those quoted for specific elements of the service (Table 1), we have reason to believe that respondents are less satisfied with the unmeasured elements of care than with those they were expressly questioned about in the survey. By examining the effect of personal characteristics in the regression equation for overall NHS satisfaction, we know only how satisfaction with unmeasured components of the NHS varies with changes in these explanatory variables, but nothing more about the level of satisfaction expressed for these components. This said, interpretation of results is at times straightforward.

The inverse relationships between income and satisfaction with omitted elements of NHS activities and between educational qualifications and satisfaction with omitted elements of NHS activities are likely to be interrelated. As education levels increase, for example, respondents will become better informed about treatments and perhaps less diffident towards those providing these treatments. That is, as education levels increase, so expectations in terms of the quality of service provided and the way in which it is delivered are likely to increase. At the same time a positive correlation between education and income levels exists and the relationship between incomes and satisfaction will reinforce that between education and satisfaction. As discussed above, an inverse relationship between income and satisfaction is consistent with *a priori* expectations for the reasons outlined above.

Table 3a shows that Catholics were less satisfied with omitted elements of health services than were non-Catholics, which on face value may seem a strange result. Given that income, education and geographic location in terms of board area (and thus differences in expenditure levels) have been controlled for, Catholics' lower levels of satisfaction with health services may appear illogical. However, the possibility of a variable such as this acting as a proxy for some excluded variable must be borne in mind. For example, differences in income, geographic location and education are only partial elements of need. If other important elements of need have been omitted which would indicate that Catholics are in greater need than non-Catholics, the fact that health service resources are limited and therefore rationed will result in a greater pool of unmet needs existing among Catholics than non-Catholics. This being the case, the greater degree of dissatisfaction among Catholics can be explained in terms of omitted variables without reference to any real or imagined religious discrimination.

Support for this interpretation of results does exist. For example, Catholics are more likely to be unemployed, long-term sick or disabled and to occupy poorer quality housing than non-Catholics (Northern Ireland Census of Population, 1991). It has been argued that these variables are positively correlated with health needs (Gravelle, 1985) and evidence exists to suggest that some of them at least are related to mortality and morbidity (Metcalf and Nicholl, 1979; Fox and Goldblatt, 1982; Banks and Jackson, 1982). The effect of need on satisfaction may be being poorly captured in variables such as education and income with religion instead capturing this effect. This is an area where some further work is required.

The negative correlation between a belief that the NHS discriminates on the basis of religion and satisfaction with the NHS is consistent with a positive value being attached to equity of treatment by the NHS on the basis of need. This is consistent with *a priori* expectations and the contention in the introduction that positive externalities are associated with the treatment of others.

Explaining the positive relationship between location in the Eastern, Northern and Western health boards (relative to being in the Southern) in terms of degree of satisfaction is less straightforward. As with religion, differences could be explained by reference to differences in needs relative to per capita 'other' expenditure levels, though equally differences in expectations or fears concerning changes in services could explain the results. (A major campaign has been ongoing in the Southern Board area to maintain service at a hospital threatened with closure.) In reality a combination of factors is probably involved here. For example, not only may needs and anxiety levels concerning services differ but so too may the types of service on offer. Further work is required to identify these factors and establish the relative weights that attach to them.

## Satisfaction with GP Services

The significant groups of variables determining satisfaction with GP services are, in order of importance: whether the individual could choose the hospital to which they would be referred for an operation; their educational qualifications; expenditure on GP services per capita in the board area; the number of GPs per capita in the board area; per capita prescription expenditures in the area; the perceived ease with which individuals could change GPs; and income.

Taking these in the order presented, the greater the perceived freedom of choice with respect to hospital, the greater was the satisfaction expressed with GP services. This is in line with *a priori* expectations. Thus, the more patients perceive themselves as having influence with respect to which hospital they are treated in, the more responsive will GPs appear to patient wishes. Assuming choice to have positive utility associated with it, the positive correlation is consistent with economic theory. A similar line of argument could explain the relationship between prescription expenditures and satisfaction. Higher prescription expenditures will reflect higher input levels and should be associated with greater satisfaction, *ceteris paribus*. Further, if they are indicative of a more liberal prescribing policy on the part of GPs, the observed positive correlation between prescriptions and satisfaction may reflect patient experiences of the ease with which they have obtained prescriptions from their GPs. The more responsive the GP, the greater the satisfaction of the patient.

The negative correlation between satisfaction and education, as above, can be explained in terms of differences in expectations. As this was discussed at length earlier no further discussion is necessary here.

The greater the expenditure on GPs per head, the greater the satisfaction with GP services. This is as one would expect, greater expenditure being associated with a greater quantity and/or quality of service. It is somewhat surprising, however, that the degree of satisfaction is negatively correlated with the number of GPs per head. It could be that the quality of GP services is negatively related to the number of GPs per head, deteriorating quality explaining the decrease in degree of satisfaction. Or it may be patients faced with a greater quantity of GPs have a greater choice and therefore greater expectations.

## Satisfaction with Inpatient Services

The variables explaining satisfaction with inpatient services may be listed in order of importance as: patient's perceptions of whether they would be sent home from hospital only when well enough to go; education; whether nurses would take seriously complaints from patients; if there would be a particular nurse to deal with problems; if an operation would happen when booked for; the person's religion; if the doctor kept the patient well informed and the individual's level of experience of health services. Variables that were notably absent included the doctor's taking the respondent's view of treatment seriously; the doctor's taking any complaints seriously and whether the patient would have a say as to the hospital in which an operation would be performed.

The positive relationship between satisfaction and confidence as to being sent home only when well enough to go; operations happening when they are supposed to; nurses taking complaints seriously; having a particular nurse to deal with problems and doctors keeping patients well informed are in line with expectations. That is, the first two highlight elements of quality respondents are likely to be concerned with. The more assured they are with respect to these elements of quality, the more satisfied are they likely to be with services. The last three, in as much as they are conducive to quality assurance and thus quality, would also be expected to be positively correlated with satisfaction. The fact that doctors taking patients' views of treatments or their complaints seriously is not associated with satisfaction levels may be indicative of the strong principal agent relationship between doctor and patient, which is not the case between nurse and patient. That is, patients may not view themselves as qualified to offer informed opinions on the aspects of care they receive from doctors. With nurses on the other hand, who to a much greater extent are perceived as providing more general caring services, patients may feel better qualified to offer opinions and complaints.

The negative correlation between education and satisfaction may be explained, as above, in terms of a combination of greater expectations and a reduction in the diffidence with which better educated individuals will approach the health service. The positive correlation between 'risk' and satisfaction indicates that the more likely an individual is to have had experience of inpatient services, the more satisfied he or she is with services. Finally, the fact that Catholics had a lower degree of satisfaction with inpatient services than non-Catholics could again be attributable to some unaccounted for aspect of need.

## Satisfaction with Outpatient Services

In descending order of importance, the significant groups of determinants of satisfaction with outpatient services were: the respondent's age; if the patient would be seen within half an hour of the appointment time; if the patient would be able to complain about treatment; the patient's education; if the patient would receive an appointment within three months; the proportion of specialities not catered for in every board, but catered for in the respondent's area; if the respondent was a Catholic; if the respondent had insurance and the number of clinics held in the respondent's board area per capita.

The positive correlation between degree of satisfaction and how confident the respondent was about receiving prompt treatment is as one would expect. That is, it reflects an aspect of service quality and, as quality improves, so would one expect satisfaction to rise. A similar argument probably lies in the relationship between the number of clinics per capita and satisfaction. The increased frequency of clinics makes prompt treatment more likely.

The positive correlation between respondents' perceptions of the ease with which complaints can be made and their degree of satisfaction probably relates to how open and responsive they believe the service is to their opinions. A more open and/or responsive service has greater utility than one which is less so.

The relationships between religion, education and degree of satisfaction are negative, as with other aspects of the NHS. The relationships between these variables and satisfaction is probably along the lines of the arguments given in the discussion of other services. No further discussion is felt warranted here.

That the degree of satisfaction fell as the number of specialities catered for increased is not as one would expect. Moreover, it is difficult to find a rational explanation as to why this may be the case, other than that the variable is proxying for one which has been omitted from the function and whose negative effect dominates the positive one we would expect here. For example, it could be that those areas where more specialities are offered are also those areas where consultation times are lowest, where the consultants seen are the least qualified, where the staff are the least friendly or where clinics are most crowded because of those from other areas having to travel to the areas where services are provided for treatment. That is, the number of services offered could be positively correlated to some negative aspect of quality which has not been accounted for or to congestion which has not been accounted for. Further work is required here.

Respondents holding insurance were less satisfied with NHS outpatient services than those without such insurance. Given that the privately insured would have access to a wider range of substitutes, this is as one would expect.

Finally, respondents in the 30–50 age group had a lower degree of satisfaction with services than those in other age groups. It is not immediately clear why this should be the case. Were it related to the opportunity cost of waiting time, the income variable should pick this up. Further, there appears no reason why expectations in this age group should differ from those in other groups. It may be that this age group have the greatest exposure to services, not just attending clinics themselves for treatment but also accompanying elderly or young relatives. Their tolerance of any negative aspect of service may be much lower than that of other age groups even allowing for differences in income. It could also be that the types of outpatient services used by this group differ from those of other groups and that the quality of care differs between services. Without further work it is impossible to draw more definite conclusions.

## Satisfaction with NHS Dentists

In descending order of importance determinants of satisfaction with dentist services may be listed as: sex of the respondent; the number of dentists per capita in the respondent's board area; dental expenditure per head; the respondent's age. Females were more satisfied with NHS dentists than were males. This may be because they have greater exposure to, and perhaps more positive experiences of, these services in their capacity as mothers. Further, the fact that females receive free dental treatment during and for one year after pregnancy may influence their perceptions of dental services.

As the number of dentists per capita increases so the degree of satisfaction falls. As above, the explanation for this may lie in changes in the expectations of respondents as the number of dentists per capita increases and/or the quality of dentistry decreasing as their number increases.

As expenditure per capita increases so too does satisfaction. This result is in line with expectations, as an increase in expenditure is probably associated with an increase in the quantity and/or quality of dental care.

Finally, those under 50 were more satisfied than older respondents with dental services. The result here may be explained, as with females, in terms of the experiences of dental care received by different age groups, and also in this case by outdated perceptions of dental care.

## Conclusions: Policy Implications and Issues Raised

When considering possible policy implications arising from this analysis, it is important to bear in mind that the stated satisfaction of consumers is not the only, nor perhaps always the most appropriate, measure of success of policies. An argument could be made for the use of more objective, purely medical measures of success since consumer satisfaction will to some extent reflect the delivery or packaging of services, which may be viewed as cosmetic features, as well as an assessment of their medical or life-saving value. But however limited the medical knowledge of consumers is, as patients or potential patients in the system their views on the services they receive are entirely valid. This view has been endorsed by the government's publication of the Patient's Charter.

The discussion above comments on the importance of variables in affecting satisfaction with the NHS and its various components. Obviously many of these explanatory variables are under the direct control or influence of health authorities. In particular expenditure on and provision of each component of service are controlled by health authorities, so that it is possible to make some judgement on whether increasing expenditure or the level of provision of services will add to satisfaction of consumers. Other variables measure the beliefs of individuals about whether their rights as patients will be granted and we can judge whether the Patient's Charter has focused on issues that are relevant to satisfaction.

## Table 4
### Percentage who state health as the priority for extra government spending

|              | 1989 | 1990 | 1991 | 1993 | 1994 |
|--------------|------|------|------|------|------|
| 1st priority | 56   | 55   | 49   | 51   | 56   |
| 2nd priority | 23   | 25   | 24   | 23   | 23   |

On the issue of expenditure, Table 4 shows that since 1989 around 75 per cent of individuals surveyed consistently recommended the NHS as either their first or second priority for additional government spending. Therefore individuals are signalling the belief that increased expenditure on the NHS would bring positive benefits. Our analysis supports this belief; higher expenditure on GPs and dental care and increased numbers of outpatient clinics raise satisfaction with the services. While results with respect to availability of services in particular areas may appear to conflict with this view (for example, with respect to the number of local doctors, dentists or number of outpatient specialities catered for in an individual's board area) plausible explanations of these apparent anomalies have been offered in terms of differing levels of expectations, unaccounted for aspects of need and differences in the quality of service provided. The conclusion to be drawn from this is that were increased government spending to become available, a majority of individuals would prefer the health service to be given a priority status in the allocation of such moneys and that these should raise consumer satisfaction.

In general, it appears that the Patient's Charter targets issues relevant to the satisfaction of consumers or potential consumers of health care, specifically in stressing the rights of the individual to be kept informed and to be consulted and emphasising issues such as efficiency and speed in provision of treatment.

It is important that the individual feels that he or she is fully informed of all information relevant to his or her treatment and is involved in the decisions affecting the treatment. This applies in particular to the patient's relationships with his or her own doctor and with nurses in hospitals, whose direct involvement with patients is probably greater than that of doctors in hospitals. The insignificance of whether doctors take the respondent's view of treatments seriously and whether doctors would take complaints seriously may reflect both the lesser degree of direct involvement with the patient and the a higher degree of diffidence towards hospital doctors. The importance to consumers of health care of having their views taken seriously is emphasised also by the fact that a perceived ability to complain about both inpatient and outpatient treatment and the ability to change local doctors easily will lead to an increase in satisfaction. These are pointers that the providers of health care should not ignore.

Finally, the government's move towards introducing standards for waiting times and reducing waiting lists for treatment, if successful, should lead to a higher level of satisfaction with the NHS. The analysis shows that reduction in time spent waiting for treatment increases overall satisfaction. The more confident individuals are that they will receive an outpatient appointment within three months of referral, will not have to wait more than half an hour to be attended to at that appointment, and if booked for an operation on a particular day will have it performed, then the greater is their satisfaction with services.

To conclude, it is clear that a high level of satisfaction with health services generally, and those the respondents were questioned about in particular, exists in Northern Ireland. The level of satisfaction has remained high despite rapid change within the health service and growing concerns over its ability to cope with the increasing demands placed upon it. Government emphasis on patient rights as an area of concern is not misplaced and genuine assurances with respect to these offer a cost-effective means of raising satisfaction with the health service. What remains to be seen is whether or not, within the context of growing demands upon the health service and upon the exchequer generally, satisfaction will remain high and assurances regarding quality of care will be treated credibly by the public.

**References**

BANKS, M.H. and JACKSON, P.R. 1982. 'Unemployment and risk of minor psychiatric disorder in young people: cross-sectional and longitudinal evidence', *Psychological Medicine*, **12**, 789–798.

CAMPBELL, R. and ROBINSON, G. 1993. 'Who cares for the National Health Service?', in Stringer, P. and Robinson, G. (eds), *Social Attitudes in Northern Ireland: the Third Report*, Blackstaff Press, Belfast.

CENSUS OFFICE 1991. *Northern Ireland Census of Population*.

DRUMMOND, M. 1991. *'Assessing Efficiency in the New National Health Service'*, York Discussion Paper 75.

FOX, A. J. and GOLDBLATT, P. O. 1982. *Longitudinal Study: Socio-Demographic Mortality Differences,* HMSO, London.

GRAVELLE, H. 1985. 'Does Unemployment Kill?', in *Nuffield/York Portfolios,* Folio 9, Nuffield Provincial Hospitals Trust.

HAM, C. 1994. *Management and Competition in the New NHS,* Radcliffe Medical Press, Oxford.

HM TREASURY 1979. *Needs Assessment Study – Report,* HMSO, London.

METCALF, D. and NICHOLL, S. J. 1979. 'Notes on the incidence of unemployment and sickness spells of three months or more', *Working Paper No. 79,* London School of Economics.

NEWCHURCH HEALTH BRIEFINGS 1993. *Strategic change in the NHS – Unleashing the market,* Newchurch and Company, London.

NORTHERN IRELAND ECONOMIC COUNCIL (NIEC) 1994. *The Reform of Health and Social Care in Northern Ireland,* Report 110, NIEC, Belfast.

NORTHERN IRELAND HEALTH AND PERSONAL SOCIAL SERVICES 1992. *A Charter for Patients and Clients.*

## Appendix A

### Table A1
### Health service staff

|  | Rate per 10,000 of population | | | |
| --- | --- | --- | --- | --- |
|  | 1981 | 1986 | 1991 | 1993 |
| England | 183.9 | 178.1 | 176.2 | 168.5 |
| Wales | 176.0 | 184.6 | 185.5 | 189.5 |
| Scotland | 221.4 | 229.6 | 221.3 | 223.4 |
| Northern Ireland | 258.2 | 245.7 | 241.7 | 223.1 |

### Table A2a
### Percentage who reported limiting long-standing illnesses

|  | Northern Ireland | | England | |
| --- | --- | --- | --- | --- |
| Age band | 1986 | 1993 | 1986 | 1993 |
| 16–44 | 20 | 11 | 24 | 14 |
| 45–64 | 42 | 30 | 45 | 28 |
| 64+ | 62 | 47 | 63 | 44 |

### Table A2b
### Percentage of people over 16 who smoke

|  | Male | | Female | |
| --- | --- | --- | --- | --- |
|  | 1986 | 1992 | 1986 | 1992 |
| England | 34 | 29 | 31 | 27 |
| Wales | 33 | 32 | 30 | 33 |
| Scotland | 37 | 34 | 35 | 34 |
| Northern Ireland | 35 | 31 | 31 | 29 |

## Table A2c

### Infant mortality rate

| | Rate per 1000 | |
| --- | --- | --- |
| | 1986 | 1993 |
| England | 9.5 | 6.3 |
| Wales | 9.5 | 5.5 |
| Scotland | 8.8 | 6.5 |
| Northern Ireland | 10.2 | 7.1 |

# Appendix B: Variable Names and Descriptions

| Variable | Description |
|---|---|
| | For the following 5 variables coding is: 1 = very satisfied, 2 = quite satisfied, 3 = neither satisfied nor dissatisfied, 4 = quite dissatisfied, 5 = very dissatisfied.<br>Dummy variables $SAT_{ij} = 1$ if $SAT_i = j$ for i = 1...4, j = 1, 2, 4, 5 are created for use as regressors in equations. |
| SAT0 | Satisfaction with the NHS |
| SAT1 | Satisfaction with local doctors/GPs |
| SAT2 | Satisfaction with being an inpatient |
| SAT3 | Satisfaction with being an outpatient |
| SAT4 | Satisfaction with NHS dentists |
| | For the following 11 variables coding is: 1 = definitely would, 2 = probably would, 3 = probably wouldn't, 4 = definitely wouldn't.<br>Dummy variables $INPAT_{ij} = 1$ if $INPAT_i = j$ for i = 1...7, j = 1...3<br>$OUTPAT_{ij} = 1$ if $OUTPAT_i = j$ for i=1...3, j=1...3<br>$WCHHOSP_j = 1$ if WCHHOSP = j for j= 1...3 for use as regressors |
| INPAT1 | Would doctor tell all you feel you need to know? |
| INPAT2 | Doctor take respondent's view of treatment seriously? |
| INPAT3 | Operation happen when booked for? |
| INPAT4 | Home only when really well enough to go? |
| INPAT5 | Nurses take seriously any complaints? |
| INPAT6 | Doctors take seriously any complaints? |
| INPAT7 | Particular nurse to deal with problems? |
| OUTPAT1 | Appointment within three months? |
| OUTPAT2 | Wait to be seen in less than 1/2 hour? |
| OUTPAT3 | Able to complain about treatment? |
| WCHHOSP | Can choose hospital for operation? |
| NHSPREJ | = 1 if respondent believes NHS treats Protestants and Catholics differently, 0 otherwise |

| | |
|---|---|
| PRIVMED | = 1 if respondent holds insurance, 0 otherwise |
| AGE | respondent's age (subdivided into 3 dummies for <30 years, 30–49 years, 50–64 years; base category 65+ years) |
| SEX | = 1 if male, 0 if female |
| INCOME | respondent's income (subdivided into 5 dummies for < £6000, £6000 – £11999, £12000 – £17999, £18000 – £25999, £26000 – £34999, the base being greater than £34999) |
| HED | Highest educational qualification of respondent (subdivided into 3 dummies for CSE + O-levels, above O-level up to and including A-level, and degree level and above, the base being no qualifications). |
| CATH | = 1 if brought up as a Catholic, 0 otherwise |
| RISK | = 1 if respondent is disabled, is a carer or lives with child under 5 or adult over 75 |
| N | =1 if respondent lives in Northern Board area, 0 otherwise |
| E | =1 if respondent lives in Eastern Board area, 0 otherwise |
| W | =1 if respondent lives in Western Board area, 0 otherwise |
| | The remaining variables are all defined for Health Boards. |
| PRES | Expenditure per head of population on prescriptions |
| GPPH | Number of GPs per capita |
| GPEXPPH | Expenditure on GPs per capita |
| HOSBEDPH | No. of beds per capita available for specialities catered for in every board |
| INSPEC | Proportion of inpatient specialities catered for in each board, not available in every board |
| CLINICPH | No. of outpatient clinics held per capita for specialities catered for in every board |
| OUTSPEC | Proportion of inpatient specialities catered for in each board, not available in every board |
| DENTPH | No. of dentists per capita |
| DENTEXPH | Expenditure on dental care per capita |

## Appendix C: Model and Method

### The Model

Let $SAT_0^*$ represent satisfaction with the NHS as a whole, and $SAT_1^*, ..., SAT_4^*$ satisfaction with each of the four components of the NHS: GPs, inpatient care, outpatient care and dentists, respectively. In principle, satisfaction could be measured along a continuous scale. Assume

$$SAT_i^* = X_i \, \beta_i + \varepsilon_i \, , \quad i = 0, 1, 2, 3, 4$$

$$\quad nx1 \quad\quad nxk_i \; k_ix1 \quad nx1$$

where $\varepsilon_i \sim N(0,1)$.

That is, the continuous variable 'satisfaction with component i' can be written as a linear combination of the explanatory variables $x_1$, $x_2$, ...., $x_{ki}$ and an unknown error $\varepsilon_i$ assumed normally distributed with mean 0 and standard deviation 1. Since we wish to assess the importance of various factors in influencing the degree of satisfaction with the NHS and its component parts, we are interested in the signs, magnitudes and significance of the parameters in $\beta_i$, $i = 0,...,4$. However, precise measurements on the continuous variable $SAT_i^*$ are unobserved. Rather, the observed variables, $SAT_i$, $i = 0,...,4$, as measured in the NISA survey, are ordinal variables with five classifications, ranging from very satisfied through to very dissatisfied.

These satisfaction measurements are the observed counterparts of the latent continuous variables $SAT_i^*$. Faced with only five categories available to indicate satisfaction, individuals choose the category that most closely reflects their feelings. Thus each measurement on $SAT_i$ indicates a particular interval of $SAT_i^*$ along which the corresponding continuous scale (or precise) satisfaction measurement lies as follows:

$SAT_i = 0$ (very satisfied)                      if $SAT_i^* \leq \mu_0$
           $= 1$ (quite satisfied)                        if $\mu_0 < SAT_i^* \leq \mu_1$
           $= 2$ (neither satisfied or dissatisfied)     if $\mu_1 < SAT_i^* \leq \mu_2$
           $= 3$ (quite dissatisfied)                  if $\mu_2 < SAT_i^* \leq \mu_3$
           $= 4$ (very dissatisfied)                   if $\mu_3 < SAT_i^*$

where $\mu_0 < \mu_1 < \mu_2 < \mu_3$.

Therefore the probability that $SAT_i$ takes the value j equals the probability that the value of $SAT_i^*$ lies in the $j^{th}$ interval. Given $\mu_0$ set to 0 and recalling $\varepsilon_i \sim N(0, 1)$, we have

$$P(SAT_i = 0) = P(SAT_i^* \leq 0) = P(\varepsilon_i \leq -X_i\beta_i) = \Phi(-X_i\beta_i)$$
$$P(SAT_i = 1) = P(0 < SAT_i^* \leq \mu_1) = \Phi(\mu_1 - X_i\beta_i) - \Phi(-X_i\beta_i)$$
$$P(SAT_i = 2) = P(\mu_1 < SAT_i^* \leq \mu_2) = \Phi(\mu_2 - X_i\beta_i) - \Phi(\mu_1 - X_i\beta_i)$$
$$P(SAT_i = 3) = P(\mu_2 < SAT_i^* \leq \mu_3) = \Phi(\mu_3 - X_i\beta_i) - \Phi(\mu_2 - X_i\beta_i)$$
$$P(SAT_i = 4) = P(SAT_i^* > \mu_3) = 1 - \Phi(\mu_3 - X_i\beta_i)$$

Maximisation of the likelihood function

$$L = \prod_{SAT_i=0} P(SAT_i = 0) \prod_{SAT_i=1} P(SAT_i = 1) \prod_{SAT_i=2} P(SAT_i = 2)$$

$$\prod_{SAT_i=3} P(SAT_i = 3) \prod_{SAT_i=4} P(SAT_i = 4)$$

therefore allows estimation of all $\beta_i$ coefficients and $\mu_1$, $\mu_2$ and $\mu_3$.

## Method

*Function specification*

As regards the appropriate set of regressors, it seems sensible to assume that an individual's satisfaction with any service is an amalgam of satisfaction with each component part of that service. Satisfaction with the NHS as a whole, $SAT_0^*$, could therefore be represented by a function where $X_0 = [x_{10}, x_{20}, ..., x_{k0}]$ represents degrees of satisfaction with each of the $k_0$ components of the NHS, including GPs, dentists, inpatient care and outpatient care. For all components of the NHS, satisfaction will depend on the level of provision of the service as regards numbers treated and specialities provided, whether various standards are met in the provision of the service (indicated by inpat1 ...inpat7 in the case of inpatient care for example), and the characteristics of the respondent. Since satisfaction measures are not available for all components of the NHS, we attempt to capture the effect of the 'non-measured' components by including dummies for health boards (to capture disparities in levels of provision for these missing services) and personal characteristics of the individual.

The following functions were therefore investigated.

**F(0)** $SAT_0^* = f(SAT_1, SAT_2, SAT_3, SAT_4,$ nhsprej, risk, age, sex, cath, income, hed, privmed, N, E, W)

**F(1)** $SAT_1^* = f($wchhosp, gpchange, pres, gpph, gpexpph, nhsprej, risk, age, sex, income, cath, hed, privmed)

**F(2)** $SAT_2^* = f($inpat1 ... inpat7, wchhosp, hosbedph, inspec, nhsprej, risk, age, sex, income, cath, hed, privmed)

**F(3)** $SAT_3^* = f($outpat1 ... outpat3, wchhosp, clinicph, outspec, nhsprej, age, sex, income, cath, hed, privmed)

**F(4)** $SAT_4^* = f($dentph, dentexph, nhsprej, age, sex, income, cath, hed, privmed)

(Note that $SAT_1$, $SAT_2$, $SAT_3$, $SAT_4$, inpat1 ...inpat7, outpat1 ...outpat3, wchhosp, gpchange, age, income and hed are all entered as sets of dummy variables when used as independent variables in the analysis. For example, $SAT_i$ comprises $SAT_{i1}$, $SAT_{i2}$, $SAT_{i4}$, $SAT_{i5}$ where $SAT_{ij} = 1$ if $SAT_i = j$, 0 otherwise, so that the comparison is with individuals who are neither satisfied nor dissatisfied with service i. See Appendix B for descriptions of all variables, or sets of dummies, used.)

*Regressions and tests*
A maximum likelihood estimation, using only observations for those individuals who expressed an opinion for all variables included in the regression, was carried out for each of the ordered probit functions F0 to F4 above and the log-likelihood value ($L_i$) was noted. The significance of each variable was then ascertained by omitting that variable (or the set of dummies representing the variable) from the regression and recalculating the log-likelihood ($L_i^*$, say). The likelihood ratio statistic, $LR = -2 (L_i^* - L_i)$ was derived and tested. In effect then, we can decide whether the presence of a particular variable in the regression adds to the explanatory power of the regression as a whole, given the presence of all the other variables, and can make some attempt at ordering the importance of various variables in explaining the satisfaction measures.

# 7

# National Identity

Karen Trew

**Introduction**

The conflict in Northern Ireland has been described as identity-driven, as sectarian differences are assumed to be accompanied by deep socio-political divisions which are not tempered by either a common national identity or shared alternative identities (for example, social class). In the early 1990s, it was suggested that this simple model of sectarian division in which religious, political and national identities coincided to create conflict had been modified as the old identities had fragmented (Pollack, 1993). The evidence from the Northern Ireland Social Attitude (NISA) surveys provides an opportunity to examine whether patterns of identification have changed over time and to explore the relationships between religious community background, national identity and a range of political and social attitudes.

Moxon-Browne (1991) provided a detailed account of the polarisation between Catholic Irishness and Protestant Britishness in his analysis of the data on national identity included in the 1989 NISA survey. He also charted the changing patterns of identification of Catholics and Protestants between 1968 and 1989. This chapter aims to build upon his analysis by exploring the stability and changes in Catholics' and Protestants' patterns of identification from 1968 to 1994, taking into account the evidence reviewed by Moxon-Browne, as well as the subsequent NISA surveys conducted in 1991,1993 and 1994.

In the light of these findings, further analysis of the 1994 data aims to establish a more detailed picture of the distinctive features of each identity by examining: (i) the characteristics of those who identify themselves as Irish, British, Ulster or Northern Irish; (ii) the relationship between these national identities and political allegiances; (iii) the association between national identity and attitudes to the relationship between the United Kingdom and Europe, and (iv) the similarities and differences between Protestants and Catholics who share the Northern Irish identity. The chapter concludes by examining the characteristics and national identifications of a particular group of 'outsiders' who report no religious group allegiances but who were brought up in the Protestant community.

**Religion and National Identities 1968–1994**

Moxon-Browne (1991) started his review of the survey evidence on choice of national identity with Rose's (1971) seminal study, which was carried out a few months before the troubles began in 1968. Rose's survey introduced a question on national identity which was repeated in the survey by Moxon-Browne ten years later and subsequently in four NISA surveys. This question asked:

*Which of these (terms) best describes the way you usually think of yourself?*

Some evidence on the changing pattern of national allegiance can be gained from the response categories which have been used in these six surveys. The terms Irish, British, and Ulster have been included in all the surveys but the Northern Irish label was not used in the 1968 and 1978 surveys. Apparently, it was not seen as an valid self-descriptor by either Protestants or Catholics. Moxon-Browne (1983) noted that the term used by the Northern Ireland Parliament after partition to describe the region it governed and its institutions was Ulster. Accordingly, the Ulster identity implies an identification with Northern Ireland as a political region and an acceptance of its legitimacy. He also suggested that in the 1970s the term acquired a hint of anti-Britishness in such usages as Ulster Defence Association, Ulster Volunteer Force and so on.

It seems that the term Northern Irish began to gain acceptance for both Catholics and Protestants during the 1970s. As Moxon-Browne (1983) indicated, in a discussion on the attempts to create a new non-sectarian focus of loyalty in Northern Ireland, this might not have been by accident as:

*...In the 1970s, The Peace People often invoked the unity of the 'Northern Irish' people, significantly omitting the term Ulster as being too divisive.* (Moxon-Browne, 1983, p. 5)

The 1989 NISA survey, which introduced the Northern Irish label as one of the possible response categories, dropped the term Anglo-Irish. The category 'sometimes Irish, sometimes British' was retained for use in the initial NISA surveys but it too was dropped in the 1994 NISA questionnaire.

In comparing the six surveys which span the period of the troubles (Table 1), a clear pattern emerges. In 1968 less than two-fifths of the people who described their religious background as Protestant identified themselves as British, a fifth saw themselves as Irish and a third saw themselves as having an Ulster identity. After a decade of the troubles only 8 per cent chose to describe themselves as Irish,

### Table 1

**Choice of national identity 1968–1994 for Protestants and Catholics (%)**

|      | Protestant ||||| Catholic |||||
|------|---------|-------|--------|-----------|-------|---------|-------|--------|-----------|-------|
|      | British | Irish | Ulster | N. Irish | Other | British | Irish | Ulster | N. Irish | Other |
| 1968 | 39 | 20 | 32 | –  | 9 | 15 | 76 | 5 | –  | 4  |
| 1978 | 67 | 8  | 20 | –  | 5 | 15 | 69 | 6 | –  | 10 |
| 1989 | 68 | 3  | 10 | 16 | 3 | 10 | 60 | 2 | 25 | 4  |
| 1991 | 66 | 2  | 15 | 14 | 3 | 10 | 62 | 2 | 25 | 1  |
| 1993 | 70 | 2  | 16 | 11 | 3 | 12 | 61 | 1 | 25 | 2  |
| 1994 | 71 | 3  | 11 | 15 | – | 10 | 62 | – | 28 | –  |

*Notes:* Northern Irish identity offered as an alternative from 1986. Other includes 'Anglo-Irish' and 'sometimes British, sometimes Irish'. Respondents who said they had 'no religion' are excluded from this analysis.

while two-thirds identified themselves as British and 20 per cent chose the Ulster identity. Subsequent surveys have shown a decreasing proportion of Protestants describing themselves as Irish and an increasing proportion seeing themselves as British.

The attractiveness of the Ulster identity to Protestants declined strongly between 1968 and 1989 and the availability of the Northern Irish label in the NISA surveys seemed to provide a viable alternative for those who felt a strong identification with their locality. The 1991 and 1993 NISA surveys found the Ulster identity growing in popularity in comparison with the 1989 findings; however, the patterns of identification found in 1994 are remarkably similar to those found in 1989, with 11 per cent of Protestants identifying themselves as Ulster and 15 per cent as Northern Irish.

Few Catholic respondents chose the Ulster identity in any of the national surveys carried out between 1968 and 1994. At the same time, the proportion of Catholics choosing to describe themselves as Irish has fallen from over three-quarters in 1968 to 62 per cent in 1994, but a sizeable minority of Catholic respondents have chosen to describe themselves as Northern Irish in the NISA surveys in which this option has been available. Moxon-Browne (1991) argues that the ambiguity of the Northern Irish label serves to make it less divisive than other possible national labels available to Protestants and Catholics. For Catholics it does not legitimise political boundaries or compromise their aspirations as the term can refer to the geographically northern part of the island of Ireland. Similarly, the

Northern Irish identity does not compromise the British identity of Protestants as the term can be seen as derived from 'Northern Ireland', an officially designated region of the United Kingdom.

In general, the evidence suggests that the onset of political violence in the early 1970s was associated with a major shift in identification among Protestants away from the Irish identity towards the British identity. Following this shift, the pattern of identification of Protestants and Catholics has remained relatively stable for at least 16 years with Protestants identifying themselves as British, Ulster or Northern Irish and Catholics mainly identifying themselves as Irish, Northern Irish or British.

**Characteristics of Those Choosing each National Identity**

There are variations in the demographic characteristics of respondents who identified themselves as Irish, Northern Irish, Ulster and British which help to clarify the unique features of these identities (Table 2). The 'Ulsterman' (and it is more likely to be a man) is less likely to live in Belfast and more likely to be a manual worker. Along with those declaring themselves British, those in this group are more likely to be older than others in the sample (reflecting the age distribution among the Protestant and Catholic populations).

Using the 1978 and 1989 surveys, Moxon-Browne (1991) also found that the Ulster label was more widely adopted by working-class than middle-class respondents. He suggested that class differences among Protestants might be associated with the rejection of British identity and a protest against 'what are seen as alien English policies' by working-class Protestants. It would seem that this may still be the case. The most notable characteristic of men and women choosing the Northern Irish identity is the higher percentage of non-manual workers in this group compared with others (though it is not significantly higher than those choosing the British option) and the lower percentage of those with no qualifications.

**National Identities and Political Allegiances**

As Table 3 indicates, the majority of those with British and Ulster identities considered that they were Unionist and the majority of those who identified themselves as Irish considered they were Nationalist. However, over a third of respondents considered they were neither Unionist or Nationalist. Forty per cent of those with an Irish identity and 45 per cent of those with a Northern Irish identity, but only 22 per cent of those who identified themselves as Ulster, refused

### Table 2
**Residential area, gender, age and social class of those with British, Irish, Ulster and Northern Irish identities (%)**

|  | British | Irish | Ulster | Northern Irish |
|---|---|---|---|---|
| *Residential area* | | | | |
| Belfast | 16 | 28 | 10 | 21 |
| East | 57 | 22 | 57 | 42 |
| West | 27 | 50 | 32 | 38 |
| *Gender* | | | | |
| Male | 48 | 50 | 57 | 53 |
| Female | 52 | 50 | 43 | 47 |
| *Age* | | | | |
| 18–34 | 30 | 39 | 30 | 41 |
| 35–59 | 42 | 41 | 40 | 44 |
| 60+ | 28 | 20 | 29 | 15 |
| *Social class* | | | | |
| Non-manual | 51 | 43 | 35 | 54 |
| Manual | 49 | 57 | 66 | 46 |
| *Education* | | | | |
| Degree | 6 | 6 | 4 | 8 |
| Higher education/'A' level | 23 | 18 | 25 | 30 |
| GCSE/CSE | 32 | 29 | 28 | 30 |
| No qualifications | 40 | 47 | 43 | 31 |

### Table 3
**Respondents defining themselves as Unionist, Nationalist or neither (%)**

|  | British | Irish | Ulster | N. Irish | All |
|---|---|---|---|---|---|
| Unionist | 67 | 2 | 75 | 29 | 42 |
| Nationalist | 2 | 56 | 0 | 25 | 20 |
| Neither Unionist nor Nationalist | 31 | 40 | 22 | 45 | 37 |

to label themselves in this way.

Table 4 reveals only a few surprises concerning party allegiance and national identity (see also Chapter 2). Those with a British or Ulster identity generally

## Table 4
### Respondent's political partisanship, Northern Ireland parties only (%)

|  | British | Irish | Ulster | N. Irish | All |
|---|---|---|---|---|---|
| Alliance | 12 | 6 | 2 | 15 | 11 |
| Democratic Unionist | 18 | 1 | 36 | 6 | 12 |
| Official Unionist | 43 | 2 | 38 | 16 | 26 |
| Sinn Fein | 0 | 15 | 0 | 1 | 4 |
| SDLP | 4 | 50 | 1 | 32 | 21 |
| Other party | 3 | 3 | 4 | 5 | 3 |
| None | 12 | 18 | 11 | 16 | 15 |
| Other answer | 7 | 6 | 7 | 9 | 7 |

support the Official Unionist Party and the Democratic Unionist Party. A further 12 per cent of the British support the Alliance party. The Irish support the Social Democratic and Labour Party and Sinn Fein; while a third of the Northern Irish support the Social Democratic and Labour Party and minorities opt for the Alliance and Official Unionist parties. The Irish and Northern Irish show slightly higher levels of political disengagement in that a higher proportion say they support no political party.

In sum, the evidence reviewed in this section of the chapter suggests that the relationship between national identity and political ideology and allegiance is less clear cut than might be expected. There is an association between choice of national identity and ideology but there are a large minority of respondents, including 40 per cent of those who identify themselves as Irish and a quarter of the British, who are not willing to describe themselves as either Unionists or Nationalists. Political allegiances are associated to some extent with choice of national identity but it is notable that one in five of the respondents, including a quarter of those with a Northern Irish identity, either could not, or would not, nominate a political party which they supported.

**National Identity and Attitude to the European Union**

After 20 years of membership of the European Community, the BSA and NISA surveys indicate that the public in Great Britain and Northern Ireland is divided in its attitude to integration with Europe (Evans, 1995; Smith and Corrigan, 1995). In Great Britain, education, class and age are important predictors of attitudes to integration (Evans, 1995). In Northern Ireland, unlike the rest of the United

146 KAREN TREW

Kingdom, primary political identification is closely associated with clear and unambiguous views on the relationship with Europe. As Smith and Corrigan (1995) noted, opposition to European federalism almost inevitably follows from the political ideology of the two main Unionist parties, which are both committed to maintenance of British sovereignty. In contrast, European integration and co-operation is seen by the SDLP as the basis for resolving the sovereignty problem and a solution to the conflict in Northern Ireland. How does national identification relate to attitudes to Europe?

From Table 5, it would seem as if there is a split in attitudes between the Irish

Table 5

**Attitudes to Europe (%)**

*Should the UK do all it can to unite fully with the European Community or, do all it can to protect its independence from the European Community?*

|  | Catholic | Protestant | British | Irish | Ulster | N. Irish | All | GB |
|---|---|---|---|---|---|---|---|---|
| Unite with EC | 70 | 32 | 34 | 73 | 25 | 58 | 48 | 40 |
| Independence | 19 | 59 | 57 | 17 | 61 | 31 | 41 | 53 |
| Don't know | 11 | 10 | 10 | 10 | 14 | 10 | 10 | 7 |
| *The UK's relationship with the European Community should be ...* | | | | | | | | |
| Closer | 62 | 32 | 35 | 62 | 23 | 54 | 45 | 37 |
| Less close | 3 | 17 | 14 | 5 | 21 | 5 | 10 | 23 |
| About right | 27 | 45 | 45 | 23 | 49 | 36 | 38 | 34 |
| Don't know | 9 | 6 | 6 | 11 | 8 | 5 | 7 | 7 |

Catholic and the Ulster or British Protestants, with the Northern Irish identifiers showing characteristics of both patterns. The majority of Protestants are protective of the sovereignty of the UK with 61 per cent of those with an Ulster identity and 57 per cent of those with a British identity saying that 'the UK should do all it can to protect its independence from the EC'. In contrast, 70 per cent of Catholics and 73 per cent of the Irish consider that 'the UK should do all it can to unite fully with the European Community'.

Looking at the results for Great Britain as reported by Evans (1995), Protestants' concern for British sovereignty is shared by the majority of the British sample. However it would be unwise to categorise Protestant attitudes in Northern Ireland as 'eurosceptic' in the same way that respondents in Great Britain may be regarded. On a further question about Europe (that did not raise the sovereignty issue) Protestant respondents appear slightly more accepting of links with Europe than are their British counterparts. Only 17 per cent favour less close links compared with 23 per cent of people in Britain. A solid 45 per cent are happy with things the way they are compared with just 34 per cent in a rather more divided British sample. As might be expected, the majority of Catholics and Irish identifiers, unlike the respondents in Great Britain, support a closer relationship with the European Community.

The Northern Irish identifiers show less consensus in their views than those with Irish, British or Ulster identities, though a majority favour closer ties with Europe and a united Europe over the maintenance of independencefor the United Kingdom.

**The Northern Irish and the 'Outsiders'**

This chapter has shown that Catholics mainly identify themselves as Irish, Northern Irish or British and Protestants identify themselves as British, Ulster or Northern Irish. It would seem that in terms of identity, Protestants and Catholics do not present monolithic groups. The sectarian groups overlap most obviously in their choice of the Northern Irish label. How similar are the Protestants and Catholics who select this label to each other and to those who share their community background? Do they represent a middle ground or are the group percentages merely a reflection of an average between two extremes?

Table 6 presents a range of background and attitudinal variable for Protestants and Catholics who label themselves Northern Irish in order to assess if these groups share characteristics beyond the common national identification.

Table 6 shows that the Catholics who identify themselves as Northern Irish differ very little in either background characteristics or attitudes from all Catholics, except that that they are slightly more likely to be well educated, of non-manual status and to want to retain the Union with Britain. However, Protestants who identify themselves as Northern Irish do differ significantly from Protestants in general. The Protestants with a Northern Irish identity are more likely to be younger and female, to come from a non-manual background, to have a degree or 'A' levels and to support the Alliance party. They are less likely than other Protestants to consider themselves Unionists and/or more likely to believe that the United Kingdom should unite with Europe, though they do not differ from other Protestants in their view that Northern Ireland should remain part of the United Kingdom.

Table 6 also includes responses from a group of 'outsiders' who have not figured

Table 6

Characteristics of Northern Irish Protestants and Catholics, Protestants only by family background and all the sample from Protestant and Catholic family backgrounds (%)

|  | N. Irish Protestant | N. Irish Catholic | All of Protestant background | All of Catholic background | Protestant *only* by family background |
|---|---|---|---|---|---|
| *National dentity* | | | | | |
| British | * | * | 70 | 11 | 67 |
| Irish | * | * | 3 | 60 | 5 |
| Ulster | * | * | 10 | < 1 | 6 |
| Northern Irish | * | * | 15 | 27 | 16 |
| *Considers self:* | | | | | |
| Unionist | 62 | 2 | 71 | 1 | 34 |
| Nationalist | 0 | 47 | – | 51 | 1 |
| Neither | 38 | 52 | 28 | 48 | 65 |
| *Gender* | | | | | |
| Male | 60 | 47 | 53 | 47 | 58 |
| Female | 40 | 53 | 47 | 54 | 42 |
| *Age* | | | | | |
| 18–34 | 43 | 39 | 31 | 39 | 49 |
| 35–59 | 41 | 45 | 42 | 43 | 39 |
| 60+ | 16 | 16 | 27 | 18 | 13 |
| *Social class* | | | | | |
| Non-manual | 59 | 45 | 49 | 40 | 46 |
| Manual | 36 | 47 | 45 | 52 | 48 |
| Never had a job | 4 | 6 | 6 | 8 | 6 |
| *Education* | | | | | |
| Degree | 12 | 4 | 7 | 5 | 8 |
| Higher Education/ 'A' level | 33 | 29 | 25 | 21 | 29 |
| GCSE/CSE | 33 | 26 | 32 | 28 | 34 |
| No qualifications | 22 | 41 | 37 | 46 | 29 |

## Table 6 continued

|  | N. Irish Protestant | N. Irish Catholic | All of Protestant background | All of Catholic background | Protestant *only* by family background |
|---|---|---|---|---|---|
| *Attitudes to Europe* | | | | | |
| UK should unite with EC | 43 | 69 | 34 | 69 | 50 |
| UK should protect independence | 43 | 23 | 56 | 20 | 35 |
| *Long-term policy for NI* | | | | | |
| Remain part of UK | 85 | 32 | 87 | 27 | 67 |
| Reunify Ireland | 6 | 56 | 7 | 57 | 19 |
| Independent state | 4 | 2 | 1 | 1 | 4 |
| *Party allegiance* | | | | | |
| Alliance | 25 | 8 | 13 | 8 | 20 |
| Democratic Unionist | 13 | 0 | 21 | >1 | 20 |
| Official Unionist | 36 | 1 | 54 | >1 | 27 |
| Sinn Fein | – | 3 | – | 10 | – |
| SDLP | 1 | 59 | 1 | 53 | 4 |
| Other party | 3 | 1 | 1 | 1 | 9 |
| None | 11 | 19 | 11 | 20 | 19 |
| Other answer | 1 | 1 | 1 | 1 | 13 |

in this chapter so far. In all analyses that examine the attitudes of Protestants and Catholics, respondents who say that they have 'no religion' are systematically excluded. Yet these respondents who reject their religious identity are an interesting group. There were too few respondents from a Catholic background who now professed to have 'no religion' to allow for separate analyses, but Table 6 shows the results for those people who were brought up as Protestant but no longer hold any religious identity. These respondents are mainly male and young, but they do not differ significantly in their social class from others with a Protestant background. Although they mainly identify themselves as British, the *majority* do not see themselves as either Unionists or Nationalists. Half of the group favour a united Europe and almost a fifth favour a reunified Ireland.

Similarly, a fifth of this group do not have any political allegiance.

In sum, this section of the report has been about the smaller groups in the sample. It has shown that whereas the Northern Irish identity would seem to be a broadly acceptable alternative to the Irish identity for Catholics, the Protestants who identify themselves as Northern Irish differ in background and beliefs from Protestants in general. The Protestant Northern Irish identifiers are younger and have had more experience of education than is generally the case for Protestants. This is consistent with a 1992 survey finding that among university students, 41 per cent of the Protestants and 25 per cent of the Catholics chose to describe themselves as Northern Irish (Benson and Trew, 1995).

The comparison between Catholic and Protestant Northern Irish identifiers provided little evidence to suggest that that there is a shared political ideology or broadly shared attitudes among Protestants and Catholics who have adopted the overlapping Northern Irish category, but it did highlight the range of attitudes among Protestants with British, Northern Irish and Ulster identities. These Protestants all share a commitment to the union with Britain but otherwise they represent a spectrum of opinion with the Northern Irish and Ulster regional identities representing opposite ends of the spectrum of unionist beliefs.

The group of men and women who were Protestant only by religious background mainly described themselves as British, but they would seem to be outside the continuum in terms of their attitudes, with one in five advocating a united Ireland. However, the most notable characteristic of this group is their lack of commitment to traditional political groupings or ideologies.

## Conclusion

This chapter has been about self-identification and the relationship between national identity and a range of demographic and attitudinal variables. It has been concerned with how people choose to label themselves given a limited choice of national identities. One of the most suprising results of the review of the evidence is that despite the turbulence of events in Northern Ireland, the pattern of identification has remained relatively stable for the last 16 years. In Northern Ireland, because national identity is contested, the debate about identity is more public than in most countries. This has been most notable in recent years when the relationship between the British and Irish governments has fluctuated and grown during attempts to devise a constitutional solution which is acceptable to the people of Northern Ireland. In these circumstances it might have been expected that the attraction of the British identity for Protestants and the Irish identity for

Catholics might have reflected such major events as the Anglo-Irish agreement in 1985 or the Downing Street declaration in 1993; but there is no evidence that these, or any other events altered the pattern of identity choices demonstrated in the NISA surveys.

Although there has been stability in the pattern of identity choices, this does not imply that the meaning of the labels (Irish, Northern Irish, Ulster and British) and their evaluations have remained static over this period. There is evidence from more qualitative small-scale research studies that there is considerable 'rebuilding' (Miller, 1995) of these national identities. For example, O'Connor (1993) highlights the confusion and debate about the meaning of Irishness for Catholics in Northern Ireland in the 1990s; while Trew (1995) found that the centrality of socio-political identity among Protestant students had increased significantly between 1992 and 1994.

By exploring the association between the choice of an identity label and a range of attitudinal and belief variables it can be seen that any simplistic linking of Irish, Catholics and nationalism as compared with the association of British, Protestants and unionism is not supported by the evidence. Nevertheless it is also true, as Moxon-Browne (1991) concluded, that 'the polarisation between Catholic Irishness and Protestant Britishness is as strong as before'. This paradox arises because there are considerable minorities among Catholics and Protestants who seem not to be represented by any of the the political parties in Northern Ireland. Although Protestants tend to see themselves as British and Catholics as Irish, this identification is not necessarily political or automatically associated with either nationalism or unionism. It may relate more to cultural identity which, for many people, may be as important as national identity.

## References

BENSON, D.E. & TREW, K. 1995. 'Facets of self in Northern Ireland: Explorations and further questions' in Wicklund, A and Oosterwegal, B (eds), *The self in European and North American Culture*, Kluwer Academic Publishers, Dordrecht.

EVANS, G. 1995. 'The state of the Union: Attitudes towards Europe', in Jowell, R., Curtice, J., Park, A., Brook, L. and Ahrendt, D. with Thomson, K. (eds), *British Social Attitudes: The Twelfth Report*. Dartmouth, Aldershot.

MILLER, D. 1995. 'Reflections on British national identity', *New Community*, 21: 153–166.

MOXON-BROWNE, E. 1983. *Nation, Class and Creed in Northern Ireland*. Gower, Aldershot.

MOXON-BROWNE, E. 1991. 'National identity', in Northern Ireland, in Stringer, P. and Robinson, G. (eds), *Social Attitudes in Northern Ireland*. Blackstaff Press, Belfast.

O'CONNOR, F. 1993. *In Search of a State: Catholics in Northern Ireland*. Blackstaff Press, Belfast.

POLLACK, A. 1993. *A Citizens' Inquiry: The Opsahl Report on Northern Ireland*. The Lilliput Press, Dublin.

ROSE, R. 1971. *Governing without Consensus: An Irish perspective*. Faber & Faber, London.

SMITH, M. L. and CORRIGAN, J. 1995. Relations with Europe, in Breen, R., Devine, P. and Robinson, G. (eds), *Social Attitudes in Northern Ireland: The Fourth Report*. Appletree Press, Belfast.

TREW, K. 1995. *Preliminary report comparing student identity choices in October 1992 and October 1994*. The Queen's University of Belfast.

## 8

# Gender Discrimination among Married Full-time Employees in Northern Ireland: Some Initial Findings

J. E. Spencer, M. Trainor and B. Black

**Introduction**

Legislative measures to combat gender discrimination in Northern Ireland were passed over twenty years ago. While there is overwhelming support for such laws (Kiernan, 1992; Davies and Downey, 1993), over 80 per cent of the Northern Ireland Social Attitudes (NISA) sample in 1991 still believed that women were likely to face discrimination in the workplace (Davies and Downey, 1993). 'Discrimination' can cover a multitude of unfair practices, but in this chapter we focus exclusively on the issue of equal pay. Because of the complexities involved in comparing levels of pay between women and men, it is worth making some points clear at the outset.

Different wage rates or earnings for men and women are not themselves evidence of discrimination if they are the result of different levels of productivity. Therefore, in measuring discrimination, we take into account those differences in productivity which arise from differences in education and work experience. Having done this, the issue becomes a question of whether or not there are differences in earnings for men and women with the same productivity characteristics. If so, we define this as discrimination in the market.

There remain a number of difficulties with our definition. First, our measure of educational qualifications may not be sufficiently precise. For example, a person may have a degree, but we do not know if that degree is in engineering or in the humanities and that may be relevant to an individual's future earnings. If women's education is bunched in subject areas which yield a lower return, discrimination will be overestimated.

Second, differences in education and work experience may themselves be the result of discrimination. Women may have less education than men, or may specialise in less remunerative subjects than men, if they expect a lower future return from their educational investment because of discrimination in pay or employment. Third, women may acquire less human capital because of the division of labour in the family. The social convention is for married women to take most of the responsibility for childcare and housework and they are thus likely to seek less demanding jobs in the labour market and, for that matter, to spend less time in it (see Chapter 4). As a result, our measure of discrimination may greatly underestimate total societal discrimination against women.

A number of studies have attempted to estimate a measure of gender discrimination for Great Britain (for example, Chiplin and Sloane, 1976; Greenhalgh, 1980; Siebert and Sloane, 1981; Zabalza and Arrufat, 1985; Joshi and Newell, 1987; Miller, 1987; Wright and Ermisch, 1991; Black, Spencer and Trainor, 1995). Wright and Ermisch (1991) used data from the Women and Employment Survey, collected in 1980, which contained detailed work histories and earnings data for women. They were therefore able to estimate a discrimination index based on real work experience data for women, unlike earlier studies which had to rely on 'potential work experience' (defined as age minus age at which the employee left full-time education) or 'imputed work experience' (which is estimated econometrically from the dataset) in their earnings equations. Their data for males were based on potential experience.

Wright and Ermisch found that the extent of gender discrimination using imputed experience for married women differed little from that based on actual experience. They estimated gender pay discrimination between married men and married women to be about 20 per cent in 1980, that is, non-discriminatory pay for the married women sampled would have been some 20 per cent more than their actual pay. This was almost four times the highest estimate of Zabalza and Arrufat (1985), based on 1975 data, and slightly higher than the highest estimate of Miller (1987), based on 1980 data. It was less than the 32 per cent found for 1977–78 by Joshi and Newell (1987), who used cohort data for workers born in 1946. The Wright and Ermisch estimate was also much less than the Blanchflower and Oswald (1989) estimate, which used data from the International Social Survey Programme (ISSP) for all employees for 1985–87, and relied entirely on potential work experience, and also less than the estimate of 31 per cent of Black, Spencer and Trainor (1995) using ISSP data for 1989 and imputed experience for married women.

This chapter follows quite closely the methodology of Zabalza and Arrufat and Wright and Ermisch. We calculate a gender discrimination index for Northern Ireland using a sample of married men and married women working as full-time employees and using an estimate of imputed experience for married women. We then compare our discrimination index with the various estimates for Great Britain mentioned above, including our own. Our sample sizes are smaller than are desirable but we try to counter this by subjecting the results to some statistical tests. We would, nonetheless, stress the desirability of checking our findings against further data in due course.

**The Model**
Our analysis is based on the theory of human capital, where it is assumed that individuals seek to maximise their wealth through their choice of investment in 'human capital' (notably education and training) and through the career paths that they choose. People make these choices subject to their own preferences and to budgetary constraints. At its simplest this results in a model in which hourly earnings are taken to depend upon an individual's level of education and his or her degree of experience of work (see Appendix A for further details). While earnings are expected to be greater for those with higher levels of education (all else being equal), this is not true of experience. Hourly earnings characteristically increase early in a person's working life, peak in early middle age when human capital is greatest, but then decline.

Within this framework discrimination is measured in a relatively straightforward way. Men and women have, on average, different levels of education and different amounts of labour force experience. On these bases alone we should expect their hourly earnings to differ. Most measures of discrimination try to assess whether the difference between male and female earnings is such as would be expected on the basis of their different levels of education and experience or whether it is actually greater than this. One method of doing this – which we adopt in this chapter – is to compute what women would earn if their attributes (notably education and experience) were rewarded at the same rate as those of men and compare this with what they actually earn. Our measure of discrimination is based on the difference between these two figures. Formally it measures discrimination as the percentage increase in women's hourly earnings that they would receive if there were no discrimination against them (the details are given in Appendix A).

We have pointed out above that this measure may underestimate discrimination if women choose career paths or levels of investment in education because of the existence of discrimination. Two other problems, standard in this approach to estimating gender discrimination, are particularly worthy of mention.

First, at any given time most adult men will be in the labour force but a large proportion of women will not. Those women who are in the labour force are not a random sample of all women and thus estimates based on women currently in the labour force may not yield results that can be applied to women in general. Technically this problem is called 'sample selection bias'. Methods to overcome this require that we not only model hourly earnings but that we also have a model predicting whether or not individuals (most importantly, women) are or are not in the labour force. This is sometimes called the participation equation. Whether or not a woman participates in the labour force is assumed to depend on whether the wage she can earn if she does participate exceeds the minimum (or 'reservation') wage that would persuade her to enter the labour force. The amount of this reservation wage will vary from woman to woman, depending on things like how many children she has, what their ages are, what other sources of income there are in the household, and so on. What she can expect to earn will depend, as we have already seen, on experience and education.

Second, we have no direct measures of experience for men or women in the dataset. For men we use potential experience (defined in the next section) as a proxy, but such a proxy would not be adequate for women with children in either the participation or earnings equations. We therefore adopt a technique pioneered by Zabalza and Arrufat (1985) which seeks to overcome this difficulty by estimating the work experience for each working woman. This is described more fully later in the chapter.

### Data and Choice of Variables

This chapter uses data from the 1994 NISA survey and the Great Britain component of the 1989 ISSP. Because the work experience of married women and single women is very different, it is customary in the literature to compare earnings differences between married women and married men. For married males, the samples used to derive the estimate of gender discrimination consisted of those between 18 and 64 years, who were working as full-time employees (defined as working 30 hours or more per week). When allowances were made for missing information on one or more of the regression variables and when data on high and low earners were dropped for reasons explained below, the resulting sample size in Northern Ireland was 218 and in Great Britain was 194.

Ideally, all married females of working age (between 18 and 59 years) should be included in the analysis. However, female work experience and time spent out of the labour market are conventionally considered to be important variables in estimating female earnings. As our datasets contain neither of these variables, they had to be estimated using a technique which was based on Zabalza and Arrufat (1985) and is described in the next section. Whether or not the individual female has children to look after is a critical variable in this calculation of estimated work experience and time spent out of the labour market. It is clear that the technique will not work for women aged 45 years or over, because these women may well have had children who no longer live at home, and such children are not referred to in the sample surveys. Accordingly, the child rearing experience of a 50 year old female, say, in either survey will not be known precisely. Hence, our estimates have to be constrained to the samples of married women aged 18–44 years in 1994 in Northern Ireland and aged 18–44 years in 1989 in Great Britain.

We are also restricting our samples to full-time employees, mainly because the earnings of over half of the married female part-time employees in each sample fell in the lowest earnings band. Hourly earnings are normally represented by the band mid-point but this is unlikely to be adequate in the lowest band. Both Callan (1991), using Republic of Ireland data, and Wright and Ermisch (1990) found that the discrimination index for married full-time workers was slightly smaller than that for all workers. Based on these results we would expect this restriction to full-time employees to reduce our estimates of discrimination by a small margin.

After taking account of missing values in the regression variables, there were 171 married females aged 18–44 years in the NISA 1994 sample, of whom 94 were in employment. In Great Britain there were 203 married females aged 18–44 years in the ISSP 1989 sample of whom 117 were in employment. There were 56 full-time employees in Northern Ireland and 65 full-time employees in Great Britain after we dropped from each sample two full-time employees whose earnings fell in the lowest band, for the reasons discussed above. Robustness checks were carried out in each case, but the coefficients were not significantly altered as a result.

To summarise, the variables that were considered to be important in the wage equations included potential experience, imputed experience, time spent at home, education, trade union membership, public sector employment and region.

*(1) Wages*
The dependent variable is the natural logarithm of hourly earnings, calculated by dividing annual income by annual hours worked. Respondents were asked how many hours a week they normally worked in their main job. It was assumed they were paid for 52 weeks per year. Each person's annual earnings were given as

earnings from all sources before income tax and national insurance, that is, gross earnings.

Employees' responses to the question on earnings were banded, as is the normal practice in surveys. We have taken the mid-points of the bands to represent average earnings in the band. Respondents in the lowest earnings band were excluded because the mid-point of this band (£2,000 in Northern Ireland and £1,000 in Great Britain) was not considered to be representative of the employees in this group. This resulted in two female full-time employees and one male full-time employee being dropped from the Northern Ireland sample and two female full-time employees being dropped from the Great Britain sample. Similarly, since the upper earnings band in Northern Ireland was open-ended above £41,000, and therefore its mid-point was indeterminate, five males in this band were dropped from the male sample. There were 29 males in Great Britain in the upper band (above £23,000) and they were dropped on the same basis. After these adjustments, the average gross hourly earnings of married females in full-time employment in Northern Ireland was 78.4 per cent of the male figure. The comparable Great Britain figure was 76.1 per cent.

## (2) *Experience*

'Potential experience' (POTEXP) is defined in Northern Ireland as respondent's age minus age on completing full-time education up to age 18 years. In Great Britain, potential experience is defined as age minus years at school minus five. For those respondents with a degree, an additional three years were subtracted from potential experience.

For females, 'imputed experience' (IMPEXP) was calculated using the back-casting method of Zabalza and Arrufat (1985) – see next section. 'Home time' (HOME) for married (and cohabiting) women is potential experience (as above) minus imputed experience.

## (3) *Education*

We have used five education dummy variables: CSE for CSE or equivalent, for example, NVQ; OLEVEL for 'O'-level or equivalent, for example, City and Guilds part 1; ALEVEL for 'A'-level or equivalent, for example, ONC/OND; HIGHER for higher education below degree level, for example, HND, HNC, nursing, teacher training; DEGREE for degree. The reference category was no qualifications.

# GENDER DISCRIMINATION AMONG MARRIED FULL-TIME EMPLOYEES

*(4) Trade Union*

The binary variable TU denoted current membership of a trade union.

*(5) Public Sector*

The binary variable PUBSEC denoted current employment in the public sector.

*(6) Region I*

For Northern Ireland two dummy variables EAST and WEST were used for the east and west of the province outside Belfast, which formed the reference category. For Great Britain the binary variable REST had a value of 1 for all regions except Greater London and the South East which formed the reference category.

Additional variables included in the probit participation equations are as follows:

*(1) Non-employment Income*

The variable NONEMPIN was defined as respondent's family income less respondent's earnings. Family income is before income tax and national insurance. In backcasting, allowance was made for the impact of economic growth on real earnings.

*(2) Husband's Professional Group*

As a proxy for husband's professional qualifications, we have used dummy variables for husband's professional group in his present or last job. For Northern Ireland, PROF is professional; INTER is intermediate; JUNIOR is junior; SKILL is skilled; SSKILL is semi-skilled. For Great Britain, PROF is professional; INTER is intermediate; SKILL is skilled; PSKILL is partly skilled and the armed forces. The reference category in both countries was unskilled.

*(3) Children*

In Northern Ireland, three dummy variables were used for the age of the youngest child: CH0TO5 indicates a youngest child aged 0–5 years; CH6TO10 indicates a youngest child aged 6–10 years; CH11TO16 indicates a youngest child aged 11–16 years. In Great Britain, five dummy variables were used for the age of the youngest child: CH0TO2, CH3TO4, CH5, CH6TO10 and CH11TO16. In both equations, two other dummy variables were used to indicate the presence of additional children; NOTH010 is other children aged from 0 to 10 years;

NOTH1116 is other children aged from 11 to 16 years.

*(4) Accommodation*

The dummy variable ACCOM had a value of 1 if the respondent lived in privately-owned or privately-rented accommodation.

*(5) Region II*

Regional dummies were not used in the probit equation for Northern Ireland. For Great Britain, dummy variables were used for the 10 standard regions: SCOT is Scotland; NORTH is Northern; NWEST is North West; YANDH is Yorkshire and Humberside; WMIDS is West Midlands; EMIDS is East Midlands; EANGLIA is East Anglia; SWEST is South West; SEAST is South East; and WALES. The reference category was Greater London.

**Estimation and Results**

The basis of our analysis is a technique called ordinary least squares regression or OLS. This provides us with estimates of how the value of a dependent variable (in our case, log hourly earnings), varies according to the values of one or more explanatory variables, such as education and experience. The information is reported as the coefficient estimates for each of the explanatory variables.

We begin by using OLS to estimate wage equations for married males in Northern Ireland and Great Britain. The results are shown in the first and third columns of Table 1 and further information about the variables is contained in Appendix B. We include, among our explanatory variables, both potential experience and potential experience squared. This allows us to take account of the concavity of the relationship between earnings and experience, that is, of the fact that earnings first increase with experience and then decline. The positive coefficient for experience and the negative coefficient for experience squared confirm that this is the case for our data also. For Northern Ireland, these effects were highly statistically significant. For Great Britain, the coefficients were less significant but, given the strength of our *a priori* expectation on the signs and given their quite high t-ratios, we chose to retain them, bearing in mind that wrongly excluding variables leads to biases in all coefficient estimates. Broadly similar results are reported for Great Britain in Wright and Ermisch (1991) and Black, Spencer and Trainor (1995). For Northern Ireland, all the education variables had significant positive coefficients, as did the trade union and public sector variables. Regional dummies for the west and the east of the province relative to Belfast were

## Table 1
### Parameter estimates of male–female earnings equations, full-time employees, Northern Ireland 1994 and Great Britain 1989

|  | Northern Ireland Male | Northern Ireland Female | Great Britain Male | Great Britain Female |
|---|---|---|---|---|
| Potential experience | 0.632 | – | 0.123 | – |
| ($\div 10$) | (5.82) |  | (1.14) |  |
| Potential experience$^2$ | –1.064 | – | –0.218 | – |
| ($\div 1000$) | (4.91) |  | (1.06) |  |
| Imputed experience | – | 0.218 | – | 0.191 |
| ($\div 10$) |  | (2.71) |  | (3.29) |
| CSE | 0.199 | – | – | – |
|  | (2.50) |  |  |  |
| OLEVEL | 0.367 | 0.296 | 0.150 | 0.399 |
|  | (4.74) | (2.90) | (2.05) | (4.84) |
| ALEVEL | 0.549 | 0.533 | 0.416 | 0.789 |
|  | (6.62) | (4.10) | (5.39) | (4.09) |
| HIGHER | 0.548 | 0.669 | 0.336 | 0.627 |
|  | (6.78) | (5.80) | (4.86) | (7.23) |
| DEGREE | 0.773 | 0.900 | 0.613 | 0.894 |
|  | (8.94) | (7.17) | (4.84) | (7.48) |
| TU | 0.160 | 0.332 | 0.099 | 0.118 |
|  | (3.18) | (4.28) | (1.91) | (1.81) |
| PUBSEC | 0.144 | – | – | – |
|  | (2.42) |  |  |  |
| REST | – | – | –0.164 | –0.142 |
|  |  |  | (3.01) | (1.95) |
| Constant | 0.584 | 0.779 | 1.345 | 0.760 |
|  | (4.34) | (6.78) | (9.60) | (6.80) |
| $R^2$ | 0.472 | 0.693 | 0.290 | 0.663 |
| N | 218 | 56 | 194 | 65 |
| SE | 0.352 | 0.282 | 0.345 | 0.254 |
| Mean log (hourly earnings) | 1.831 | 1.582 | 1.633 | 1.355 |

*Note: Figures in brackets are t-values.*

found to be statistically insignificant. For Great Britain, all the education variables except CSE had positive and significant coefficients. The trade union coefficient while positive, was much smaller than for Northern Ireland. The public sector coefficient was statistically insignificant. The earnings equation for Northern Ireland shows earnings increasing very rapidly as potential experience increases, peaking at 29.7 years of potential experience. In Great Britain the peak in earnings occurs at 28.3 years of potential experience, that is, an estimate quite close to the 26.5 years of Wright and Ermisch (1991).

The results for the married females are also reported in Table 1 and in Appendices B and C. Various steps are involved, as discussed above. First, an equation was developed to derive the probability of a married female in Northern Ireland in 1994, with certain characteristics, working (full-time or part-time, which were not distinguished at this stage). Given the estimated coefficients, it is then possible to estimate for each female the probability of her working the year before (1993), the year before that (1992) and so on. Using the approach of Zabalza and Arrufat (1985), as adapted in Black, Spencer and Trainor (1995), these probabilities, after some adjustments, are then summed, starting at the point at which her potential experience was zero and carrying on as far as 1994. This yields an estimate of work experience for each woman. The same procedure was followed for Great Britain. The equations predicting the probability of a female working were then re-estimated replacing age and age squared with this new measure of imputed experience (IMPEXP) and imputed experience squared (IMPEXPSQ). From these separate equations for Northern Ireland and Great Britain it is possible to compute a new variable for each country (called 'lambda') which can then be entered into the earnings equation regression model to try to offset the selectivity bias arising from the fact that our samples consist only of women whose earnings are greater than their reservation wage (see Appendix A for technical details of this procedure).

The fact that our samples had to be restricted to married women aged 18–44 years at the sample survey dates not only reduced the sample sizes in the participation and the earnings equations, but it also made it unreasonable to expect the curvature of the wage–experience function to be clearly captured in the estimates, given the sample sizes available. Graphing typical estimates from other studies of earnings against experience, the graphs look linear for experience between zero and 15–20 years. Thus we do not expect squared terms to be significant in estimating the impact of experience on earnings among the women in our sample. Our estimates will be useful over a smaller range than is standard, perhaps around five years experience on either side of the mean of female experience. Hence we estimate discrimination at $\overline{X}_F$, the mean of female experience, and not, for example at $\overline{X}_M$, the mean of male experience.

Returning to the two female wage equations in Table 1, imputed experience was significant in both equations but imputed experience squared was not statistically significant in either and was deleted. In neither Northern Ireland nor Great Britain did home time (HOME) or its square prove to be statistically significant and these variables were also dropped. In Northern Ireland, education proved as important for females as for males, with the males obtaining slightly higher earnings given lower level qualifications, especially CSE, and the females doing slightly better from higher education at degree or sub-degree level. This pattern was different in Great Britain, where females obtained higher returns to all qualifications.

The mark-up in earnings associated with trade union membership (TU) was much higher in Northern Ireland for both males and females, and dramatically favoured females whose earnings were increased by 33 per cent if they were trade union members. The public sector dummy was significant for males in Northern Ireland, but not for females. It was not statistically significant for either males or females in Great Britain. The lambda variable was not statistically significant in either Northern Ireland or Great Britain so that selectivity bias is deemed absent. (The presumption that imputed experience and its square are exogenous in the earnings equations was checked in that Hausman–Wu tests were applied in the earnings equations, including lambda. Some experimentation was tried, by including the home time variables with the imputed experience variables and lambda. The relevant F test was invariably insignificant.)

Before turning to the implied estimates of discrimination, it might be of interest to examine the estimated effects on earnings of extra education allied to

Table 2

Estimated hourly earnings in £s, other things being equal, for men and women with 10 years' experience, Northern Ireland 1994 and Great Britain 1989

|  | Northern Ireland ||| Great Britain |||
| --- | --- | --- | --- | --- | --- | --- |
| Education | Male | Female | M/F | Male | Female | M/F |
| No qualifications | 4.11 | 3.78 | 1.09 | 4.69 | 2.91 | 1.61 |
| 'O'-level | 5.93 | 5.08 | 1.17 | 5.45 | 4.34 | 1.26 |
| 'A'-level | 7.12 | 6.44 | 1.11 | 7.11 | 6.41 | 1.11 |
| Degree | 8.90 | 9.29 | 0.96 | 8.65 | 7.12 | 1.21 |

average experience. In Northern Ireland, the average value of experience for the women in our sample is 10.35 years while in Great Britain it is 12.64 years. Taking a hypothetical person with 10 years' experience, Table 2 gives the estimated hourly earnings for such a person given different levels of education. We assume the person is in a trade union, in the public sector and lives in the reference region.

These results suggest that educational qualifications make little difference to relative earnings in Northern Ireland, except at degree level. However, in Great Britain, the possession of educational qualifications at 'O'-level and above very much reduces the male-female differential at average experience.

The parameter estimates can now be used to calculate the discrimination measures for Northern Ireland and Great Britain. The male–female differential in

Table 3

**Decomposition of male–female earnings differentials: married persons, full-time employees, Northern Ireland 1994 and Great Britain 1989**

|  | Northern Ireland | Great Britain |
|---|---|---|
| Observed earnings gap $\overline{\log W_M} - \overline{\log W_F}$ | 0.2490 | 0.2784 |
| Attributes $\hat{\beta}_M'(\overline{X}_M - \overline{X}_F)$ | 0.1745 | 0.0401 |
| Discrimination exponent (d) $(\hat{\beta}_M - \hat{\beta}_F)'\overline{X}_F$ | 0.0746 | 0.2383 |
| Discrimination (D) $100 [\exp(\hat{\beta}_M - \hat{\beta}_F)'\overline{X}_F - 1]$ | 7.7% | 26.9% |
| Estimated standard error of discrimination exponent | 0.0599 | 0.0541 |
| 95% confidence interval for D | −4.2% to 21.2% | 14.1% to 41.0% |

observed average hourly earnings (the 'observed earnings gap') can be decomposed into two parts. One part arises because men and women have, on average, different levels of education, different amounts of experience and have different rates of trade union membership and so forth (this is labelled 'Attributes' in Table 3). The other part is what remains when the differences in attributes have been taken into account (this is labelled 'Discrimination exponent' (d) in Table 3). Table 3 also reports our measure of discrimination (D) which, as noted earlier, is the percentage increase in women's earnings that would have to occur in the absence of discrimination. Another way of expressing this is to say that it tells us by how much women's earnings are depressed as a result of discrimination. Thus, the more discrimination that exists, the higher this figure will be.

The Northern Ireland estimate of this – 7.7 per cent – is very low. In the absence of discrimination, women's average hourly earnings would be only 7.7 per cent higher than they actually are. The Great Britain estimate, at 26.9 per cent, is much higher and is quite similar to that of Wright and Ermisch (1991) who with 1980 data (and including part-time as well as full-time employees) found, using imputed experience for females, a figure of 22.1 per cent and using actual experience, a figure of 21.2 per cent.

The measures of gender discrimination reported are estimated at the point of female means. They thus estimate average discrimination, given the characteristics of the females sampled. It is possible, in principle, to measure discrimination corresponding to any level of human capital and other attributes including experience. Thus, for example, given the rapidly rising estimated returns to potential experience to Northern Ireland males referred to above, it is likely that an estimate of discrimination for females of higher than average experience would be higher than the average D reported here.

We cannot pursue this point very far, however, since our female equations are linear approximations in imputed experience and should not be assumed to have reasonable validity too far from the average. Furthermore, we do not have a sufficient sample size to try to refine our estimates for particular classes of individuals. Perhaps it is enough to point out that the low Northern Ireland discrimination figure is certainly heavily influenced by the rapidly rising estimated returns to male potential experience, returns which we suggest below might be underestimated, so that discrimination may be higher for higher levels of female experience.

## Conclusion

Our results suggest that gender discrimination, given the theory used, is considerably lower in Northern Ireland than in Great Britain. Of course, the results depend not only on the assumed theory but also on the particular sample analysed. Thus, the results are obviously subject to sampling variation and it would therefore be valuable, especially given the smallish samples, to subject the results to statistical testing (see Appendix A). In Table 3 we have reported approximate confidence intervals for D showing that the sample value of gender discrimination in Northern Ireland is not significantly different from zero and we turn now to the hypothesis that gender discrimination is the same in the two countries. Using the approximate test outlined in Appendix D, the difference between the discrimination exponents turns out to be statistically significant at the 5 per cent level and we conclude that the discrimination exponent (d) and hence gender discrimination (D) is lower in Northern Ireland in 1994 than in Great Britain in 1989.

We would again emphasise that this statement is statistically based and is dependent on assumptions including, crucially, the validity of the *a priori* earnings model and is based on a comparison of 1994 data with 1989 data. It should also be noted that the deletion of low earners and high earners from the samples, on the practical grounds that their hourly earnings are too indeterminate to be usable, may be biasing. As stated above, five males in Northern Ireland and 29 males in Great Britain in the top earnings bracket were deleted. No females were in this bracket. Thus discrimination may be underestimated, a possibility increased by the fact that four of the five individuals dropped on account of their being in the lowest earnings bracket were female. The authors are currently working on maximum likelihood techniques for allocating earnings to points in the interval other than the mid-point. This should provide checks on the robustness of our estimates, but it seems highly unlikely that the gap between the discrimination measures between Northern Ireland and Great Britain will be reduced. While both estimates might rise, the Northern Ireland estimate should rise less, given that the number of high earners dropped from the Northern Ireland sample was much smaller.

It is also worth commenting on the implications for discrimination measures of the use of potential experience for men as a proxy for actual experience. Clearly there must be a tendency for such a proxy to lead to an underestimation of discrimination. Since males will be credited with more experience than they actually have, their returns to experience will tend to be underestimated leading to an underestimate of gender discrimination. This point may apply particularly to Northern Ireland, given the high and persistent levels of unemployment there in the past.

It is impossible to quantify this effect in the absence of work histories for males. A large random sample drawn in 1987 in the Republic of Ireland shows that potential experience is, on average, little more than actual experience for all married male employees (the figures are 25.7 and 24.8 years, respectively; Callan and Wren, 1994, Table A42). Yet the effects on the discrimination measures are not negligible in that between 4 and 5 percentage points are added to D.

This suggests that our estimates of discrimination for both Northern Ireland and Great Britain are likely to be too low. Because unemployment in Northern Ireland typically exceeds that in Great Britain we might expect the difference between potential experience and actual experience to be greater in Northern Ireland, and the upward adjustment to be correspondingly higher. If so, the difference between the two discrimination measures may have been overestimated. To resolve this problem satisfactorily we need actual work histories for males.

Nonetheless, despite these caveats, our results suggesting statistically significant different levels of gender discrimination between the two country samples are striking, especially since the approximate standard errors in these models can be quite large (that is, differences are not usually significant). It will be interesting to see, in due course, if the results stand up to further scrutiny, with fresh datasets and possibly alternative models.

That part of the male–female earnings difference attributed to discrimination (the Discrimination exponent (d) shown in Table 3) can itself, of course, be decomposed into various elements. Our results for Great Britain in Tables 1 and 2 suggest that average discrimination would be much higher were it not for the effects of education favouring females. This benefit was not in evidence in Northern Ireland. The Wright and Ermisch results, when decomposed, suggest that education contributes, but only slightly, to discrimination. We would not wish to emphasise any detailed decomposition of this type at this stage of our work, however, particularly in view of data limitations and small samples.

It is of importance to ask if our estimates of discrimination are fairly robust to different specifications of the equations. This is worth checking, given the data problems, since the statistical tests will be less powerful the smaller the sample size. In fact, for various specifications, the measures changed quite little. We illustrate this with the specification for Great Britain females involving imputed experience and home time and their squares. When all these variables are included together with the variables of Table 1, the Great Britain female equation is as follows (t-ratios are in parentheses):

$$\log^{\wedge} W_F = 0.6006 + 0.0475 \text{ IMPEXP} - 0.000908 \text{ IMPEXPSQ} - 0.0232 \text{ HOME}$$
$$\phantom{\log^{\wedge} W_F =\ }(2.91)\phantom{xx}(1.62)\phantom{xxxxxxxxx}(-0.91)\phantom{xxxxxxxxxx}(-1.18)$$

$$+ 0.001557 \text{ HOMESQ} + 0.40172 \text{ OLEVEL} + 0.73191 \text{ ALEVEL}$$
$$\phantom{xx}(1.21)\phantom{xxxxxxxxxxxx}(4.49)\phantom{xxxxxxxxxx}(3.55)$$

$$+ 0.62971 \text{ HIGHER} + 0.87866 \text{ DEGREE} - 0.13687 \text{ REST} + 0.12180 \text{ TU}$$
$$\phantom{xx}(6.63)\phantom{xxxxxxxxxx}(6.66)\phantom{xxxxxxxxx}(-1.83)\phantom{xxxxxxx}(1.79)$$

The imputed experience and home variables are all of correct sign but the coefficients of IMPEXPSQ, HOME and HOMESQ are individually and jointly insignificant at the 5 per cent level. Nonetheless, retaining all these variables and making a comparison with males yields the following result: a difference in average log hourly earnings of 0.2784 is decomposed into that part due to attributes (0.0401), that part due to the effects of depreciation of human capital from home time (0.0306) and the remainder due to discrimination (0.2075). The discrimination exponent (d) implies a discrimination index D of 23.1 per cent, a figure close to our previous estimate for Great Britain of 26.9 per cent.

## References

BERNDT, E. R. 1991. *Econometrics*, Addison Wesley, Wokingham.

BLACK, B., SPENCER, J. E. and TRAINOR, M. 1995. 'Gender discrimination in earnings in West Germany, The Netherlands and Great Britain: a comparative study', *Queen's University of Belfast, Department of Economics Working Paper*, 54 (July).

BLANCHFLOWER, D. G. AND OSWALD, A. J. 1989. 'International patterns of work', in Jowell, R., Witherspoon, S. and Brook, L. (eds), *British Social Attitudes Special International Report*, Gower, London.

BLINDER, A.S. 1973. 'Wage discrimination: reduced form and structural estimates', *Journal of Human Resources*, **8**, 436–455.

CAIN, G. G. 1986. 'Labor market discrimination', in Ashenfelter, O. and Layard, R. (eds), *Handbook of Labor Economics*, Vol. 1, North-Holland, Amsterdam, pp. 693–785.

CALLAN, T. 1991. 'Male–female wage differentials in Ireland', *Economic and Social Review*, **23**, 55–72.

CALLAN, T. and WREN, A. 1994. 'Male–female wage differentials: analysis and policy issues', *Economic and Social Research Institute*, 163 (February).

CHIPLIN, B. and SLOANE, P. J. 1976. 'Personal characteristics and sex differentials in professional employment', *Economic Journal*, **86**, 729–745.

COTTON, J. 1988. 'On the decomposition of wage differentials', *The Review of Economics and Statistics*, **70**, 236–243.

DAVIES, C. and DOWNEY, A. 1993. 'Women's rights or responsibilities? Reconciling the demands of home and work' in Stringer, P. and Robinson, G. (eds), *Social Attitudes in Northern Ireland: the Third Report*, Blackstaff, Belfast.

GREENE, W. H. 1990. *Econometric Analysis*, Macmillan, New York.

GREENE, W. H. 1992. *Limdep Version 6.0*, Econometric Software Inc, Bellport, New York.

GREENHALGH, C. A. 1980. 'Male–female wage differentials in Great Britain: is marriage an equal opportunity?', *Economic Journal*, **90**, 751–775.

HAUSMAN, J. A. 1978. 'Specification Tests in Econometrics', *Econometrica*, **46**, 1251–1271.

HECKMAN, J. J. 1979. 'Sample selection bias as a specification error', *Econometrica*, **47**, 143–161.

JOSHI, H. E. and NEWELL, M. 1987. 'Pay differences between men and women: longitudinal evidence from the 1946 birth cohort', *Centre for Economic Policy Research Discussion Paper*, 156.

KIERNAN, K. 1992. 'Men and women at work and at home', in Jowell, R., Brook, L., Prior, G. and Taylor, B. (eds), *British Social Attitude: the Ninth Report*, Aldershot, Dartmouth.

KILLINGSWORTH, M. R. and HECKMAN, J. J. 1986. 'Female labor supply: a survey', in Ashenfelter, O. and Layard, R. (eds), *Handbook of Labor Economics, Vol. 1*, North-Holland, Amsterdam, pp. 103–204.

MILLER, P. 1987. 'The wage effect of the occupational segregation of women in Britain', *Economic Journal*, **97**, 885–896.

MINCER, J. 1974. *Schooling, Experience and Earnings*, National Bureau of Economic Research, Columbia University Press, New York.

NEUMARK, D. 1988. 'Employers' discriminatory behavior and the estimation of wage discrimination', *Journal of Human Resources*, **23**, 279–295.

OAXACA, R. 1973. 'Male–female wage differentials in urban labor markets', *International Economic Review*, **14**, 693–709.

SIEBERT, W. S. and SLOANE, P. J. 1981. 'The measurement of sex and marital status discrimination at the workplace', *Economica*, **48**, 125–141.

STEWART, M. 1987. 'Collective bargaining arrangements, closed shops and relative pay', *Economic Journal*, **97**, 140–156.

WEISS, Y. and GRONAU, R. 1981. 'Expected interruptions in labor force participation and sex-related differences in earnings growth', *Review of Economic Studies*, **48**, 607–619.

WILLIS, R. J. 1986. 'Wage determinants: a survey and reinterpretation of human capital earnings functions', in Ashenfelter, O. and Layard, R. (eds), *Handbook of Labor Economics*, Vol. 1, North-Holland, Amsterdam, pp. 525–602.

WRIGHT, R. E. and ERMISCH, J. F. 1990. 'Male–female wage differentials in Great Britain' *Birkbeck College, University of London, Discussion Paper in Economics*, 10/90.

WRIGHT, R. E. and ERMISCH, J. F. 1991. 'Gender discrimination in the British labour market: a reassessment', *Economic Journal* **101**, 508–522.

WU, D. 1973. 'Alternative tests of independence between stochastic regressors and disturbances', *Econometrica*, **41**, 733–750.

WU, D. 1974. 'Alternative tests of independence between stochastic regressors and disturbances: final sample results', *Econometrica*, **42**, 529–546.

ZABALZA, A. and ARRUFAT, J. L. 1985. 'The extent of sex discrimination in Great Britain', in Zabalza, A. and Tzannatos, Z. (eds), *Women and equal pay: The effects of legislation on female employment and wages in Britain*, Cambridge University Press, Cambridge, pp. 70–98.

## Appendix A

The underlying theory of human capital statistical earnings functions is derived on the basis of individuals maximising a wealth variable, and choosing career paths and forms of human capital formation subject to their preferences and intertemporal budget constraints (Willis, 1986; Berndt, 1991). Using a number of simplifications, which rely principally on the work of Mincer (for example, Mincer, 1974), and which are described in Willis (op. cit.), we can derive estimable equations of the form

$$\log W = \beta_0 + \beta_1 \text{Education} + \beta_3 \text{Experience} + \beta_4 \text{Experience}^2 + u \qquad (1)$$

where W is hourly earnings, Education stands for education variables (for example, 'O'-levels), Experience stands for experience at work including on-the-job training and u is a random disturbance term. The expectation of human capital theory that earnings should be a concave function of experience is taken account of by including the square of Experience. On the assumption that experience yields general, not specific, on-the-job training, we expect hourly earnings to increase early in life and to peak near mid-life when human capital is largest, prior to its net depreciation. (Berndt, 1991, pp. 155–157 summarises this literature, which is also surveyed in detail by Willis, 1986.)

Discrimination is generally measured, following the work of Blinder (1973) and Oaxaca (1973), by comparing differences in the estimated regression coefficients as follows (ignoring disturbance terms).

$$W_F(ND) = \text{female earnings in the absence of discrimination}$$
$$= \exp(X'_F \beta_M)$$

where $X'_F$ are a female's characteristics (education etc.) and $\beta_M$ are the male coefficients. Actual female earnings, on the other hand, are given by $W_F = \exp(X'_F \beta_F)$, where $\beta_F$ are the female coefficients. Discrimination is then measured as

$$D = 100(W_F(ND) - W_F)/W_F$$
$$= 100(\exp(X'_F(\beta_M - \beta_F)) - 1) \qquad (2)$$

where D can be interpreted as the percentage increase in the hourly wage rate that women would receive if they were remunerated like men, that is, so that there was no direct discrimination.

In practice $X_F$ is often measured at the means and the $\beta$s are replaced by the estimated coefficients. It is also possible, of course, to measure discrimination using $X_M$ as weights. It will be clear that the validity of these ways of estimating discrimination depends on the validity of the assumption that the $\beta$s would be the same in the absence of discrimination.

Assuming that the Xs are non-stochastic,

$$\text{var}(X'_F(\hat{\beta}_M - \hat{\beta}_F)) = X'_F(\text{var cov}\hat{\beta}_M + \text{var cov}\hat{\beta}_F)X_F$$

if the samples of males and females are assumed to be independent. This expression can be estimated. In practice, the Xs are unlikely to be non-stochastic and for this and other reasons (see below on selectivity bias) the above formula can be seen as an asymptotic approximation (Stewart, 1987). We, in fact, measure at $X_F = \overline{X}_F$ and assume normality to obtain an approximate 95 per cent confidence interval for $\overline{X}'_F(\hat{\beta}_M - \hat{\beta}_F)$ and hence obtain an approximate 95 per cent (asymmetric) confidence interval for D.

Corresponding to the two measures of discrimination (measuring at $\overline{X}_F$ or $\overline{X}_M$) are two estimated decompositions of the difference between average male and female earnings,

$$\overline{\log W}_M - \overline{\log W}_F = (\overline{X}_M - \overline{X}_F)'\hat{\beta}_M + \overline{X}'_F(\hat{\beta}_M - \hat{\beta}_F)$$
$$= (\overline{X}_M - \overline{X}_F)'\hat{\beta}_F + \overline{X}'_M(\hat{\beta}_M - \hat{\beta}_F). \qquad (3)$$

In fact, a third decomposition is possible

$$\overline{\log W}_M - \overline{\log W}_F = (\overline{X}_M - \overline{X}_F)'\beta^* + [\overline{X}'_M(\beta_M - \beta^*) - \overline{X}'_F(\beta_F - \beta^*)]$$

where $\beta^*$ is defined as the no-discrimination wage structure and the discrimination component consists of the two separate elements in the square brackets (Neumark, 1988; Cotton, 1988). We do not use this decomposition as we do not wish, partly on account of the small and restricted samples available, to have to estimate $\beta^*$, but instead we concentrate on the more standard measure in (3) using $\overline{X}_F$ as weights for reasons associated with the use of the imputed experience variable and explained earlier in this chapter.

It is important to emphasise that this approach may underestimate discrimination if, for example, women choose specific careers or work profiles not because of endowments or preferences but because of expectations of discrimination in other possible careers. Such discrimination might lead females to underinvest in education or to choose jobs in which they expect future discrimination to be low – or, indeed, to spend more time out of the labour force. This sort of endogeneity leads to $\overline{X}'_F(\beta_M - \beta_F)$ tending to understate discrimination (Berndt 1991, pp.189–190; Cain, 1986; Weiss and Gronau, 1981) and may be a particular problem with the experience variable. This is discussed later in this appendix.

In principle statistical earning functions for males and females should be similar but in practice age–earnings profiles for females tend to be flatter. This is generally accepted as reflecting the view that, for females, incentives to invest in human capital are less because with child rearing there will be less time to recoup the benefits of experience and because of the depreciation of skills in time spent outside the labour market rearing children. Consequently it will be important, if the effect of experience is not to be underestimated, to include in the female earnings functions a variable for time out of the labour market (HOME) and its square (HOMESQ).

A further more subtle difficulty in estimating earnings functions for females arises from this fact that many women spend time out of the labour force. It is now well known that naive regressions of earnings on their determinants may suffer from sample selectivity bias, a bias which can be corrected asymptotically by inserting an extra variable in the earnings equation. This extra variable lambda, sometimes known as the inverse Mills ratio, can be generated, following the work of Heckman (1979), by a probit equation estimated on all women, working and non-working, in the sample.

The probit equation estimates the probability of working, that is, the probability that an individual's earning power (W) exceeds her reservation wage (W*). W will depend on variables such as education and experience following the human capital model, while W* will depend on variables such as number and age of children, non-earned income etc. The problem of selectivity bias and its solution via probit is discussed concisely by Killingsworth and Heckman (1986) and Greene (1990).

Two other important issues complicate the estimation of female earnings. First, experience is often unknown and hence not available as a variable in the participation equation (the probit) or the earnings equation. This is overcome following a technique pioneered by Zabalza and Arrufat (1985), which is used to estimate experience and is described earlier in this chapter.

The second problem, referred to above, is that experience may not be exogenous in that experience depends on participation and hence on earnings. The Hausman–Wu test (Hausman, 1978; Wu, 1973, 1974) checks for endogeneity of a set of variables on the right hand side of a regression equation in the sense that it tests whether or not that set is independent of the disturbance term of the equation. If the null of independence is rejected, an instrumental variables type estimator is called for.

In studies of women's earnings, it is generally thought likely that experience and experience squared are possible candidates for offending non-zero correlations with the disturbance term in the probit or earnings equations. It can be argued that this problem does not arise in our work, however, at least with experience and its square. For experience is not available and is replaced with imputed experience, the latter being based, as described above, on variables such as age etc which can perhaps be taken as exogenous. However, as a check and safeguard, we applied the Hausman–Wu test to each female earnings equation. The test results supported the null hypothesis of zero correlations and instrumental variables were accordingly not used.

## Appendix B

### Means and standard deviations of the variables

|  | Mean Male | Mean Female | Standard deviation Male | Standard deviation Female |
|---|---|---|---|---|
| *Northern Ireland, 1994* | | | | |
| log (hourly earnings) | 1.831 | 1.582 | 0.474 | 0.481 |
| POTEXP | 22.202 | – | 10.344 | – |
| POTEXPSQ | 599.42 | – | 513.02 | – |
| IMPEXP | – | 10.352 | – | 4.844 |
| IMPEXPSQ | – | 130.22 | – | 117.89 |
| HOME | – | 4.609 | – | 4.297 |
| HOMESQ | – | 39.380 | – | 59.769 |
| CSE | 0.156 | 0.125 | 0.364 | 0.334 |
| OLEVEL | 0.193 | 0.286 | 0.395 | 0.456 |
| ALEVEL | 0.142 | 0.125 | 0.350 | 0.334 |
| HIGHER | 0.151 | 0.179 | 0.359 | 0.386 |
| DEGREE | 0.138 | 0.143 | 0.345 | 0.353 |
| TU | 0.482 | 0.536 | 0.501 | 0.503 |
| PUBSEC | 0.243 | 0.446 | 0.430 | 0.502 |
| EAST | 0.569 | 0.589 | 0.496 | 0.496 |
| WEST | 0.317 | 0.214 | 0.466 | 0.414 |
| *Sample size* | *218* | *56* | | |
| | | | | |
| *Great Britain, 1989* | | | | |
| log (hourly earnings) | 1.633 | 1.355 | 0.401 | 0.413 |
| POTEXP | 25.144 | – | 10.951 | – |
| POTEXPSQ | 751.55 | – | 578.60 | – |
| IMPEXP | – | 12.644 | – | 5.563 |
| IMPEXPSQ | – | 190.35 | – | 160.17 |
| HOME | – | 4.079 | – | 4.985 |
| HOMESQ | – | 41.107 | – | 75.704 |
| CSE | 0.072 | 0.108 | 0.259 | 0.312 |
| OLEVEL | 0.186 | 0.323 | 0.390 | 0.471 |
| ALEVEL | 0.180 | 0.031 | 0.386 | 0.174 |

|  | Mean | | Standard deviation | |
| --- | --- | --- | --- | --- |
|  | Male | Female | Male | Female |
| HIGHER | 0.216 | 0.262 | 0.413 | 0.443 |
| DEGREE | 0.046 | 0.092 | 0.211 | 0.292 |
| TU | 0.515 | 0.477 | 0.501 | 0.503 |
| PUBSEC | 0.268 | 0.369 | 0.444 | 0.486 |
| REST | 0.686 | 0.723 | 0.465 | 0.451 |
| *Sample size* | *194* | *65* | | |

## Appendix C

**Probit equations used to derive imputed experience and home time for married females aged 18–44 years**

*Northern Ireland, 1994 (N=171)*

| Variable | Coefficient | t-value | Mean | Standard deviation |
| --- | --- | --- | --- | --- |
| AGE | 0.1374 | 0.74 | 32.778 | 6.193 |
| AGESQ | -0.0023 | 0.80 | 1112.5 | 407.57 |
| NONEMPIN | -0.00006 | 2.90 | 12506.0 | 7669.8 |
| CSE | 0.1948 | 0.52 | 0.135 | 0.342 |
| OLEVEL | 0.204 | 0.63 | 0.298 | 0.459 |
| ALEVEL | -0.034 | 0.08 | 0.105 | 0.308 |
| HIGHER | 1.083 | 2.37 | 0.111 | 0.315 |
| DEGREE | 0.821 | 1.45 | 0.064 | 0.246 |
| PROF | 0.528 | 1.04 | 0.205 | 0.405 |
| INTER | 0.802 | 1.41 | 0.123 | 0.329 |
| JUNIOR | 1.175 | 1.83 | 0.082 | 0.275 |
| SKILL | 0.447 | 0.988 | 0.380 | 0.487 |
| SSKILL | 0.031 | 0.06 | 0.135 | 0.342 |
| CH0TO5 | -0.397 | 1.06 | 0.485 | 0.501 |
| CH6TO10 | -0.253 | 0.623 | 0.199 | 0.400 |
| CH11TO16 | 0.548 | 1.15 | 0.140 | 0.348 |
| NOTH010 | -0.366 | 1.97 | 0.596 | 0.830 |
| NOTH1116 | -0.118 | 0.76 | 0.433 | 0.812 |
| ACCOM | 1.130 | 3.70 | 0.754 | 0.432 |
| Constant | -2.212 | 0.745 | | |

*Great Britain, 1989 (N=203)*

| Variable | Coefficient | t-value | Mean | Standard Deviation |
|---|---|---|---|---|
| AGE | 0.0254 | 0.10 | 33.621 | 6.656 |
| AGESQ | −0.00058 | 0.16 | 1174.40 | 442.42 |
| NONEMPIN | −0.0001 | 3.57 | 12507.0 | 6546.6 |
| CSE | 1.392 | 2.89 | 0.123 | 0.329 |
| OLEVEL | 0.706 | 1.98 | 0.286 | 0.453 |
| ALEVEL | 0.809 | 1.11 | 0.044 | 0.206 |
| HIGHER | 0.847 | 2.02 | 0.192 | 0.395 |
| DEGREE | 1.424 | 1.63 | 0.059 | 0.236 |
| PROF | −0.475 | 0.43 | 0.074 | 0.262 |
| INTER | −0.919 | 0.92 | 0.276 | 0.448 |
| SKILL | −0.976 | 1.05 | 0.488 | 0.501 |
| PSKILL | −1.495 | 1.57 | 0.153 | 0.361 |
| CH0TO2 | −3.251 | 5.40 | 0.212 | 0.410 |
| CH3TO4 | −2.840 | 4.23 | 0.118 | 0.324 |
| CH5 | −1.465 | 1.52 | 0.020 | 0.139 |
| CH6TO10 | −1.798 | 3.00 | 0.182 | 0.387 |
| CH11TO16 | −1.302 | 2.48 | 0.217 | 0.413 |
| NOTH010 | −0.245 | 0.99 | 0.335 | 0.679 |
| NOTH1116 | 0.593 | 2.37 | 0.310 | 0.595 |
| SCOT | −0.116 | 0.16 | 0.064 | 0.245 |
| NORTH | −0.428 | 0.68 | 0.064 | 0.245 |
| NWEST | 0.109 | 0.19 | 0.094 | 0.292 |
| YANDH | 0.019 | 0.03 | 0.094 | 0.292 |
| WMIDS | 0.495 | 0.83 | 0.143 | 0.351 |
| EMIDS | −0.489 | 0.75 | 0.079 | 0.270 |
| EANGLIA | −0.399 | 0.54 | 0.044 | 0.206 |
| SWEST | −0.468 | 0.73 | 0.089 | 0.285 |
| SEAST | 0.958 | 1.69 | 0.197 | 0.399 |
| WALES | 1.616 | 2.03 | 0.049 | 0.217 |
| ACCOM | 0.646 | 1.73 | 0.818 | 0.387 |
| Constant | 2.691 | 0.623 | | |

## Appendix D

An approximate test that discrimination is the same between the two countries is available as follows. Write

$$\hat{d} = (\hat{\beta}_M - \hat{\beta}_F)'\overline{X}_F$$

the discrimination exponent, one for Great Britain and one for Northern Ireland ($d_{GB}$ and $d_{NI}$, say).

Assuming $\overline{X}_F$ is fixed (or conditioning on $\overline{X}_F$), the variation in $\hat{d}$ arises through the variation in $\hat{\beta}_M$ and $\hat{\beta}_F$, the estimated coefficients in the country's earnings equations. From Appendix A we can readily estimate $\text{var}\,\hat{d}$ and the null hypothesis, $H_0 : d_{NI} = d_{GB}$, can be tested using the statistic

$$(\hat{d}_{NI} - \hat{d}_{GB})/\sqrt{(\hat{\text{var}}\,\hat{d}_{NI} + \hat{\text{var}}\,\hat{d}_{GB})}$$

noticing that $\hat{d}_{NI}$ and $\hat{d}_{GB}$ are independent. On $H_0$, and assuming $\overline{X}_F$ to be non-stochastic in each country, the statistic is for large samples approximately standard normal. In our samples, this statistic is evaluated to be

$$(0.0746 - 0.2383)/\sqrt{(0.0599^2 + 0.0541^2)} = -2.03.$$

This is significant at the 5 per cent level using a one-tailed test.

# 9

# Community Relations, Equality and the Future

Tony Gallagher

## Introduction

All of the Northern Ireland Social Attitudes (NISA) surveys have included a module of questions on community relations and each book published in the series has included a report on this module (Gallagher, 1991; 1992a, b; 1993; 1995a; Gallagher and Dunn, 1991; Curtice and Gallagher, 1990). This chapter addresses the community relations issues explored in the 1994 survey. Clearly the circumstances in Northern Ireland have changed dramatically since the survey was administered. In particular, the paramilitary cease-fires have brought the first real promise of an end to violence after a quarter century of bloodshed, and undoubtedly this will have an impact on perceptions of community relations. In this context the 1994 survey forms both the end of one time-series and the beginning of another. This chapter brings up-to-date the ongoing pattern of results from each of the survey years and provides an important baseline measure by which the impact of the hoped-for end of violence will be assessed.

The remainder of the chapter is divided into three main sections. The first section examines briefly some of the results relating to identity issues in Northern Ireland. The second section focuses on attitudes to equality. The 1994 survey

## Table 1
### Political partisanship, Northern Ireland parties only (%)

|  | Catholic ||||| Protestant |||||
| --- | --- | --- | --- | --- | --- | --- | --- | --- | --- | --- |
|  | 1989 | 1990 | 1991 | 1993 | 1994 | 1989 | 1990 | 1991 | 1993 | 1994 |
| Unionist parties | 2 | 1 | – | 1 | 0 | 69 | 70 | 65 | 68 | 69 |
| Nationalist parties | 51 | 51 | 59 | 52 | 64 | – | – | 1 | 1 | 0 |
| Other party | 12 | 10 | 11 | 14 | 10 | 12 | 8 | 10 | 9 | 12 |
| None | 28 | 24 | 16 | 22 | 19 | 10 | 13 | 14 | 12 | 10 |

contained many questions relating to this issue, in part because of a review of the 1989 Fair Employment Act, and the likelihood of anti-discrimination legislation on the basis of 'race'. The results on the second of these topics are explored in greater detail in Chapter 5 of this volume, but here we are concerned with the responses of Protestants and Catholics to these issues as an indication of their broader views on equity. In the third and final part of this chapter we examine our respondents' perceptions of the current and future state of relations between the two main religious communities in Northern Ireland.

**Identity**

The survey includes a number of variables through which we can examine aspects of identity. These include political partisanship, national identity and attitudes to the constitutional future of Northern Ireland. We have examined these data in previous reports on the survey; here we bring the picture up to date. From Table 1 we can see that political identification remains firmly entrenched, with most Catholics identifying with nationalist political parties and most Protestants with unionist political parties. Only around one-in-ten of our sample identifies with political parties which explicitly seek cross-community support and a slightly higher proportion say they identify with no political party.

Table 2
Would you describe yourself as ... (%)

|  | Catholic |  |  |  | Protestant |  |  |  |
| --- | --- | --- | --- | --- | --- | --- | --- | --- |
|  | 1986 | 1989 | 1993 | 1994 | 1986 | 1989 | 1993 | 1994 |
| ... British | 9 | 8 | 12 | 9 | 65 | 68 | 69 | 70 |
| ... Irish | 61 | 60 | 61 | 62 | 3 | 3 | 2 | 3 |
| ... Ulster | 1 | 2 | 1 | – | 14 | 10 | 15 | 11 |
| ... Northern Irish | 20 | 25 | 24 | 28 | 11 | 16 | 11 | 15 |

Table 2 shows the data for national identity where our survey asked respondents to select their preferred identity label. In 1994, as in past years, the favoured national label among Protestants was British, while that among Catholics was Irish. Over the survey years a minority from both communities have selected other labels, with Protestants fluctuating between Ulster and Northern Irish, while Catholics tend to prefer the Northern Irish label. The important point to emphasise, however, is the continuing fundamental difference between Catholics and Protestants in their identification with Britain or Ireland.

### Table 3
#### Percentage in Northern Ireland saying that ...

|  | Catholic 1991 | Catholic 1993 | Catholic 1994 | Protestant 1991 | Protestant 1993 | Protestant 1994 |
|---|---|---|---|---|---|---|
| ... there should be a united Ireland: | 53 | 49 | 60 | 4 | 5 | 6 |
| ... the Union should be maintained: | 35 | 36 | 25 | 92 | 90 | 91 |
| ... British troops should be withdrawn: | 49 | 47 | 51 | 11 | 10 | 13 |
| ... British troops should not be withdrawn: | 38 | 39 | 37 | 86 | 85 | 84 |

We now turn from perceptions of identity in politics and nationality towards aspirations in these areas by looking at our respondents' views on the future of Northern Ireland. Table 3 shows the pattern of perceptions on the constitutional future of Northern Ireland. As indicated above, the key point here relates to the difference in perception between Protestants and Catholics which has been evident in each survey. Thus, while most Protestants support the retention of the Union between Northern Ireland and Great Britain, the more popular option for Catholics is a united Ireland. Similarly, while most Protestants would not support the withdrawal of the British troops, around one-half of Catholics say they would favour such a withdrawal. An additional aspect of this pattern is that there is a stronger consensus among Protestants on these issues. It is perhaps worth noting also the increase in 1994, in comparison with previous survey years, in the proportion of Catholics saying they would support a united Ireland.

### Table 4
#### Percentage saying they would trust government just about always or most of the time

|  | Catholic 1989 | Catholic 1991 | Catholic 1993 | Catholic 1994 | Protestant 1989 | Protestant 1991 | Protestant 1993 | Protestant 1994 |
|---|---|---|---|---|---|---|---|---|
| British government under direct rule | 15 | 22 | 19 | 17 | 32 | 40 | 30 | 27 |
| Stormont government under local assembly | 20 | 31 | 31 | 24 | 67 | 73 | 65 | 65 |
| Irish government in united Ireland | 36 | 45 | 37 | 38 | 10 | 14 | 11 | 12 |

The final area to be examined in this section deals with perceptions of potential political arrangements in Northern Ireland. As with the tables above, the data here are consistent with previous surveys and are included mainly for the purposes of updating. Table 4 shows our respondents' accounts of how far they would trust government under three alternative scenarios. The pattern found in past years is repeated in 1994, in that a majority of Protestants say they would trust a locally elected government, but under a third would trust the British government under direct rule and only about one-in-ten would trust an Irish government under a united Ireland. The pattern of responses among Catholics differs mainly in that none of the three alternatives attracts a majority view.

In this section of the chapter we have seen that the 1994 survey highlights a continuing pattern of difference among Catholics and Protestants. This difference is found in their preferred identities, both political and national. In addition, it is found in their aspirations and judgements for the political and constitutional future of Northern Ireland. As has been argued in previous reports on the survey, these fundamental differences provide the bedrock upon which all other attitudes to community relations must be placed. That said, it is perhaps worth reiterating that the views illustrated here represent the period just before the cease-fires. For many years a seemingly interminable stasis had afflicted the political context in the province. With the announcement of the Downing Street Declaration towards the end of 1993, the stasis appeared to start breaking. However, it was only after the cease-fires, in the late summer of 1994, that the political context became subject to rapid change and it seems reasonable to suppose that attitudes on some of the areas examined above may begin to shift. While the data above provide a pre-cease-fire baseline, however, the measurement of change must await future NISA surveys.

## Attitudes to Equality

Current government policy on community relations identifies three objectives: the encouragement of greater contact between Protestants and Catholics, the

Table 5

Percentage saying Protestants and Catholics are treated equally by ...

|  | Catholic | Protestant |
| --- | --- | --- |
| ... the National Health Service in treating patients | 93 | 90 |
| ... Government unemployment schemes in treating applicants for a place | 81 | 72 |
| ... the NI Housing Executive in treating applicants for a home | 67 | 65 |
| ... central government in Stormont in treating job applicants | 47 | 60 |
| ... local district councils in treating job applicants | 45 | 59 |
| ... the Fair Employment Commission | 82 | 62 |

encouragement of greater tolerance of cultural pluralism and the promotion of equality of opportunity (Gallagher, 1995b). In each year of the survey questions have been incorporated to examine aspects of these policy objectives. In 1994 the questions included in the survey had a strong focus on equality issues, not least because of review of the 1989 Fair Employment Act and the likelihood of anti-discrimination legislation on the basis of 'race'. The 'race' issue is explored at greater length in Chapter 5 of this volume, but here we look at the comparative attitudes of Protestants and Catholics on these issues. We begin by examining attitudes to fair employment issues.

In each administration of the NISA survey we have asked respondents for their perceptions of the extent to which a variety of public bodies treat Protestants and Catholics equally. In 1994 we asked a similar question but included, for the first time, the Fair Employment Commission (FEC) as one of the listed public bodies. We can see from Table 5 that the general public perception is that the FEC does treat members of both communities equitably, although it is notable that this view is held by a higher proportion of Catholics in our survey than Protestants.

We now turn to a series of questions designed to gauge our respondents' perception of the extent of fairness or unfairness in the labour market more generally. Previous administrations of the survey have included questions related

Table 6

**Percentage saying that the chances of Protestants and Catholics getting a job are ...**

|  | Catholic |  |  |  | Protestant |  |  |  |
|---|---|---|---|---|---|---|---|---|
|  | 1989 | 1991 | 1993 | 1994 | 1989 | 1991 | 1993 | 1994 |
| ... the same | 30 | 29 | 41 | 42 | 60 | 62 | 61 | 57 |
| ... different | 60 | 59 | 55 | 55 | 30 | 30 | 32 | 38 |

Table 7

**If the chances are different, which group is more likely to get a job? (%)**

|  | Catholic |  |  |  | Protestant |  |  |  |
|---|---|---|---|---|---|---|---|---|
|  | 1989 | 1991 | 1993 | 1994 | 1989 | 1991 | 1993 | 1994 |
| Protestant | 89 | 82 | 86 | 88 | 34 | 26 | 28 | 30 |
| Catholic | 1 | 2 | 2 | – | 43 | 49 | 41 | 42 |
| Don't know/depends | 10 | 16 | 12 | 12 | 22 | 25 | 31 | 28 |

to this topic, but in 1994 additional items were included for the first time. Tables 6 and 7 show details of responses to a question which has been asked regularly on the survey. We asked our respondents whether or not they felt that the chances of Protestants and Catholics getting a job were the same or different. For those who felt that the chances were different, we then asked which group they felt was at an advantage. From Table 6 we can see that the 1994 results are consistent with previous surveys in that most Catholics feel that the chances of getting a job are different, while most Protestants feel that the chances of getting a job are the same. It is noteworthy that the proportion of Catholics who feel there is inequity has declined slightly over the survey years, while the proportion of Protestants perceiving inequity has increased slightly.

From Table 7 we can see that the religious difference in the perception of the direction of inequity in 1994 is also consistent with past surveys. Among those Catholics who feel that the chances of getting a job are different, a clear majority perceive that Protestants are at an advantage. By contrast, among the minority of Protestants who feel that the chances of getting a job are different there is a more mixed picture: while two-in-five feel that Catholics are at an advantage, a little under a third feel that Protestants are at an advantage.

Further insight into this issue was obtained from a question asked for the first time in 1994. We asked our respondents directly whether they felt Protestants had a better chance of getting jobs in Northern Ireland, or Catholics had a better chance, or both groups had the same chance. The results reflect the pattern discussed above. Whereas 51 per cent of Catholics feel that Protestants have the better chance of getting jobs, this is so for only 13 per cent of Protestants in our survey. While 18 per cent of Protestants feel that Catholics have the better chance of getting jobs, almost no Catholics in our survey express this view. Finally, while 57 per cent of Protestants say that the chances for both groups are the same, this is so for only 42 per cent of Catholics in our survey.

In summary, the emergent picture can be described as follows: while most Protestants feel that the employment market in Northern Ireland is, by and large, fair to both communities, most Catholics feel that it is not fair. Furthermore, most Catholics believe that the unfairness in employment operates to their disadvantage. Within these overall patterns, it should be noted that the minority position in both communities is increasing: thus, in 1994 more Catholics than in previous surveys say that the labour market is fair, and more Protestants than in previous surveys say that the labour market is unfair.

Questions asked in previous surveys have examined whether or not respondents feel that some employers take religion into account in their employment decisions. In past years a majority of respondents from both communities thought that this was true, and the results in 1994 are no different. A little under two-thirds of the Protestants in our survey say that there are employers who will give a preference to one or other of the two main religious communities. Most of our Catholic respondents concur with this view, but somewhat more say that there are employers who will advantage Protestants in comparison with employers who will advantage Catholics (81 per cent and 57 per cent, respectively).

However, in 1994 we asked an additional series of questions to try to assess why people believe these processes to operate. One question asked directly whether our respondents felt these processes occurred because of discrimination or some other process. The results were clear: about four-in-five of our respondents say that any advantage which members of either religious community obtain in employment is due to discrimination. This is despite the finding that only five per cent or fewer of our respondents say that they themselves have experienced discrimination in employment, promotion or in relations between work mates.

One explanation that is sometimes offered to explain differences in the composition of workforces lies in the so-called 'chill factor'. This implies that some people will be put off applying for or accepting a job because of their perception that they would not receive fair treatment in that workplace. In order to test the role of the chill factor we asked our respondents two types of questions. First, we asked if they applied for a job would it matter whether or not all of their potential work mates were of the same religion. Following this, we asked whether or not they would avoid applying for a job in either a Protestant or a Catholic area. The results suggest that the chill factor does play a role for some people. While about three-quarters of both groups say that the religious composition of a workforce would not be a matter of concern in a job application, 58 per cent of Catholics in our survey say they would avoid applying for a job in Protestant areas, while 48 per cent of Protestants say they would avoid applying for a job in Catholic areas.

This relatively high level of avoidance may explain an apparent conumdrum in the data outlined above. On the one hand our survey results suggest that a relatively large proportion of respondents believe that discrimination operates in the labour market, or at least that religion is a factor which influences employment opportunity. At the same time only a very small proportion claim to have experienced directly the consequences of any discrimination. If, as we have seen, a significant proportion of people avoid applying for jobs in certain areas then they might believe that they have avoided those situations where they might have faced discrimination. Thus, they can continue to believe that discrimination exists despite a lack of direct experience, given that they consciously avoid those situations where they perceive that this direct experience is most likely to be found.

The data above outline some of the perceptions that respondents in our survey have on aspects of fair employment, but we also asked for their views on measures which are, or could, be taken against discrimination in employment. On the simple principle of fairness there is a clear and unambiguous consensus: almost all our respondents say that there should be equal opportunities in employment and all but a small minority say they support laws against religious discrimination. However, the consensus between the two main communities began to break down a little once we started asking about more specific measures. Thus, while more than three-in-four Catholics say that they would support a law requiring the recording of religion, this is so for only one-in-two Protestants. The current Fair Employment Act (1989) does require employers to monitor annually the religious composition of their workforces and, while 90 per cent of Catholics say they think this law treats both communities fairly, this is so for only 65 per cent of Protestants. These differences should be noted, but should not, perhaps, be over-exaggerated, not least because evidence from past surveys suggests that support for fair employment measures has grown in recent years.

Indeed, it may be that now, any concerns about fair employment legislation relate more to the possible consequences of these measures rather than any existing requirements of the legislation. It is not only in Northern Ireland that some concern is occasionally expressed about affirmative action, especially where this is interpreted as providing a sanction for some form of reverse discrimination. We sought the views of our respondents on this issue by asking whether or not they agreed with the idea that, if one religious community is under-represented in a workplace, members of that community should be given preference in new job opportunities. Almost four-in-five Protestants disagree with this suggestion, as do just over half of Catholics. As with the previous discussion, there is a difference in the extent to which an opinion is held between the two groups, but no difference in the direction of the opinion held.

Of course, community relations in Northern Ireland involves more than the two main religious communities. As is increasingly being recognised, the right to equal opportunities extends to ethnic minority communities in Northern Ireland, whose interests have, arguably, been ignored over the years. Indeed, it seems likely that by the time this book is published draft legislation on race relations will be well advanced. As a further insight into views on equality, our survey included a number of items dealing with attitudes to other minority communities. Here we examine briefly the views of Catholics and Protestants on these issues, but the range of items relevant to this are considered at somewhat greater length in Chapter 5 of this volume.

### Table 8
**In the UK have we gone too far, far enough or not far enough on equal opportunities for ... (%)**

|  | Catholic | Protestant |
|---|---|---|
| *Women* | | |
| Too far | 5 | 14 |
| About right | 52 | 55 |
| Not far enough | 42 | 30 |
| *Blacks and Asians* | | |
| Too far | 7 | 15 |
| About right | 38 | 51 |
| Not far enough | 49 | 27 |
| *Gays and lesbians* | | |
| Too far | 51 | 69 |
| About right | 35 | 22 |
| Not far enough | 11 | 7 |

We asked our respondents whether they felt that legislation on equal opportunities had gone too far, not far enough, or was about right for a range of groups. The items of interest here are summarised in Table 8. We can see from this table that Catholics tend to be a little more liberal than Protestants on these issues, but that both groups are particularly illiberal with regard to gays and lesbians. This comparative pattern for the religious communities was found on some other issues as well: while 53 per cent of Catholics feel that more needs to be done to provide sites for gypsies and travellers, this is so for only 34 per cent of Protestants. Conversely, three-in-four respondents from both communities feel that the law has gone too far in allowing the right to show nudity and sex in films.

Additional questions examined whether respondents felt there was prejudice against a series of named ethnic minority communities in Northern Ireland. Over four-in-five say that there is prejudice against travellers. Thereafter the views of Protestants and Catholics begin to diverge. Thus, while 48 per cent of Catholics say there is prejudice against Chinese people, only 34 per cent of Protestants concur. Similarly 52 per cent of Catholics, in comparison with 40 per cent of Protestants, say there is prejudice against Asians. Using a variation on a social distance scale we found that a little over a third of our respondents say that most people would mind having a Chinese boss and over half say that most people would mind a close relative marrying someone of Chinese origin. Under both scenarios the proportions are a little higher when we asked about Asians. All of these figures are lower than the responses obtained from comparable questions asked of British samples in different years of the Social Attitudes survey. However, while only about a third of respondents in Northern Ireland say there is prejudice against Chinese and Asian people in the job market, over two-thirds say they would support a law against racial discrimination.

**Optimists and Pessimists**
For the third and final part of the chapter we turn to our respondents' views on the general state of community relations in Northern Ireland. In each administration of the survey we have asked our respondents whether they felt relations between Protestants and Catholics were better, worse or about the same as they had been five years previously, and whether they felt they would be better, worse or about the same in five years time. Reports on previous surveys noted an emergent optimism over the years in that there was a small rise in the proportion saying that community relations were getting, and would get, better, and a more marked decline in the proportion saying that community relations were getting, and would get, worse. The report on the 1993 survey noted a slight retrenchment in this pattern and it was suggested that this might have been attributable to the changing nature and extent of political violence at that time.

The context of the survey is important for the present data also. The survey was administered in the Spring and early Summer of 1994. Thus, at the time our respondents were expressing their views Northern Ireland had just come through a particularly bloody period, even by its own standards, and the air was rife with rumours of deals, agreements and cease-fires, not least because of the apparently new situation created by the Downing Street Declaration. As events turned out the IRA cessation of violence did not become official until the end of August, 1994, to be closely followed by a cease-fire announcement from the Loyalist paramilitary

### Table 9

**Perceptions of relations between Protestants and Catholics now compared with five years ago (%)**

|  | Catholic | | | Protestant | | |
|---|---|---|---|---|---|---|
|  | Better | About the same | Worse | Better | About the same | Worse |
| 1989 | 23 | 44 | 31 | 20 | 50 | 26 |
| 1991 | 31 | 50 | 16 | 28 | 53 | 15 |
| 1993 | 27 | 46 | 24 | 24 | 46 | 28 |
| 1994 | 26 | 44 | 26 | 26 | 45 | 26 |

### Table 10

**Perceptions of relations between Protestants and Catholics in five years time (%)**

|  | Catholic | | | Protestant | | |
|---|---|---|---|---|---|---|
|  | Better | About the same | Worse | Better | About the same | Worse |
| 1989 | 30 | 51 | 16 | 22 | 56 | 16 |
| 1991 | 40 | 50 | 4 | 29 | 55 | 10 |
| 1993 | 32 | 51 | 11 | 26 | 47 | 21 |
| 1994 | 36 | 43 | 18 | 30 | 45 | 18 |

groups. This means that the 1994 NISA survey may be the last collected in a period of violence, thus providing an important benchmark for assessing attitudinal change as a consequence of the end of political violence.

We can see from Table 9 that our respondents' view of the current state of community relations in comparison with 'five years ago' is little different from the view expressed in 1993. A similar picture emerges from Table 10 where we asked for our respondents' view on the state of community relations 'in five years time' in comparison to now. Such movement as can be seen between 1993 and 1994 is generally in a positive direction for Protestants and more mixed for Catholics, but the differences are small.

In 1991 our survey evidence suggested that people were becoming quite optimistic about the state of community relations but as we moved into the 1990s this optimism may have become tempered by events. In 1994 this situation still

## Table 11
### Community relations in 5 years time

|  |  | Community relations in 5 years time compared to now |  |  |
|---|---|---|---|---|
|  |  | Better | The same | Worse |
| Community relations | Better | 1 | 1 | 2 |
| now compared | The same | 1 | 2 | 3 |
| with five years ago | Worse | 2 | 3 | 3 |

seemed to hold: thinking back to that period there was a sense that Northern Ireland was on something of a knife-edge, and our survey results are consistent with this.

It was decided to explore these data a little further by combining responses to both questions and examining which categories of respondents were more or less optimistic with regard to their view of community relations. Table 11 shows the way in which we defined the combined pattern of responses. Respondents whose combined responses fell into cells marked '1' were defined as optimists, respondents whose responses fell into cells marked '2' were defined as neutral and those whose responses fell into cells marked '3' were defined as pessimists. This procedure involved responses from 92 per cent of our total sample. Of those who were included, 36 per cent were defined as optimists, 36 per cent were defined as neutral and 28 per cent were defined as pessimists. A comparison with the data above will indicate that the procedure used here may understate slightly the proportion who fall into the neutral category.

While recognising the limitations of the procedure outlined above, what does it tell us about the type of people who are more likely to be optimistic regarding community relations? The emergent pattern is that the level of optimism appears to be linked to a number of factors including one's perception of equal opportunity in employment, political identification, age and economic position. Interestingly there is little difference in the level of optimism or pessimism indicated by these data for Protestants and Catholics.

Those who feel that equal opportunity in employment exists are likely to be more optimistic than those who feel that equality does not exist. Of those who say that the chances of Protestants and Catholics getting a job are the same, 40 per cent were optimists and only 22 per cent pessimists. By contrast, among those who feel that the chances of Protestants and Catholics getting a job are not the same, 32 per cent were optimists and 33 per cent were pessimists. When we turn to political identification we find that a little under a third of those who identify with unionist or nationalist parties, or who say they identify with no party, are optimists, but the proportion of optimists among those who say they identify with the Alliance party is much higher at 44 per cent. The age pattern is interesting in that the most optimistic group is the youngest cohort in the survey, those aged between 18 and 24 years, while the least optimistic are those aged between 35 and 44 years. Whether it is significant or not, this is the age cohort who would have been in their teenage years when the violence broke out in Northern Ireland. Finally, among those who work in non-manual occupations 33 per cent were defined as optimists and only 21 per cent were defined as pessimists. By contrast, among those in manual occupations 28 per cent were optimists while 34 per cent were pessimists.

Clearly the points above merely touch on the surface of these data and some of the variables briefly considered here will, in all likelihood, be inter-related. That said, it is perhaps worthy of note that of the various groups considered above, the most optimistic group comprised the youngest age group. Let us hope that their apparent high level of optimism for the future will be realised.

## Conclusion

This chapter has examined three aspects of the evidence from the 1994 NISA survey. These dealt with issues of identity and aspirations for the future, attitudes to equality, both between the two main religious communities and for ethnic minority communities, and the relative extent of optimism that existed for the future.

The survey highlights a continuing pattern of difference among Catholics and Protestants in their preferred identities, both political and national. In addition, it is found in their aspirations and judgements for the political and constitutional future of Northern Ireland. As has been argued in previous reports on the survey, these fundamental differences provide the bedrock upon which all other attitudes to community relations must be placed. However, we noted also that the 1994 survey may turn out to be the last carried out during a period of violence and it seems possible that some of these attitudes may now begin to shift.

The section on attitudes to equality examined a number of areas. As regards attitudes to fair employment, the emergent picture is that while most Protestants feel that the employment market in Northern Ireland is, by and large, fair to both communities, most Catholics feel that it is not fair. Furthermore, most Catholics believe that the unfairness in employment operates to their disadvantage.

However, it was noted that in 1994 more Catholics than in previous surveys say that the labour market is fair, and more Protestants than in previous surveys say that the labour market is unfair. In 1994 we asked a series of new questions relating to fair employment issues. Included among these were questions dealing with the 'chill factor'. This evidence suggested that while most respondents say they would not be put off applying for a job on the basis of the religious composition of the workforce, a significant proportion would be put off applying for jobs in areas where the other community is predominant. This avoidance strategy may help to explain why so many respondents believe that discrimination operates in the labour market while at the same time so few claim any direct experience of discrimination.

Other new questions in 1994 dealt with attitudes to 'race' issues. Overall, respondents in Northern Ireland believe there to be less prejudice against ethnic minority communities in comparison with attitudes in Britain. In addition, Catholics appear to be somewhat more tolerant than Protestants. Possible explanations for these patterns are examined further by Brewer and Dowds in Chapter 5 of this volume.

Finally we looked at the extent of optimism and pessimism regarding community relations among our respondents. Previous surveys suggested evidence of growing optimism at the beginning of the 1990s, with a degree of retrenchment as the decade advanced. The 1994 survey suggests a similar pattern to that found in 1993, although there is some movement towards optimism among Protestants. A number of factors were found to influence the relative degree of optimism and pessimism. It was noteworthy that the most optimistic group were the youngest age group in our survey. We must all hope that their optimism is fulfilled.

## References

CURTICE, J. and GALLAGHER, A. M. 1990. 'The Northern Irish Dimension', in Jowell, R., Witherspoon, S. and Brook, L. (eds), *British Social Attitudes: the Seventh Report*, Gower, Aldershot.

GALLAGHER, A. M. 1991. 'Justice and the Law in Northern Ireland', in Jowell, R, Brook, L and Taylor, B. (eds), *British Social Attitudes: the Eighth Report*, Dartmouth, Aldershot.

GALLAGHER, A. M. 1992a. 'Community Relations in Northern Ireland', in Jowell, R., Brook, L., Prior, G. and Taylor, B. (eds), *British Social Attitudes: the Ninth Report*. Avebury, Aldershot.

GALLAGHER, A. M. 1992b. 'Civil Liberties and the State', in Stringer, P. and Robinson, G. (eds.), *Social Attitudes in Northern Ireland; the Second Report*, Blackstaff Press, Belfast.

GALLAGHER, A. M. 1993. 'Community Relations', in Stringer, P. and Robinson, G. (eds.), *Social Attitudes in Northern Ireland; the Third Report*, Blackstaff Press, Belfast.

GALLAGHER, A. M. 1995a. 'Equity, contact and pluralism: attitudes to community relations', in Breen, R., Devine, P. and Robinson, G. (eds), *Social Attitudes in Northern Ireland: the Fourth Report*, Appletree Press, Belfast.

GALLAGHER, A. M. 1995b. 'The approach of government: community relations and equity', in Dunn, S. (ed.), *Facets of the Conflict in Northern Ireland*, Macmillan/St Martin's Press, London/New York.

GALLAGHER, A. M. and DUNN, S. 1991. 'Community Relations in Northern Ireland: attitudes to contact and integration', in Stringer, P. and Robinson, G. (eds.), *Social Attitudes in Northern Ireland: the First Report*, Blackstaff Press, Belfast.

# Appendix 1:
# Technical Details of the Survey

Alan McClelland

---

**Background to the Survey**

The Northern Ireland Social Attitudes (NISA) survey was funded by the Nuffield Foundation and the Central Community Relations Unit for the third consecutive year in 1991. Subsequent funding for the NISA survey was secured for a further three years (1993–1995) with contributions from Government departments in Northern Ireland.

As in previous years, both the British Social Attitudes (BSA) survey and the NISA survey consisted of 'core' questions and of 'modules' on specific topic areas. Due to an increase in the demand for information from the NISA survey, two parallel versions of the questionnaire were fielded in Northern Ireland. Both versions of the questionnaire contained common core questions and topic modules specific to each parallel version of the questionnaire. Modules in the two Northern Ireland questionnaires were selected from the larger number that were used in the three versions of the British questionnaire. The one exception to this was a module dealing with issues specific to Northern Ireland which was included only in the NISA. However, some of these Northern Ireland module questions were, for comparative purposes, also asked in Great Britain.

An advisory panel, consisting of representatives from Social and Community Planning Research (SCPR), the Policy Planning and Research Unit (PPRU) and the Central Community Relations Unit (CCRU), was responsible for constructing the basic content of the questionnaire used in Northern Ireland. The panel both planned the Northern Ireland module and advised on which modules from the British questionnaire might be most usefully incorporated into the Northern Ireland version.

Final responsibility for the construction and wording of the questionnaire remained with SCPR. Responsibility for sampling and fieldwork rested with the

Central Survey Unit of PPRU.

As with the 1993 NISA survey, fieldwork was completed by interviewers employing Computer Assisted Interviewing (CAI) (see Sweeney and McClelland, 1994).

**Content of the Questionnaire**
The basic schema of each of the NISA questionnaires mirrored that of the British survey. Each had two components. The first consisted of the main questionnaire administered by interviewers. The second component was a self-completion supplement which was filled in by respondents after the interview, and was either collected by interviewers or returned by post.

Each year the questionnaire includes a number of core questions on topics such as the economy and labour market participation, as well as a range of background and classificatory questions. It also contains questions (or modules) on attitudes to other issues. These are repeated less frequently, on a two- or three-year cycle, or at longer intervals.

As two versions of the questionnaire were fielded in 1994, it was possible to include a wider range of topic modules than was possible in previous years. The core modules, Northern Ireland module and classification questions were asked of all respondents. In addition, half of respondents were asked the topic modules in version A of the questionnaire while the remainder were asked the topic modules in version B of the questionnaire.

The self-completion supplements consisted of the module designed for the International Social Survey Programme (ISSP) (for further details see Jowell, Witherspoon and Brook, 1989), as well as items from the British questionnaire and the Northern Ireland module which were most appropriately asked in that format.

Two versions of the self-completion questionnaire were used in association with the two versions of the main questionnaire administered by interviewers, with core questions asked in both versions and with each version concentrating on its specific topic modules.

**The Sample**
As with the BSA survey, the NISA survey was designed to yield a representative sample of all adults aged 18 and over, living in private households (for further details of the BSA see Jowell, Curtice, Park, Brook, Ahrendt and Thomson, 1995).

The sample in Northern Ireland was drawn from the rating list, in contrast to that in Great Britain which is based on the Postcode Address File (PAF) and

## Contents of the 1994 Northern Ireland Social Attitudes survey questionnaire

| | |
|---|---|
| **Core questions** (*Common to both versions of the questionnaire*) | Newspaper readership |
| | Government spending |
| | Labour market participation |
| | Religion |
| | Housing |
| | Classification |
| | ISSP module (women and the family) |
| **Topic Module Version A** | Social class and race |
| | Trust in the politcal process |
| | International relations |
| | Civil liberties |
| **Topic Module Version B** | Economic prospects |
| | Poverty |
| | Countryside/environment |
| | Informal carers |
| **Northern Ireland Module** | Community relations |
| | Perceptions of religious prejudice |
| | Protestant–Catholic relations |
| | Segregation and integration |
| | Even-handedness of institutions |
| | Equal opportunities in employment |
| | Education/integrated schools |
| | Political partisanship |
| | Community/national identity |
| | Trust in government structures |
| | Party politcal identification |

involves a multi-stage sample design. The rating list provided by the Rates Collection Agency (NI) is the most up-to-date listing of private households in Northern Ireland and is made available to the Central Survey Unit (CSU) for research purposes.

The rating list available to CSU was limited to those addresses that had a domestic-rated portion. It excluded people in institutions (but not those who live in private households at such institutions). The CSU list was updated twice yearly, following rate-billing in April and September. The list did not include newly built properties which have been occupied since the last update. Contained within the list, inevitably, were a proportion of 'non-viable' addresses which may have been, for example, derelict or vacant. The size of the allocated sample was adjusted to compensate for this wastage.

As the sampling frame was one of addresses, a further stage of sampling was required to select individual adults for interview. Consequently, weighting of the achieved sample was necessary to compensate for the effect of household size on the probability of an individual being selected as a respondent.

## Sample Design and Selection of Addresses

Several factors common to Northern Ireland, including the generally low population density outside greater Belfast and its small geographical area, allow the use of an unclustered, simple random sample design. In addition, the extensive coverage of CSU's field force enables this sample design to be used effectively. The benefits gained from using a simple random sample include: its effectiveness in generating representative samples of the population for surveys at any given sample size; and the greater precision of survey estimates compared to those of a clustered design.

The NISA sample was therefore a simple random sample of all addresses contained on the rating list. Addresses were selected from the computer-based copy of the rating list using a routine for the generation of random numbers. Addresses selected for household surveys by CSU are excluded from further sampling for a period of two years.

Prior to drawing the sample, Northern Ireland as a whole was stratified into three geographical areas. This stratification, based on district council boundaries consisted of Belfast – Belfast District Council; East – most of the remaining district council areas east of the river Bann, excluding Moyle and Newry and Mourne; West – the remaining district council areas. Within each of these three areas, a simple random sample of addresses was selected from the rating list, with probability proportionate to the number of addresses in that stratified area.

Figure 1 shows the distribution of addresses on the rating list, of selected

## Figure 1
### Geographical distribution of the sample

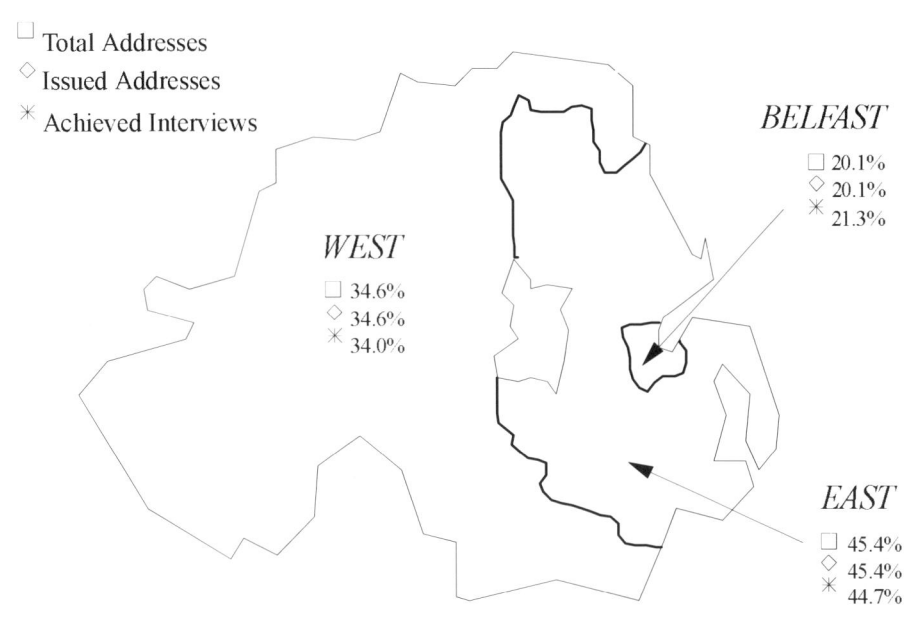

☐ Total Addresses
◇ Issued Addresses
✳ Achieved Interviews

BELFAST
☐ 20.1%
◇ 20.1%
✳ 21.3%

WEST
☐ 34.6%
◇ 34.6%
✳ 34.0%

EAST
☐ 45.4%
◇ 45.4%
✳ 44.7%

addresses and the distribution of addresses at which interviews were achieved.

### Selection of Individuals

The rating list is a good up-to-date source of private addresses in Northern Ireland. The list does not, however, include information about the number of adults living at each address. Only one individual was to be selected at each address at which interviewers were successful in achieving initial co-operation. To achieve this, the interviewers entered anonymised details of all the adults in the household currently aged 18 or over into the laptop computer. From the list of eligible adults, the computer selected one respondent through a Kish grid random selection procedure.

### Weighting of the Achieved Sample

It is not possible using the rating list to select addresses in Northern Ireland with probability proportionate to the size of the household. To compensate for this potential source of bias, the data was weighted prior to analysis. The weighting adjusted the data for the fact that individuals living in larger households had a lower chance of being included in the sample than individuals living in smaller households. The data were weighted in relation to the number of eligible adults at that address, derived from the details of household structure recorded by the interviewers. In order to retain the actual number of interviews, the weighted

| | | Weighting of the sample | | |
|---|---|---|---|---|
| No. of adults 18 and over | Weight | No. | % | Scaled weight |
| 1 | 1 | 248 | 16.3 | 0.5127 |
| 2 | 2 | 777 | 51.2 | 1.0253 |
| 3 | 3 | 280 | 18.4 | 1.5380 |
| 4 | 4 | 127 | 8.4 | 2.0506 |
| 5 | 5 | 77 | 5.1 | 2.5633 |
| 6 | 6 | 6 | 0.4 | 3.0759 |
| 7 | 7 | 4 | 0.2 | 3.5886 |

sample was scaled back to the originally achieved sample size, yielding a total of 1519 interviews and an average weight of 1.

**Fieldwork**

Prior to commencement of the fieldwork, advance letters were sent to each household selected in the sample. The letter informed the household that they had been selected for inclusion in the survey and contained a brief description of the nature of the survey.

The fieldwork was conducted by 66 interviewers from CSU's panel. They were fully briefed and familiarised with the survey procedures. The first briefing session was held on 3 May 1994 with fieldwork beginning immediately afterwards. The main field period extended until 8 July 1994. A small proportion of interviews were carried out in the period between 8 July and 12 August 1994.

The survey was conducted as an SCPR survey, with all survey documents clearly identifying that research organisation. Interviewers, however, carried and presented their normal CSU identity cards. To avoid any confusion on the part of respondents, interviewers also carried, and left with respondents, a letter of introduction from the research team at SCPR. The letter clearly identified the relationship between PPRU and SCPR in the context of the survey. Respondents were given the London telephone number of the Social Attitudes research team at

# APPENDIX 1: TECHNICAL DETAILS OF THE SURVEY

SCPR as well as a Belfast telephone number, in case they had any queries or uncertainties about the survey or the interviewer. The Belfast telephone number was a direct telephone line manned by PPRU field staff during office hours, and otherwise covered by an answering machine. Only a very small number of respondents used either method of contact.

A total of 2,400 addresses were selected. They were assigned to interviewers using CSU's normal allocation procedures which ensure minimum travelling distances for each interviewer. The field work was supervised by CSU using the standard quality control methods employed on all government surveys in Northern Ireland. Interviewers were required to make at least three calls at an address (normal procedure allows for additional calls to be made should the interviewer be passing the address while working in the area), before declaring it a non-contact and returning the allocation sheet to headquarters. The timing of the initial contact calls is left to the discretion of the interviewer, based on knowledge of the area, to maximise the likelihood of finding someone at home. Before declaring an address to be a non-contact, at least one call must have been made in the morning, afternoon and evening or weekend. Non-contact addresses were returned to headquarters and, if possible, were re-issued before the end of the field period for (up to) three more calls.

Field staff at CSU monitored the return of work and quality assured the data which were returned on a weekly basis by the interviewers. Staff at CSU maintained telephone contact with all interviewers and dealt with any problems that arose in the field initially by this means.

|  | Response rate | |
|---|---|---|
|  | Northern Ireland | |
|  | No. | % |
| Addresses issued | 2400 |  |
| Vacant, derelict etc. | 233 |  |
| In scope | 2167 | 100 |
| Interview achieved | 1519 | 70 |
| Interview not achieved | 648 | 30 |
| Refused | 439 | 20 |
| Non-contact | 108 | 5 |
| Unproductive interview | 101 | 5 |

## Figure 2
### Summary of response to the survey

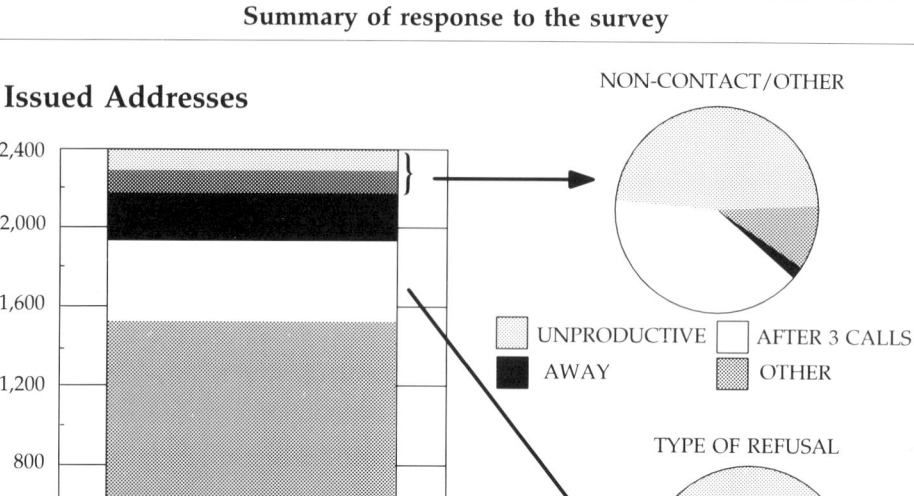

[Figure 2: Bar chart of Issued Addresses broken down by Interviewed, Refusal, Vacant/Derelict etc, Non-contact, Unproductive interview; with pie charts showing Non-contact/Other (Unproductive, Away, After 3 calls, Other) and Type of Refusal (Outright, Letter, Circumstantial).]

An overall response rate of 70 per cent was achieved, based on the total number of issued addresses which were within the scope of the survey (that is, occupied, private addresses).

Refusals were obtained at 20 per cent of eligible addresses. At 5 per cent of addresses interviewers could not contact either the household or the selected respondent within the field period. Unproductive interviews were obtained at a further 5 per cent of addresses.

### Self-Completion Questionnaire

At the end of the face-to-face interview, interviewers introduced the self-completion questionnaire. Where possible, the selected respondent completed the questionnaire while the interviewer was still in the house. If this was not possible, the questionnaire was either collected by the interviewer at a later date, or posted by the respondent to a Northern Ireland Post Office Box. The self-

| Response rate for the self-completion questionnaires | | |
|---|---|---|
| Achieved interviews | 1519 | 100% |
| Self-completion returned | 1315 | 87% |
|   Version A | 663 | |
|   Version B | 652 | |
| Not returned | 204 | 13% |

completion questionnaire was then forwarded, through CSU to SCPR.

The return of self-completion questionnaires was monitored by CSU field staff. Up to two reminder letters were sent at two-weekly intervals after the initial interview. In all, 87 per cent of the self-completion questionnaires were returned.

## Data Processing and Coding

Disks containing interview information were returned by the field force on a weekly basis. The information contained on the returned disks was transferred onto an office Field Management System on a weekly basis. This procedure meant that the progress of the fieldwork could be monitored on a week by week basis. After the completion of the fieldwork period, final checks were made on the information contained on the return disks prior to the datafiles being sent to SCPR for checking, coding and editing. For the self-completion questionnaire, SCPR conducted all checking, editing, coding, keying and computer editing.

## Analysis Variables

The analysis variables in the Northern Ireland dataset are the same as those in the British survey. However, the questions on party identification use Northern Irish political parties. A number of analysis variables were coded by SCPR from the current or last job held by the respondent (and spouse or partner). Summary variables derived from these and some further derived variables are included in the dataset. The principal analysis variables available in the dataset are listed in the following table.

| | |
|---|---|
| **Coded analysis variables** | Standard Occupational Classification (1990) |
| | Employment status |
| | Socio-economic group (SEG) |
| | Registrar General's Social Class (I to V) |
| | Goldthorpe class schema |
| | Standard Industrial Classification (SIC, 1980) |
| | Standard Occupational Code |
| **Derived analysis variables** | Age within sex |
| | Party political identification |
| | Current economic position |
| | Area |
| | Highest educational qualification |
| | Accomodation tenure |
| | Marital status |

**Sampling Errors**

No sample is likely to reflect precisely the characteristics of the population it is drawn from, because of both sampling and non-sampling errors. An estimate of the amount of error due to the sampling process can be calculated.

For a simple random sample design, in which every member of the sampled population has an equal and independent chance of inclusion in the sample, the sampling error of any percentage, $p$, can be calculated by the formula

$$s.e. (p) = \sqrt{\frac{p(100-p)}{n}}$$

where $n$ is the number of respondents on which the percentage is based. The sample for the NISA survey is drawn as a simple random sample, and thus this formula can be used to calculate the sampling error of any percentage estimate from the survey. A confidence interval for the population percentage can be calculated by the formula

$$95 \text{ per cent confidence interval} = p \pm 1.96 \times s.e. (p)$$

If 100 similar, independent samples were chosen from the same population, 95 of them would be expected to yield an estimate for the percentage, $p$, within this confidence interval.

The absence of design effects in the Northern Ireland survey, and therefore, of

# APPENDIX 1: TECHNICAL DETAILS OF THE SURVEY

the need to calculate complex standard errors, means that the standard error and confidence intervals for percentage estimates from the survey are only slightly greater than for the British survey, despite the smaller sample size. It also means that standard statistical tests of significance (which assume random sampling) can be applied directly to the data.

A percentage estimate of 10 per cent (or 90 per cent) which is based on all respondents to the Northern Ireland survey has a standard error of 0.8 per cent and a 95 per cent confidence interval of ±1.5 per cent. A percentage estimate of 50 per cent has a standard error of 1.3 and a 95 per cent confidence interval of ±2.5 per cent. Sampling errors for proportions based on sub-groups within the sample are somewhat larger than they would have been had the questions been asked of everyone.

Table A1 provides examples of the sampling errors and confidence intervals for typical percentage estimates from the NISA survey.

## Representativeness of the Sample

In any survey, there is a possibility of non-response bias. Non-response bias arises if the characteristics of non-respondents differ significantly from those of respondents, in such a way that they are reflected in the responses given in the survey. Accurate estimates of non-response bias can only be obtained by comparing characteristics of the achieved sample with the distribution of the same characteristics in the population at the time of sampling. Such comparisons are usually made to current Census of Population data.

It is not possible to estimate directly whether any non-response bias exists in the NISA survey. However, Tables A2–A5 compare the characteristics of both the households and individuals sampled with those sampled in the Continuous Household Survey (CHS) for the 1993–94 year (the survey year running from April 1993 to March 1994). The CHS has a much larger sample (over 3000 households are interviewed) and uses the same simple random sample design. All adults aged 16 or over are interviewed. No weighting is required to compensate for the effect of household size on probability of selection. The CHS has been running for ten years and produces consistent estimates from year to year.

Where available, figures from the 1991 Census of Population for Northern Ireland have been shown for comparison.

## References

JOWELL, R., CURTICE, J., PARK, A., BROOK, L. and AHRENDT, D. WITH THOMSON, K. (EDS), 1995. *British Social Attitudes: the Twelfth Report*, Dartmouth, Aldershot.

JOWELL, R., WITHERSPOON, S. and BROOK, L. (EDS), 1989. *British Social Attitudes: Special International Report*, Gower, Aldershot.

THE NORTHERN IRELAND CENSUS 1991. *Summary Report 1992*, HMSO, Belfast.

SWEENEY, K. and MCCLELLAND, A. 1995. 'Technical details of the survey', in Breen, R., Devine, R. and Robinson, G. (eds), *Social Attitudes in Northern Ireland: The Fourth Report*, Appletree Press, Belfast.

## Table A1
### Standard errors and confidence limits

| | % (p) | Standard error of p (%) | 95% confidence interval +/− | 95% confidence limits |
|---|---|---|---|---|
| *Classification variables, n = 1519* | | | | |
| **Derived religion** | | | | |
| Protestant | 53.4 | 1.3 | 2.5 | 50.9–55.9 |
| Roman Catholic | 35.9 | 1.2 | 2.4 | 33.5–38.3 |
| Other | 10.7 | 0.8 | 1.5 | 9.2–12.2 |
| **(Tenure 2) Housing tenure*** | | | | |
| Owns | 63.9 | 1.2 | 2.4 | 61.5–66.3 |
| Rent from NIHE | 27.8 | 1.1 | 2.2 | 25.6–30.0 |
| **Derived employment status** | | | | |
| Economically active | 53.1 | 1.3 | 2.5 | 50.6–54.4 |
| Unemployed | 6.4 | 0.6 | 1.2 | 5.2–7.6 |
| *Attitudinal variables (all), n = 1519* | | | | |
| (**Gpchange**) Consider it not difficult to change GP | 72.1 | 1.2 | 2.2 | 69.9–74.3 |
| *Version B, n = 754* | | | | |
| (**ECGBCLSE**) The UK should have closer links with the European Community | 44.7 | 1.8 | 3.5 | 41.2–48.2 |
| *Employees only, n = 651* | | | | |
| (**Indrel**) Not good relations between management and employees | 16.3 | 1.4 | 2.8 | 13.5–19.1 |
| *Self-completion (Version A), n = 663* | | | | |
| (**Videodem**) Police should have the right to video demonstrations | 59.7 | 1.9 | 3.7 | 56.0–63.4 |
| *Self-completion (Version B), n = 652* | | | | |
| (**Petitenv**) Signed a petition about the environment in the past five years | 31.1 | 1.8 | 3.6 | 27.5–34.7 |

* Unweighted data

## Table A2
### Comparison of household characteristics

|  |  | NISA Survey (1994)* | Continuous Household Survey (1993/94) | Northern Ireland Census (1991) |
|---|---|---|---|---|
| *Characteristics of sampled households* | | | | |
| Tenure | Owner occupied | 64 | 64 | 62 |
|  | Rented, NIHE | 28 | 28 | 29 |
|  | Rented, other | 8 | 7 | 8 |
|  | Rent free | 1 | 1 | 1 |
| Type of home | Detached | 32 | 31 | 31 |
|  | Semi-detached | 24 | 22 | 23 |
|  | Terraced | 36 | 38 | 37 |
|  | Purpose-built flat | 5 | 7 | 6 |
|  | Converted-flat | 1 | 1 | 2 |
|  | Other | 1 | 2 | – |
| Household income (£) | Less than 4000 | 11 | 14 | |
|  | 4000–7999 | 24 | 25 | |
|  | 8000–11,999 | 14 | 12 | |
|  | 12,000–17,999 | 15 | 13 | |
|  | 18,000–19,999 | 4 | 4 | |
|  | 20,000 and over | 19 | 18 | |
|  | Unknown | 13 | 13 | |
| Base = 100% | | 1519 | 3182 | 530,369 |

* Household characteristics are based on unweighted data from the NISA survey.

## Table A3
### Comparison of individual characteristics (%)

| Characteristics of sampled individuals aged 18 and over | | NISA Survey (1994) | Continuous Household Survey (1993–94) | Northern Ireland Census (1991) |
|---|---|---|---|---|
| Sex | Male | 50 | 47 | 48 |
| | Female | 50 | 53 | 52 |
| Age | 18–24 | 15 | 13 | 16 |
| | 25–34 | 20 | 20 | 21 |
| | 35–44 | 19 | 18 | 18 |
| | 45–54 | 17 | 16 | 15 |
| | 55–59 | 7 | 7 | 6 |
| | 60–64 | 5 | 6 | 6 |
| | 65 and over | 18 | 19 | 18 |
| Marital status | Single | 23 | 24 | 28 |
| | Married/cohabiting | 62 | 60 | 59 |
| | Widowed | 9 | 10 | 9 |
| | Divorced/separated | 6 | 5 | 3 |
| Economic activity | Working | 53 | 49 | 49* |
| | Unemployed | 6 | 6 | 9 |
| | Inactive | 39 | 40 | 42 |
| | Refused/missing | 1 | 3 | |
| Base = 100% | | 1519 | 6131 | 1,117,221** |

\* Based on total population aged 16 and over (base = 1,167,938).
\*\* Persons aged 18 and over.

## Table A4
### Stated religious denomination (%)

| Religious denomination of persons aged 18 years and over | NISA Survey (1994) | Continuous Household Survey (1993–94)* | Northern Ireland Census (1991)** |
|---|---|---|---|
| Protestant | 56 | 60 | 50 |
| Roman Catholic | 36 | 36 | 38 |
| Non-Christian | – | – | – |
| No religion | 10 | 2 | 4 |
| Unwilling to say | 1 | 1 | 7 |
| Base = 100% | 1519 | 5158 | 1,577,836 |
| (Undefined CHS)* |  | (15%) |  |

\* Religion remains undefined in the CHS for individuals who did not fully co-operate in the survey and were, therefore, not asked their denomination. The base for this percentage is the total number of adults aged 18 and over in the sampled households (6058).
\*\* Usually resident population (all ages).

## Table A5
### Redefined religious denomination (%)

| Religious denomination* of persons aged 18 years and over | NISA Survey (1994) | Continuous Household Survey (1993–94) |
|---|---|---|
| Protestant | 60 | 59 |
| Roman Catholic | 38 | 38 |
| Non-Christian | – | – |
| No religion | 1 | 2 |
| Unwilling to say | 1 | 1 |
| Base = 100% | 1519 | 6058 |

\* Religious denomination has been redefined, in both surveys, for all those who stated 'No religion' or were unwilling to specify their denomination. In the NISA survey denomination was calculated from the religion in which the respondent was brought up. In the CHS denomination was redefined using the denomination specified by other members of the household.

# Appendix 2:
# Using Northern Ireland Social Attitudes Survey Data

All survey datasets are deposited and can be obtained from the ESRC Data Archive at Essex University. In addition, the survey years 1989–1991 are available as a fully documented *combined* dataset. Although the annual book covers many topics in depth, it cannot hope to provide time-series data for all questions included in that survey round; for this reason we would encourage interested parties to use the data directly.

The core of the survey is the community relations module which has been included in every survey round except for 1990 when a module on attitudes to crime and the police was fielded instead. The list on the following page shows the modules fielded in every survey year.

Topics covered* in Northern Ireland Social Attitudes surveys 1989–1995

| TOPICS (excluding 'core' ones) | SURVEY YEAR ||||||
| --- | --- | --- | --- | --- | --- | --- |
|  | 1989 | 1990 | 1991 | 1993 | 1994 | 1995 |
| AIDS | ✔ |  |  |  |  |  |
| Attitudes to work (ISSP) | ✔ |  |  |  |  |  |
| Changing gender roles (ISSP) |  |  |  |  | ✔ |  |
| Charitable giving |  |  | ✔ | ✔ |  |  |
| Childcare |  |  |  |  | ✔ | ✔ |
| Civil liberties |  | ✔ |  |  | ✔ |  |
| Community relations | ✔ |  | ✔ | ✔ | ✔ | ✔ |
| Countryside and the environment |  | ✔ |  | ✔ | ✔ | ✔ |
| Crime and the police |  | ✔ |  |  |  |  |
| Diet and health | ✔ |  |  |  |  |  |
| Drugs |  |  |  |  |  | ✔ |
| Economic prospects | ✔ | ✔ | ✔ | ✔ |  | ✔ |
| Education |  |  |  | ✔ |  | ✔ |
| Family networks |  |  |  |  |  | ✔ |
| Gender issues at the workplace |  |  | ✔ |  | ✔ |  |
| Gender roles |  |  | ✔ |  | ✔ |  |
| Global environmental issues (ISSP) |  |  |  | ✔ |  |  |
| Health and lifestyle |  |  | ✔ |  |  |  |
| Informal carers |  |  |  |  | ✔ |  |
| National identity (ISSP) |  |  |  |  |  | ✔ |
| National Health Service | ✔ | ✔ | ✔ | ✔ | ✔ | ✔ |
| Political trust |  |  |  |  | ✔ |  |
| Poverty | ✔ |  |  |  | ✔ |  |
| Race and immigration |  |  |  |  | ✔ |  |
| Religious beliefs (ISSP) |  |  | ✔ |  |  |  |
| Role of government (ISSP) |  | ✔ |  |  |  |  |
| Single parenthood and child support |  |  |  | ✔ | ✔ | ✔ |
| Sexual morality | ✔ | ✔ |  |  |  |  |
| Social class | ✔ | ✔ |  |  | ✔ |  |
| Taxation and public spending (long) |  |  |  |  |  | ✔ |
| Transport |  |  |  |  |  | ✔ |
| UK's relations with Europe/other countries | ✔ | ✔ | ✔ | ✔ | ✔ | ✔ |
| Welfare state |  |  |  | ✔ |  | ✔ |

* Excluded are 'core topics' such as public spending, workplace issues and economic prospects, and standard classificatory items such as economic activity, newspaper readership, religious denomination and party identification, all of which are asked every year.

# Appendix 3:
# The Questionnaires

As explained in Appendix 1, two different versions of the NISA questionnaire (A and B) were fielded in 1994, each with its own self-completion supplement. In the following pages we reproduce first version A of the interview questionnaire in full, then those parts of version B that differ. The two versions of the self-completion questionnaire follow.

As the survey was carried out using Computer Assisted Interviewing (CAI), the two questionnaires reproduced here are derived from the Blaise program in which they were written. The keying codes have been removed and the percentage distribution of answers to each question inserted instead. The SPSS variable name is also included, bracketed and in italics, beside each question. Routeing directions are given above each question and any routeing instruction should be considered as staying in force until the next routeing instruction. Percentages in the main questionnaire are based on the total sample (765 weighted and unweighted in version A, 754 weighted and unweighted in version B). In the self-completion questionnaire they are based on the 663 (weighted) in version A and 652 (weighted) in version B who returned the forms.

For further details on the questionnaires readers are referred to Jowell et al. (1995).

## References

JOWELL, R., CURTICE, J., PARK, A., BROOK, L. and AHRENDT, D. with THOMSON, K. (EDS) 1995. *British Social Attitudes: the Twelfth Report*. Dartmouth, Aldershot.

# NORTHERN IRELAND SOCIAL ATTITUDES SURVEY 1994

## VERSION A QUESTIONNAIRE

n=1519

### NEWSPAPER READERSHIP/ POLITICS

**ASK ALL**

Q47 [ReadPap]
Do you normally read any daily **morning** newspaper at least 3 times a week?

%
55.0 Yes
45.0 No
- (Don't Know)
- (Refusal/NA)

Q48 **IF 'Yes' AT** [Readpap]
[WhPaper]
Which one do you normally read?
**IF MORE THAN ONE ASK:** Which one do you read **most** frequently?
**ONE CODE ONLY**

%
2.4 (Scottish) Daily Express
2.9 Daily Mail
11.0 Daily Mirror/Record
2.5 Daily Star
13.4 The Sun
1.6 Today
1.6 Daily Telegraph
- Financial Times
0.5 The Guardian
0.6 The Independent
0.6 The Times
- Morning Star
9.6 The News Letter
6.9 The Irish News
0.6 The Irish Times
0.7 Other Irish/Northern Irish/Scottish regional or local daily morning paper **(WRITE IN)**
0.2 Other **(WRITE IN)**
- (Don't Know)
- (Refusal/NA)

n=1519

**ASK ALL**

Q52 [Voted92]
Now I would like to ask some questions about politics. Talking to people, we have found that a lot people don't manage to vote. How about you? Did you manage to vote in the last general election in **April 1992**?

%
73.3 Yes, voted
21.3 No
2.9 Too young to vote
1.8 Not eligible/not on register
0.4 (Don't Know)
0.2 (Refusal/NA)

Q53 [VoteResn]
**CARD**
Which of the four statements on this card comes closest to the way you vote in a 'Westminster' election?

%
36.6 I vote for a party regardless of the candidate
37.6 I vote for a party only if I approve of the candidate
7.7 I vote for a candidate regardless of his or her party
17.3 I do not generally vote at all
0.5 (Don't Know)
0.3 (Refusal/NA)

Q54 [Politics]
How much interest do you generally have in what is going on in politics ... **READ OUT** ...

%
8.0 .. a great deal,
16.0 quite a lot,
28.5 some,
32.9 not very much,
14.4 or none at all?
0.0 (Don't Know)
0.2 (Refusal/NA)

212

# PUBLIC SPENDING, WELFARE BENEFITS AND HEALTH CARE

ASK ALL

**Q55** *[Spend1]*
CARD
Here are some items of government spending. Which of them, if any, would be your highest priority for **extra** spending?
Please read through the whole list before deciding.
ENTER ONE CODE ONLY FOR HIGHEST PRIORITY

**Q56** *[Spend2]*
And which next?
ENTER ONE CODE ONLY FOR NEXT HIGHEST

|  | [Spend1] % | [Spend2] % |
|---|---|---|
| Education | 18.7 | 33.7 |
| Defence | 0.9 | 3.4 |
| Health | 55.0 | 22.9 |
| Housing | 4.8 | 11.1 |
| Public Transport | 0.6 | 1.2 |
| Roads | 3.4 | 4.3 |
| Police and prisons | 1.2 | 2.4 |
| Social security benefits | 8.7 | 11.6 |
| Help for industry | 4.9 | 7.9 |
| Overseas aid | 1.1 | 0.8 |
| (None of these) | 0.3 | 0.3 |
| (Don't Know) | 0.2 | 0.3 |
| (Refusal/NA) | - | - |

**Q57** *[SocBen1]*
CARD
Thinking now only of the government's spending on **social benefits** like those on the card.
Which, if any, of these would be your highest priority for **extra** spending?
ENTER ONE CODE ONLY FOR HIGHEST PRIORITY

**Q58** *[SocBen2]*
And which next?
ENTER ONE CODE ONLY FOR NEXT HIGHEST

|  | [SocBen1] % | [SocBen2] % |
|---|---|---|
| Retirement pensions | 41.2 | 22.5 |
| Child benefits | 15.0 | 19.4 |
| Benefits for the unemployed | 11.6 | 12.8 |
| Benefits for disabled people | 24.4 | 35.8 |
| Benefits for single parents | 7.2 | 8.0 |
| (None of these) | 0.4 | 1.0 |
| (Don't Know) | 0.2 | 0.4 |
| (Refusal/NA) | - | - |

**Q59** *[FalseClm]*
I will read two statements. For each one please say whether you agree or disagree.
Large numbers of people these days **falsely** claim benefits.
IF AGREE OR DISAGREE: Strongly or slightly?

**Q60** *[FailClm]*
(And do you agree or disagree that ....)
Large numbers of people who are eligible for benefits these days **fail** to claim them.
IF AGREE OR DISAGREE: Strongly or slightly?

|  | [FalseClm] % | [FailClm] % |
|---|---|---|
| Agree strongly | 50.3 | 36.4 |
| Agree slightly | 28.0 | 45.1 |
| Disagree slightly | 8.8 | 11.2 |
| Disagree strongly | 7.6 | 3.4 |
| (Don't Know) | 5.1 | 3.8 |
| (Refusal/NA) | - | - |

**Q61** *[Dole]*
Opinions differ about the level of benefits for the unemployed. Which of these two statements comes closest to your own view ... READ OUT ....

| | % |
|---|---|
| ..benefits for the unemployed are **too low** and cause hardship, | 51.0 |
| or, benefits for the unemployed are **too high** and discourage them finding jobs, | 29.8 |
| (Neither) | 12.3 |
| Other answer (WRITE IN) | 4.0 |
| (Don't Know) | 2.7 |
| (Refusal/NA) | 0.0 |

**Q63** *[TaxSpend]*
CARD
Suppose the government had to choose between the three options on this card. Which do you think it should choose?

| | % |
|---|---|
| Reduce taxes, spend **less** on health, education and social benefits | 6.7 |
| Keep taxes and spending on these services at the **same** level as now | 37.5 |
| Increase taxes and spend **more** on health, education and social benefits | 49.6 |
| (None of these) | 4.9 |
| (Don't Know) | 1.2 |
| (Refusal/NA) | 0.1 |

| | | n=1519 |
|---|---|---|
| Q64 | **[NHSSat]** **CARD** All in all, how satisfied or dissatisfied would you say you are with the way in which the National Health Service runs nowadays? Choose a phrase from this card. | |
| Q65 | **[GPSat]** **CARD AGAIN** From your own experience, or from what you have heard, please say how satisfied or dissatisfied you are with the way in which each of these parts of the National Health Service runs nowadays. First, local doctors or GPs? | |
| Q66 | **[DentSat]** **CARD AGAIN** (And how satisfied or dissatisfied are you with the NHS as regards ...:) National Health Service dentists? | |

| | [NHSSat] | [GPSat] | [DentSat] |
|---|---|---|---|
| | % | % | % |
| Very satisfied | 8.4 | 37.0 | 23.3 |
| Quite satisfied | 40.2 | 47.7 | 47.4 |
| Neither satisfied not dissatisfied | 16.8 | 6.0 | 13.9 |
| Quite dissatisfied | 20.7 | 6.0 | 8.6 |
| Very dissatisfied | 13.5 | 2.7 | 3.6 |
| (Don't know) | 0.4 | 0.6 | 3.2 |
| (Not answered) | - | - | - |

| | | |
|---|---|---|
| Q67 | **[InPatSat]** **CARD AGAIN** (And how satisfied or dissatisfied are you with the NHS as regards ...:) Being in hospital as an **in-patient**? | |
| Q68 | **[OutPaSat]** **CARD AGAIN** (And how satisfied or dissatisfied are you with the NHS as regards ...:) Attending hospital as an **out-patient**? | |

| | [InPatSat] | [OutPatSat] |
|---|---|---|
| | % | % |
| Very satisfied | 27.0 | 16.2 |
| Quite satisfied | 42.2 | 45.8 |
| Neither satisfied not dissatisfied | 13.0 | 12.4 |
| Quite dissatisfied | 9.9 | 15.5 |
| Very dissatisfied | 3.0 | 5.6 |
| (Don't know) | 4.8 | 4.5 |
| (Not answered) | - | - |

| | | n=1519 |
|---|---|---|
| Q69 | **[PrivMed]** Are you covered by a private health insurance scheme, that is an insurance scheme that allows you to get private **medical treatment**? ADD. IF NECESSARY: For example, BUPA and PPP. Yes No (Don't Know) (Refusal/NA) | % 7.7 92.3 - - |
| Q70 | **IF 'Yes' at [PrivMed]** **[PrivPaid]** Does your employer (or your partner's employer) pay the majority of the cost of membership of this scheme? Yes No (Don't Know) (Refusal/NA) | % 2.8 4.8 0.1 - |
| Q71 | **ASK ALL** **[NHSLimit]** It has been suggested that the National Health Service should be available **only to those with lower incomes**. This would mean that contributions and taxes could be lower and most people would then take out medical insurance or pay for health care. Do you support or oppose this idea? Support Oppose (Don't Know) (Refusal/NA) | % 19.6 77.6 2.8 - |
| Q72 | **[InPat1]** **CARD** Now, suppose you had to go into a local NHS hospital for observation and maybe an operation. From what you know or have heard, please say whether you think the hospital doctors would tell you all you feel you need to know? | |
| Q73 | **[InPat2]** **CARD AGAIN** (And please say whether you think ...) ...the hospital doctors would take seriously any views you may have on the sorts of treatment available? | |
| Q74 | **[InPat3]** **CARD AGAIN** (And please say whether you think ...) ...the operation would take place on the day it was booked for? | |

n=1519

|  | [InPat1] % | [InPat2] % | [InPat3] % |
|---|---|---|---|
| Definitely would | 16.9 | 8.3 | 11.1 |
| Probably would | 49.4 | 43.3 | 57.0 |
| Probably would not | 24.1 | 34.2 | 22.1 |
| Definitely would not | 8.4 | 9.7 | 5.2 |
| (Don't Know) | 1.0 | 4.5 | 4.6 |
| (Refusal/NA) | - | - | - |

Q75 *[InPat4]*
**CARD AGAIN**
(And please say whether you think ...)
...you would be allowed home only when you were really well enough to leave?

Q76 *[InPat5]*
**CARD AGAIN**
(And please say whether you think ...)
...the nurses would take seriously any complaints you may have?

Q77 *[InPat6]*
**CARD AGAIN**
(And please say whether you think ...)
...the hospital doctors would take seriously any complaints you may have?

|  | [InPat4] % | [InPat5] % | [InPat6] % |
|---|---|---|---|
| Definitely would | 11.3 | 21.6 | 16.1 |
| Probably would | 39.5 | 59.1 | 57.6 |
| Probably would not | 34.7 | 14.3 | 20.1 |
| Definitely would not | 13.4 | 3.5 | 3.8 |
| (Don't Know) | 1.1 | 1.5 | 2.4 |
| (Refusal/NA) | - | - | - |

Q78 **CARD AGAIN**
(And please say whether you think ...)
...there would be a particular nurse responsible for dealing with any problems you may have?

Q79 *[OutPat1]*
**CARD AGAIN**
Now suppose you had a back problem and your GP referred you to a hospital out-patients' department.
From what you know or have heard, please say whether you think...
...you would get an appointment within three months?

n=1519

Q80 *[OutPat2]*
**CARD AGAIN**
(And please say whether you think ...)
...when you arrived, the doctor would see you within half an hour of your appointment time?

|  | [InPat7] % | [OutPat1] % | [OutPat2] % |
|---|---|---|---|
| Definitely would | 12.0 | 9.1 | 5.9 |
| Probably would | 41.2 | 41.6 | 30.3 |
| Probably would not | 31.4 | 28.4 | 36.0 |
| Definitely would not | 8.7 | 16.5 | 26.3 |
| (Don't Know) | 6.7 | 4.4 | 1.6 |
| (Refusal/NA) | - | - | - |

Q81 *[OutPat3]*
**CARD AGAIN**
(And please say whether you think ...)
...if you wanted to complain about the treatment you received, you would be able to without any fuss or bother?

Q82 *[WhchHosp]*
**CARD AGAIN**
Now suppose you needed to go into hospital for an operation. Do you think you would have a say about which hospital you went to?

|  | [OutPat3] % | [WhchHosp] % |
|---|---|---|
| Definitely would | 6.9 | 6.8 |
| Probably would | 44.3 | 27.2 |
| Probably would not | 30.1 | 40.5 |
| Definitely would not | 12.4 | 21.7 |
| (Don't Know) | 6.2 | 3.7 |
| (Refusal/NA) | 0.1 | - |

Q83 *[GpChange]*
Suppose you wanted to change your GP and go to a different practice, how difficult or easy do you think this would be to arrange? Would it be ... **READ OUT** ...

%
5.4 ...very difficult,
15.1 fairly difficult,
35.8 not very difficult,
36.3 or, not at all difficult?
7.4 (Don't Know)
- (Refusal/NA)

## ECONOMIC ACTIVITY, THE LABOUR MARKET, GENDER ISSUES AT THE WORKPLACE AND CHILDCARE

**ASK ALL** [n=1519]

Q88 [REconAct] (figures refer to first answer on the list)
CARD
Which of these descriptions applies to what you were doing last week, that is, in the seven days ending last Sunday?
CODE ALL THAT APPLY
PROBE: Any others?
%
3.6  In full-time education (not paid for by employer, including on vacation)
1.3  On government training/employment programme (eg. Employment Training, Youth Training, etc
51.5  In paid work (or away temporarily) for at least 10 hours in week
0.2  Waiting to take up paid work already accepted
5.4  Unemployed and registered at a benefit office
0.7  Unemployed, not registered, but actively looking for a job
0.3  Unemployed, wanting a job (of at least 10 hrs per week) but not actively looking for a job
5.6  Permanently sick or disabled
14.9  Wholly retired from work
15.3  Looking after the home
0.9  (Doing something else) (WRITE IN)
-  Respondent refusal
0.1  (Don't Know)
-  (Refusal/NA)

**ASK ALL IN PAID WORK (IF 'in paid work' AT [REconAct])** [n=784]

Q89 [REmploye]
In your (main) job are you ... READ OUT ...
%
83.0  ... an employee,
16.8  or, self-employed?
-  (Don't Know)
0.2  (Refusal/NA)

**ASK ALL EMPLOYEES (IF 'employee'/DK AT [REmploye])** [n=651]

Q90 [EmploydT]
For how long have you been continuously employed by your present employer?
ENTER NUMBER. THEN SPECIFY MONTHS OR YEARS
Range: 1 ... 60
Median: 72 months

Q92 [ESrJbTim]
In your present job, are you working ... READ OUT ...
RESPONDENT'S OWN DEFINITION
%
83.9  ... full-time,
16.1  or, part-time?
-  (Don't Know)
-  (Refusal/NA)

Q93 [EJbHours] [n=651]
How many hours a week do you normally work in your (main) job?
IF RESPONDENT CANNOT ANSWER, ASK ABOUT LAST WEEK.
ROUND TO NEAREST HOUR.
CODE 95 FOR 95+
Range: 10 ... 95
Median: 39 hours

Q94 [EJbHrCat] (CALCULATED BY PROGRAM)
HOURS WORKED - CATEGORISED
%
5.0  10-15 hours a week
6.5  16-23 hours a week
4.5  24-29 hours a week
83.9  30 or more hours a week
0.2  (Don't Know)
-  (Refusal/NA)

Q95 [WageNow]
How would you describe the wages or salary you are paid for the job you do - on the low side, reasonable, or on the high side?
IF LOW: Very low or a bit low?
%
10.7  Very low
23.2  A bit low
59.8  Reasonable
5.7  On the high side
0.5  Other answer (WRITE IN)
-  (Don't Know)
-  (Refusal/NA)

Q98 [PayGap]
CARD
Thinking of the highest and the lowest paid people at your place of work, how would you describe the @bgap@D between their pay, as far as you know?
Please choose a phrase from this card.
%
26.4  Much too big a gap
39.0  About right
3.7  Too small
0.6  Much too small a gap
3.4  (Don't Know)
0.2  (Refusal/NA)

Q99 [WageXpct]
If you stay in this job, would you expect your wages or salary over the coming year to .. READ OUT ...
%
9.3  ... rise by more than the cost of living,
41.3  rise by the same as the cost of living,
31.3  rise by less than the cost of living,
15.6  or, not to rise at all?
1.1  (Will not stay in job)
1.4  (Don't Know)
-  (Refusal/NA)

Q100 **IF 'Not rise at all' AT [WageXpct]** n=651
[WageDrop]
Would you expect your wages or salary to stay the same, or in fact to go down?
%
13.9 Stay the same
1.7 Go down
- (Don't Know)
- (Refusal/NA)

Q101 **ASK ALL EMPLOYEES (IF 'Employee'/DK AT [REmploye])**
[NumEmp]
Over the coming year do you expect your workplace to be ... **READ OUT** ...
%
19.1 ... increasing its number of employees,
19.8 reducing its number of employees,
59.8 or, will the number of employees stay about the same?
0.6 Other answer **(WRITE IN)**
0.8 (Don't Know)
- (Refusal/NA)

Q104 [LeaveJob]
Thinking now about your own job. How likely or unlikely is it that you will leave this employer over the next year for any reason?
Is it ... **READ OUT** ...
%
9.1 ... very likely,
8.3 quite likely,
28.3 not very likely,
53.5 or, not at all likely?
0.9 (Don't Know)
- (Refusal/NA)

Q105 **IF 'very likely' OR 'quite likely' AT [LeaveJob]**
**CARD**
Why do you think you will leave? Please choose a phrase from this card or tell me what other reasonthere is.
**CODE ALL THAT APPLY**
Multicoded (Maximum of 9 codes)
%
0.8 Firm will close down [WhyGo1]
2.2 I will be declared redundant [WhyGo2]
2.0 I will reach normal retirement age [WhyGo3]
1.6 My contract of employment will expire [WhyGo4]
0.5 I will take early retirement [WhyGo5]
8.0 I will decide to leave and work for another employer [WhyGo6]
0.9 I will decide to leave and work for myself, as self-employed [WhyGo7]
0.3 I will leave to look after home/children/relative [WhyGo10]
3.6 Other answer **(WRITE IN)** [WhyGo8]
0.9 (Don't Know)
0.1 (Refusal/NA)

Q117 **ASK ALL EMPLOYEES (IF 'employee'/DK AT [REmploye])** n=651
[EUnemp]
During the last **five years** - that is since March 1989 - have you been unemployed and seeking work for any period?
%
19.9 Yes
80.1 No
- (Don't Know)
- (Refusal/NA)

Q118 **IF 'yes' AT EUnemp**
[EUnempT]
For how many **months** in total during the last five years?
Range: 0 ... 60
**Median: 8 months**

Q119 **ASK ALL EMPLOYEES (IF 'employee'/DK AT [REmploye])**
[WpUnions]
At your place of work are there unions, staff associations, or groups of unions recognised by the management for negotiating pay and conditions of employment?
**IF YES, PROBE FOR UNION OR STAFF ASSOCIATION**
%
49.7 Yes : trade union(s)
6.3 Yes : staff association
43.1 No, none
2.7 (Don't Know)
0.9 (Refusal/NA)

Q120 **IF 'yes' AT [WpUnions]**
[WpUnionW]
On the whole, do you think (these unions do their/this staff association does its) job well or not?
%
27.6 Yes
25.7 No
2.7 (Don't Know)
0.9 (Refusal/NA)

Q121 [TUShould]
CARD
Listed on the card are a number of things trade unions or staff associations can do. Which, if any, do you think is the **most important** thing they should try to do at **your workplace?**
UNIONS OR STAFF ASSOCIATIONS SHOULD TRY TO:

%
10.3  Improve working conditions
13.4  Improve pay
21.2  Protect existing jobs
2.2   Have more say over how work is done day-to-day
5.6   Have more say over management's long-term plans
1.0   Work for equal opportunities for women
-     Work for equal opportunities for ethnic minorities
1.1   Reduce pay differences at the workplace
0.9   (NONE OF THESE)
0.3   (Don't Know)
0.9   (Refusal/NA)

ASK ALL EMPLOYEES (IF 'Employee'/DK AT [REmployee])

Q122 [IndRel]
In general how would you describe relations between management and other employees at your workplace ...
READ OUT ...
%
31.7  ... very good,
51.7  quite good,
12.4  not very good,
3.9   or, not at all good?
0.2   (Don't Know)
-     (Refusal/NA)

Q123 [WorkRun]
And in general, would you say your workplace was ...
READ OUT ...
%
28.3  ... very well managed,
56.3  quite well managed,
15.1  or, not well managed?
0.3   (Don't Know)
-     (Refusal/NA)

Q124 [ELookJob]
Suppose you lost your job for one reason or another would you start looking for another job, would you wait for several months or longer before you started looking, or would you decide **not** to look for another job?
%
90.9  Start looking
4.9   Wait several months or longer
3.8   Decide not to look
0.4   (Don't Know)
-     (Refusal/NA)

n=651

Q125 IF 'Start looking' AT [ELookJob]
[EFindJob]
How long do you think it would take you to find an acceptable replacement job?
IF 'NEVER' PLEASE CODE 96
ENTER NUMBER. THEN SPECIFY MONTHS OR YEARS
Range: 1 ... 96
Median: 6 months

ASK ALL EMPLOYEES (IF 'Employee'/DK AT [REmployee])

Q127 [ESelfEm]
For any period during the last five years, have you worked as a **self-employed** person as your main job?
%
1.8   Yes
98.2  No
-     (Don't Know)
-     (Refusal/NA)

Q128 IF 'Yes' AT [ESelfEm]
[ESelfEmT]
In total, for how many months during the last five years have you been self-employed?
Range: 1 ... 60
Median: 24 months

Q129 IF 'no' AT [ESelfEm]
[ESelfSer]
How seriously in the last five years have you considered working as a self-employed person.. ... READ OUT ...
%
3.9   ... very seriously,
8.8   quite seriously,
11.9  not very seriously,
73.5  or, not at all seriously?
-     (Don't Know)
-     (Refusal/NA)

ASK ALL EMPLOYEES (IF 'Employee'/DK AT [REmployee])

Q130 [EmpEarn]
Now for some more general questions about your work. For some people their job is simply something they do in order to earn a living. For others it means much more than that. On balance, is your present job ... READ OUT
%
36.7  ... just a means of earning a living,
63.3  or, does it mean much more to you than that?
-     (Don't Know)
-     (Refusal/NA)

n=651

Q131 **IF 'just a means of earning a living' AT [EmpEarn]**   n=651
[EmpLiv]
Is that because ... READ OUT ...
%
15.7 ... there are no better jobs around here,
9.5 you don't have the right skills to get a better job,
10.7 or, because you would feel the same about **any** job you had?
0.8 (Don't Know)
- (Refusal/NA)

Q132 **ASK ALL EMPLOYEES (IF 'Employee'/DK AT [REmployeI])**
[EPrefJob]
If without having to work, you had what you would regard as a reasonable living income, do you think you would still prefer to have a paid job or wouldn't you bother?
%
76.9 Still prefer paid job
21.7 Wouldn't bother
0.6 Other answer **(WRITE IN)**
0.9 (Don't Know)
- (Refusal/NA)

Q135 [PrefHour]
Thinking about the number of hours you work each week including regular overtime, would you prefer a job where you worked ... READ OUT ...
%
3.5 ... more hours per week,
26.7 fewer hours per week,
69.8 or, are you happy with the number of hours you work at present?
- (Don't Know)
- (Refusal/NA)

Q136 **IF 'more hours per week' AT [MoreHour]**
Is the reason why you don't work more hours because ... READ OUT ...
%
2.8 ... your employer can't offer you more hours,
0.5 or, your personal circumstances don't allow it?
- (Both)
0.2 Other answer **(WRITE IN)**
- (Don't Know)
- (Refusal/NA)

Q139 **IF 'fewer hours per week' AT [PrefHour]**
[FewHour]
In which of these ways would you like your working hours to be shortened ... READ OUT ...
%
11.7 ... shorter hours each day,
14.0 or, fewer days each week?
0.9 Other answer **(WRITE IN)**
- (Don't Know)
- (Refusal/NA)

Q142 [EarnHour]
Would you still like to work fewer hours, if it meant earning less money as a result?
%
8.5 Yes
17.2 No
1.0 It depends
- (Don't Know)
- (Refusal/NA)

Q143 **ASK ALL EMPLOYEES (IF 'Employee'/DK AT [REmployeI])**
[EWkHrd] CARD
Which of these statements best describes your feelings about your job?
%
12.5 In my job :
39.3 I only work as hard as I have to
    I work hard, but not so that it interferes with the rest of my life
48.2 I make a point of doing the best I can, even if it sometimes does interfere with the rest of my life
- (Don't Know)
- (Refusal/NA)

Q144 [EWrkArrA] CARD
Please use this card to say whether any of the following arrangements are available to you, at your workplace ... Part-time working, allowing you to work less than the full working day?

Q145 [EWrkArrB]
(Is this available to you at your workplace?)
.. flexible hours, so that you can adjust your own daily working hours?

Q146 [EWrkArrC]
(Is this available to you at your workplace?)
.. job-sharing schemes, where part-timers share one full-time job?

| | EWrkArrA % | EWrkArrB % | EWrkArrC % |
|---|---|---|---|
| Not available - and I would **not** use it if it were | 45.4 | 25.3 | 62.5 |
| Not available - but I **would** use it if it were | 17.8 | 52.8 | 20.9 |
| Available - but I do **not** use it | 20.9 | 5.7 | 14.6 |
| Available - and I **do** use it | 15.9 | 16.2 | 1.7 |
| (Don't Know) | - | - | 0.3 |
| (Refusal/NA) | - | - | - |

| | | EWrkArrD % | EWrkArrE % | EWrkArrF % |
|---|---|---|---|---|
| Q147 | [EWrkArrD] (Is this available to you at your workplace?) ... working from home at least some of the time? | | | |
| Q148 | [EWrkArrE] (Is this available to you at your workplace?) ... term-time contracts, allowing parents special time off during school holidays? | | | |
| Q149 | [EWrkArrF] (Is this available to you at your workplace?) ... nurseries provided by your employer for the young children of employees? | | | |
| | | | | n=651 |
| Not available - and I would not use it if it were | | 57.2 | 59.7 | 67.0 |
| Not available - but I would use it if it were | | 30.5 | 32.3 | 28.7 |
| Available - but I do not use it | | 2.3 | 2.3 | 3.6 |
| Available - and I do use it | | 9.9 | 4.7 | 0.6 |
| (Don't Know) | | 0.2 | 1.0 | - |
| (Refusal/NA) | | - | - | - |

Q150 [EWrkArrG]
(Is this available to you at your workplace?)
... arrangements by your employer for the care of children during school holidays?

Q151 [EWrkArrH]
(Is this available to you at your workplace?)
... childcare allowances towards the cost of child care?

**ASK ALL FEMALE EMPLOYEES (IF 'Employee'/DK AT [REmploye] AND 'Female' AT [RSex])** n=284
Q152 [EWrkArrI]
(Is this available to you at your workplace?)
... 'career breaks', that is keeping women's jobs open for a few years so that mothers can return to work after caring for young children?

| | EWrkArrG % | EWrkArrH % | EWrkArrI % |
|---|---|---|---|
| Not available - and I would not use it if it were | 65.6 | 56.1 | 34.2 |
| Not available - but I would use it if it were | 31.1 | 41.6 | 36.2 |
| Available - but I do not use it | 2.0 | 1.3 | 23.0 |
| Available - and I do use it | 1.0 | 0.3 | 4.7 |
| (Don't Know) | 0.3 | 0.8 | 2.0 |
| (Refusal/NA) | - | - | - |

**ASK ALL MALE EMPLOYEES (IF 'Employee'/DK AT [REmploye] AND 'Male' AR [RSex])** n=368
Q153 [EWrkArrJ]
(Is this available to you at your workplace?)
... paternity leave, allowing fathers extra leave, when their children are born?

**ASK ALL EMPLOYEES** n=651
Q154 [EWrkArrL]
(Is this available to you at your workplace?)
... time off, either paid or unpaid, to care for sick children?

| | EWrkArrJ % | EWrkArrL % |
|---|---|---|
| Not available - and I would not use it if it were | 41.6 | 33.5 |
| Not available - but I would use it if it were | 31.9 | 32.5 |
| Available - but I do not use it | 12.6 | 16.4 |
| Available - and I do use it | 11.9 | 13.5 |
| (Don't Know) | 2.1 | 4.0 |
| (Refusal/NA) | - | - |

**ASK ALL MALE EMPLOYEES (IF 'Employee'/DK AT [REmploye] AND 'Male' AR [RSex])** n=368
Q156 [EMSmeWrk]
Where you work, are there any women doing the same sort of work as you?

| | |
|---|---|
| Yes | 41.6 |
| No | 57.9 |
| (Work alone) | - |
| (No-one else doing the same job) | 0.6 |
| (Don't Know) | - |
| (Refusal/NA) | - |

Q157 [EMSexWrk]
Do you think of your work as ... READ OUT ...
    mainly men's work,
    mainly women's work,
    or, work that either men or women do?
    Other answer (WRITE IN)
    (Don't Know)
    (Refusal/NA)

%
35.1
0.6
63.7
0.6
-
-

IF 'mainly men's work'/other/DK/Refusal AT [EMSexWrk]    n=368
Q160 [EMWomCld]
Do you think that women could do the same sort of work as you?
    Yes
    No
    (Don't Know)
    (Refusal/NA)

%
17.9
17.0
64.9
0.3

IF 'Yes'/DK AT [EMWomCld]
Q161 [EMWomWld]
Do you think that women would be willing to do the same sort of work as you?
    Yes
    No
    (Don't Know)
    (Refusal/NA)

%
8.1
9.5
0.3
-

ASK ALL FEMALE EMPLOYEES (IF 'Employee'/DK AT [REmploye] AND 'Female' AT [RSexi])    n=284
Q162 [EWSmeWrk]
Where you work, are there any men doing the same sort of work as you?
    Yes
    No
    (Work alone)
    (No-one else doing the same job)
    (Don't Know)
    (Refusal/NA)

%
50.5
48.8
-
0.7
-
-

Q163 [EWSexWrk]
Do you think of your work as ... READ OUT ...
    mainly women's work,
    mainly men's work,
    or, work that either men or women do?
    Other answer (WRITE IN)
    (Don't Know)
    (Refusal/NA)

%
26.9
2.9
70.2
-
-
-

IF 'mainly women's work'/other/DK/Refusal at [EWSexWrk]    n=284
Q166 [EWMenCld]
Do you think that men could do the same sort of work as you?
    Yes
    No
    (Don't Know)
    (Refusal/NA)

%
21.9
5.1
73.1
-

IF 'Yes'/DK AT [EWMenCld]    n=132
Q167 [EWMenWld]
Do you think that men would be willing to do the same sort of work as you?
    Yes
    No
    (Don't Know)
    (Refusal/NA)

%
11.9
9.9
-
-

ASK ALL SELF-EMPLOYED (IF 'self-employed' AT [REmploye])
Q168 [SsrJbTim]
In your present job, are you working ... READ OUT ...
RESPONDENT'S OWN DEFINITION
    ... full-time,
    or, part-time?
    (Don't Know)
    (Refusal/NA)

%
84.0
16.0
-
-

Q169 [SJbHours]
How many hours a week do you normally work in your (main) job?
IF RESPONDENT CANNOT ANSWER, ASK ABOUT LAST WEEK.
ROUND TO NEAREST HOUR
CODE 95 FOR 95+
Range: 10 ... 95
Median: 50 hours

Q170 [SJbHrCat] (CALCULATED BY PROGRAM)
SELF-EMPLOYED HOURS WORKED - CATEGORISED
    10-15 hours a week
    16-23 hours a week
    24-29 hours a week
    30 or more hours a week
    (Don't Know)
    (Refusal/NA)

%
5.4
3.5
1.9
88.3
0.8
-

Q171 [SUnemp]
During the last five years - that is since March 1989 - have you been unemployed and seeking work for any period?
    Yes
    No
    (Don't Know)
    (Refusal/NA)

%
22.2
77.8
-
-

| | | | | | |
|---|---|---|---|---|---|
| Q172 | **IF 'yes' AT [SUnemp]**<br>[SUnempT]<br>For how many months in total during the last five years (have you been unemployed) ?<br>ENTER NUMBER OF MONTHS<br>Range: 0 ... 60<br>Median: 6 months | n=132 | Q177 | [BusIFut]<br>And over **the coming year**, do you think your business will do ... READ OUT ...<br>... better,<br>about the same,<br>or, worse than this year?<br>Other answer (WRITE IN)<br>(Don't Know)<br>(Refusal/NA) | n=132 |
| Q173 | **ASK ALL SELF-EMPLOYED (IF 'self-employed' AT [REmployel])**<br>[SEmplee]<br>Have you, for any period in the last five years, worked as an **employee** as your main job rather than as self-employed?<br>% Yes<br>22.6 Yes<br>77.4 No<br>- (Don't Know)<br>- (Refusal/NA) | | | %<br>29.2<br>59.9<br>9.7<br>1.2<br>-<br>- | |
| | | | Q180 | [SPartnrs]<br>In your work or business, do you have any partners or other self-employed colleagues?<br>NOTE: **DOES NOT INCLUDE EMPLOYEES**<br>Yes, has partner(s)<br>No<br>(Don't Know)<br>(Refusal/NA) | |
| Q174 | **IF 'yes' AT [SEmplee]**<br>[SEmpleeT]<br>In total for how many months during the last five years have you been an employee<br>Range: 1 ... 60<br>Median: 30 months | | | %<br>31.5<br>68.5<br>-<br>- | |
| | | | Q181 | [SNumEmp]<br>And in your work or business, do you have any employees, or not?<br>NOTE: **FAMILY MEMBERS MAY BE EMPLOYEES ONLY IF THEY RECEIVE A REGULAR WAGE OR SALARY**<br>Yes, has employee(s)<br>No<br>(Don't Know)<br>(Refusal/NA) | |
| Q175 | **IF 'no' AT [SEmplee]**<br>[SEmplSer]<br>How seriously in the last five years have you considered getting a job as an **employee** ... READ OUT ...<br>%<br>1.6 ... very seriously,<br>5.4 quite seriously,<br>7.0 not very seriously,<br>63.4 or, not at all seriously?<br>18.1 (Business not in existence then)<br>3.5 (Don't Know)<br>- (Refusal/NA) | | | %<br>38.1<br>61.9<br>-<br>- | |
| | | | Q182 | [SEmpEarn]<br>Now for some more general questions about your work. For some people their job is simply something they do in order to earn a living. For others it means much more than that. On balance, is your present job ...<br>... READ OUT ...<br>... just a means of earning a living,<br>or, does it mean much more to you than that?<br>(Don't Know)<br>(Refusal/NA) | |
| Q176 | **ASK ALL SELF-EMPLOYED (IF 'self-employed' AT [REmployel])**<br>[BuslOKJ]<br>Compared with a year ago, would you say your business is doing ... READ OUT ...<br>%<br>9.7 ... very well,<br>26.5 quite well,<br>52.5 about the same,<br>5.4 not very well,<br>2.3 or, not at all well?<br>3.5 (Business not in existence then)<br>- (Don't Know)<br>- (Refusal/NA) | | | %<br>21.8<br>78.2<br>-<br>- | |
| | | | Q183 | **IF 'just a means of earning a living' AT [SEmpEarn]**<br>[SEmpLiv]<br>Is that because ... READ OUT ...<br>... there are no better jobs around here,<br>you don't have the right skills to get a better job,<br>or, because you would feel the same about **any** job you had?<br>(Don't Know)<br>(Refusal/NA) | |
| | | | | %<br>3.9<br>5.1<br>11.3<br>1.6<br>- | |

**ASK ALL SELF-EMPLOYED**
(IF 'self-employed' AT [REmploye])
[SPrefJob] n=132
Q184 If without having to work, you had what you would regard as a reasonable living income, do you think you would still prefer to have a paid job or wouldn't you bother?
%
89.1 Still prefer paid job
10.5 Wouldn't bother
0.4 Other answer (WRITE IN)
- (Don't Know)
- (Refusal/NA)

[SWkHrd]
Q187 CARD
Which of these statements best describes your feelings about your job?
%
7.8 In my job :
25.7 I only work as hard as I have to
 I work hard, but not so that it interferes with the rest of my life
65.8 I make a point of doing the best I can, even if it sometimes does interfere with the rest of my life
- (Don't Know)
0.8 (Refusal/NA)

**ASK ALL NOT IN PAID WORK** (IF NOT 'in paid work' AT [REconAct])
[NPWork10] n=736
Q188 In the seven days ending last Sunday, did you have any paid work of less than 10 hours a week?
%
5.2 Yes
94.5 No
- (Don't Know)
0.3 (Refusal/NA)

**ASK ALL LOOKING AFTER THE HOME** (IF 'looking after the home' AT [REconAct]) n=233
[EverJob]
Q189 Have you, during the last five years, ever had a full- or part-time job of 10 hours or more a week?
%
23.1 Yes
76.9 No
- (Don't Know)
- (Refusal/NA)

IF 'no' AT [EverJob]
[FtJobSer] n=233
Q190 How seriously in the past five years have you considered getting a full-time job ... READ OUT ...
PROMPT, IF NECESSARY: FULL-TIME IS 30+ HOURS A WEEK

IF 'not very seriously'/'not at all seriously' AT [FtJobSer]
[PtJobSer]
Q191 How seriously, in the past five years, have you considered getting a part-time job ... READ OUT ...

                                  [FtJobSer]  [PtJobSer]
                                      %           %
... very seriously,                  3.5         1.1
quite seriously,                     4.4         3.5
not very seriously,                  6.6         6.4
or, not at all seriously?           62.3        57.9
(Don't Know)                          -           -
(Refusal/NA)

**ASK ALL IN PAID WORK** (INCLUDING RESPONDENTS LOOKING AFTER THE HOME WHO HAVE HAD PAID WORK OF LESS THAN 10 HOURS IN THE LAST WEEK (IF 'in paid work' AT [REconAct] PLUS THOSE 'looking after the home' at [REconAct] AND 'yes' AT [NPWork10])
[WChdLt5] n=791
Q192 Can I just check, do you have any children under five living at home?
%
19.8 Yes
80.2 No
- (Don't Know)
- (Refusal/NA)

IF 'no' AT [WChd512]
[WChd512]
Q193 Do you have any children over five but under twelve living at home?
%
16.3 Yes
64.0 No
- (Don't Know)
- (Refusal/NA)

Q193  **ASK ALL WHO ARE WORKING AND HAVE CHILDREN UNDER 12 (IF 'yes' AT [WChdLt5] OR AT [WChd512])**  n=285
**CARD**
Which of the following **best** describes the way you arrange for your children to be looked after while you are at work? Any others? **CODE ALL THAT APPLY**
Multicoded (Maximum of 12 codes)
%
8.5    I work only while they are at school *[WChArr01]*
1.8    They look after themselves until I get home *[WChArr02]*
1.1    I work from home *[WChArr03]*
7.7    A mother's help or nanny looks after them at home *[WChArr04]*
-      They go to a workplace nursery *[WChArr05]*
1.8    They go to a day nursery *[WChArr06]*
10.6   They go to a child-minder *[WChArr07]*
23.7   A relative looks after them *[WChArr08]*
7.2    A friend or neighbour looks after them *[WChArr09]*
49.5   My husband / wife / partner looks after them *[WChArr10]*
1.1    (None of these) *[WChArr11]*
-      Other answer **(WRITE IN)** *[WChArr00]*
-      (Refusal/NA)
-      (Don't know)

**IF 'day nursery' AT [WChArr05]**
Q197   *[WNursry]*
Is that day nursery a private nursery, or does it receive funds from the local council?
%
1.1    Private nursery only
0.7    Council-funded nursery only
-      (Both - use both kinds)
-      (Don't Know)
-      (Refusal/NA)

**ASK ALL WHO ARE WORKING AND HAVE CHILDREN UNDER 12 (IF 'yes' AT [WChdLt5] OR AT [WChd512])**
Q198   *[WChdCon]*
How convenient are the arrangements you now have for looking after your children? Are they ... **READ OUT** ...
%
77.0   ... very convenient,
18.0   fairly convenient,
4.5    not very convenient,
0.2    or, not at all convenient?
0.4    (Don't Know)
-      (Refusal/NA)

Q199   *[WChdSat]*
And how satisfied overall are you with these arrangements?
Are you ... **READ OUT** ...
%
77.2   ... very satisfied,
19.2   fairly satisfied,
2.5    not very satisfied,
0.7    or, not at all satisfied?
-      (Don't Know)
-      (Refusal/NA)

Q200   *[WChdPr1]*
**CARD**
Suppose you could choose from **any** of the types of childcare on the card. Which would be your first choice for childcare while you are at work?
Please read the whole list before deciding.
**ENTER ONE CODE ONLY FOR FIRST CHOICE**

Q203   *[WChdPr2]*
**CARD**
... and which would be your second choice?
**ENTER ONE CODE ONLY FOR SECOND CHOICE**

|   | [WChdPr1] % | [WChdPr2] % |
|---|---|---|
| I would work only while they are at school | 16.2 | 6.1 |
| They would look after themselves until I got home | 0.4 | 1.1 |
| I would work from home | 1.1 | 5.4 |
| A mother's help or nanny would look after them at home | 9.0 | 5.4 |
| They would go to a workplace nursery | 3.1 | 2.9 |
| They would go to a council-funded day nursery | 1.8 | 2.7 |
| They would go to a private day nursery | 2.2 | 4.1 |
| They would go to a child-minder | 8.6 | 10.6 |
| A relative would look after them | 13.1 | 33.5 |
| A friend or neighbour would look after them | 5.6 | 11.2 |
| My husband / wife / partner would look after them | 38.3 | 12.4 |
| (None of these) | 0.4 | 3.6 |
| Other answer **(WRITE IN)** | - | - |
| (Don't Know) | 0.4 | 0.7 |
| (Refusal/NA) | - | - |

Q206 [WPrfWrkJ] | n=285

And if you did have the childcare arrangement of your choice, would you prefer to ... READ OUT ...

%
11.2 ... work more hours than now,
12.2 work fewer hours than now,
76.3 or, are you happy with the hours you work at present
- (Don't Know)
0.4 (Refusal/NA)

IF WOULD PREFER TO WORK MORE HOURS AND CURRENTLY NOT FULL-TIME (IF 'work more hours' AT [WPrfWrk] AND LESS THAN [EJbHrCat] OR AT [SJbHrCat] PLUS THOSE 'looking after the home' AT [REconAct] AND 'yes' AT [NPWork10])

Q207 [WPtFull] | n=276

Do you think you might work full-time then, or not?

%
5.6 Yes, might work full-time
2.6 No, would not
- (Don't Know)
0.4 (Refusal/NA)

ASK ALL WHO ARE WORKING AND HAVE CHILDREN UNDER 12 (IF 'yes' AT [WChdLt5] OR AT [WChd512])

Q208 [WScFull] | n=285

When all your children have gone to secondary school, which do you think you are most likely to do ... READ OUT ...

%
82.6 ... work full-time,
17.1 work part-time,
0.4 or, not have a paid job at all?
- (Don't Know)
- (Refusal/NA)

ASK ALL IN PAID WORK (IF 'paid work' at [REconAct])

Q209 [ESOldRsp] | n=784

Some people have responsibilities for looking after a disabled, sick, or elderly friend or relative. Is there anyone like this who depends on you to provide some regular care for them?

%
13.9 Yes
85.9 No
- (Don't Know)
0.2 (Refusal/NA)

IF 'yes' AT [ESOldRsp]

Q210 [ESOldAfH]

Does this responsibility ... READ OUT ...

%
1.5 ... prevent you from working longer hours in your job,
12.4 or, does it make no difference to your working hours?
- (Don't Know)
0.2 (Refusal/NA)

27

ASK ALL WHO ARE LOOKING AFTER THE HOME WITH NO PAID WORK (IF 'looking after the home' AT [REconAct] AND 'no' AT [NPWork10]) | n=225

Q211 [HChdLt5]

Can I just check, do you have any children under five living at home?

%
31.7 Yes
68.3 No
- (Don't Know)
- (Refusal/NA)

IF 'no' AT [HChdLt5]

Q212 [HChd512]

Do you have any children over five but under twelve living at home?

%
15.3 Yes
53.0 No
- (Don't Know)
- (Refusal/NA)

ASK ALL WHO ARE LOOKING AFTER THE HOME WITH NO PAID JOB AND HAVE CHILDREN UNDER 12 (IF 'yes' AT [HChdLt5] OR AT [HChd512]) | n=106

Q213 CARD

Do you regularly use any of these childcare arrangements for your child or children during the day?
Multicoded (Maximum of 8 codes)

%
2.4 A mother's help or nanny looks after them at home [HChArr04]
18.0 They go to a day-nursery [HChArr06]
1.5 They go to a child-minder [HChArr07]
10.2 A relative looks after them [HChArr08]
2.4 A friend or neighbour looks after them [HChArr09]
8.3 My husband / wife / partner looks after them [HChArr10]
0.5 Other answer (WRITE IN) [HChArr11]
64.6 None of these [HChArr00]
- (Don't Know)
- (Refusal/NA)

IF 'day nursery' AT [HChArrF1]

Q216 [HNursry]

Is that day nursery a private nursery, or does it receive funds from the local council?

%
4.9 Private nursery only
13.1 Council-funded nursery only
- (Both - use both kinds)
- (Don't Know)
- (Refusal/NA)

28

**IF LOOKING AFTER THE HOME WITH NO PAID JOB AND USING CHILDCARE REGULARLY (IF 'nanny' OR 'day-nursery' OR 'child-minder' OR 'relative' OR 'friend or neighbour' OR 'husband/wife/partner' OR 'other' AT [HChArr0-7])**  n=106

Q217 *[HChdCon]*
How convenient are the arrangements you now have for looking after your children? Are they ... READ OUT ...
%
18.9 ... very convenient,
13.1 fairly convenient,
3.4 not very convenient,
- or, not at all convenient?
- (Don't Know)
- (Refusal/NA)

Q218 *[HChdSat]*
And how satisfied overall are you with these arrangements? Are you ... READ OUT ...
%
23.8 ... very satisfied,
9.7 fairly satisfied,
1.9 not very satisfied,
- or, not at all satisfied?
- (Don't Know)
- (Refusal/NA)

**ASK ALL WHO ARE LOOKING AFTER THE HOME WITH NO PAID JOB AND HAVE CHILDREN UNDER 12 (IF 'yes' AT [HChdLt5] OR AT [HChd512])**

Q219 *[HChdPr1]*
CARD
Suppose you decided to take a job outside the home, and you could choose from any of the types of childcare on the card. Which would be your first choice for child-care while you were at work?
Please read through the whole list before deciding.
**ENTER ONE CODE ONLY FOR FIRST CHOICE**

Q222 *[HChdPr2]*
CARD
... and which would be your second choice?
**ENTER ONE CODE ONLY FOR SECOND CHOICE**

n=106

|  | [HChdPr1] % | [HChdPr2] % |
|---|---|---|
| I would work only while they are at school | 55.8 | 7.8 |
| They would look after themselves until I got home | 1.0 | 0.5 |
| I would work from home | 0.5 | 15.5 |
| A mother's help or nanny would look after them at home | 4.9 | 4.4 |
| They would go to a workplace nursery | 3.9 | 6.3 |
| They would go to a council-funded day nursery | 3.4 | 4.9 |
| They would go to a private day nursery | - | 3.9 |
| They would go to a child-minder | 3.9 | 10.7 |
| A relative would look after them | 20.9 | 27.2 |
| A friend or neighbour would look after them | 1.5 | 7.8 |
| My husband / wife / partner would look after them | 4.4 | 10.7 |
| NONE OF THESE **(WRITE IN)** | - | - |
| (Don't Know) | - | 0.5 |
| (Refusal/NA) | - | - |

Q225 *[HWChoic]*
And if you did have the childcare arrangement of your choice, would you prefer to ... READ OUT ...
%
59.2 ... work full-time
17.5 work part-time
22.8 or, would you choose not to work outside the home?
0.5 (Either full-time or part-time)
- (Don't Know)
- (Refusal/NA)

Q226 *[HScFull]*
When all your children have gone to secondary school, which do you think you are most likely to do ... **READ OUT** ...
%
45.1 ... work full-time
44.2 work part-time
9.7 or, not have a paid job at all?
1.0 (Don't Know)
- (Refusal/NA)

Q227 *[HOldRspl]*
Some people have responsibilities for looking after a disabled, sick, or elderly friend or relative. Is there anyone like this who depends on you to provide some regular care for them?
%
30.6 Yes
69.4 No
- (Don't Know)
- (Refusal/NA)

**IF 'yes' AT [HOldResp]**

Q228 [HOldAfh1]
Does this responsibility ... READ OUT ...
- 13.1  ... prevent you from getting a paid job,
- 17.5  ... or, would you not want a paid job anyway?
-       (Don't Know)
-       (Refusal/NA)

**ASK ALL WHO ARE LOOKING AFTER THE HOME WITH NO PAID JOB AND HAVE CHILDREN UNDER 12 (IF 'yes' AT [HChdLt5] OR AT [HChd512])**

Q229 [ParnWrk1]
CARD
I am going to read out some reasons parents of young children give for not working, or not working many hours. Please use this card to say how important each of these reasons is for **you personally**.
... I enjoy spending time with my children more than working.

n=106

Q230 [ParnWrk2]
... It's better for the children if I am home to look after them.
(How important is this reason for you personally?)

Q231 [ParnWrk3]
... It would cost too much to find suitable childcare.
(How important is this reason for you personally?)

|  | [ParnWrk1] % | [ParnWrk2] % | [ParnWrk3] % |
|---|---|---|---|
| Very important | 73.3 | 78.2 | 40.8 |
| Fairly important | 22.8 | 18.9 | 31.1 |
| Not very important | 1.9 | 1.9 | 9.2 |
| Not at all important | 1.9 | 1.0 | 9.7 |
| Does not apply to me | - | - | 8.7 |
| (Don't Know) | - | - | 0.5 |
| (Refusal/NA) | - | - | - |

Q232 [ParnWrk4]
... I cannot find the kind of childcare I would like.
(How important is this reason for you personally?)

Q233 [ParnWrk5]
... My life would be too difficult if I had to combine childcare and paid work.
(How important is this reason for you personally?)

Q234 [ParnWrk6]
... My partner would not want me to work.
(How important is this reason for you personally?)

|  | [ParnWrk4] % | [ParnWrk5] % | [ParnWrk6] % |
|---|---|---|---|
| Very important | 31.1 | 31.6 | 17.0 |
| Fairly important | 12.6 | 31.1 | 8.3 |
| Not very important | 15.0 | 17.0 | 14.6 |
| Not at all important | 7.8 | 9.7 | 14.6 |
| Does not apply to me | 32.0 | 10.7 | 44.2 |
| (Don't Know) | 1.5 | - | 1.5 |
| (Refusal/NA) | - | - | - |

Q235 [ParnWrk7]
... I cannot find the kind of work I want with suitable hours.
(How important is this reason for you personally?)

Q236 [ParnWrk8]
... I cannot find the kind of work I want near my home.
(How important is this reason for you personally?)

|  | [ParnWrk7] % | [ParnWrk8] % |
|---|---|---|
| Very important | 29.1 | 27.7 |
| Fairly important | 18.4 | 21.8 |
| Not very important | 10.7 | 10.2 |
| Not at all important | 10.7 | 9.7 |
| Does not apply to me | 31.1 | 30.6 |
| (Don't Know) | - | - |
| (Refusal/NA) | - | - |

**ASK ALL UNEMPLOYED (IF 'unemployed and registered at a benefit office'/'unemployed, not registered at a benefit office'/'unemployed, wanting a job but not actively looking for a job' AT [REconAct])**

n=97

Q237 [UUnempT]
In total how many months in the last five years - that is, since March 1989 - have you been unemployed and seeking work?
Range: 1 ... 60
**Median: 36 months**

Q238 [CurUnemp]
How long has this **present** period of unemployment and seeking work lasted so far?
ENTER NUMBER THEN SPECIFY MONTHS OR YEARS
Range: 1 ... 60
**Median: 24 months**

Q240 [JobQual]
How confident are you that you will find a job to match your qualifications ...
READ OUT ...
%
5.3    ... very confident,
19.0   quite confident,
29.6   not very confident,
46.0   or, not at all confident?
-      (Don't Know)
-      (Refusal/NA)

Q241 [UFindJob]
Although it may be difficult to judge, how long from now do you think it will be before you find an acceptable job?
ENTER NUMBER THEN SPECIFY MONTHS OR YEARS
CODE 96 FOR NEVER
Range: 1 ... 96
Median: 6 months

IF THREE MONTHS OR MORE/NEVER/DK AT [UfindJob]
Q243 [URetrain]
How willing do you think you would be in these circumstances to retrain for a different job ... READ OUT ...

Q244 [UJobMove]
How willing would you be to move to a different area to find an acceptable job ... READ OUT ...

Q245 [UBadJob]
And how willing do you think you would be in these circumstances to take what you now consider to be an unacceptable job ... READ OUT ...

|  | [URetrain] | [UJobMove] | [UBadJob] |
|---|---|---|---|
|  | % | % | % |
| ... very willing, | 17.5 | 6.3 | 7.9 |
| quite willing, | 25.4 | 6.3 | 16.4 |
| or, not very willing? | 16.9 | 47.1 | 33.3 |
| (Don't Know) | - | - | 2.1 |
| (Refusal/NA) | 31.2 | 31.2 | 31.2 |

n=97

ASK ALL UNEMPLOYED (IF 'unemployed and registered at a benefit office'/'unemployed, not registered at a benefit office'/'unemployed, wanting a job but not actively looking for a job' At [REconAct])
Q246 [ConMove]
Have you ever actually considered moving to a different area - an area other than the one you live in now - to try to find work?
%
27.5   Yes
72.5   No
-      (Don't Know)
-      (Refusal/NA)

Q247 [UJobChnc]
Do you think that there is a real chance nowadays that you will get a job in this area, or is there no real chance nowadays?
%
40.7   Real chance
55.6   No real chance
3.7    (Don't Know)
-      (Refusal/NA)

Q248 [FPtWork]
Would you prefer full- or part-time work, if you had the choice?
%
75.7   Full-time
21.2   Part-time
1.1    Not looking for work
2.1    (Don't Know)
-      (Refusal/NA)

IF 'part-time' AT [FPtWork]
Q249 [PartTime]
About how many hours per week would you like to work?
PROBE FOR BEST ESTIMATE
Range: 1...30
Median: 20 Hours

ASK ALL UNEMPLOYED (IF 'unemployed and registered at a benefit office'/'unemployed, not registered at a benefit office'/'unemployed, wanting a job but not actively looking for a job' At [REconAct])
Q250 [UnemEarn]
For some people work is simply something they do in order to earn a living. For others it means much more than that. In general, do you think of work as ... READ OUT ...
%
49.2   ... just a means of earning a living,
50.8   or, does it mean much more to you than that?
-      (Don't Know)
-      (Refusal/NA)

Q251 **IF 'just a means of earning a living' AT [UnemLiv]** n=97
[UnempLiv]
Is that because ... READ OUT ...
%
17.5 ... there are no good jobs around here,
9.5 ... you don't have the right skills to get a good job,
22.2 or, because you would feel the same about **any** job you had?
- (Don't Know)
- (Refusal/NA)

**ASK ALL WHOLLY RETIRED**
**(IF 'wholly retired' AT [REconAct])** n=227
Q252 [REmplPen]
Do you receive a pension from any past employer?
%
43.0 Yes
57.0 No
- (Don't Know)
- (Refusal/NA)

Q253 [MsCheck]
May I just check, are you ... READ OUT ...
%
52.7 ... married,
47.3 or, not married?
- (Don't Know)
- (Refusal/NA)

Q254 **IF 'married' AT [MsCheck]**
[SEmplPen]
Does your (husband/wife) receive a pension from any past employer?
%
15.2 Yes
37.6 No
- (Don't Know)
- (Refusal/NA)

Q255 **ASK ALL WHOLLY RETIRED**
**(IF 'wholly retired' AT [REconAct])**
[PrPenGet]
And do you receive a pension from any **private** arrangements you have made in the past, that is **apart** from the state pension or one arranged through an employer?
%
7.0 Yes
92.8 No
0.2 (Don't Know)
- (Refusal/NA)

Q256 **IF 'married' AT [MsCheck]**
[SPrPnGet]
And does your (husband/wife) receive a pension from any **private** arrangements (he/she) has made in the past, that is **apart** from the state pension or one arranged through an employer?
%
0.5 Yes
52.3 No
- (Don't Know)
- (Refusal/NA)

Q257 **ASK ALL WHOLLY RETIRED (IF 'wholly retired' AT [REconAct])**
[RetAge]
(Can I just check) are you over *(sixty-five/sixty)*?
%
91.0 Yes
9.0 No
- (Don't Know)
- (Refusal/NA)

Q258 **IF 'yes' AT [RetAge]**
[RPension]
On the whole would you say the present **state** pension is on the low side, reasonable, or on the highside?
IF 'ON THE LOW SIDE': Very low or a bit low?
%
27.6 Very low
40.3 A bit low
22.2 Reasonable
- On the high side
0.9 (Don't Know)
- (Refusal/NA)

Q259 [RPenInYr]
Do you expect your state pension in a year's time to purchase **more** than it does now, **less**, or about the **same**?
%
1.6 More
67.4 Less
20.8 About the same
1.1 (Don't Know)
- (Refusal/NA)

Q260 **ASK ALL WHOLLY RETIRED**
**(IF 'wholly retired' AT [REconAct])**
[RetirAg2]
At what age did you retire from work?
NEVER WORKED, CODE: 00
Range: 0 ... 80
**Median: 61 years**

## ASK ALL ON GOVERNMENT PROGRAMME OR WAITING TO TAKE UP WORK (IF 'on government training scheme' OR 'waiting to take up work' AT [REconAct])

n=24

Q261 [WgUnemp]
During the last five years - that is since March 1989 have you been unemployed and seeking work for any period?

Numbers:
15 Yes
8 No
- (Don't Know)
- (Refusal/NA)

Q262 [WgEarn]
For some people work is simply something they do in order to earn a living. For others it means much more than that.
In general, do you think of work as ... READ OUT ...

Numbers:
5 ... just a means of earning a living,
16 or, does it mean much more to you than that?
3 (Don't Know)
- (Refusal/NA)

IF 'just a means of earning a living' AT [WgEarn]

Q263 [WgLiv]
Is that because ... READ OUT ...

Numbers:
3 ... there are no good jobs around here,
- you don't have the right skills to get a good job,
3 or - because you would feel the same about **any** job you had?
- (Don't Know)
3 (Refusal/NA)

## ASK ALL IN FULL-TIME EDUCATION (IF 'in full-time education' AT [REconAct])

n=55

Q264 [EdUnemp]
During the last five years - that is since March 1989 have you been unemployed and seeking work for any period?

Numbers:
10 Yes
45 No
- (Don't Know)
- (Refusal/NA)

230

## COMMUNITY RELATIONS IN NORTHERN IRELAND

n=1519

ASK ALL

Q266 [PrejRC]
Now I would like to ask some questions about religious prejudice against both Catholics and Protestants in Northern Ireland.
First thinking of **Catholics** - do you think there is a lot of prejudice against them in Northern Ireland nowadays, a little, or hardly any?

Q267 [PrejProt]
And now, thinking of **Protestants** - do you think there is a lot of prejudice against them in Northern Ireland nowadays, a little, or hardly any?

|  | [PrejRC] % | [PrejProt] % |
|---|---|---|
| A lot | 29.3 | 22.0 |
| A little | 46.2 | 51.0 |
| Hardly any | 21.9 | 24.0 |
| (Don't Know) | 2.2 | 2.5 |
| (Refusal/NA) | 0.5 | 0.5 |

Q268 [SRlPrej]
%
How would you describe yourself ... READ OUT ...
0.8 ... as very prejudiced against people of other religions,
11.2 a little prejudiced,
87.2 or, not prejudiced at all?
0.5 Other answer **(WRITE IN)**
0.1 (Don't Know)
(Refusal/NA)

Q272 [RlRelAgo]
What about relations between Protestants and Catholics? Would you say they are **better** than they were 5 years ago, **worse**, or about the **same** now as then?
**IF 'IT DEPENDS':** On the whole...
%
26.3 Better
27.3 Worse
42.9 About the same
2.1 Other answer **(WRITE IN)**
1.3 (Don't Know)
0.1 (Refusal/NA)

38

n=1519

Q276 [RIRelFut]
And what about in 5 years time?
Do you think relations between Protestants and Catholics will be **better** than now, **worse** than now, or about the **same** as now?
**IF 'IT DEPENDS'**: On the whole...

%
32.2 Better than now
18.1 Worse than now
43.8 About the same
1.1 Other answer (WRITE IN)
4.8 (Don't Know)
0.1 (Refusal/NA)

Q280 [RelgAlwy]
Do you think that religion will **always** make a difference to the way people feel about each other in Northern Ireland?

%
85.6 Yes
10.4 No
2.6 Other answer (WRITE IN)
1.3 (Don't Know)
0.2 (Refusal/NA)

Q284 [NHSRlGPJ]
CARD
For each of the next questions, please use this card to say whether you think **Catholics** are treated better than **Protestants** in Northern Ireland, or whether **Protestants** are treated better than **Catholics**, or whether both are treated equally.
First, the **National Health Service** in Northern Ireland.
How does it treat Catholic and Protestant patients?

Q285 [NIHRlGPJ]
CARD
What about the **Northern Ireland Housing Executive** - how does it treat Catholics and Protestants who apply for a home?

Q286 [DCRlGPJ]
CARD
What about your **local district council** - how does it treat Catholics and Protestants who apply for jobs?

231

---

n=1519

|  | [NHSRlGPJ] % | [NIHRlGPJ] % | [DCRlGPJ] % |
|---|---|---|---|
| Catholics treated much better | 1.1 | 2.5 | 0.9 |
| Catholics treated a bit better | 2.5 | 8.0 | 6.2 |
| Both treated equally | 91.2 | 65.0 | 53.6 |
| Protestants treated a bit better | 1.2 | 6.8 | 15.9 |
| Protestants treated much better | 0.3 | 1.6 | 4.8 |
| (It depends/Can't say) | 1.6 | 6.7 | 7.5 |
| (Don't Know) | 2.2 | 9.1 | 10.8 |
| (Refusal/NA) | 0.2 | 0.3 | 0.3 |

Q287 [StrRlGPJ]
CARD
And what about **central government** in Stormont - how does it treat Catholics and Protestants who apply for jobs?

Q288 [GSURlGPJ]
CARD
What about **government programmes for the unemployed** - how do they treat Catholics and Protestants who apply for places?

Q289 [FECRlGPJ]
And what about the **Fair Employment Commission** - how does it treat Catholics and Protestants?

|  | [StrRlGPJ] % | [GSURlGPJ] % | [FECRlGPJ] % |
|---|---|---|---|
| Catholics treated much better | 1.5 | 1.7 | 6.2 |
| Catholics treated a bit better | 7.7 | 6.0 | 12.8 |
| Both treated equally | 55.1 | 75.1 | 69.5 |
| Protestants treated a bit better | 13.7 | 2.9 | 1.8 |
| Protestants treated much better | 4.2 | 0.4 | 0.5 |
| (It depends/Can't say) | 6.3 | 4.5 | 3.5 |
| (Don't Know) | 11.3 | 9.1 | 5.5 |
| (Refusal/NA) | 0.3 | 0.2 | 0.2 |

Q290 [JbRLGCh1]    n=1519
Thinking now about employment...
On the whole, do you think the Protestants and Catholics in Northern Ireland who apply for the same jobs have the **same** chance of getting a job or are their chances of getting a job different?
IF 'IT DEPENDS', PROMPT: On the whole ....
%
50.6  Same chance
44.6  Different chance
4.6   (Don't Know)
0.2   (Refusal/NA)

Q291 [JbRlGCh2]
IF 'different chance/DK AT JBR1GCh1
Which group is **more** likely to get a job - Protestants or Catholics?
IF 'IT DEPENDS', PROMPT: On the whole ....
%
27.8  Protestants
10.8  Catholics
10.4  (Don't Know)
0.4   (Refusal/NA)

Q292 [JobRlGCh]
Are (Protestants/Catholics) **much** more likely or just a **bit** more likely to get a job?
%
9.1   (Protestants much more likely)
18.6  (Protestants a bit more likely)
50.6  (Same chance)
8.1   (Catholics a bit more likely)
2.7   (Catholics much more likely)
6.3   (Don't know which is more likely)
4.1   (Don't know whether they have the same chance)
0.4   (Refusal/NA)

ASK ALL
Q293 [JobRlGSh]
And do you think Protestants and Catholics in Northern Ireland who apply for the same jobs **should** have the same chance of getting a job or should Protestants have a better chance, or should Catholics have a better chance?
%
98.0  Same chance
0.8   Protestants better
0.4   Catholics better
0.6   (Don't Know)
0.1   (Refusal/NA)

Q294 [ProtJob]    n=1519
Now I'm going to ask **separately** about employment chances of Protestants and Catholics.
Some people think that many employers are **more** likely to give jobs to Protestants than to Catholics.
Do you think this happens ... READ OUT ...
IF 'IT DEPENDS': In **general**, what would you say?
%
17.2  ... a lot,
51.9  a little,
26.0  or, hardly at all?
4.6   (Don't Know)
0.3   (Refusal/NA)

Q295 [YProtJob]
IF 'a lot' OR 'a little' AT [ProtJob]
Why do you think this happens? -
Do you think it is **mainly** because employers discriminate against Catholics or **mainly** because Catholics are not as well qualified as Protestants?
IF 'BOTH', PROBE BEFORE CODING
%
55.0  Mainly because employers discriminate
4.1   Mainly because Catholics aren't qualified
6.1   Both (AFTER PROBE)
3.9   (Don't Know)
5.0   (Refusal/NA)

ASK ALL
Q296 [RCJob]
Some people think that many employers are **more** likely to give jobs to Catholics than to Protestants.
Do you think this happens ... READ OUT ...
IF 'IT DEPENDS': In **general**, what would you say?
%
10.5  ... a lot,
49.6  a little,
34.5  or, hardly at all?
5.1   (Don't Know)
0.3   (Refusal/NA)

Q297 [YRCJob]
IF 'a lot' OR 'a little' AT [RCJob]
Why do you think this happens? -
Do you think it is **mainly** because employers discriminate against Protestants or **mainly** because Protestants are not as well qualified as Catholics?
IF 'BOTH', PROBE BEFORE CODING
%
50.0  Mainly because employers discriminate
1.9   Mainly because Protestants aren't qualified
3.9   Both (AFTER PROBE)
4.1   (Don't Know)
5.6   (Refusal/NA)

n=1519

**Q298 ASK ALL**
[FELSupp]
Do you generally support or oppose having Fair Employment Laws in Northern Ireland, to help prevent **religious** discrimination?

| % | |
|---|---|
| 86.4 | Support |
| 11.1 | Oppose |
| 2.3 | (Don't Know) |
| 0.2 | (Refusal/NA) |

**Q299** [FELEmp]
At present the Fair Employment Law in Northern Ireland requires employers to keep records on the religion of their employees to help prevent discrimination.
Do you generally support or oppose the law requiring employers to keep such records?
**IF 'SUPPORT' OR 'OPPOSE': STRONGLY OR JUST A BIT?**

| % | |
|---|---|
| 30.9 | Support strongly |
| 28.4 | Support just a bit |
| 14.0 | Oppose just a bit |
| 24.1 | Oppose strongly |
| 2.4 | (Don't Know) |
| 0.1 | (Refusal/NA) |

**Q300** [FELEqual]
Do you feel that the present Fair Employment Law treats Protestants better than Catholics, treats Catholics better than Protestants or treats Protestants and Catholics equally?

| % | |
|---|---|
| 1.5 | Treats Protestants better |
| 17.8 | Treats Catholics better |
| 74.8 | Treats both equally |
| 5.8 | (Don't Know) |
| 0.2 | (Refusal/NA) |

**Q301** [JbApplRl]
Suppose you were applying for a job, how much would it matter to you how many people there were of your own religion at the workplace?
Would it matter ... **READ OUT** ...

| % | |
|---|---|
| 5.6 | ...a lot |
| 19.5 | a bit |
| 74.1 | or, not at all? |
| 0.5 | (Don't Know) |
| 0.2 | (Refusal/NA) |

**Q302** [AvoidP]
Suppose you were applying for a job, would you avoid workplaces situated in a mainly **Protestant** area?
**IF 'YES' OR 'NO': Is this definitely or probably?**

**Q303** [AvoidRC]
And suppose you were applying for a job, would you avoid workplaces situated in a mainly **Catholic** area?
**IF 'YES' OR 'NO': Is this definitely or probably?**

| | [AvoidP] | [AvoidRC] |
|---|---|---|
| | % | % |
| Yes, definitely | 11.5 | 12.5 |
| Yes, probably | 13.3 | 20.0 |
| Probably not | 23.2 | 28.9 |
| Definitely not | 51.0 | 37.6 |
| (Don't Know) | 0.8 | 0.8 |
| (Refusal/NA) | 0.2 | 0.2 |

**Q304** [JobRefus]
Have **you yourself** in the last ten years been refused a job for reasons which you think were to do with your religion?

| % | |
|---|---|
| 4.4 | Yes |
| 82.9 | No |
| 12.4 | Have not worked in last ten years |
| 0.2 | (Don't Know) |
| 0.1 | (Refusal/NA) |

**Q305 IF 'yes'/'no'/DK/Refusal AT [JobRefus]**
[JbUnfair]
And have **you yourself** in the last ten years been treated unfairly when applying for a promotion or a move to a better position for reasons which you think had to do with your religion?

| % | |
|---|---|
| 2.9 | Yes |
| 84.5 | No |
| 0.2 | (Don't Know) |
| 0.1 | (Refusal/NA) |

**Q306** [ThreatRl]
Have you yourself in the last ten years been treated unfairly at work by your workmates or colleagues for reasons which you think were to do with your religion?

| % | |
|---|---|
| 3.1 | Yes |
| 84.3 | No |
| 0.2 | (Don't Know) |
| 0.1 | (Refusal/NA) |

**Q307 ASK ALL**
[FairRep]
If a particular religion is under-represented in a firm, do you think the firm should give preferential treatment to people from that religion when filling posts?

| % | |
|---|---|
| 25.3 | Yes |
| 70.5 | No |
| 4.1 | (Don't Know) |
| 0.1 | (Refusal/NA) |

Q308 [GovMxSch]
Thinking now about **mixed** or **integrated** schooling, that is, schools with fairly large numbers of both Catholic and Protestant children: do you think the government should **encourage** mixed schooling, **discourage** mixed schooling or leave things as they are?

%
75.0 Encourage it
22.2 Discourage it
21.9 Leave things as they are
0.7 (Don't Know)
0.1 (Refusal/NA)

Q309 [ChRlGRsp]
CARD
Do you think the government and public bodies should or should not ... do more to teach Catholic and Protestant children greater respect for each other?

Q310 [IntegHse]
CARD
Do you think the government and public bodies should or should not ... do more to create integrated housing?

Q311 [BtrComRl]
CARD
Do you think the government and public bodies should or should not ... do more to create better community relations generally?

Q312 [IntegWrk]
CARD
Do you think the government and public bodies should or should not ... do more to create integrated workplaces?

| | [ChRlGRsp] | [IntegHse] | [BtrComRl] |
|---|---|---|---|
| | % | % | % |
| Definitely should | 81.7 | 51.0 | 70.1 |
| Probably should | 15.1 | 32.0 | 26.3 |
| Probably should not | 1.3 | 10.4 | 1.7 |
| Definitely should not | 0.8 | 4.2 | 0.7 |
| (Don't Know) | 1.0 | 2.5 | 1.1 |
| (Refusal/NA) | 0.1 | 0.1 | 0.1 |

| | [IntegWrk] |
|---|---|
| | % |
| Definitely should | 61.0 |
| Probably should | 30.4 |
| Probably should not | 5.0 |
| Definitely should not | 2.1 |
| (Don't Know) | 1.5 |
| (Refusal/NA) | 0.1 |

Q313 [GBImpNI]
CARD
For each of the following, please say how active you think each should be in trying to improve relations between the communities in Northern Ireland. Firstly, the British government?

Q314 [IRImpNI]
CARD
... the government of the Irish Republic?

Q315 [UImpNI]
CARD
... Unionist politicians?

Q316 [NatImpNI]
CARD
... Nationalist politicians?

| | [GBImpNI] | [IRImpNI] | [UImpNI] |
|---|---|---|---|
| | % | % | % |
| Much more active than now | 55.9 | 37.1 | 55.3 |
| A little more active than now | 22.8 | 19.4 | 22.4 |
| About the same as now | 15.8 | 15.4 | 14.2 |
| A little less active than now | 1.7 | 9.6 | 3.9 |
| Much less active than now | 1.3 | 15.6 | 1.6 |
| (Don't Know) | 2.3 | 2.7 | 2.3 |
| (Refusal/NA) | 0.2 | 0.2 | 0.3 |

| | [NatImpNI] |
|---|---|
| | % |
| Much more active than now | 50.3 |
| A little more active than now | 22.6 |
| About the same as now | 14.6 |
| A little less active than now | 6.1 |
| Much less active than now | 3.6 |
| (Don't Know) | 2.5 |
| (Refusal/NA) | 0.3 |

Q317 [NISupPty]
Generally speaking, do you think of yourself as a supporter of any one political party?

%
40.8 Yes
58.8 No
- (Don't Know)
0.4 (Refusal/NA)

n=1519

**Q319** **IF 'no'/DK AT [NISupPty]**
[NIClsPty]
Do you think of yourself as a little closer to one political party than to the others?

%
22.2 Yes
36.6 No
- (Don't Know)
0.4 (Refusal/NA)

**Q322** **IF 'yes' AT [NISupPty] OR AT [NIClsPty]:** Which One?
**IF 'no'/DK AT [NISupPty] OR [NIClsPty]:** If there were a general election tomorrow, which political party do you think you would be most likely to support?
[NIPtyID1]

%
7.4 Conservative
6.1 Labour
1.1 Liberal Democrat
0.3 Other Party
1.0 Other answer
12.8 None
7.9 Alliance (Northern Ireland)
10.8 DUP/Democratic Unionist Party
21.8 OUP/Official Unionist
0.9 Other Unionist party
3.9 Sinn Fein
19.2 SDLP
0.6 Workers Party
0.2 Campaign for Equal Citizenship
0.6 Green Party
2.0 (Don't Know)
3.4 (Refusal/NA)

**Q328** **IF 'Conservative', 'Labour' OR 'Liberal Democrat' AT [NIPtyID1]**
[NIPtyID3]
If there were a general election in which only Northern Ireland parties were standing, which one do you think you would be most likely to support?
**CODE ONE ONLY**

%
2.6 Alliance
1.5 DUP/Democratic Unionist Party
4.4 OUP/Official Unionist Party
0.5 Other Unionist party
- Sinn Fein
2.1 SDLP
0.4 Workers Party
- Campaign for Equal Citizenship
0.2 Green Party
0.1 Other Party
0.3 Other answer
2.1 None
0.4 (Don't Know)
5.4 (Refusal/NA)

n=1519

**Q333** **IF NORTHERN IRELAND PARTY MENTIONED AT [NIPtyID1]**
[NIdStrn]
Would you call yourself very strong ... (name of Northern Ireland party) ... fairly strong, or not very strong?

%
9.1 Very strong (name of Northern Ireland party)
26.0 Fairly strong
42.6 Not very strong
- (Don't Know)
5.8 (Refusal/NA)

**ASK ALL**

**Q334** [NINatID]
**CARD**
Which of these **best** describes the way you usually think of yourself?

%
45.9 British
25.4 Irish
6.3 Ulster
19.9 Northern Irish
1.8 Other **(WRITE IN)**
0.2 (Don't Know)
0.4 (Refusal/NA)

**Q337** [BrtIRSde]
When there is an argument between Britain and the Republic of Ireland, do you generally find yourself on the side of the British or of the Irish government?
**IF 'IT DEPENDS':** On the whole ...

%
49.3 Generally British government
14.0 Generally Irish government
22.0 It depends **(AFTER PROBE)**
13.5 Neither
0.7 (Don't Know)
0.5 (Refusal/NA)

**Q338** [GovIntNI]
**CARD**
Under direct rule from Britain, as now, how much do you generally trust **British governments** of **any** party to act in the best interests of Northern Ireland?
**CODE ONE ONLY**

**Q339** [StrIntNI]
**CARD AGAIN**
If there was self-rule, how much do you think you would generally trust a **Stormont government** to act in the best interests of Northern Ireland?
**CODE ONE ONLY**

Q340 [IreIntNI]
CARD AGAIN
And if there was a united Ireland, how much do you think you would generally trust an **Irish government** to act in the best interests of Northern Ireland?
**CODE ONE ONLY**

|  | [GovIntNI] | [StrIntNI] | [IreIntNI] |
|---|---|---|---|
|  | % | % | % |
| Just about always | 2.9 | 9.6 | 2.2 |
| Most of the time | 19.3 | 37.6 | 19.2 |
| Only some of the time | 41.4 | 28.9 | 33.3 |
| Rarely | 23.2 | 12.1 | 20.6 |
| Never | 11.4 | 7.7 | 20.0 |
| (Don't Know) | 1.6 | 3.8 | 4.2 |
| (Refusal/NA) | 0.4 | 0.4 | 0.5 |

Q341 [UntdIrel]
At any time in the next 20 years, do you think it is likely or unlikely that there will be a united Ireland?
**PROBE: Very likely/unlikely or quite likely/unlikely**

%
6.9 Very likely
23.7 Quite likely
26.6 Quite unlikely
34.0 Very unlikely
5.0 (Even chance)
3.6 (Don't Know)
0.3 (Refusal/NA)

n=1519

## CLASS AND RACE (VERSION A)

**VERSION A: ASK ALL**

Q343 [SCOpport]
To what extent do you think a person's social class affects his or her opportunities in Northern Ireland today ... **READ OUT** ...

%
20.0 ... a great deal
38.8 quite a lot
33.4 not very much
6.3 or - not at all?
- Other answer **(WRITE IN)**
0.9 (Don't Know)
0.5 (Refusal/NA)

Q346 [SCImpAgo]
Do you think social class is **more** or **less** important now in affecting a person's opportunities than it was 10 years ago, or has there been no real change?

%
17.3 **More** important now
35.2 **Less** important now
45.3 No change
1.6 (Don't Know)
0.5 (Refusal/NA)

Q347 [SCImpFut]
Do you think that in 10 years' time social class will be more or less important than it is now in affecting a person's opportunities, or will there be no real change?

%
16.0 **More** important in 10 years' time
31.3 **Less** important in 10 years' time
49.8 No change
2.3 (Don't Know)
0.5 (Refusal/NA)

Q348 [SRSocCl]
CARD
Most people see themselves as belonging to a particular social class. Please look at this card and tell me which social class you would say **you** belong to?

Q349 [PrSocCl]
And which social class would you say your **parents** belonged to when you started at primary school?

|  | [SRSocCl] | [PrSocCl] |
|---|---|---|
|  | % | % |
| Upper middle | 1.3 | 2.1 |
| Middle | 27.5 | 17.8 |
| Upper working | 18.4 | 14.4 |
| Working | 49.6 | 57.8 |
| Poor | 1.9 | 7.2 |
| (Don't Know) | 0.5 | 0.1 |
| (Refusal/NA) | 0.7 | 0.7 |

n=765

Q350 **ASK ALL**
[RaceOrNI]
CARD
To which of these groups do you consider you belong?       n=1519
%
0.0 BLACK: of African or Caribbean or other origin
0.0 ASIAN: of Indian origin
     – ASIAN: of Pakistani origin
     – ASIAN: of Bangladeshi origin
0.2 ASIAN: of Chinese origin
0.2 ASIAN: of other origin **(WRITE IN)**
99.3 WHITE
0.1 MIXED: of mixed origin **(WRITE IN)**
0.0 (Don't Know)
0.1 (Refusal/NA)

**VERSION A: ASK ALL**                                    n=765
Q355 [PrejChn]
Firstly thinking of **Chinese** people – that is people whose families were originally from China or Hong Kong – who now live in Northern Ireland. Do you think there is a lot of prejudice against them in Northern Ireland nowadays, a little, or hardly any?

Q356 [PrejAs]
And **Asians** – that is, people whose families were originally from India, Pakistan or Bangladesh – who now live in Northern Ireland. Do you think there is a lot of prejudice against them in Northern Ireland nowadays, a little, or hardly any?

Q357 [PrjTrav]
And what about **travellers** – that is people who have no permanent home but travel from site to site. Do you think there is a lot of prejudice against them in Northern Ireland nowadays, a little or hardly any?

|  | [PrejChn] | [PrejAs] | [PrjTrav] |
|---|---|---|---|
|  | % | % | % |
| A lot | 7.2 | 9.6 | 45.1 |
| A little | 33.6 | 36.1 | 37.4 |
| Hardly any | 53.8 | 49.4 | 14.3 |
| (Don't Know) | 5.0 | 4.6 | 2.8 |
| (Refusal/NA) | 0.3 | 0.3 | 0.3 |

Q358 [PrejNow]
Do you think there is generally **more** racial prejudice in Northern Ireland now than there was 5 years ago, **less**, or about the **same** amount?
%
12.1 More now
19.0 Less now
63.3 About the same
4.2 Other answer **(WRITE IN)**
0.9 (Don't Know)
0.6 (Refusal/NA)

Q361 [PrejFut]
Do you think there will be **more, less** or about the **same** amount of racial prejudice in Northern Ireland in 5 years time compared with now?
%
10.6 More in 5 years
17.6 Less
65.8 About the same
0.9 Other answer **(WRITE IN)**
4.4 (Don't Know)
0.6 (Refusal/NA)

Q364 [SRPrej]
How would you describe yourself ... **READ OUT** ...
%
0.7 ...as very prejudiced against people of other races,
10.2 a little prejudiced,
87.7 or – not prejudiced at all?
0.4 Other answer **(WRITE IN)**
0.3 (Don't Know)
0.6 (Refusal/NA)

Q367 [ChnJob]
On the whole, do you think people of Chinese origin in Northern Ireland are **not** given jobs these days **because** of their race ... **READ OUT** ...

Q368 [AsJob]
And on the whole, do you think people of Asian origin in Northern Ireland are **not** given jobs these days **because** of their race ... **READ OUT** ...

|  | [ChnJob] | [AsJob] |
|---|---|---|
|  | % | % |
| ... a lot, | 5.2 | 5.7 |
| a little, | 22.6 | 26.9 |
| or, hardly at all? | 56.8 | 52.6 |
| (Don't Know) | 14.7 | 14.2 |
| (Refusal/NA) | 0.6 | 0.6 |

Q369 [RacLawNI]
In Britain there is a law **against** racial discrimination, that is against giving unfair preference to a particular race in housing, jobs and so on. Do you generally **support** or **oppose** the idea of a law for this purpose in Northern Ireland?
%
69.3 Support
26.1 Oppose
4.0 (Don't Know)
0.6 (Refusal/NA)

Q370 [RaceVILw]  n=765
Some people say there should be a special law against attacks on people because of their race. Others say these attacks should be treated by the law like any other attacks. Do you think there should be a special law against racial violence or not?
**PROBE:** Is that definitely or probably should/should not?

%
23.8 Definitely should
26.9 Probably should
25.3 Probably should not
19.7 Definitely should not
3.8 (Don't Know)
0.6 (Refusal/NA)

**IF 'White' AT [RaceOrig]**

Q371 [OBossCh]
Do you think most white people in Northern Ireland would mind or not mind if a suitably qualified person of **Chinese** origin were appointed as their boss?
**IF 'WOULD MIND':** A lot or a little?

Q374 [SBossCh]
And would you personally? Would you mind or not mind?
**IF 'WOULD MIND':** A lot or a little?

|  | [OBossCh] % | [SBossCh] % |
|---|---|---|
| Mind a lot | 10.8 | 3.5 |
| Mind a little | 23.0 | 6.8 |
| Not mind | 61.6 | 87.4 |
| Other answer **(WRITE IN)** | 0.2 | - |
| (Don't Know) | 3.5 | 1.2 |
| (Refusal/NA) | 0.3 | 0.3 |

Q377 [OMarCh]
Do you think that **most** white people in Northern Ireland would mind or not mind if one of their close relatives were to marry a person of **Chinese** origin?
**IF 'WOULD MIND':** A lot or a little?

Q380 [SMarCh]
And you personally? Would you mind or not mind?
**IF 'WOULD MIND':** A lot or a little?

|  | [OMarCh] % | [SMarCh] % |
|---|---|---|
| Mind a lot | 18.9 | 10.2 |
| Mind a little | 35.9 | 21.6 |
| Not mind | 38.5 | 64.8 |
| Other answer **(WRITE IN)** | 0.3 | 0.3 |
| (Don't Know) | 5.2 | 1.7 |
| (Refusal/NA) | 0.6 | 0.6 |

53

Q383 [OBossAs]  n=765
Do you think most white people in Northern Ireland would mind or not mind if a suitably qualified person of **Asian** origin were appointed as their boss?
**IF 'WOULD MIND':** A lot or a little?

Q386 [SBossAs]
And would you personally?
**IF 'WOULD MIND':** A lot or a little?

|  | [OBossAs] % | [SBossAs] % |
|---|---|---|
| Mind a lot | 11.1 | 4.9 |
| Mind a little | 31.9 | 13.4 |
| Not mind | 50.8 | 79.3 |
| Other answer **(WRITEIN)** | 0.5 | - |
| (Don't Know) | 4.4 | 1.1 |
| (Refusal/NA) | 0.6 | 0.6 |

Q389 [OMarAs]
Do you think that **most** white people in Northern Ireland would mind or not mind if one of their close relatives were to marry a person of **Asian** origin?
**IF 'WOULD MIND':** A lot or a little?

Q389 [SMarAs]
And you personally?
**IF 'WOULD MIND':** A lot or a little?

|  | [OMarAs] % | [SMarAs] % |
|---|---|---|
| Mind a lot | 18.6 | 12.3 |
| Mind a little | 41.9 | 24.4 |
| Not mind | 34.3 | 60.8 |
| Other answer **(WRITE IN)** | 0.5 | 0.3 |
| (Don't Know) | 3.4 | 1.0 |
| (Refusal/NA) | 0.6 | 0.6 |

54

## POLITICAL TRUST (VERSION A)

### VERSION A: ASK ALL

**Q396** [GovtWork]
CARD
Which of these statements best describes your opinion on the present system of governing the UK?

%
3.5 Works extremely well and could not be improved
30.9 Could be improved in small ways but mainly works well
40.3 Could be improved quite a lot
23.2 Needs a great deal of improvement
1.8 (Don't Know)
0.3 (Refusal/NA)

**Q397** [Lords]
Do you think that the House of Lords should remain as it is or is some change needed?

30.4 Remain as is
57.1 Change needed
12.1 (Don't Know)
0.3 (Refusal/NA)

**IF WANTING CHANGE IN THE HOUSE OF LORDS (IF 'change needed' AT [Lords])**

**Q398** [LordShow]
Do you think the House of Lords should be ... READ OUT

%
16.1 ... replaced by a different body,
21.9 abolished and replaced by nothing,
18.2 or, should there be some other kind of change?
0.9 (Don't Know)
12.5 (Refusal/NA)

### VERSION A: ASK ALL

**Q399** [Monarchy]
How about the monarchy or the royal family in the UK? How important or unimportant do you think it is for the UK to continue to have a monarchy ... READ OUT ...

%
29.7 ... very important,
27.0 quite important,
16.3 not very important,
12.1 not at all important,
13.3 or, do you think the monarchy should be abolished?
1.1 (Don't Know)
0.5 (Refusal/NA)

**Q400** CARD
Suppose a law was being considered by Parliament which you thought was really unjust and harmful. Which, if any, of the things on this card do you think you would do?
Any others?
CODE ALL THAT APPLY
Multicoded (Maximum of 8 codes)

%
50.3 Contact my MP [DoMP]
12.0 Speak to an influential person [DoSpk]
9.2 Contact a government department [DoGov]
11.1 Contact radio, TV or newspaper [DoTV]
54.3 Sign a petition [DoSign]
7.1 Raise the issue in an organisation I already belong to [DoRais]
13.3 Go on a protest or demonstration [DoProt]
5.9 Form a group of like-minded people [DoGrp]
12.9 (No, none of these) [DoNone]
0.6 (Don't know)
0.5 (Refusal/NA)

**Q401** CARD
And have you ever done any of the things on this card about a government action which you thought was unjust and harmful? Which ones? Any others?
CODE ALL THAT APPLY
Multicoded (Maximum of 8 codes)

%
13.1 Contacted my MP [DoneMP]
2.5 Spoke to an influential person [DoneSpk]
2.4 Contacted a government department [DoneGov]
3.4 Contacted radio, TV or newspaper [DoneTV]
33.8 Signed a petition [DoneSign]
3.5 Raised the issue in an organisation I already belong to [DoneRais]
11.3 Gone on a protest or demonstration [DoneProt]
0.8 Formed a group of like-minded people [DoneGrp]
55.3 (No, none of these) [DoneNone]
0.7 (Don't know)
- (Refusal/NA)

**Q402** [BreakLaw]
Are there any circumstances in which **you** might break a law to which you were very strongly opposed?

%
26.2 Yes
70.8 No
2.7 (Don't Know)
0.3 (Refusal/NA)

Q403 [CoalitIn]
Which do you think is generally better for the UK ...
READ OUT ...
%
41.0  ... to have a government formed by one political party,
52.3  or, for two or more parties to get together to form a
       government?
6.4   (Don't Know)
0.3   (Refusal/NA)

Q404 [VoteSyst]
Some people say that we should change the **parliamentary**
voting system to allow smaller political parties to get
a fairer share of MPs. Others say that we should keep
the voting system as it is, to produce more effective
government. Which view comes closest to your own ...
READ OUT ...
IF ASKED, REFERS TO 'PROPORTIONAL REPRESENTATION'
%
38.2  ... that we should change the voting system,
57.1  or, ...keep it as it is?
4.4   (Don't Know)
0.3   (Refusal/NA)

Q405 [ObeyLaw]
In general would you say that people should obey the law
without exception, or are there exceptional occasions on
which people should follow their consciences even if it
means breaking the law?
%
51.4  Obey law without exception
46.2  Follow conscience on occasions
2.1   (Don't Know)
0.3   (Refusal/NA)

Q406 [GovNoSay]
CARD
Please choose a phrase from this card to say how much
you agree or disagree with the following statements.
People like me have no say in what the government does.

Q407 [LoseTch]
Generally speaking, those we elect as MPs lose touch
with people pretty quickly

Q408 [VoteIntr]
Parties are only interested in people's votes, not in
their opinions

                          [GovNoSay]  [LoseTch]  [VoteIntr]
                              %           %          %
Agree strongly               31.1       29.5       29.5
Agree                        43.1       49.1       47.1
Neither agree nor disagree   10.4        9.6        8.8
Disagree                     12.9       10.8       13.0
Disagree strongly             1.7         -         0.3
(Don't Know)                  0.4        0.7        0.9
(Refusal/NA)                  0.4        0.3        0.3

n=765

Q409 [VoteOnly]
Voting is the only way people like me can have any say
about how the government runs things

Q410 [GovComp]
Sometimes politics and government seem so complicated
that a person like me cannot really understand what is
going on

Q411 [PtyNtMat]
It doesn't really matter which party is in power, in the
end things go on much the same

Q412 [InfPolit]
I think I am better informed than most people about
politics and government

                          [VoteOnly]  [GovComp]  [PtyNtMat]
                              %           %          %
Agree strongly               19.0       21.7       17.9
Agree                        54.0       49.6       51.6
Neither agree nor disagree   11.1        9.8        7.4
Disagree                     13.1       15.8       20.1
Disagree strongly             1.9        2.4        2.2
(Don't Know)                  0.4        0.1        0.2
(Refusal/NA)                  0.6        0.6        0.6

                          [InfPolit]
                              %
Agree strongly                2.1
Agree                        16.9
Neither agree nor disagree   25.3
Disagree                     43.6
Disagree strongly            11.5
(Don't Know)                   -
(Refusal/NA)                  0.6

Q413 [GovTrust]
CARD
How much do you trust UK governments of **any** party to
place the needs of the nation above the interests of
their own political party?

Q414 [ClrTrust]
And how much do you trust local councillors of **any** party
to place the needs of their area above the interests of
their own political party?

Q415 [PapTrust]
How much do you trust journalists on national newspapers
to pursue the truth above getting a good story?

|  | [GovTrust] | [ClrTrust] | [PapTrust] |
|---|---|---|---|
|  | % | % | % |
| Just about always | 1.9 | 2.8 | 1.0 |
| Most of the time | 18.9 | 29.7 | 8.0 |
| Only some of the time | 52.1 | 47.8 | 38.4 |
| Almost never | 24.6 | 17.3 | 50.8 |
| (Don't Know) | 1.8 | 1.7 | 1.0 |
| (Refusal/NA) | 0.6 | 0.6 | 0.7 |

Q416 [PolTrust]
And how much do you trust police not to bend the rules in trying to get a conviction?

Q417 [CSTrust]
And how much do you trust top civil servants to stand firm against a minister who wants to provide false information to parliament?

Q418 [MpsTrust]
How much do you trust politicians of **any** party in the UK to tell the truth when they are in a tight corner?

|  | [PolTrust] | [CSTrust] | [MpsTrust] |
|---|---|---|---|
|  | % | % | % |
| Just about always | 7.1 | 4.4 | 0.9 |
| Most of the time | 39.6 | 26.0 | 9.1 |
| Only some of the time | 33.7 | 38.0 | 40.6 |
| Almost never | 16.6 | 24.4 | 46.9 |
| (Don't Know) | 2.4 | 6.6 | 1.9 |
| (Refusal/NA) | 0.6 | 0.6 | 0.6 |

# EUROPE AND INTERNATIONAL RELATIONS (VERSION A)      n=765

**VERSION A: ASK ALL**

Q420 [ECGBClse]
Now a few questions about the UK's relationships with other countries.
As a member state, would you say that the UK's relationship with the European Community should be ... **READ OUT** ...

%
44.7  ... closer,
10.3  less close,
37.0  or, is it about right?
7.4   (Don't Know)
0.6   (Refusal/NA)

Q421 [ECLnkInf]
Do you think that closer links with the European Community would give the UK ... **READ OUT** ...

%
40.7  ... **more** influence in the world,
9.2   **less** influence in the world,
44.3  or, would it make no difference?
5.2   (Don't Know)
0.6   (Refusal/NA)

Q422 [ECLnkStr]
And would closer links with the European Community make the UK ... **READ OUT** ...

%
47.6  ... **stronger** economically,
12.3  **weaker** economically,
32.0  or, would it make no difference?
7.4   (Don't Know)
0.6   (Refusal/NA)

Q423 [Nation]
On the whole, do you think the UK's interests are better served by ... **READ OUT** ...

%
41.1  ... closer links with Western Europe,
15.3  or, closer links with America?
26.1  (Both equally)
9.2   (Neither)
7.6   (Don't Know)
0.6   (Refusal/NA)

Q424 [UnitEEC]
Which of these comes closer to your views ... **READ OUT** ...

%
47.8  ...the UK should do all it can to unite fully with the European Community,
41.1  or, the UK should do all it can to protect its independence from the European Community?
10.6  (Don't Know)
0.6   (Refusal/NA)

Q425 [ECPolicy]
**CARD**
Do you think the UK's long-term policy should be ...
**READ OUT** ...
%
6.2   ... to leave the European Community, 
23.5  to stay in the EC and try to **reduce** its powers,
23.4  to leave things as they are,
26.9  to stay in the EC and try to **increase** the EC's powers,
12.0  or, to work for the formation of a single European government?
7.3   (Don't Know)
0.6   (Refusal/NA)

n=765

Q426 [EcuView]
**CARD**
And here are three statements about the future of the pound in the European Community. 
Which **one** comes closest to your view?
%
25.3  **Replace** the pound by a single currency
15.1  Use **both** the pound and a new European currency in the UK
54.5  Keep the pound as the **only** currency for the UK
4.4   (Don't Know)
0.6   (Refusal/NA)

Q427 [ECVotRes]
**CARD**
Which of the four statements on this card comes closest to the way you would vote in an European election?
%
31.9  I would vote for a party regardless of the candidate
37.4  I would vote for a party only if I approved of the candidate
9.9   I would vote for a candidate regardless of his or her party
18.3  I would generally not vote
1.6   (Don't Know)
0.9   (Refusal/NA)

Q428 [NIreland]
Do you think the long-term policy for Northern Ireland should be for it ... **READ OUT** ...
%
62.7  ... to remain part of the United Kingdom,
26.7  or, to reunify with the rest of Ireland?
4.8   Other **(WRITE IN)**
4.0   (Don't Know)
0.5   (Refusal/NA)

242

Q431 [DecFutNI]
And who do you think should have the right to decide what the long-term future of Northern Ireland should be? Should it be ...
%
62.8  ... the people in Northern Ireland on their own,
24.4  or, the people of Ireland, both north and south,
10.0  or, the people both in Northern Ireland and in Britain?
1.7   Other answer **(WRITE IN)**
1.0   (Don't Know)
0.3   (Refusal/NA)

n=765

Q434 [TroopOut]
Some people think that government policy towards Northern Ireland should include a complete withdrawal of British troops.
Would you personally **support** or **oppose** such a policy?
**PROBE:** Strongly or a little?
%
12.6  Support strongly
15.4  Support a little
48.6  Oppose strongly
15.4  Oppose a little
2.2   Other **(WRITE IN)**
5.2   (Don't Know)
0.6   (Refusal/NA)

## CIVIL LIBERTIES (VERSION A)

n=765

**Q439** [PaprDef]
Suppose a newspaper got hold of confidential government defence plans and wanted to publish them ... **READ OUT** ...

%
19.7 Should the newspaper be allowed to publish the plans,
75.6 or, should the government have the power to prevent publication?
4.1 (Don't Know)
0.6 (Refusal/NA)

**Q440** [LeakDef]
CARD
Suppose the government wanted to find out the name of the person who had leaked these confidential defence plans. Should the paper have the legal right to keep the person's name secret, or not?

%
25.9 Definitely should have the legal right to keep name secret
13.3 Probably should
18.6 Probably should **not**
37.3 Definitely should **not** have the legal right
4.4 (Don't Know)
0.6 (Refusal/NA)

**Q441** [PaprEcon]
Now suppose a newspaper got hold of confidential government economic plans ... **READ OUT** ...

%
43.7 Should the newspaper be allowed to publish the plans,
50.9 or, should the government have the power to prevent publication?
4.8 (Don't Know)
0.6 (Refusal/NA)

**Q442** [LeakEcon]
CARD
Suppose the government wanted to find out the name of the person who had leaked these confidential economic plans. Should the paper have the legal right to keep the person's name secret, or not?

%
28.0 Definitely should have the legal right to keep name secret
18.0 Probably should
17.9 Probably should **not**
30.7 Definitely should **not** have the legal right
4.8 (Don't Know)
0.6 (Refusal/NA)

n=765

**Q443** [VCRoads]
CARD
Some people say that there ought to be video cameras in public places to detect criminals. Others say this cuts down on everyone's privacy. Do you think video cameras **should** or **should not** be allowed in the following places?
...on roads to detect speeding drivers?

**Q444** [VCFootbl]
CARD AGAIN
(Should or should not video cameras be allowed...)
..at football grounds to detect troublemakers?

**Q445** [VCVandal]
CARD AGAIN
(Should or should not video cameras be allowed...)
..on housing estates to detect vandals?

|  | [VCRoads] | [VCFootbl] | [VCVandal] |
|---|---|---|---|
|  | % | % | % |
| Definitely be allowed | 65.4 | 82.6 | 63.8 |
| Probably be allowed | 23.2 | 14.0 | 20.1 |
| Probably **not** be allowed | 5.9 | 1.7 | 10.6 |
| Definitely **not** be allowed | 4.8 | 1.1 | 4.6 |
| (Don't Know) | 0.4 | 0.2 | 0.7 |
| (Refusal/NA) | 0.3 | 0.3 | 0.3 |

**Q446** [RaceGlty]
Suppose two people - one white, one black - each appear in court, charged with a crime they did **not** commit. What do you think their chances are of being found **guilty**? ... **READ OUT** ...

%
0.9 ... the white person is more likely to be found guilty,
52.8 they have the same chance,
41.5 or, the black person is more likely to be found guilty?
4.3 (Don't Know)
0.6 (Refusal/NA)

**Q447** [RichGlty]
Now suppose another two people from different backgrounds - one rich, one poor - each appear in court charged with a crime they did **not** commit. What do you think their chances are of being found **guilty**?
... **READ OUT** ...

%
1.1 ... the rich person is more likely to be found guilty,
38.9 they have the same chance,
57.1 or, the poor person is more likely to be found guilty?
2.1 (Don't Know)
0.7 (Refusal/NA)

Q448 [RelgGlty]
Now suppose another two people of different religions - one Protestant, one Catholic - each appear in court charged with a crime they did **not** commit. What do you think their chances are of being found **guilty**?
... READ OUT ...

%
1.7   The Protestant is more likely to be found guilty
78.4  they have the same chance
14.5  or, the Catholic is more likely to be found guilty?
4.8   (Don't Know)
0.6   (Refusal/NA)

Q449 [ChOppWom]
CARD
Now I want to ask about some changes that have been happening in the UK over the years. For each one, please tell me whether you think it has gone too far, or not gone far enough.
How about attempts to give equal opportunities to women in the UK?

Q450 [ChOppMin]
Attempts to give equal opportunities to black people and Asians in the UK?
(Has it gone too far, or not far enough?)

Q451 [ChNudSex]
The right to show nudity and sex in films and magazines?
(Has it gone too far, or not far enough?)

|  | [ChOppWom] | [ChOppMin] | [ChNudSex] |
|---|---|---|---|
|  | % | % | % |
| Gone much too far | 1.8 | 2.4 | 34.0 |
| Gone too far | 7.5 | 8.9 | 37.2 |
| About right | 51.8 | 44.6 | 20.7 |
| Not gone far enough | 33.2 | 34.2 | 4.7 |
| Not gone nearly far enough | 3.0 | 2.5 | 1.7 |
| (Don't Know) | 2.1 | 6.8 | 1.1 |
| (Refusal/NA) | 0.6 | 0.6 | 0.6 |

Q452 [ChOppHom]
Attempts to give equal opportunities to homosexuals - that is, gays and lesbians?
(Has it gone too far, or not far enough?)

Q453 [ChGypTrv]
Providing sites for gypsies and travellers to stay?
(Has it gone too far, or not far enough?)

Q454 [ChRgtDem]
The right of people to go on protest marches and demonstrations?
(Has it gone too far, or not far enough?)

|  | [ChOppHom] | [ChGypTrv] | [ChRgtDem] |
|---|---|---|---|
|  | % | % | % |
| Gone much too far | 29.7 | 5.2 | 2.8 |
| Gone too far | 29.7 | 13.2 | 16.8 |
| About right | 27.5 | 35.4 | 64.3 |
| Not gone far enough | 7.9 | 36.7 | 11.3 |
| Not gone nearly far enough | 1.2 | 4.8 | 1.7 |
| (Don't Know) | 3.3 | 4.1 | 2.5 |
| (Refusal/NA) | 0.6 | 0.6 | 0.6 |

Q455 [ChLwStrk]
Laws to make it difficult for people to go on strike?
(Has it gone too far, or not far enough?)

Q456 [ChLegAid]
Giving Legal Aid - that is, financial help with the cost of going to court?
(Has it gone too far, or not far enough?)

|  | [ChLwStrk] | [ChLegAid] |
|---|---|---|
|  | % | % |
| Gone much too far | 4.4 | 4.2 |
| Gone too far | 26.3 | 15.1 |
| About right | 54.1 | 45.8 |
| Not gone far enough | 9.9 | 24.4 |
| Not gone nearly far enough | 0.2 | 3.8 |
| (Don't Know) | 4.5 | 6.1 |
| (Refusal/NA) | 0.6 | 0.6 |

# HOUSING

**ASK ALL**

Q566 *[Hometype]*
Now a few questions on housing
INTERVIEWER CODE FROM OBSERVATION AND CHECK WITH RESPONDENT
Would I be right in describing this accommodation as a ...
READ OUT ONE YOU THINK APPLIES

%
36.0 ... detached house or bungalow,
25.1 ... semi-detached house or bungalow,
34.2 ... terraced house,
3.4 ... self-contained, purpose built flat/maisonette (inc. in tenement block),
0.7 ... self-contained converted flat/maisonette,
- ... room(s) not self-contained.
0.5 Other (**WRITE IN**)
- (Don't Know)
- (Refusal/NA)

Q569 *[HomeEst]*
May I just check, is your home part of a housing estate?
NOTE: MAY BE PUBLIC OR PRIVATE, BUT IT IS THE RESPONDENT'S VIEW WE WANT

%
42.6 Yes, part of estate
57.4 No
- (Don't Know)
- (Refusal/NA)

Q570 *[Tenure1]*
Does your household own or rent this accomodation?
PROBE AS NECESSARY
IF OWNS: Outright or on a mortgage?
IF RENTS: From whom?

%
31.7 OWNS: Own (leasehold/freehold) outright
37.6 OWNS: Buying (leasehold/freehold) on mortgage
23.4 RENTS: Housing executive
0.8 RENTS: Housing Association
0.6 RENTS: Property company
0.5 RENTS: Employer
0.3 RENTS: Other organisation
0.5 RENTS: Relative
3.7 RENTS: Other individual
0.2 Housing Trust
0.7 Rent free, squatting, etc
- (Don't Know)
0.1 (Refusal/NA)

# RELIGION

**ASK ALL**

Q772 *[Religion]*
And now for some questions on some other topics....
Do you regard yourself as belonging to any particular religion?
IF YES: Which?
CODE ONE ONLY - DO NOT PROMPT

%
9.7 No religion
2.6 Christian - no denomination
35.9 Roman Catholic
16.2 Church of Ireland/Anglican
1.1 Baptist
3.9 Methodist
24.7 Presbyterian
0.3 Other Christian
- Hindu
0.0 Jewish
0.2 Muslim
- Sikh
- Buddhist
- Other non-Christian
1.3 Free Presbyterian
1.0 Brethren
0.6 United Reform Church (URC)/Congregational
1.7 Other Protestant
- (Don't Know)
0.7 (Refusal/NA)

Q580 IF NOT REFUSAL AT [Religion]
*[FamRelig]*
In what religion, if any, were you brought up?
PROBE IF NECESSARY: What was your family's religion?
CODE ONE ONLY - DO NOT PROMPT

%
0.6 No religion
1.2 Christian - no denomination
38.6 Roman Catholic
20.4 Church of Ireland/Anglican
0.7 Baptist
4.9 Methodist
28.8 Presbyterian
0.2 Other Christian
- Hindu
0.0 Jewish
0.2 Muslim
- Sikh
- Buddhist
- Other non-Christian
0.4 Free Presbyterian
1.4 Brethren
1.0 United Reform Church (URC)/Congregational
0.8 Other Protestant
- (Don't Know)
0.8 (Refusal/NA)

Q587 **IF GIVING A RELIGION AT [Religion] OR AT [FamRelig]**  [n=1519]
[ChAttend]
Apart from such special occasions as weddings, funerals and baptisms, how often nowadays do you attend services or meetings connected with your religion?
**PROBE AS NECESSARY**

%
45.5 Once a week or more
7.3 Less often but at least once in two weeks
12.1 Less often but at least once a month
8.4 Less often but at least twice a year
3.6 Less often but at least once a year
17.8 Never or practically never
0.2 Varies too much to say
0.1 (Don't Know)
0.8 (Refusal/NA)

## CLASSIFICATION  [n=1519]

Q24 **ASK ALL**
[NumAdult]
**INTERVIEWER: YOU ARE GOING TO ASK ABOUT ALL THE ADULTS AGED 18 OR OVER IN THE HOUSEHOLD. STARTING WITH THE HOH, LIST ALL ADULTS IN DESCENDING ORDER OF AGE.**
Including yourself, how many adults are there in your household, that is, people aged 18 and over whose main residence this is and who are catered for by the same person as yourself or share living accommodation with you?
**ENTER NUMBER OF PERSONS AGED 18 AND OVER**

%
16.3 1 person
51.2 2 persons
18.4 3 persons
8.4 4 persons
5.1 5 persons
0.4 6 persons
0.2 7 persons

Q33 [NumChild]
And how many people are there in your household aged under 18 (INCLUDING CHILDREN)?

%
16.2 1 child
16.8 2 children
8.5 3 children
2.7 4 children
1.0 5 children
0.4 6 children
0.2 7 children

dv [Household]
NUMBER OF PERSONS IN HOUSEHOLD INCLUDING RESPONDENT.

%
12.2 1 person
25.1 2 persons
20.5 3 persons
19.4 4 persons
13.4 5 persons
5.7 6 persons
1.7 7 persons
1.1 8 persons
0.9 9 persons

dv [MarStatNI]
RESPONDENT'S MARITAL STATUS.

%
60.0 Married
1.6 Cohabiting
20.9 Single, no children
2.1 Single parent
9.1 Widowed
2.9 Divorced
3.4 Separated

n=1519

| | | |
|---|---|---|
| dv | | [RSex] |
| | | RESPONDENT'S SEX |
| % | 50.3 | Male |
| | 49.7 | Female |

| | | |
|---|---|---|
| dv | | [RAge] |
| | | RESPONDENT'S AGE LAST BIRTHDAY |
| | | **Median: 42 years** |

| | | |
|---|---|---|
| dv | | [RResp] |
| | | WHETHER RESPONDENT HAS LEGAL RESPONSIBILITY FOR THE ACCOMMODATION (INCLUDING JOINT OR SHARED RESPONSIBILITY) |
| % | 77.2 | Legally responsible |
| | 22.8 | Not legally responsible |

Q614 [SlfMxSch]
Did you ever attend a mixed or integrated school, that is, a school with fairly large numbers of **both** Catholic **and** Protestant children?
IF YES: In Northern Ireland or somewhere else?
%
15.2 Yes, in Northern Ireland
4.2 Yes, somewhere else
80.5 No, did not
0.1 (Don't Know)
0.1 (Refusal/NA)

Q615 [OthChld]
Apart from people you have already mentioned who live in your household, have you any (other) children, including stepchildren, who grew up in your household? 'CHILDREN' MEANS THOSE THEN AGED UNDER 18, AND INCLUDES THOSE NO LONGER LIVING.
%
23.4 Yes
76.6 No
- (Don't Know)
- (Refusal/NA)

IF THERE ARE CHILDREN UNDER 18 IN THE HOUSEHOLD OR ANSWERED 'Yes' AT [OthChild]
Q616 [ChdMxSch]
And have any of your children ever attended a mixed or integrated school, with fairly large numbers of both Catholics and Protestants attending?
IF YES: In Northern Ireland or somewhere else?
%
11.2 Yes, in Northern Ireland
0.9 Yes, somewhere else
51.5 No, did not
0.1 (Don't Know)
0.1 (Refusal/NA)

247

n=1519

Q617 [DutyResp]
ASK ALL
Who is the person mainly responsible for general domestic duties in this household?
%
44.9 Respondent mainly
41.3 Someone else mainly
13.8 Duties shared equally
- (Don't Know)
- (Refusal/NA)

IF 'someone else mainly' OR 'duties shared equally' AT [DutyResp]
Q618 PLEASE SPECIFY THIS PERSON'S/THESE PEOPLE'S RELATIONSHIP TO RESPONDENT
Multicoded (Maximum of 6 codes)
%
32.4 Wife/female partner of respondent [DutyWife]
13.8 Mother/mother-in-law of respondent [DutyMum]
3.3 Husband/male partner of respondent [DutyHusb]
3.5 Other female in household [DutyFem]
1.3 Other male in household [DutyMale]
2.0 Other answer [DutyOthr]
- (Don't know)
- (Refusal/NA)

IF THERE ARE CHILDREN UNDER 18 IN THE HOUSEHOLD
Q620 [ChldResp]
Who is the person mainly responsible for the general care of the child(ren) here?
%
18.5 Respondent mainly
18.9 Someone else mainly
8.4 Care shared equally
0.0 (Don't Know)
- (Refusal/NA)

IF 'someone else mainly' OR 'care shared equally' AT [Chldresp]
Q621 PLEASE SPECIFY THIS PERSON'S/THESE PEOPLE'S RELATIONSHIP TO RESPONDENT
Multicoded (Maximum of 6 codes)
%
18.1 Wife/female partner of respondent [ChldWife]
5.9 Mother/mother-in-law of respondent [ChldMum]
2.0 Husband/male partner of respondent [ChldHusb]
0.9 Other female in household [ChldFem]
0.3 Other male in household [ChldMale]
0.5 Other answer [ChldOthr]
0.0 (Don't know)
- (Refusal/NA)

n=1519

Q623 **ASK ALL**
[TEA]
How old were you when you completed your continuous full-time education?
PROBE IF NECESSARY

%
35.1 15 or under
29.3 16
12.0 17
8.7 18
11.1 19 or over
1.3 Still at school
2.4 Still at college, polytechnic or university
- Other answer (WRITE IN)
- (Don't Know)
0.1 (Refusal/NA)

Q626 [SchQual]
CARD
Have you passed any of the examinations on this card?

%
47.1 Yes
52.9 No
- (Don't Know)
- (Refusal/NA)

Q627 IF 'yes' AT [SchQual]
Which ones? PROBE: Any others?
CODE ALL THAT APPLY
Multicoded (Maximum of 16 codes)

%
11.0 CSE Grades 2-5  [EdQual1]
- - - - - - - - - - - - - - - - - - - - - - - - - - - - - - -
- GCSE Grades D-G
- - - - - - - - - - - - - - - - - - - - - - - - - - - - - - -
38.8 CSE-Grade 1  [EdQual2]
- GCE 'O' level
- GCSE - Grades A-C
- School Certificate
- Scottish (SCE) Ordinary
- Scottish School-leaving Certificate lower grade
- SUPE Ordinary
- Northern Ireland Junior Certificate
- - - - - - - - - - - - - - - - - - - - - - - - - - - - - - -
17.1 GCE 'A' level/'S' level  [EdQual3]
- Higher school certificate
- Matriculation
- Scottish SCE/SLC/SUPE at Higher Grade
- Northern Ireland Senior Certificate
- - - - - - - - - - - - - - - - - - - - - - - - - - - - - - -
0.6 Overseas school leaving exam or certificate  [EdQual4]
- - - - - - - - - - - - - - - - - - - - - - - - - - - - - - -
- (Don't know)
- (Refusal/NA)

n=1519

Q628 **ASK ALL**
[PSchQual]
CARD
And have you passed any of the exams or got any of the qualifications on this card?

%
45.7 Yes
54.3 No
- (Don't Know)
- (Refusal/NA)

Q628 IF 'yes' AT [PSchQual]
Which ones? PROBE: Any others?
CODE ALL THAT APPLY
Multicoded (Maximum of 12 codes)

%
8.0 Recognised trade apprenticeship completed  [EdQual5]
15.7 RSA/other clerical, commercial qualification  [EdQual6]
9.5 City & Guilds Certificate - Craft/Intermediate/Ordinary/Part I  [EdQual7]
5.0 City & Guilds Certificate - Advanced/Final/ Part II or Part III  [EdQual8]
1.6 City & Guilds Certificate - Full technological  [EdQual9]
3.2 BEC/TEC General/Ordinary National Certificate (ONC) or Diploma (OND)  [EdQual10]
3.2 BEC/TEC Higher/Higher National Certificate (HNC) or Diploma (HND)  [EdQual11]
2.3 Teacher training qualification  [EdQual12]
2.6 Nursing qualification  [EdQual13]
2.6 Other technical or business qualification/certificate  [EdQual14]
6.5 University or CNAA degree or diploma  [EdQual15]
5.1 Other recognised academic or vocational qualification (WRITE IN)  [EdQual16]
0.0 (Don't know)
- (Refusal/NA)

Q633 IF NOT 'in paid work' OR 'waiting to take up paid work' AT [REconAct]
[JobChk]
May I just check, have you ever had a job?

%
41.8 Yes
6.4 No never
- (Don't Know)
- (Refusal/NA)

ASK ALL WHO HAVE EVER WORKED (IF 'in paid work' OR 'waiting to take up paid work' AT [REconAct] OR 'Yes' AT [JobChk]) n=1421

Q634 [RTitle] (NOT ON THE DATA FILE)
IF IN PAID WORK (IF 'in paid work' AT [REconAct]): Now I want to ask you about your present job.
What is your job?
PROBE IF NECESSARY: What is the name or title of the job?
IF WAITING TO TAKE UP PAID WORK (IF 'waiting to take up paid work' AT [REconAct]): Now I want to ask you about your future job.
What is your job?
PROBE IF NECESSARY: What is the name or title of the job?
IF NOT IN PAID WORK (OR WAITING TO TAKE UP PAID WORK) BUT EVER HAD JOB IN THE PAST (IF 'Yes' AT [JobChk]): Now I want to ask you about your last job.
What was your job?
PROBE IF NECESSARY: What was the name or title of the job?
Open Question (Maximum of 50 characters)

Q635 [RTypeWk] (NOT ON THE DATA FILE)
What kind of work (do/will/did) you do most of the time?
IF RELEVANT: What materials/machinery (do/will/did) you use?
Open Question (Maximum of 50 characters)

Q636 [RTrain] (NOT ON THE DATA FILE)
What training or qualifications (are/were) needed for that job?
Open Question (Maximum of 50 characters)

[RSuper]
(Do/Will/Did) you directly supervise or (are you/will you be/were you) directly responsible for the work of any other people?
%
30.2   Yes
69.6   No
0.2    (Don't Know)
0.1    (Refusal/NA)

IF 'Yes' AT [RSuper]
[RMany]
Q638   How many?
       Median: 5

ASK ALL WHO HAVE EVER WORKED (IF 'in paid work' OR 'waiting to take up paid work' AT [REconAct] OR 'Yes' AT [JobChk]) n=1421

Q639 [RSupMan]
Can I just check, (are you/will you be/were you) a ...
READ OUT ...
%
15.3   ...manager,
13.3   ...foreman or supervisor,
71.4   or not?
-      (Don't Know)
-      (Refusal/NA)

Q640 [REmplyee]
Can I just check: (are you/will you be/were you) ...
READ OUT ...
%
86.8   ... an employee
13.2   or, self-employed?
-      (Don't Know)
-      (Refusal/NA)

IF EMPLOYEE IN CURRENT OR LAST JOB
(IF 'employee' AT [REmplyee] )

Q641 [Premises]
(Is/was) where you (work/will work/worked) your employer's only premises, or (are/were) there other premises elsewhere?
%
28.5   Employer's only premises
58.2   Employer has other premises elsewhere
-      (Don't Know)
-      (Refusal/NA)

ASK ALL WHO HAVE EVER WORKED (IF 'paid work' OR 'waiting to take up paid work' AT [REconAct] OR 'Yes' AT [JobChk])

Q642 [REmpMake] (NOT ON THE DATA FILE)
What (does/did) your employer/you make or do at the place where you usually (work/will work/worked) (from)?
Open Question (Maximum of 50 characters)

Q643 [REmpWork]
Including yourself, how many people (are/were) employed at the place where you usually (work/will work/worked) (from)?
IF SELF-EMPLOYED: (do/will/did) you have any employees?
IF YES: PROBE FOR CORRECT PRECODE
%
3.6    None
23.4   Under 10
14.9   10-24
23.0   25-99
21.6   100-499
13.0   500 or more
0.4    (Don't Know)
0.1    (Refusal/NA)

Q644 [RPartFul]
(Is/Was) the job ... READ OUT ...
% 
82.7 ...full-time (30+ HOURS)
17.2 or, part-time (10-29 HOURS)?
- (Don't Know)
0.1 (Refusal/NA)

**ASK ALL**
Q659 [UnionSA]
Are you **now** a member of a trade union or staff association?
**CODE FIRST TO APPLY**
%
21.0 Yes, trade union
4.8 Yes, staff association
74.0 No
0.2 (Don't Know)
- (Refusal/NA)

**IF 'no' AT [UnionSA]**
Q660 [TUSAEver]
Have you **ever** been a member of a trade union or staff association?
**CODE FIRST TO APPLY**
%
20.3 Yes, trade union
2.7 Yes, staff association
51.0 No
0.1 (Don't Know)
0.2 (Refusal/NA)

n=1421

n=1519

Q664 **IF MARRIED OR COHABITING**
[SEconAct] (Figures refer to the first answer on the list)
Which of these descriptions applied to what your (husband/wife/partner) was doing last week, that is the seven days ending last Sunday?
PROBE: Any others?
**CODE ALL THAT APPLY**
Multicoded (Maximum of 11 codes)
%
0.7 In full-time education (not paid for by employer, including on vacation)
0.2 On government training/employment programme (eg. Employment Training, Youth Training, etc)
52.5 In paid work (or away temporarily) for at least 10 hours in week
- Waiting to take up paid work already accepted
5.9 Unemployed and registered at a benefit office
0.2 Unemployed, **not** registered, but actively looking for a job
0.7 Unemployed, wanting a job (of at least 10 hrs a week), but **not** actively looking for a job
5.5 Permanently sick or disabled
13.0 Wholly retired from home
21.0 Looking after the home
0.2 (Doing something else) (WRITE IN)
- (Don't know)
0.2 (Refusal/NA)

n=935

Q665 **IF SPOUSE/PARTNER IS NOT IN WORK** (IF 'in full-time education', 'on government training scheme', 'unemployed', 'permanently sick', 'wholly retired', 'looking after home', 'doing something else' AT [SEconAct])
[SLastJob]
How long ago did your (husband/wife/partner) last have a paid job (other than the government programme you mentioned) of at least 10 hours a week?
%
4.1 Within past 12 months
11.8 Over 1, up to 5 years ago
10.4 Over 5, up to 10 years ago
10.3 Over 10, up to 20 years ago
7.7 Over 20 years ago
2.9 Never had a paid job of 10+ hours a week
0.3 (Don't Know)
- (Refusal/NA)

n=908

ASK ALL WHOSE SPOUSE/PARTNER HAS EVER WORKED
(IF 'in paid work'/'waiting to take up paid work' AT
[SEconAt] OR 'Within past 12 months'/'Over 1, up to 5
years ago'/ 'Over 5, up to 10 years ago'/ 'Over 10, up to
20 years ago'/ 'Over 20 years ago' AT [SLastJob])

Q666 [STitle] (NOT ON THE DATA FILE)
IF SPOUSE/PARTNER IN PAID WORK (IF 'paid work' AT
[SEconAct]): Now I want to ask you about your
(husband's/wife's/partner's) present job.
What is (his/her) job?
PROBE IF NECESSARY: What is the name or title of that
job?
IF SPOUSE/PARTNER IS WAITING TO TAKE UP PAID WORK (IF
'waiting to take up paid work' AT [SEconAct]): Now I
want to ask you about your (husband's/wife's/partner's)
future job.
What is (his/her) job?
PROBE IF NECESSARY: What is the name or title of that
job?
IF SPOUSE/PARTNER IS NOT IN PAID WORK (OR WAITING TO
TAKE UP PAID WORK) BUT HAS EVER WORKED IN THE PAST (IF
'Within past 12 months'/ 'Over 1, up to 5 years go'/
'Over 5, up to 10 years ago'/ 'Over 10, up to 20 years
ago' AT [SLastJob]): Now I want to ask you about your (husband's/wife/partner's) past
job.
What was (his/her) job?
PROBE IF NECESSARY: What was the name or title of that
job?
Open Question (Maximum of 50 characters)

Q667 [STypeWk] (NOT ON THE DATA FILE)
What kind of work (does/will/did) (he/she) do most of
the time?
IF RELEVANT: What materials/machinery (does/will/did)
(he/she) use?
Open Question (Maximum of 50 characters)

Q668 [STrain] (NOT ON THE DATA FILE)
What training or qualifications (are/were) needed for
that job?
Open Question (Maximum of 50 characters)

Q670 [SSuper]
(Does/Will/Did) (he/she) directly supervise or
(is/will/was) (he/she) (be) directly responsible for the
work of any other people?
%
28.1  Yes
69.8  No
2.0   (Don't Know)
0.1   (Refusal/NA)

n=908

Q670 IF 'Yes' AT [SSuper]
[SMaryj]
How many?
Range: 1 ... 9999
Median: 5

ASK ALL WHOSE SPOUSE/PARTNER HAS EVER WORKED (IF 'in
paid work'/'waiting to take up paid work' AT [SEconAt]
OR 'Within past 12 months'/ 'Over 1, up to 5 years go'/
'Over 5, up to 10 years ago'/ 'Over 10, up to 20 years
ago'/ 'Over 20 years ago' AT [SLastJob])

Q671 [SSupMan]
Can I just check, (is/will/was) (he/she) (be) ...
READ OUT ...
14.5  ...a manager,
13.7  a foreman or supervisor,
71.6  or not?
 -    (Don't Know)
0.3   (Refusal/NA)

Q672 [SEmploye]
(Is/Will/Was) (he/she) (be) ... READ OUT ...
88.5  ...an employee
11.2  or, self-employed?
 -    (Don't Know)
0.3   (Refusal/NA)

Q673 [SEmpMake] (NOT ON DATA FILE)
What (does/will/was) the employer (IF SELF-EMPLOYED:
(he/she)) make or do at the place where (he/she) usually
(works/will work/worked)?
Open Question (Maximum of 50 characters)

Q674 [SEmpWork]
Including (himself/herself), roughly how many people
(are/were) employed at the place where (he/she) usually
(works/will work/worked) (from)?
IF SELF-EMPLOYED: (does/will/did) (he/she) have any
employees?
IF YES: PROBE FOR CORRECT PRECODE
%
4.7   None
18.9  Under 10
17.0  10-24
21.3  25-99
22.4  100-499
13.1  500 or more
2.3   (Don't Know)
0.3   (Refusal/NA)

Q675 [SPartFul]
(Is/Was) the job ... **READ OUT** ...
%
80.6 ... full-time (30+ HOURS)
19.0 or, part-time (10-29 HOURS)?
- (Don't Know)
0.4 (Refusal/NA)

**IF MARRIED OR COHABITING**
Q690 [ReligSam]
Is your (husband/wife/ partner) the same religion as you?
**PROBE IF NECESSARY**
%
90.2 Yes, same religion
7.1 No, not same religion
2.2 No religion at all
0.1 (Don't Know)
0.3 (Refusal/NA)

**ASK ALL**   n=1519
Q691 [CarOwn]
Do you, or does anyone else in your household, own or have the regular use of a car or a van?
%
74.4 Yes
25.6 No
- (Don't Know)
- (Refusal/NA)

Q692 [AnyBNew]
**CARD**
Do you or does your (wife/husband/ partner) receive any of the **state** benefits on this card at present?
%
34.3 Yes
65.3 No
- (Don't Know)
0.5 (Refusal/NA)

**IF 'yes' AT [AnyBNew]**
Q693 Which ones?
Any others?
**CODE ALL THAT APPLY**
%
Multicoded (Maximum of 12 codes)
1.6 Unemployment benefit [BenftN1]
16.0 Income support [BenftN2]
3.6 One-parent benefit [BenftN3]
2.6 Family credit [BenftN4]
9.6 Housing benefit (rent-rebate) [BenftN5]
0.8 Statutory sick pay/sickness benefit [BenftN6]
7.3 Invalidity benefit [BenftN7]
5.0 Disability living allowance [BenftN8]
2.6 Widow's pension [BenftN10]
3.1 Attendance allowance [BenftN13]
0.6 Severe disablement allowance [BenftN14]
1.2 Other state benefit(s) (**PLEASE SAY WHAT**) [BenftN12]
0.1 (Don't know)
0.5 (Refusal/NA)

---

**ASK ALL**   n=1519
Q708 [Disab]
Do you have any long-standing health problems or disabilities which limit what you can do at work, at home or in your leisure time?
**INTERVIEWER: 'LONG-STANDING' MEANS HAVE HAD PROBLEM FOR 3 YEARS OR MORE OR EXPECT PROBLEM TO LAST FOR 3 YEARS OR MORE**
%
20.7 Yes
79.2 No
- (Don't Know)
0.1 (Refusal/NA)

Q709 [EvrLivGB]
Have you **ever** lived in mainland Britain for more than a year?
%
16.9 Yes
83.1 No
- (Don't Know)
- (Refusal/NA)

Q710 [EvrLivER]
And have you **ever** lived in the Republic of Ireland for more than a year?
%
4.6 Yes
95.4 No
- (Don't Know)
- (Refusal/NA)

Q711 [UniNatID]
Generally speaking, do you think of yourself as a unionist, a nationalist or neither?
%
42.3 Unionist
20.0 Nationalist
36.8 Neither
0.3 (Don't Know)
0.6 (Refusal/NA)

**IF 'Unionist' OR 'Nationalist' AT [UniNatID]**
Q712 [UniNatSt]
Would you call yourself a very strong (unionist/nationalist), fairly strong, or not very strong?
%
9.3 Very strong
26.9 Fairly strong
26.2 Not very strong
- (Don't Know)
0.9 (Refusal/NA)

**ASK ALL**

Q713 *[HhIncome]*
CARD
Which of the letters on this card represents the total income of your household from **all** sources **before** tax? Please just tell me the letter.
**NOTE: INCLUDES INCOME FROM BENEFITS, SAVINGS, ETC.**

n=1519

**ASK ALL RESPONDENTS WHO ARE WORKING
(IF 'in paid work' AT [REconAct])**

n=784

Q714 *[REarn]*
CARD
Which of the letters on this card represents your **own** gross or total **earnings**, before deduction of income tax and national insurance?

|  | [HhIncome] % | [REarn] % |
|---|---|---|
| less than £3,999 | 6.4 | 8.6 |
| £4,000 - £5,999 | 10.9 | 12.9 |
| £6,000 - £7,999 | 8.7 | 12.5 |
| £8,000 - £9,999 | 7.2 | 10.5 |
| £10,000 - £11,999 | 7.0 | 11.0 |
| £12,000 - £14,999 | 9.7 | 12.2 |
| £15,000 - £17,999 | 6.8 | 8.3 |
| £18,000 - £19,999 | 4.1 | 3.6 |
| £20,000 - £22,999 | 4.8 | 3.5 |
| £23,000 - £25,999 | 4.8 | 3.6 |
| £26,000 - £28,999 | 2.2 | 2.2 |
| £29,999 - £31,999 | 2.6 | 1.6 |
| £32,000 - £34,999 | 2.5 | 1.0 |
| £35,000 - £37,999 | 1.4 | 0.5 |
| £38,000 - £40,999 | 0.7 | 0.1 |
| £41,000 or more | 3.4 | 1.6 |
| (Don't Know) | 11.8 | 1.4 |
| (Refusal/NA) | 5.0 | 5.0 |

**ASK ALL**

n=1519

Q715 *[OwnShare]*
Do you (or your husband/wife/ partner) own any shares quoted on the Stock Exchange, including unit trusts?
%
14.4 Yes
84.4 No
0.1 (Don't Know)
1.1 (Refusal/NA)

83

# VERSION B QUESTIONNAIRE

ECONOMIC PROSPECT (VERSION B)

**VERSION B: ASK ALL**

n=754

Q459 *[Prices]*
Now I'd like to ask you about two economic problems - **inflation** and **unemployment**.
First, **inflation**: in a year from now, do you expect prices generally to have gone up, to have stayed the same, or to have gone down?
**IF GONE UP OR GONE DOWN:** By a lot or a little?

Q460 *[Unemp]*
Second, **unemployment**:
in a year from now, do you expect unemployment to have gone up, to have stayed the same, or to have gone down?
**IF GONE UP OR GONE DOWN:** By a lot or a little?

|  | [Prices] % | [Unemp] % |
|---|---|---|
| To have gone up by a lot | 31.9 | 11.4 |
| To have gone up by a little | 52.7 | 29.7 |
| To have stayed the same | 12.0 | 35.3 |
| To have gone down by a little | 2.3 | 20.1 |
| To have gone down by a lot | 0.1 | 1.6 |
| (Don't Know) | 0.8 | 1.8 |
| (Refusal/NA) | 0.1 | 0.1 |

Q461 *[UnempInf]*
If the government **had** to choose between keeping down inflation or keeping down unemployment, to which do you think it should give highest priority?
%
30.3 Keeping down inflation
66.7 Keeping down unemployment
0.1 Other answer **(WRITE IN)**
2.2 (Don't Know)
0.1 (Refusal/NA)

Q464 *[Concern]*
Which do you think is the most concern to **you and your family** ... READ OUT ...
%
58.9 ... inflation,
39.1 or, unemployment?
0.5 Other answer **(WRITE IN)**
0.5 (Don't Know)
0.1 (Refusal/NA)

84

Q467 [Industry]
Looking ahead over the next year, do you think the UK's general industrial performance will improve, stay much the same, or decline?
**IF IMPROVE OR DECLINE:** By a lot or a little?

%
2.9 Improve a lot
22.7 Improve a little
52.6 Stay much the same
12.4 Decline a little
2.4 Decline a lot
6.8 (Don't Know)
0.2 (Refusal/NA)

Q468 [IncomGap]
Thinking of income levels generally in the UK today, would you say that the **gap** between those with high incomes and those with low incomes is ... **READ OUT** ...

%
85.6 ... too large,
9.5 about right,
2.4 or, too small?
2.4 (Don't Know)
0.1 (Refusal/NA)

Q469 [TaxHi]
**CARD**
Generally, how would you describe **levels of taxation**?
Firstly, for those with **high** incomes?
Please choose a phrase from this card.

Q470 [TaxMid]
Next for those with **middle** incomes?
Please choose a phrase from this card.

Q471 [TaxLow]
Next for those with **low** incomes?
Please choose a phrase from this card.

|  | [TaxHi] | [TaxMid] | [TaxLow] |
|---|---|---|---|
|  | % | % | % |
| Much too high | 3.7 | 4.9 | 34.4 |
| Too high | 11.0 | 31.3 | 45.9 |
| About right | 30.4 | 51.4 | 16.9 |
| Too low | 35.2 | 7.8 | 0.3 |
| Much too low | 15.7 | 0.3 | 0.2 |
| (Don't Know) | 3.9 | 4.1 | 2.1 |
| (Refusal/NA) | 0.1 | 0.1 | 0.1 |

Q472 [SRInc]
Among which group would you place yourself ... **READ OUT**

%
2.0 ... high income,
47.3 middle income,
49.9 or, low income?
0.6 (Don't Know)
0.1 (Refusal/NA)

n=754

Q473 [HIncDiff]
**CARD**
Which of the phrases on this card would you say comes closest to your feelings about your household's income these days?

%
27.6 Living comfortably on present income
53.5 Coping on present income
13.6 Finding it difficult on present income
5.0 Finding it very difficult on present income
0.1 Other answer **(WRITE IN)**
- (Don't Know)
0.1 (Refusal/NA)

Q476 [HIncPast]
Looking back over the **last year** or so, would you say your household's income has ... **READ OUT** ...

%
49.3 ... fallen behind prices,
45.2 kept up with prices,
4.3 or, gone up by more than prices?
1.2 (Don't Know)
0.1 (Refusal/NA)

Q477 [HIncXpct]
And looking forward to the **year ahead**, do you expect your household's income will ... **READ OUT** ...

%
45.8 ... fall behind prices,
46.9 keep up with prices,
4.9 or, go up by more than prices?
2.2 (Don't Know)
0.1 (Refusal/NA)

# POVERTY/SINGLE PARENTS (VERSION B)

## VERSION B: ASK ALL

**Q479** *[UB1Poor]*
Now some questions about welfare benefits.
Think of a 25-year-old unemployed woman living alone.
Her only income comes from state benefits. Would you say
that she ... **READ OUT** ...

%
2.2 ... has more than enough to live on,
20.9 has enough to live on,
56.4 is hard up,
14.1 or, is really poor?
6.2 (Don't Know)
0.1 (Refusal/NA)

**Q480** *[MumPoor]*
What about an unemployed single mother with a young
child. Their only income comes from state benefits.
Would you say they ... **READ OUT** ...

%
1.7 ... have more than enough to live on,
19.6 have enough to live on,
50.7 are hard up,
22.2 or, are really poor?
5.6 (Don't Know)
0.1 (Refusal/NA)

**Q481** *[UB1On45]*
Now thinking again of that 25-year-old unemployed woman
living alone. After rent, her income is £45 a week.
Would you say that she ... **READ OUT** ...

%
1.4 ... has more than enough to live on,
20.3 has enough to live on,
53.9 is hard up,
23.3 or, is really poor?
1.1 (Don't Know)
0.1 (Refusal/NA)

**Q482** *[MumOn77]*
And thinking again about that unemployed single mother
with a young child. After rent, their income is £77 a
week. Would you say they ... **READ OUT** ...

%
2.4 ... have more than enough to live on,
28.4 have enough to live on,
50.1 are hard up,
17.3 or, are really poor?
1.5 (Don't Know)
0.1 (Refusal/NA)

**Q483** *[MtUnmar1]*
Imagine an unmarried couple who split up. They have a
child at primary school who remains with the mother. Do
you think that the father should always be made to make
maintenance payments to support the child?

**Q484** *[MtUnmar2]*
If he **does** make maintenance payments for the child,
should the amount depend on his income, or not?

**Q485** *[MtUnmar3]*
Do you think the amount of maintenance should depend on
the **mother's** income, or not?

|        | [MtUnmar1] % | [MtUnmar2] % | [MtUnmar3] % |
|--------|---|---|---|
| Yes    | 87.3 | 90.1 | 67.3 |
| No     | 10.3 | 8.6  | 31.4 |
| (Don't Know) | 2.2 | 1.1 | 1.2 |
| (Refusal/NA) | 0.1 | 0.1 | 0.1 |

**Q486** *[MtUnmar4]*
Suppose the mother now marries someone else. Should the
child's natural father go on paying maintenance for the
child, should he stop, or should it depend on the
step-father's income?

%
37.6 Continue
18.8 Stop
41.0 Depends
2.5 (Don't Know)
0.1 (Refusal/NA)

**Q487** *[WorseOff]*
**CARD**
Please look at this card and say, as far as money is
concerned, what you think happens when a marriage breaks
up.

%
23.4 The woman nearly always comes off worse than the man
23.6 The woman usually comes off worse
20.5 The woman and the man usually come off about the same
18.6 The man usually comes off worse
4.4 The man nearly always comes off worse than the woman
5.5 (Varies/depends)
0.7 Other answer **(WRITE IN)**
3.1 (Don't Know)
0.1 (Refusal/NA)

**Q490** *[MuchPov]*
Some people say there is very little **real** poverty in the
UK today. Others say there is quite a lot. Which comes
closest to **your** view ... **READ OUT** ...

%
37.2 ... that there is very little real poverty in the UK,
61.0 or, that there is quite a lot?
1.6 (Don't Know)
0.1 (Refusal/NA)

Q491 [PastPov]
Over the last ten years, do you think that poverty in the UK has been increasing, decreasing or staying at about the same level?
%
54.1  Increasing
9.1   Decreasing
34.6  Staying at same level
2.1   (Don't Know)
0.1   (Refusal/NA)

Q492 [FuturPov]
And over the **next** ten years, do you think that poverty in the UK will ... **READ OUT** ...
%
48.2  ... increase,
10.8  decrease,
37.3  or, stay at about the same level?
3.5   (Don't Know)
0.1   (Refusal/NA)

Q493 [Poverty1]
Would you say someone in the UK **was** or **was not** in poverty if ...
... they had enough to buy the things they really needed, but not enough to buy the things most people take for granted?

Q494 [Poverty2]
(Would you say someone in the UK **was** or **was not** in poverty if ...)
... they had enough to eat and live, but not enough to buy other things they needed?

Q495 [Poverty3]
(Would you say someone in the UK **was** or **was not** in poverty if ...)
... they had not got enough to eat and live without getting into debt?

|  | [Poverty1] | [Poverty2] | [Poverty3] |
|---|---|---|---|
|  | % | % | % |
| Was in poverty | 32.6 | 68.6 | 90.6 |
| Was not | 65.9 | 29.9 | 8.4 |
| (Don't Know) | 1.4 | 1.4 | 0.9 |
| (Refusal/NA) | 0.1 | 0.1 | 0.1 |

n=754

Q496 [WhyNeed]
**CARD**
Why do you think there are people who live in need? Of the four views on this card, which **one** comes closest to your own? **CODE ONE ONLY**
%
13.5  Because they have been unlucky
16.1  Because of laziness or lack of willpower
22.0  Because of injustice in our society
41.8  It's an inevitable part of modern life
1.1   (None of these)
3.1   Other answer **(WRITE IN)**
2.2   (Don't Know)
0.1   (Refusal/NA)

Q499 [FeelPoor]
How often do **you** and your household feel poor nowadays ... **READ OUT** ...
%
37.9  ... never,
49.0  every now and then,
6.4   often,
6.2   or, almost all the time?
0.3   (Don't Know)
0.1   (Refusal/NA)

n=754

## COUNTRYSIDE/ENVIRONMENT (VERSION B)     n=754

**ASK ALL**

Q503 *[Spoils]* (NOT ON THE DATA FILE)
Now a few questions about the countryside.
What, if anything, do you think spoils or threatens the countryside in the UK these days? PROBE UNTIL 'NO'. RECORD WORD FOR WORD.
What else? And what else? PROBE UNTIL 'NO'. RECORD WORD FOR WORD.
CONTINUE IN A NOTE (ctrl + f4), IF NECESSARY
Open Question (Maximum of 100 characters)

Q504 *[CThreat1]*
CARD
Which, if any, of the things on this card do you think is the **greatest threat** to the countryside?
If you think none of them is a threat, or something not on the card please say so.
CODE ONE ONLY
INTERVIEWER: DO NOT TRY TO CHANGE THE ANSWER AT PREVIOUS QUESTION ('Spoils')

**IF ANSWER GIVEN AT [CThreat1]**

Q507 *[CThreat2]*
And which do you think is the next greatest threat (to the countryside)?
CODE ONE ONLY

|  | [CThreat1] % | [CThreat2] % |
|---|---|---|
| Motorways and road building | 8.1 | 11.2 |
| Industrial pollution | 26.5 | 24.0 |
| Removal by farmers of traditional landscapes, such as hedgerows, woodlands | 6.1 | 7.6 |
| Too many people visiting the countryside | 0.3 | 1.8 |
| Rubbish tipping and litter | 29.2 | 22.0 |
| Urban growth and housing development | 15.0 | 12.0 |
| Use of chemicals and pesticides in farming | 12.6 | 16.9 |
| (None of these) | 0.7 | 1.8 |
| Other answer (WRITE IN) | 0.8 | 0.1 |
| (Don't Know) | 0.5 | 0.4 |
| (Refusal/NA) | 0.1 | 2.2 |

**VERSION B: ASK ALL**

Q510 *[Crowded1]*
CARD
Beauty spots and other popular places in the countryside often get crowded. Suppose one of these was visited so much that enjoying its peace and quiet was being spoiled.
Using this card, are you in favour of or against ...
...cutting down or closing car parks near the site?

Q511 *[Crowded2]*
(To limit the number of visitors, are you in favour of or against...) ...stopping anyone at all from visiting it at particular times each year?

Q512 *[Crowded3]*
(To limit the number of visitors, are you in favour of or against...) ...making visitors pay and using the the extra money to help protect it?

|  | [Crowded1] % | [Crowded2] % | [Crowded3] % |
|---|---|---|---|
| Strongly in favour | 7.5 | 4.3 | 14.3 |
| In favour | 35.2 | 34.1 | 56.7 |
| Neither in favour nor against | 25.0 | 16.7 | 13.0 |
| Against | 25.4 | 38.0 | 13.2 |
| Strongly against | 5.2 | 5.4 | 1.5 |
| (Don't Know) | 1.4 | 1.2 | 1.1 |
| (Refusal/NA) | 0.3 | 0.3 | 0.3 |

Q513 *[Crowded4]*
(To limit the number of visitors, are you in favour of or against...) ...issuing free permits in advance so people will have to plan their visits?

Q514 *[Crowded5]*
(To limit the number of visitors, are you in favour of or against...) ...cutting down on advertising and promoting it?

Q515 *[Crowded6]*
(To limit the number of visitors, are you in favour of or against...) ...advertising and promoting other popular places in the countryside instead?

|  | [Crowded4] % | [Crowded5] % | [Crowded6] % |
|---|---|---|---|
| Strongly in favour | 3.9 | 2.8 | 5.0 |
| In favour | 30.7 | 34.8 | 49.5 |
| Neither in favour nor against | 21.4 | 28.8 | 26.6 |
| Against | 38.7 | 30.1 | 15.4 |
| Strongly against | 3.2 | 1.7 | 1.1 |
| (Don't Know) | 1.8 | 1.6 | 2.2 |
| (Refusal/NA) | 0.3 | 0.3 | 0.3 |

Q516 [ConDevt]
Suppose you heard that a housing development was being planned in a part of the countryside you knew and liked. Would you be concerned by this, or not?

%
73.5  Yes, concerned
25.2  No
1.0   (Don't Know)
0.3   (Refusal/NA)

Q517  **IF 'yes' AT [ConDevt]**
**CARD**
Would you personally be likely to do any of these things about it? Any others?
**CODE ALL THAT APPLY**
Multicoded (Maximum of 8 codes)

%
12.0  (No, would take no action) [DevtDo1]
27.1  Contact an MP or councillor [DevtDo2]
13.1  Contact a government or planning department [DevtDo3]
4.8   Contact radio, TV or a newspaper [DevtDo4]
50.1  Sign a petition [DevtDo5]
4.8   Join a conservation group [DevtDo6]
11.1  Give money to a campaign [DevtDo7]
7.6   Volunteer to work for a campaign [DevtDo8]
7.0   Go on a protest march or demonstration [DevtDo9]
-     (Don't Know)
1.3   (Refusal/NA)

Q518  **VERSION B: ASK ALL**
[ConFlwr]
Now suppose you heard that a site where wildflowers grew was going to be ploughed for farmland.
Would you be concerned by this, or not?

%
36.5  Yes, concerned
62.3  No
1.0   (Don't Know)
0.3   (Refusal/NA)

Q519  **IF 'yes' AT [ConFlwr]**
**CARD**
Would you personally be likely to do any of these things about it? Any others?
**CODE ALL THAT APPLY**
Multicoded (Maximum of 8 codes)

%
7.3   (No, would take no action) [FlwrDo1]
8.6   Contact an MP or councillor [FlwrDo2]
5.0   Contact a government or planning department [FlwrDo3]
2.0   Contact radio, TV or a newspaper [FlwrDo4]
22.2  Sign a petition [FlwrDo5]
2.9   Join a conservation group [FlwrDo6]
3.5   Give money to a campaign [FlwrDo7]
2.2   Volunteer to work for a campaign [FlwrDo8]
2.2   Go on a protest march or demonstration [FlwrDo9]
-     (Don't Know)
1.4   (Refusal/NA)

n=754

Q520  **VERSION B: ASK ALL**
[CtryDone]
**CARD**
Have you ever done any of the things on the card to help protect the countryside?

%
34.8  Yes
64.4  No
0.3   (Don't Know)
0.5   (Refusal/NA)

Q521  **IF 'yes' AT [CtryDone]**
Which have you ever done to help protect the countryside? Any others?
**CODE ALL THAT APPLY**

%
5.6   Contacted MP or councillor [CtryDon1]
4.3   Contacted a government or planning department [CtryDon2]
2.0   Contacted radio, TV or a newspaper [CtryDon3]
28.4  Signed a petition [CtryDon4]
3.1   Joined a conservation group [CtryDon5]
10.0  Given money to a campaign [CtryDon6]
1.8   Volunteered to work for a campaign [CtryDon7]
1.4   Gone on a protest march or demonstration [CtryDon8]
-     (Don't Know)
0.8   (Refusal/NA)

n=754

# INFORMAL CARERS (VERSION B)

**VERSION B: ASK ALL**

n=754

Q523 [CareHome]
Now some questions about informal care, that is care for those who are sick, handicapped or elderly provided by non-professionals and generally unpaid.
Some people have extra family responsibilities because they look after someone who is sick, handicapped or elderly.
May I check, is there anyone **living with you** who is sick, handicapped or elderly whom you look after or give special help to (for example a sick, handicapped or elderly relative, husband, wife, child, friend...)?

%
5.3 Yes
94.4 No
- (Don't Know)
0.3 (Refusal/NA)

Q524 [NumHome]
**IF 'yes' AT [CareHome]**
Do you look after or help one person **living with you** or is it more than one?

%
4.9 One
0.3 Two
0.1 Three

**VERSION B: ASK ALL**

Q525 [CareSep]
What about people **not living with you**, do you provide some regular service or help for any sick, handicapped or elderly relative, friend or neighbour **not living with you**?

%
20.6 Yes
79.1 No
- (Don't Know)
0.3 (Refusal/NA)

Q526 [NumSep]
**IF 'yes' AT [CareSep]**
Do you look after or help one person **not living with you** or more than one?

%
15.4 One
3.9 Two
1.0 Three
0.1 Four
0.2 Ten

**ASK ALL CARERS (IF 'yes' AT [CareHome] OR AT [CareSep])**

n=194

Q527 [MainCare]
Now thinking of the person you mainly care for (that is the person you spend **most hours** per week caring for).
Is that person...

%
5.3 ...your husband or wife,
7.4 your child or stepchild,
- your foster child,
34.3 your parent,
8.2 your parent-in-law,
33.5 another relative,
10.3 or a friend/neighbour?
- Other (**PLEASE SAY WHICH**)
- (Don't Know)
1.1 (Refusal/NA)

Q530 [Name] **(NOT ON THE DATA FILE)**
What is the first name of that person?
**(IF NAME IS NOT GIVEN REFER TO PERSON)**
Open Question (Maximum of 20 characters)

Q532 [DepGen]
And may I just check, is (Name) male or female...

%
26.6 Male
72.3 Female
- (Don't Know)
1.1 (Refusal/NA)

Q533 [DepAge]
What is (his/her) age?
**ENTER AGE IF GIVEN OR CODE AS DON'T KNOW**
**IF LESS THAN 1 YEAR ENTER 1**
**Median: 74 years**

**IF CARING BOTH FOR SOMEONE LIVING WITH RESPONDENT AND SOMEONE NOT LIVING WITH RESPONDENT (IF 'yes' AT [CareHome] AND AT [CareSep])**

Q534 [MainLive]
May I just check, does (Name) live with you?

%
1.3 Yes
0.3 No
- (Don't Know)
1.1 (Refusal/NA)

**ASK ALL CARERS (IF 'yes' AT [CareHome] OR AT [CareSep])**

Q535 [Live] **(NOT ON THE SCREEN - COMPUTED BY PROGRAM FROM [CareHome], [CareSep] AND [MainLive]**
Where does (Name) live...?

%
20.3 With carer
78.6 Lives separately
- (Don't Know)
1.1 (Refusal/NA)

|  |  | n=194 |
|---|---|---|

| Q536 | Does *(Name)* need help as a result of ... **READ OUT** ... **CODE ALL THAT APPLY** Multicoded (Maximum of 5 codes) |
|---|---|
| % |  |
| 48.0 | Old age/frailty *[DepHelp1]* |
| 39.6 | Physical disability *[DepHelp2]* |
| 28.5 | (Physical) illness *[DepHelp3]* |
| 7.9 | Mental handicap *[DepHelp4]* |
| 4.0 | Mental illness *[DepHelp5]* |
| 1.1 | (Refusal/NA) |
| - | (Don't know) |

| Q537 | *[HelpTim]* Taking account of all the help you give, including travelling time, about how long do you spend looking after *(Name)* in an average week? **IF VARIES: ASK FOR THE NUMBER OF HOURS IN THE MOST RECENT WEEK OF CARING** |
|---|---|
| % |  |
| 16.9 | 0-2 hours per week |
| 17.7 | 3-4 hours per week |
| 21.9 | 5-9 hours per week |
| 23.0 | 10-19 hours per week |
| 5.8 | 20-29 hours per week |
| 1.6 | 30-39 hours per week |
| 1.6 | 40-59 hours per week |
| 10.0 | 60 hours plus |
| 0.5 | (Don't Know) |
| 1.1 | (Refusal/NA) |

| Q538 | *[HelpDay]* And on how many days per week do you usually look after or help *(Name)*? **IF VARIES: ASK FOR THE NUMBER OF DAYS IN THE MOST RECENT WEEK OF CARING** |
|---|---|
| % |  |
| 21.6 | One day per week |
| 13.7 | Two days per week |
| 15.6 | Three days per week |
| 5.8 | Four days per week |
| 6.6 | Five days per week |
| 2.9 | Six days per week |
| 32.7 | Seven days per week |
| - | (Don't Know) |
| 1.1 | (Refusal/NA) |

|  |  | r=194 |
|---|---|---|

| Q539 | **CARD** Which if any of the things on this card do you usually do for *(Name)*? **CODE ALL THAT APPLY** Multicoded (Maximum of 10 codes) |
|---|---|
| % |  |
| 31.4 | Help with personal care eg washing, dressing, eating, toilet *[TypHlp01]* |
| 23.2 | Physical help eg helping in/out of bed/chair, helping up/downstairs *[TypHlp02]* |
| 33.5 | Helping with paperwork/financial matters *[TypHlp03]* |
| 66.8 | Practical help, eg shopping and housework *[TypHlp04]* |
| 36.1 | Other practical help eg gardening and decorating *[TypHlp05]* |
| 58.3 | Companionship *[TypHlp06]* |
| 47.2 | Take him/her out *[TypHlp07]* |
| 16.1 | Give medicine *[TypHlp08]* |
| 21.1 | Supervision *[TypHlp09]* |
| 0.3 | Other help (**SPECIFY WHICH**) *[TypHlp10]* |
| - | (None) *[TypHlp00]* |
| - | (Don't know) |
| 1.1 | (Refusal/NA) |

| Q543 | **IF MORE THAN ONE TYPE OF HELP GIVEN AT** *[TypHlp]* *[MainHelp]* And which of these things takes up most of the time you spend caring for *(Name)*? **CARD** **CODE ONE ONLY** |
|---|---|
| % |  |
| 11.1 | Help with personal care eg washing, dressing, eating, toilet |
| 5.0 | Physical help eg helping in/out of bed/chair, helping up/downstairs |
| 0.8 | Helping with paperwork/financial matters |
| 24.8 | Practical help eg shopping and housework |
| 4.0 | Other practical help eg gardening and decorating |
| 20.1 | Companionship |
| 3.7 | Taking him/her out |
| 0.3 | Giving medicine |
| 4.2 | Supervision |
| 0.3 | Other help |
| 0.3 | (Don't Know) |
| 1.1 | (Refusal/NA) |

n=194

**ASK ALL CARERS**
(IF 'Yes' AT [CareHome] OR AT [CareSep])
[HelpMon]

Q544 About how long have you been caring for or helping (Name)?
%
4.2 Less than 6 months
6.9 6-12 months
23.0 Over 1 year, less than 3 years
15.8 3 years, less than 5 years
27.7 5 years, less than 10 years
9.8 10 years, less than 15 years
5.3 15 years, less than 20
6.3 20 years or more
- (Don't Know)
1.1 (Refusal/NA)

Q545 **CARD**
Excluding family members, friends, relatives and neighbours, does (Name) receive regular visits, at least once a month, from any of these people or services?
**CODE ALL THAT APPLY** (If dependant does not receive any regular visits - code 9)
Multicoded (Maximum of 8 codes)
%
19.3 Doctor? [DepVisi1]
25.9 Community or district nurse? [DepVisi2]
14.2 Health visitor? [DepVisi3]
9.2 Social worker? [DepVisi4]
26.9 Home helps? [DepVisi5]
3.4 Meals on wheels? [DepVisi6]
7.7 Voluntary worker? [DepVisi7]
8.7 Other visitor or service (**PLEASE SPECIFY**)? [DepVisi8]
35.9 (Does not receive any regular visits) [DepVisi0]
- (Don't Know)
1.6 (Refusal/NA)

Q549 Apart from the people and services just mentioned, is there anyone else who helps to look after (Name), for example another family member, relative, friend or neighbour? **on a regular basis,**
**CODE ALL THAT APPLY**
(If no-one else helps to care for dependant - code 6)
Multicoded (Maximum of 5 codes)
%
73.9 Relative (including husband or wife) [RelHelp1]
2.6 Friend [RelHelp2]
3.4 Neighbour [RelHelp3]
2.1 Paid helper [RelHelp4]
2.9 Someone else [RelHelp5]
20.6 Nobody else [RelHelp0]
- (Don't know)
1.1 (Refusal/NA)

n=754

**VERSION B: ASK ALL**
[DepRel]

Q550 **CARD**
Here are views that people sometimes express about people who need care. For each of these statements, please use this card to say whether you agree or disagree.
First, do you agree or disagree that...
...these days people who need care get most of their help from relatives.

Q551 [ForGrant]
(And do you agree or disagree that...)
...carers are too often taken for granted by the authorities.

Q552 [CarDuty]
(And do you agree or disagree that...)
...looking after family members is a duty and carers should not be paid by the authorities.

| | [DepRel] | [ForGrant] | [CarDuty] |
|---|---|---|---|
| | % | % | % |
| Strongly agree | 31.7 | 53.0 | 1.6 |
| Agree | 46.2 | 39.5 | 12.8 |
| Neither agree nor disagree | 6.7 | 3.0 | 11.4 |
| Disagree | 13.1 | 3.3 | 52.8 |
| Strongly disagree | 1.4 | 0.1 | 19.8 |
| (Don't Know) | 0.6 | 0.8 | 1.4 |
| (Refusal/NA) | 0.3 | 0.3 | 0.3 |

Q553 [RelWill]
(And do you agree or disagree that...)
...relatives are much less willing than they used to be to look after other members of the family.

Q554 [CarBenef]
(And do you agree or disagree that...)
...all carers should be entitled to a state benefit which recognises their work.

Q555 [GovCare]
(And do you agree or disagree that...)
...nowadays, government provides most of the help for people needing care.

| | [RelWill] | [CarBenef] | [GovCare] |
|---|---|---|---|
| | % | % | % |
| Strongly agree | 13.7 | 39.4 | 1.5 |
| Agree | 52.1 | 50.4 | 25.5 |
| Neither agree nor disagree | 8.2 | 5.9 | 9.9 |
| Disagree | 21.4 | 2.5 | 48.1 |
| Strongly disagree | 2.8 | 0.8 | 12.7 |
| (Don't Know) | 1.6 | 0.7 | 2.0 |
| (Refusal/NA) | 0.3 | 0.3 | 0.3 |

Q556 [WomCare]
(And do you agree or disagree that...)
...**women** should be prepared to give up their jobs to care for family members who are sick, disabled or elderly.

Q557 [MenCare]
(And do you agree or disagree that...)
...**Men** should be prepared to give up their jobs to care for family members who are sick, disabled or elderly.

n=754

|  | [WomCare] % | [MenCare] % |
|---|---|---|
| Strongly agree | 1.4 | 0.6 |
| Agree | 13.1 | 7.6 |
| Neither agree nor disagree | 14.6 | 12.3 |
| Disagree | 48.4 | 53.9 |
| Strongly disagree | 21.0 | 23.9 |
| (Don't Know) | 1.2 | 1.2 |
| (Refusal/NA) | 0.4 | 0.4 |

Q558 [EldCare]
Thinking now only of **elderly** people.
As the number of elderly persons needing care increases over the next few years, who in your opinion, should be expected to provide the bulk of the care that will be needed?
Should it be ... **READ OUT** ...
**CODE ONE ONLY**

%
28.4 ...relatives? (including husband or wife)
61.4 the government?
1.6 friends/neighbours?
2.5 or voluntary organisations?
2.4 Other (**WRITE IN**)
0.8 (Both government and relatives)
1.2 (Mixture of all)
0.4 (Don't Know)
0.4 (Refusal/NA)

Q562 [OwnProv]
Again, thinking of **elderly** people.
How much do you agree or disagree with each of these statements?
First, do you agree or disagree that...
...it should be everyone's responsibility to make their own provision so that they can pay for their own care when they are old.

Q563 [NotPay]
(And do you agree or disagree that...)
...people who have paid tax all their lives should **not** be expected to pay for any care they may need when they are old.

Q564 [MkRelCar]
(And do you agree or disagree that...)
...relatives should be made to care for close family members who need help.

Q565 [EldSell]
(And do you agree or disagree that...)
...if necessary, elderly people should sell their own home to meet the cost of living in an old person's home.

n=754

|  | [OwnProv] % | [NotPay] % | [MkRelCar] % |
|---|---|---|---|
| Strongly agree | 1.8 | 31.9 | 1.2 |
| Agree | 18.9 | 49.3 | 18.2 |
| Neither agree nor disagree | 10.5 | 5.0 | 12.4 |
| Disagree | 51.0 | 11.4 | 53.6 |
| Strongly disagree | 16.3 | 1.0 | 13.8 |
| (Don't Know) | 1.2 | 1.0 | 0.5 |
| (Refusal/NA) | 0.4 | 0.4 | 0.4 |

|  | [EldSell] % |
|---|---|
| Strongly agree | 0.7 |
| Agree | 14.9 |
| Neither agree nor disagree | 9.2 |
| Disagree | 46.1 |
| Strongly disagree | 28.0 |
| (Don't Know) | 0.5 |
| (Refusal/NA) | 0.5 |

# P.1345/NI

## NORTHERN IRELAND SOCIAL ATTITUDES 1994
## SELF-COMPLETION QUESTIONNAIRE

Spring 1994

**A**

n = 1315

### A2.01 To begin, we have some questions about women Do you agree or disagree ...?

PLEASE TICK **ONE** BOX ON EACH LINE

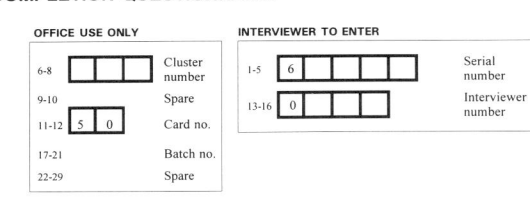

| | Strongly agree | Agree | Neither agree nor disagree | Disagree | Strongly disagree | Can't choose | (Not answered) |
|---|---|---|---|---|---|---|---|
| a. [WWRELCHD] A working mother can establish just as warm and secure a relationship with her children as a mother who does not work | % 17.3 | 46.5 | 8.8 | 20.0 | 4.7 | 1.6 | 1.1 |
| b. [WWCHDSUF] A pre-school child is likely to suffer if his or her mother works | % 6.4 | 30.9 | 16.0 | 35.3 | 8.2 | 1.9 | 1.4 |
| c. [WWFAMSUF] All in all, family life suffers when the woman has a full-time job | % 6.5 | 28.6 | 14.8 | 38.1 | 9.4 | 1.6 | 1.1 |
| d. [WANTHOME] A job is all right, but what most women really want is a home and children | % 5.7 | 27.4 | 19.1 | 32.3 | 11.0 | 2.8 | 1.7 |
| e. [HWIFEFFL] Being a housewife is just as fulfilling as working for pay | % 9.7 | 40.0 | 17.2 | 22.0 | 5.2 | 3.8 | 2.1 |
| f. [FEMJOB] Having a job is the best way for a woman to be an independent person | % 10.5 | 49.3 | 17.1 | 17.5 | 1.9 | 2.3 | 1.4 |
| g. [WOMENWRK] Most women have to work these days to support their families | % 18.2 | 61.8 | 9.3 | 7.8 | 0.8 | 1.1 | 1.0 |

### A2.02 And, do you agree or disagree ...?

PLEASE TICK **ONE** BOX ON EACH LINE

| | Strongly agree | Agree | Neither agree nor disagree | Disagree | Strongly disagree | Can't choose | (Not answered) |
|---|---|---|---|---|---|---|---|
| a. [BOTHEARN] Both the man and woman should contribute to the household income | % 23.1 | 46.6 | 16.6 | 10.8 | 1.0 | 1.2 | 0.7 |
| b. [SEXROLE] A man's job is to earn money; a woman's job is to look after the home and family | % 4.9 | 23.7 | 14.9 | 39.9 | 14.8 | 0.9 | 0.9 |
| c. [TRADROLE] It is not good if the man stays at home and cares for the children and the woman goes out to work | % 6.9 | 21.9 | 21.6 | 36.9 | 9.0 | 2.3 | 1.3 |
| d. [FAMLIFE] Family life often suffers because men concentrate too much on their work | % 6.7 | 48.2 | 20.1 | 21.0 | 1.2 | 1.8 | 1.0 |

### THANK YOU AGAIN FOR YOUR HELP.

*Social and Community Planning Research is an independent social research institute registered as a charitable trust. Its projects are funded by government departments, local authorities, universities and foundations to provide information on social issues in the UK. This survey series has been funded mainly by one of the Sainsbury Family Charitable Trusts, with contributions also from other grant-giving bodies and government departments. Please contact us if you would like further information.*

A2.03 Do you think that women should work outside the home full-time, part-time or not at all under these circumstances?
PLEASE TICK ONE BOX ON EACH LINE

N = 1315

| | | Work full-time | Work part-time | Stay at home | Can't choose | (Not answered) |
|---|---|---|---|---|---|---|
| a. | [WWCHD1] After marrying and before there are children | 83.1 | 8.4 | 3.0 | 4.4 | 1.0 |
| b. | [WWCHD2] When there is a child under school age | 6.8 | 32.9 | 53.7 | 5.1 | 1.5 |
| c. | [WWCHD3] After the youngest child starts school | 19.7 | 62.6 | 10.9 | 5.6 | 1.2 |
| d. | [WWCHD4] After the children leave home | 69.1 | 19.1 | 3.5 | 6.5 | 1.7 |

A2.04 Do you agree or disagree ....?
PLEASE TICK ONE BOX ON EACH LINE

| | | Strongly agree | Agree | Neither agree nor disagree | Disagree | Strongly disagree | Can't choose | (Not answered) |
|---|---|---|---|---|---|---|---|---|
| a. | [MARVIEW1] Married people are generally happier than unmarried people | 5.1 | 22.0 | 35.9 | 26.6 | 6.2 | 3.7 | 0.5 |
| b. | [MARVIEW3] The main advantage of marriage is that it gives financial security | 2.6 | 18.6 | 20.1 | 47.3 | 9.2 | 1.7 | 0.6 |
| c. | [MARVIEW4] The main purpose of marriage these days is to have children | 1.8 | 18.2 | 14.9 | 53.5 | 8.8 | 1.8 | 0.9 |
| d. | [MARVIEW5] It is better to have a bad marriage than no marriage at all | 0.9 | 2.3 | 2.3 | 44.4 | 47.0 | 2.2 | 0.9 |
| e. | [MARVIEW6] People who want children ought to get married | 22.7 | 46.1 | 10.1 | 14.0 | 5.2 | 1.4 | 0.6 |
| f. | [MARVIEW10] One parent can bring up a child as well as two parents together | 6.1 | 31.6 | 15.7 | 34.1 | 10.8 | 1.2 | 0.5 |
| g. | [MARVIEW11] It is all right for a couple to live together without intending to get married | 7.7 | 34.9 | 16.6 | 23.0 | 15.2 | 1.8 | 0.8 |
| h. | [MARVIEW12] It is a good idea for a couple who intend to get married to live together first | 7.3 | 30.8 | 20.5 | 24.2 | 14.2 | 2.0 | 0.9 |
| i. | [MARVIEW13] Divorce is usually the best solution when a couple can't seem to work out their marriage problems | 8.1 | 44.5 | 15.9 | 19.6 | 6.6 | 4.4 | 1.0 |

A2.05 All in all, what do you think is the ideal number of children for a family to have?
PLEASE WRITE THE NUMBER IN THE BOX → 3
(Don't know) % 1.8
(Not answered) % 4.9

A2.06 Do you agree or disagree ....?
PLEASE TICK ONE BOX ON EACH LINE

n = 1315

| | | Strongly agree | Agree | Neither agree nor disagree | Disagree | Strongly disagree | Can't choose | (Not answered) |
|---|---|---|---|---|---|---|---|---|
| a. | [CHDVIEW2] Watching children grow up is life's greatest joy | 29.3 | 52.0 | 13.0 | 3.1 | 0.3 | 1.8 | 0.5 |
| b. | [CHDVIEW3] Having children interferes too much with the freedom of parents | 1.7 | 6.3 | 14.8 | 59.5 | 15.0 | 1.8 | 0.9 |
| c. | [CHDVIEW6] People who have never had children lead empty lives | 2.9 | 16.4 | 21.8 | 43.3 | 10.4 | 4.3 | 0.8 |
| d. | [CHDVIEW7] When there are children in the family, parents should stay together even if they don't get along | 3.4 | 22.3 | 17.2 | 42.9 | 8.9 | 4.6 | 0.7 |
| e. | [CHDVIEW8] Even when there are no children, a married couple should stay together even if they don't get along | 2.1 | 7.2 | 11.4 | 54.8 | 19.1 | 4.8 | 0.7 |

A2.07 [PREPCHLD] Which of these would you say is more important in preparing children for life ....
PLEASE TICK ONE BOX

%
... to be obedient, 39.0
OR
... to think for themselves? 53.5
Can't choose 6.9
(Not answered) 0.7

A2.08 [MTHRWRKD] Did your mother ever work for pay for as long as one year, after you were born and before you were 14?
PLEASE TICK ONE BOX

%
Yes, she worked 40.9
No 57.1
Did not live with mother 0.9
(Not answered) 1.1
(Don't know) –

NI

**A2.09a** [MUMALIVE] Is your mother still alive?
PLEASE TICK ONE BOX

n = 1315

%
Yes 58.2 → PLEASE ANSWER b. BELOW
No 41.5 → GO TO Q2.10

[MUMVISIT]
**b.** IF YOU ANSWERED YES AT a.
How often do you see or visit your mother?
PLEASE TICK ONE BOX ONLY

%
She lives in the same household 15.1
I see or visit her:
... daily 8.8
... at least several times a week 12.0
... at least once a week 13.1
... at least once a month 4.2
... several times a year 3.0
... less often 1.7
(Not answered) 0.6

[DIVORCED]
EVERYONE PLEASE ANSWER
**A2.10** Have you ever been divorced?
PLEASE TICK ONE BOX

%
Yes 6.5
No 78.4
Never married 14.4
(Not answered) 0.7

[MARDNOW]
**A2.11** Are you married or living as married now?
PLEASE TICK ONE BOX

%
Yes, married 58.8 → PLEASE ANSWER Q2.12 a & b BELOW
Yes, living as married 1.9 → PLEASE ANSWER Q2.12a ONLY
No 35.5 → GO TO Q2.13
(Not answered) 3.8

OFFICE USE ONLY

SPARE

---

NI

[SDIVORCD]
**A2.12a** PLEASE ANSWER THIS QUESTION IF YOU ARE MARRIED OR LIVING AS MARRIED
Has your husband or wife or partner ever been divorced?
PLEASE TICK ONE BOX ONLY

n = 1315

%
Yes 2.2  ⎫ IF YOU ARE LIVING AS MARRIED PLEASE GO TO Q2.13
No 57.8 ⎭
(Not answered) 4.5

[COHABIT]
**b.** PLEASE ANSWER THIS QUESTION IF YOU ARE MARRIED
Did you live with your husband or wife before you got married?
PLEASE TICK ONE BOX

%
Yes 4.9
No 48.4
Not married 0.2
(Not answered) 9.1

EVERYONE PLEASE ANSWER
[NOTMARRY]
**A2.13** Did you ever live together with a partner you didn't marry?
PLEASE TICK ONE BOX ONLY

%
Yes, with a previous partner 3.5
Yes, with my present partner 2.5
Yes, both with a previous partner and with my present partner 0.4
No, never 92.4
(Not answered) 1.2

**A2.14** Do you agree or disagree ...?
PLEASE TICK ONE BOX ON EACH LINE

| | Strongly agree | Agree | Neither agree nor disagree | Disagree | Strongly disagree | Can't choose | (Not answered) |
|---|---|---|---|---|---|---|---|
| [MATLEAVE] **a.** Working women should receive paid maternity leave when they have a baby | % 43.5 | 47.9 | 3.4 | 2.9 | 0.7 | 1.2 | 0.5 |
| [CHLDCRBN] **b.** Families should receive financial benefits for child-care when both parents work | % 16.3 | 34.3 | 17.1 | 24.8 | 3.8 | 2.6 | 1.1 |
| [ABORTION] **c.** A pregnant woman should be able to obtain a legal abortion for any reason whatsoever, if she chooses not to have the baby | % 9.0 | 20.4 | 11.2 | 24.1 | 30.4 | 4.3 | 0.6 |

## N

**[PMSWRNG]**
A2.15a Do you think it is wrong or not wrong if a man and a woman have sexual relations before marriage?

PLEASE TICK ONE BOX ONLY

n = 1315

| | % |
|---|---|
| Always wrong | 28.2 |
| Almost always wrong | 6.6 |
| Wrong only sometimes | 13.1 |
| Not wrong at all | 42.9 |
| Can't choose | 8.7 |
| (Not answered) | 0.5 |

**[TNSWRNG]**
b. What if they are in their early teens, say under 16 years old? In that case is it ....

PLEASE TICK ONE BOX ONLY

| | % |
|---|---|
| ... always wrong, | 77.7 |
| almost always wrong, | 11.5 |
| wrong only sometimes, | 4.7 |
| or, not wrong at all? | 2.4 |
| Can't choose | 3.3 |
| (Not answered) | 0.4 |

**[EMSWRNG]**
c. What about a married person having sexual relations with someone other than his or her husband or wife? Is it ....

PLEASE TICK ONE BOX ONLY

| | % |
|---|---|
| ... always wrong, | 78.6 |
| almost always wrong, | 11.9 |
| wrong only sometimes, | 4.8 |
| or, not wrong at all? | 1.8 |
| Can't choose | 2.5 |
| (Not answered) | 0.4 |

**[HMSWRNG]**
d. And what about sexual relations between two adults of the same sex? Is it ....

PLEASE TICK ONE BOX ONLY

| | % |
|---|---|
| ... always wrong, | 69.8 |
| almost always wrong, | 3.6 |
| wrong only sometimes, | 4.2 |
| or, not wrong at all? | 11.1 |
| Can't choose | 10.8 |
| (Not answered) | 0.5 |

## N

**[HARASSCW]**
A2.16 Sometimes at work people find themselves the object of sexual advances, propositions, or unwanted sexual discussions from co-workers or supervisors. The advances sometimes involve physical contact and sometimes just involve sexual conversations. Has this ever happened to you?

PLEASE TICK ONE BOX

n = 1315

| | % |
|---|---|
| Yes | 11.8 |
| No | 84.1 |
| Never have worked | 3.6 |
| (Not answered) | 0.4 |

**PLEASE ANSWER Q2.17 TO Q2.19 IF YOU ARE MARRIED OR LIVING AS MARRIED. IF NOT MARRIED OR NOT LIVING AS MARRIED, PLEASE GO TO Q2.20.**

**[CPLINCOM]**
A2.17 How do you and your spouse/partner organise the income that one or both of you receive? Please choose the option that comes closest.

PLEASE TICK ONE BOX ONLY

| | % |
|---|---|
| I manage all the money and give my partner his or her share | 9.2 |
| My partner manages all the money and gives me my share | 8.7 |
| We pool all the money and each take out what we need | 31.2 |
| We pool some of the money and keep the rest separate | 6.6 |
| We each keep our own money separate | 4.6 |
| Not married or living as married | 35.5 |
| (Not answered) | 4.2 |

**PLEASE ANSWER IF YOU ARE MARRIED OR LIVING AS MARRIED**

A2.18 In your household, who does the following things?

PLEASE TICK ONE BOX ON EACH LINE

| | Always the woman | Usually the woman | About equal or both together | Usually the man | Always the man | Is done by a third person | Can't choose | (Not answered) |
|---|---|---|---|---|---|---|---|---|
| **[HHJOB1]** a. The washing and ironing % | 35.5 | 17.5 | 5.8 | 0.2 | 0.2 | 1.4 | 0.1 | 4.0 |
| **[HHJOB2]** b. Small repairs around the house % | 1.3 | 1.4 | 6.4 | 30.6 | 18.4 | 2.2 | 0.2 | 4.1 |
| **[HHJOB3]** c. Looking after sick family members % | 16.8 | 14.2 | 26.3 | 0.2 | 0.4 | 0.5 | 1.9 | 4.3 |
| **[HHJOB4]** d. Shopping for groceries % | 18.7 | 16.1 | 24.2 | 0.9 | 0.5 | 0.2 | - | 3.9 |
| **[HHJOB5]** e. Deciding what to have for dinner % | 20.5 | 18.7 | 20.0 | 0.9 | 0.1 | 0.3 | 0.1 | 3.9 |

## N1

**PLEASE ANSWER IF YOU ARE MARRIED OR LIVING AS MARRIED**           n = 1315

**A2.19a** [BOTHWORK]
Do you and your husband or wife or partner both have paid work at the moment?

| | % | |
|---|---|---|
| PLEASE TICK ONE BOX | Yes | 26.7 → PLEASE ANSWER Q2.19b |
| | No | 33.8 → PLEASE GO TO Q2.20 |
| | (Not answered) | 4.1 |

b. [EARNMOST]
Who earns more money?

PLEASE TICK ONE BOX ONLY                                         %

| | |
|---|---|
| The man earns much more | 15.4 |
| The man earns a bit more | 5.5 |
| We earn about the same amount | 3.1 |
| The woman earns a bit more | 1.6 |
| The woman earns much more | 1.0 |
| (Not answered) | 4.2 |

**PLEASE ANSWER Q2.20 AND Q2.21 IF YOU HAVE EVER HAD CHILDREN. IF YOU HAVE NEVER HAD CHILDREN, PLEASE GO TO Q2.22.**

**A2.20** Did you work outside the home full-time, part-time or not at all ...

PLEASE TICK ONE BOX ON EACH LINE

| | Worked full-time | Worked part-time | Stayed at home | Does not apply | (Not answered) |
|---|---|---|---|---|---|
| a. [RMARVWRK1] After marrying and before you had children? | % 52.7 | 3.0 | 9.9 | 4.6 | 5.2 |
| b. [RMARVWRK2] And what about when a child was under school age? | % 31.3 | 6.7 | 26.6 | 4.4 | 6.5 |
| c. [RMARVWRK3] After the youngest child started school? | % 28.4 | 12.5 | 15.5 | 12.5 | 6.5 |
| d. [RMARVWRK3] And how about after the children left home? | % 21.2 | 5.2 | 6.8 | 35.1 | 7.2 |

**A2.21** What about your spouse/partner at that time - did he/she work outside the home full-time, part-time or not at all ...

PLEASE TICK ONE BOX ON EACH LINE

| | Worked full-time | Worked part-time | Stayed at home | Does not apply | (Not answered) |
|---|---|---|---|---|---|
| a. [SMARVWRK1] After marrying and before you had children? | % 57.1 | 2.1 | 6.7 | 3.5 | 6.0 |
| b. [SMARVWRK2] And what about when a child was under school age? | % 38.6 | 6.4 | 18.8 | 4.9 | 6.8 |
| c. [SMARVWRK3] After the youngest child started school? | % 33.6 | 9.0 | 11.9 | 14.0 | 7.1 |
| d. [SMARVWRK4] And how about after the children left home? | % 23.1 | 3.1 | 6.2 | 35.3 | 7.8 |

267

## N1

**EVERYONE PLEASE ANSWER**      n = 1315

**A2.22** How much do you agree or disagree ... ?

PLEASE TICK ONE BOX ON EACH LINE

| | Strongly agree | Agree | Neither agree nor disagree | Disagree | Strongly disagree | Can't choose | (Not answered) |
|---|---|---|---|---|---|---|---|
| a. [CHLDARR] ... mothers of young children should not expect employers to make special arrangements to help them combine jobs and childcare | % 4.6 | 25.7 | 18.6 | 33.6 | 12.2 | 4.0 | 1.3 |
| b. [CHLDGOV] ... the government should provide money for childcare, so that mothers of young children can work if they want to | % 17.0 | 45.5 | 13.8 | 16.4 | 3.7 | 2.7 | 0.9 |

**A2.23** Think of a child under 3 years old whose parents both have full-time jobs.

How suitable do you think each of these childcare arrangements would be for the child?

PLEASE TICK ONE BOX ON EACH LINE

| | Very suitable | Somewhat suitable | Not very suitable | Not at all suitable | Can't choose | (Not answered) |
|---|---|---|---|---|---|---|
| a. [CHDCARE1] A state or local authority nursery? | % 28.3 | 37.2 | 14.5 | 6.0 | 6.8 | 7.1 |
| b. [CHDCARE2] A private creche or nursery? | % 37.0 | 39.0 | 9.1 | 3.0 | 5.2 | 6.7 |
| c. [CHDCARE3] A child-minder or babysitter? | % 32.9 | 40.8 | 10.9 | 3.8 | 4.3 | 7.2 |
| d. [CHDCARE4] A neighbour or friend? | % 22.4 | 37.4 | 21.8 | 6.3 | 4.4 | 7.7 |
| e. [CHDCARE5] A relative? | % 48.8 | 30.8 | 8.6 | 2.8 | 3.4 | 5.6 |
| f. [CHDCARE6] A workplace nursery or creche? | % 45.0 | 33.2 | 7.8 | 3.4 | 4.8 | 5.8 |

**A2.24** [PROTRCMX]
Some people think that better relations between Protestants and Catholics in Northern Ireland will only come about through more mixing of the two communities. Others think that better relations will only come about through more separation? Which comes closest to your views ...

PLEASE TICK ONE BOX                                           %

| | |
|---|---|
| ... better relations will come about through more mixing. | 93.8 |
| OR | |
| ... better relations will come about through more separation? | 4.3 |
| (Don't know) | 0.2 |
| (Not answered) | 1.7 |

## NI

**A2.25** And are you in favour of more mixing or more separation in ...

PLEASE TICK **ONE BOX** ON EACH LINE

n=1315

| | | Much more mixing | Bit more mixing | Keep things as they are | Bit more separation | Much more separation | (Not answered) |
|---|---|---|---|---|---|---|---|
| a. | /MIXDPRIM/ ... primary schools? | % 57.5 | 20.3 | 19.8 | 1.1 | 0.4 | 0.9 |
| b. | /MIXDGRAM/ ... secondary and grammar schools? | % 56.9 | 22.9 | 17.2 | 1.1 | 0.3 | 1.6 |
| c. | /MIXDLIV/ ... where people live? | % 48.2 | 30.6 | 16.5 | 1.9 | 0.6 | 2.1 |
| d. | /MIXDWORK/ ... where people work? | % 54.2 | 32.8 | 9.7 | 1.2 | 0.4 | 1.6 |
| e. | /MIXDLEIS/ ... people's leisure or sports activities? | % 59.6 | 27.4 | 9.8 | 1.0 | 0.3 | 1.9 |
| f. | /MIXDMARR/ ... people's marriages? | % 29.7 | 21.5 | 38.1 | 3.9 | 4.5 | 2.2 |

**A2.26** /NISPEND/ Do you think the government should spend more on trying to improve community relations in Northern Ireland, spend less or is spending about right?

PLEASE TICK **ONE BOX ONLY**

| | % |
|---|---|
| Spend much more | 43.4 |
| Spend a bit more | 29.9 |
| Spending is about right | 18.2 |
| Spend a bit less | 1.8 |
| Spend much less | 1.3 |
| Can't choose | 4.9 |
| (Not answered) | 0.5 |

## NI

**A2.27** The U.K. controls the numbers of people from abroad that are allowed to settle in this country. Please say, for each of the groups below, whether you think the U.K. should allow more settlement, less settlement, or about the same amount as now.

PLEASE TICK **ONE BOX** ON EACH LINE

n=663

| | | More settlement | Less settlement | About the same as now | (Not answered) |
|---|---|---|---|---|---|
| a. | /AUSI/MM/ Australians and New Zealanders | % 18.0 | 18.6 | 60.3 | 2.9 |
| b. | /ASIANIMM/ Indians and Pakistanis | % 5.7 | 36.9 | 54.8 | 2.3 |
| c. | /EECIMM/ People from European Community countries | % 15.8 | 23.3 | 57.5 | 3.0 |
| d. | /WIIMM/ West Indians | % 6.0 | 34.4 | 56.4 | 3.0 |
| e. | /EEUROIMM/ People from Eastern Europe | % 13.0 | 28.5 | 55.6 | 2.6 |
| f. | /CHINAIMM/ People from China and Hong Kong | % 7.7 | 31.4 | 58.1 | 2.6 |

**A2.28** /RELCONTL/ Now thinking about the families (husbands, wives, children, parents) of people who have already settled in the U.K., would you say in general that the U.K. should ...

PLEASE TICK **ONE BOX**

| | % |
|---|---|
| ... be stricter in controlling the settlement of close relatives | 35.0 |
| or - be less strict in controlling the settlement of close relatives | 14.4 |
| or - keep the controls about the same as now | 48.6 |
| Don't know | 0.4 |
| (Not answered) | 1.6 |

**A2.29** /SCOBEYLW/ In general, would you say that people should obey the law without exception, or are there exceptional occasions on which people should follow their consciences, even if it means breaking the law?

PLEASE TICK **ONE BOX**

| | % |
|---|---|
| Obey the law without exception | 47.1 |
| Follow conscience on occasions | 43.3 |
| Can't choose | 8.8 |
| (Not answered) | 0.9 |

**A2.30** There are some people whose views are considered extreme by the majority.

First, consider people who support organisations that want to change policy by planting bombs. Do you think such people should be allowed to ...

PLEASE TICK **ONE BOX** ON EACH LINE

| | | Definitely | Probably | Probably not | Definitely not | Can't choose | (Not answered) |
|---|---|---|---|---|---|---|---|
| a. | /REVTEAS1/ ... teach 15 year olds in schools? | % 3.2 | 4.3 | 9.9 | 77.6 | 3.6 | 1.5 |
| b. | /REVINTTV/ ... give interviews on television to put their case? | % 7.2 | 13.8 | 10.7 | 62.7 | 4.5 | 1.2 |
| c. | /REVCAND/ ... stand as candidates in elections? | % 7.9 | 9.3 | 9.7 | 66.6 | 5.3 | 1.2 |

## NI

**A2.31** Second, consider people who believe that whites are racially superior to all other races. Do you think such people should be allowed to ...

n = 663

| | | Definitely | Probably | Probably not | Definitely not | Can't choose | (Not answered) |
|---|---|---|---|---|---|---|---|
| a. | [PRJTEASC] ... teach 15 year olds in schools? | % 3.2 | 10.2 | 22.9 | 56.7 | 6.0 | 1.0 |
| b. | [PRJNTTV] ... give interviews on television to put their case? | % 6.6 | 19.5 | 23.0 | 43.9 | 5.9 | 1.2 |
| c. | [PRJCAND] ... stand as candidates in elections? | % 6.6 | 18.1 | 20.7 | 46.4 | 6.9 | 1.2 |

**A2.32** [JUSTICE] All systems of justice make mistakes, but which do you think is worse ...

PLEASE TICK ONE BOX

%
... to convict an innocent person, 59.0
OR
to let a guilty person go free? 21.9
Can't choose 17.9
(Not answered) 1.2

**A2.33** Suppose the police get an anonymous tip that a man with a long criminal record is planning to break into a warehouse.

Do you think the police should be allowed, without a Court Order ...

PLEASE TICK ONE BOX ON EACH LINE

| | | Definitely | Probably | Probably not | Definitely not | Can't choose | (Not answered) |
|---|---|---|---|---|---|---|---|
| a. | [CRIMIN1] ... to keep the man under surveillance? | % 70.1 | 22.2 | 2.0 | 2.6 | 1.9 | 1.2 |
| b. | [CRIMIN2] ... to tap his telephone? | % 28.8 | 30.8 | 16.7 | 18.7 | 2.9 | 2.1 |
| c. | [CRIMIN3] ... to open his mail? | % 17.8 | 25.7 | 23.6 | 27.4 | 3.5 | 2.1 |
| d. | [CRIMIN4] ... to detain the man overnight for questioning? | % 37.2 | 36.2 | 10.0 | 10.9 | 4.4 | 1.3 |

**A2.34** Now, suppose the tip is about a man *without* a criminal record.

Do you think the police should be allowed, without a Court Order ...

PLEASE TICK ONE BOX ON EACH LINE

| | | Definitely | Probably | Probably not | Definitely not | Can't choose | (Not answered) |
|---|---|---|---|---|---|---|---|
| a. | [NONCRIM1] ... to keep the man under surveillance? | % 39.5 | 33.0 | 11.7 | 12.8 | 1.7 | 1.3 |
| b. | [NONCRIM2] ... to tap his telephone? | % 8.7 | 17.2 | 31.4 | 37.3 | 3.0 | 2.4 |
| c. | [NONCRIM3] ... to open his mail? | % 7.0 | 10.7 | 31.0 | 45.2 | 3.7 | 2.4 |
| d. | [NONCRIM4] ... to detain the man overnight for questioning? | % 15.1 | 24.0 | 25.0 | 30.8 | 3.5 | 1.6 |

## NI

**A2.35** [VIDEODEM] Which of these two statements comes closer to your own view?

PLEASE TICK ONE BOX

n = 663

%
The police should have a right to take video films of people at protests or demonstrations 59.7
OR
People should have a right to *not* be videoed at protests or demonstrations without their consent 28.4
Can't choose 10.7
(Not answered) 1.1

**A2.36** [BANBLAST] Some books or films offend people who have strong religious beliefs. Should books and films that attack religions be prohibited by law or should they be allowed?

PLEASE TICK ONE BOX ONLY

%
Definitely should be prohibited 18.8
Probably should be prohibited 25.0
Probably should be allowed 28.1
Definitely should be allowed 13.5
Can't choose 13.2
(Not answered) 1.4

**A2.37** As long as there is no threat to security, should prisoners be allowed to ...

PLEASE TICK ONE BOX ON EACH LINE

| | | Definitely | Probably | Probably not | Definitely not | Can't choose | (Not answered) |
|---|---|---|---|---|---|---|---|
| a. | [PRISBKS] ... have as many books as they wish to read? | % 50.5 | 38.8 | 3.2 | 4.3 | 2.4 | 0.8 |
| b. | [PRISVIST] ... visit home occasionally, say one weekend a month? | % 11.4 | 27.0 | 22.9 | 33.7 | 3.5 | 1.5 |
| c. | [PRISLONG] ... have their wife or husband occasionally stay overnight with them at the prison? | % 9.7 | 19.1 | 19.8 | 44.7 | 5.1 | 1.5 |
| d. | [PRISJOB] ... earn a little money in prison? | % 23.6 | 45.0 | 10.0 | 16.7 | 2.9 | 1.7 |

**A2.38** [CSSILENT] Suppose a cabinet minister gives false information to the Westminster parliament about an important national issue.

PLEASE TICK ONE BOX

%
Should the law allow civil servants in the minister's department to reveal the correct facts, 77.8
OR
should civil servants be required by law to keep silent? 6.9
Can't choose 14.3
(Not answered) 1.0

N1  14

A2.39 /LAWSAY/
Some say that the courts in the U.K. should have the power to overturn laws made by the Westminster parliament. Others say that parliament should always have the final say. Which comes closest to your view?

n = 663

PLEASE TICK ONE BOX

|  | % |
|---|---|
| The courts should have the power to overturn laws made by parliament, | 41.0 |
| OR parliament should always have the final say? | 33.2 |
| Can't choose | 24.4 |
| (Not answered) | 1.4 |

A2.40 Please tick one box for each statement below to show how much you agree or disagree with it.

PLEASE TICK ONE BOX ON EACH LINE

|  |  | Agree strongly | Agree | Neither agree nor strongly | Disagree | Disagree strongly | (Not answered) |
|---|---|---|---|---|---|---|---|
| a. | /PCGUNS/ On-duty police officers should always carry guns | % 31.3 | 39.7 | 16.7 | 10.0 | 1.5 | 0.9 |
| b. | /LITESENT/ Too many convicted criminals are let off lightly by the courts | % 42.9 | 43.5 | 8.8 | 3.1 | 0.4 | 0.2 |
| c. | /CONFESSN/ A confession made during police questioning and later withdrawn should not on its own be enough to convict someone | % 17.3 | 47.9 | 21.6 | 10.0 | 1.5 | 1.5 |
| d. | /BENIDCRD/ People claiming state benefits should have to carry an identity card to help prevent fraud | % 28.7 | 41.4 | 10.3 | 15.7 | 2.9 | 1.0 |
| e. | /MAGISTRAT/ Once people are made local magistrates they lose touch with ordinary people pretty quickly | % 10.0 | 32.8 | 44.9 | 9.8 | 1.0 | 1.3 |

N1  15

A2.41 And please tick one box for each statement below to show how much you agree or disagree with it.

n = 663

PLEASE TICK ONE BOX ON EACH LINE

|  |  | Agree strongly | Agree | Neither agree nor disagree | Disagree | Disagree strongly | (Not answered) |
|---|---|---|---|---|---|---|---|
| a. | /PCNOSOLC/ The police should be allowed to question suspects for up to a week without letting them see a solicitor | % 3.4 | 8.1 | 10.4 | 51.4 | 25.1 | 1.6 |
| b. | /REFUGEES/ Refugees who are in danger because of their political beliefs should always be welcome in the U.K. | % 5.0 | 28.6 | 36.9 | 25.1 | 2.9 | 1.5 |
| c. | /PCCOMPLN/ Serious complaints against the police should be investigated by an independent body, not by the police themselves | % 36.1 | 50.8 | 8.0 | 3.2 | 0.9 | 1.1 |
| d. | /IDCARDS/ Every adult in the U.K. should have to carry an identity card | % 12.8 | 29.4 | 23.0 | 24.3 | 9.4 | 1.1 |
| e. | /CRIMSLNT/ If someone remains silent under police questioning, it should count against them in court | % 12.8 | 32.8 | 21.6 | 24.8 | 7.0 | 0.9 |
| f. | /NINPRISN/ The prisons contain too many people who ought to be given a lighter punishment | % 3.8 | 19.9 | 31.8 | 37.8 | 5.3 | 1.5 |
| g. | /NOWARRNT/ The police should not need a warrant to search the homes of suspects | % 7.8 | 16.8 | 11.6 | 44.2 | 18.2 | 1.3 |

A2.42 Some say that more decisions should be made by the European Community. Others say that more decisions should be made by individual governments. Do you think decisions about taxes should be made mostly by the European Community or mostly by individual governments?

PLEASE TICK ONE BOX ON EACH LINE

|  |  | Mostly made by the EC | Mostly made by individual governments | Made by both equally | Can't choose | (Not answered) |
|---|---|---|---|---|---|---|
| a. | /ECDEC1/ ... Decisions about taxes? | % 7.8 | 66.5 | 14.5 | 10.0 | 1.2 |
| b. | /ECDEC2/ And what about decisions about controlling pollution? | % 27.6 | 31.1 | 32.2 | 7.1 | 1.9 |
| c. | /ECDEC3/ Decisions about defence? | % 12.6 | 54.1 | 22.8 | 8.3 | 2.2 |
| d. | /ECDEC4/ Decisions about the rights of people at work? | % 19.7 | 43.8 | 27.4 | 7.5 | 1.6 |
| e. | /ECDEC5/ Decisions about immigration? | % 13.2 | 51.2 | 25.0 | 9.2 | 1.5 |

## A2.43 [PROPREP]

How much do you agree or disagree with this statement?

The U.K. should introduce proportional representation for the general elections, so that the number of MPs each party gets matches more closely the number of votes each party gets.

PLEASE TICK **ONE BOX** ONLY

n = 663

| | % |
|---|---|
| Strongly agree | 18.2 |
| Agree | 32.1 |
| Neither agree nor disagree | 20.8 |
| Disagree | 11.1 |
| Strongly disagree | 2.3 |
| Can't choose | 14.2 |
| (Not answered) | 1.2 |

## A2.44

There are many ways people or organisations can protest against a government action they strongly oppose. Please show which you think should be allowed and which should not be allowed by ticking a box on each line.

PLEASE TICK **ONE BOX** ON EACH LINE

**Should it be allowed?**

| | Definitely | Probably | Probably not | Definitely not | Can't choose | (Not answered) |
|---|---|---|---|---|---|---|
| a. [PROTEST1] Organising public meetings to protest against the government | 41.6% | 41.2 | 6.3 | 2.9 | 6.3 | 1.9 |
| b. [PROTEST2] Publishing pamphlets to protest against the government | 38.3% | 40.9 | 8.7 | 3.5 | 6.8 | 1.9 |
| c. [PROTEST3] Organising protest marches and demonstrations | 32.4% | 33.0 | 17.4 | 9.0 | 6.4 | 1.9 |
| d. [PROTEST4] Occupying a government office and stopping work there for several days | 3.8% | 9.4 | 33.0 | 46.1 | 5.5 | 2.2 |
| e. [PROTEST5] Seriously damaging government buildings | 1.1% | 1.2 | 10.7 | 82.4 | 2.8 | 1.8 |
| f. [PROTEST6] Organising a nationwide strike of all workers against the government | 9.2% | 21.8 | 21.6 | 39.1 | 6.6 | 1.6 |

## A2.45a [TUPOWER]

Do you think that trade unions in the UK have too much power or too little power?

PLEASE TICK **ONE BOX** ONLY

| | % |
|---|---|
| Far too much power | 5.6 |
| Too much power | 12.4 |
| About the right amount of power | 41.7 |
| Too little power | 22.5 |
| Far too little power | 4.9 |
| Can't choose | 11.7 |
| (Not answered) | 1.2 |

## [BUSPOWER]

b. How about business and industry? Do they have too much power or too little power?

PLEASE TICK **ONE BOX** ONLY

n = 663

| | % |
|---|---|
| Far too much power | 9.0 |
| Too much power | 22.1 |
| About the right amount of power | 42.4 |
| Too little power | 13.0 |
| Far too little power | 0.5 |
| Can't choose | 11.7 |
| (Not answered) | 1.3 |

## [GOVPOWER]

c. And what about the government? Does it have too much power or too little power?

PLEASE TICK **ONE BOX** ONLY

| | % |
|---|---|
| Far too much power | 14.9 |
| Too much power | 28.7 |
| About the right amount of power | 41.3 |
| Too little power | 5.4 |
| Far too little power | 0.2 |
| Can't choose | 8.3 |
| (Not answered) | 1.2 |

## 18

**A2.46** Some people say that the U.K. governments nowadays - of whichever party - can actually do very little to change things. Others say they can do quite a bit. Please say whether you think that U.K. governments nowadays can do very little or quite a bit ...

British governments can do:

PLEASE TICK **ONE BOX** ON EACH LINE

n = 663

| | | Very little % | Quite a bit % | (Not answered) % |
|---|---|---|---|---|
| a. /GOVTDOPR/ | ... to keep prices down? % | 38.6 | 59.9 | 1.5 |
| b. /GOVTDOUN/ | ... to reduce unemployment? % | 39.0 | 59.7 | 1.3 |
| c. /GOVTDOSK/ | ... to improve the general standard of living? % | 28.7 | 69.8 | 1.5 |
| d. /GOVTDOSS/ | ... to improve the health and social services? % | 20.9 | 76.9 | 2.0 |
| e. /GOVTDOPV/ | ... to reduce poverty? % | 29.8 | 68.2 | 1.8 |
| f. /GOVTCRM/ | ... to cut crime? % | 36.2 | 62.1 | 1.5 |

**A2.47** Listed below are some institutions. From what you know or have heard about each one, can you say whether, on the whole, you think it is well run or not well run?

PLEASE TICK **ONE BOX** ON EACH LINE

| | | Very well run | Well run | Not very well run | Not at all well run | (Not answered) |
|---|---|---|---|---|---|---|
| a. /NHSRON2/ | The National Health Service % | 4.6 | 38.4 | 43.8 | 11.9 | 1.3 |
| b. /PRESSRN2/ | The press % | 3.2 | 40.5 | 41.6 | 12.5 | 2.2 |
| c. /LGOVRUN2/ | Local government % | 1.5 | 38.4 | 49.8 | 8.0 | 2.2 |
| d. /CSRUN2/ | The civil service % | 4.9 | 54.1 | 33.1 | 4.8 | 2.7 |
| e. /MANUFRN2/ | Manufacturing industry % | 6.7 | 64.5 | 22.4 | 3.2 | 2.7 |
| f. /BANKRUN2/ | Banks % | 18.1 | 63.9 | 12.5 | 3.6 | 1.9 |
| g. /UNIONRN2/ | The trade unions % | 3.3 | 50.8 | 37.1 | 5.6 | 3.0 |
| h. /BBCRUN2/ | The BBC % | 8.3 | 57.7 | 27.3 | 4.7 | 1.9 |
| i. /POLICRN2/ | The police % | 13.4 | 56.3 | 24.1 | 4.3 | 1.6 |
| j. /UNIVRUN/ | Universities % | 15.3 | 69.9 | 11.8 | 0.6 | 2.0 |
| k. /SCHLRUN/ | State schools % | 10.0 | 65.5 | 19.9 | 2.1 | 2.1 |

**A2.48** /VOTEDUTY/ Which of these statements comes closest to your view about general elections?

PLEASE TICK **ONE BOX** ONLY

| | % |
|---|---|
| In a general election : It's not really worth voting | 16.5 |
| People should vote only if they care who wins | 24.7 |
| It is everyone's duty to vote | 57.7 |
| (Not answered) | 1.2 |

## 19

**A2.49** Please show how much you agree or disagree with each of the following statements.

PLEASE TICK **ONE BOX** ON EACH LINE

n = 663

| | | Strongly agree % | Agree % | Neither agree nor disagree % | Disagree % | Strongly disagree % | Can't choose % | (Not answered) % |
|---|---|---|---|---|---|---|---|---|
| a. | I wish it were easier for people like me to get their views across to politicians /APATHY1/ | 24.7 | 54.1 | 15.7 | 1.0 | 0.1 | 3.5 | 0.9 |
| b. | Politicians are in it just for themselves /APATHY2/ | 9.7 | 38.3 | 29.8 | 16.5 | 1.1 | 2.9 | 1.7 |
| c. | Politicians these days are simply not good enough to do the job they have to do /APATHY3/ | 11.3 | 36.8 | 30.2 | 17.6 | 0.5 | 2.4 | 1.2 |
| d. | Even the best politicians cannot have much impact because of the way government works /APATHY4/ | 9.7 | 53.3 | 19.4 | 12.2 | 0.9 | 3.1 | 1.4 |
| e. | It doesn't really matter which party is in power, in the end things go on much the same /APATHY5/ | 11.7 | 52.7 | 11.2 | 17.9 | 3.2 | 1.9 | 1.3 |

**A2.50** Are you in favour of or against the death penalty for ...
PLEASE TICK **ONE BOX** ON EACH LINE

| | | In favour % | Against % | (Don't know) % | (Not answered) % |
|---|---|---|---|---|---|
| a. /CAPPUN1/ | ... murder in the course of a terrorist act? | 56.6 | 40.0 | 0.6 | 2.8 |
| b. /CAPPUN2/ | ... murder of a police officer? | 56.0 | 40.0 | 0.6 | 3.4 |
| c. /CAPPUN3/ | ... other murders? | 49.7 | 46.1 | 0.6 | 3.6 |

**A2.51** Please tick one box for each statement to show how much you agree or disagree with it.

PLEASE TICK **ONE BOX** ON EACH LINE

n = 1315

| | | Strongly agree % | Agree % | Neither agree nor disagree % | Disagree % | Strongly disagree % | (Not answered) % |
|---|---|---|---|---|---|---|---|
| a. /WELFRESP/ | The welfare state makes people nowadays less willing to look after themselves | 8.7 | 37.9 | 20.5 | 29.2 | 2.5 | 1.1 |
| b. /WELFST(G)/ | People receiving social security are made to feel like second class citizens | 9.9 | 39.7 | 22.9 | 25.2 | 1.6 | 0.8 |
| c. /WELFHELP/ | The welfare state encourages people to stop helping each other | 3.0 | 31.1 | 28.6 | 34.3 | 2.1 | 0.9 |
| d. /MOREWELF/ | The government should spend more money on welfare benefits for the poor, even if it leads to higher taxes | 11.4 | 43.8 | 23.8 | 17.8 | 2.3 | 0.9 |
| e. /UNEMPJOB/ | Around here, most unemployed people could find a job if they really wanted one | 6.5 | 28.1 | 20.4 | 36.3 | 7.6 | 1.1 |
| f. /SOCHELP/ | Many people who get social security don't really deserve any help | 3.5 | 22.0 | 24.6 | 40.1 | 8.4 | 1.3 |
| g. /DOLEFIDL/ | Most people on the dole are fiddling in one way or another | 9.4 | 31.4 | 25.7 | 27.9 | 4.8 | 0.8 |
| h. /WELFFEET/ | If welfare benefits weren't so generous, people would learn to stand on their own two feet | 7.2 | 25.1 | 18.9 | 37.3 | 11.0 | 0.6 |

272

## N1

**A2.52** And please tick one box for each of these statements to show how much you agree or disagree with it.

n = 1315

PLEASE TICK **ONE BOX** ON EACH LINE

| | | Agree strongly | Agree | Neither agree nor disagree | Disagree | Disagree strongly | (Not answered) |
|---|---|---|---|---|---|---|---|
| a. | [REDISTRB] Government should redistribute income from the better-off to those who are less well off % | 13.4 | 36.1 | 21.0 | 24.9 | 3.5 | 1.1 |
| b. | [BIGBUSNN] Big business benefits owners at the expense of workers % | 13.7 | 44.5 | 24.0 | 14.7 | 1.3 | 1.6 |
| c. | [WEALTH1] Ordinary people get their fair share of the nation's wealth % | 1.4 | 17.1 | 25.5 | 47.0 | 7.6 | 1.3 |
| d. | [RICHLAW] There is one law for the rich and one for the poor % | 17.8 | 43.8 | 20.4 | 15.4 | 1.8 | 0.9 |
| e. | [INDUST4] Management will always try to get the better of employees if it gets the chance % | 17.1 | 45.6 | 21.1 | 14.2 | 0.8 | 1.1 |

**A2.53** And please tick one box for each of these statements to show how much you agree or disagree with it.

PLEASE TICK **ONE BOX** ON EACH LINE

| | | Agree strongly | Agree | Neither agree nor disagree | Disagree | Disagree strongly | (Not answered) |
|---|---|---|---|---|---|---|---|
| a. | [TRADVALS] Young people today don't have enough respect for traditional values % | 23.9 | 51.6 | 11.6 | 10.6 | 1.1 | 1.2 |
| b. | [STIFSENT] People who break the law should be given stiffer sentences % | 31.3 | 50.9 | 11.5 | 5.0 | 0.2 | 1.1 |
| c. | [DEATHAPP] For some crimes, the death penalty is the most appropriate sentence % | 26.2 | 29.7 | 10.0 | 21.0 | 12.0 | 1.0 |
| d. | [OBEY] Schools should teach children to obey authority % | 31.9 | 55.1 | 8.1 | 3.4 | 0.2 | 1.2 |
| e. | [WRONGLAW] The law should always be obeyed, even if a particular law is wrong % | 9.2 | 30.5 | 26.0 | 29.1 | 4.1 | 1.2 |
| f. | [CENSOR] Censorship of films and magazines is necessary to uphold moral standards % | 30.2 | 44.5 | 12.5 | 9.3 | 2.4 | 1.0 |

## N1

**A2.54a** [QTIME] To help us plan better in future, please tell us about how long it took you to complete this questionnaire.

n = 1315

PLEASE TICK **ONE BOX ONLY**

| | % |
|---|---|
| Less than 15 minutes | 3.5 |
| Between 15 and 20 minutes | 22.9 |
| Between 21 and 30 minutes | 32.4 |
| Between 31 and 45 minutes | 26.5 |
| Between 46 and 60 minutes | 8.4 |
| Over one hour | 4.9 |
| (Don't know) | 0.1 |
| (Not answered) | 1.2 |

b. [QDATE] And on what date did you fill in the questionnaire?

PLEASE WRITE IN  DATE  0  MONTH  1994

## THANK YOU VERY MUCH FOR YOUR HELP

Please keep the completed questionnaire for the interviewer if he or she has arranged to call for it. Otherwise, please post it as soon as possible in the pre-paid addressed envelope provided.

Head Office: 35 NORTHAMPTON SQUARE, LONDON EC1V 0AX
Tel: 0171 250 1866  Fax: 0171 250 1524

Field and DP Office: 100 KINGS ROAD, BRENTWOOD, ESSEX CM14 4LX
Tel: 01277 200600  Fax: 01277 214117

SCPR — SOCIAL & COMMUNITY PLANNING RESEARCH

**B**

P.1345/NI

## NORTHERN IRELAND SOCIAL ATTITUDES 1994

Spring 1994

### SELF-COMPLETION QUESTIONNAIRE

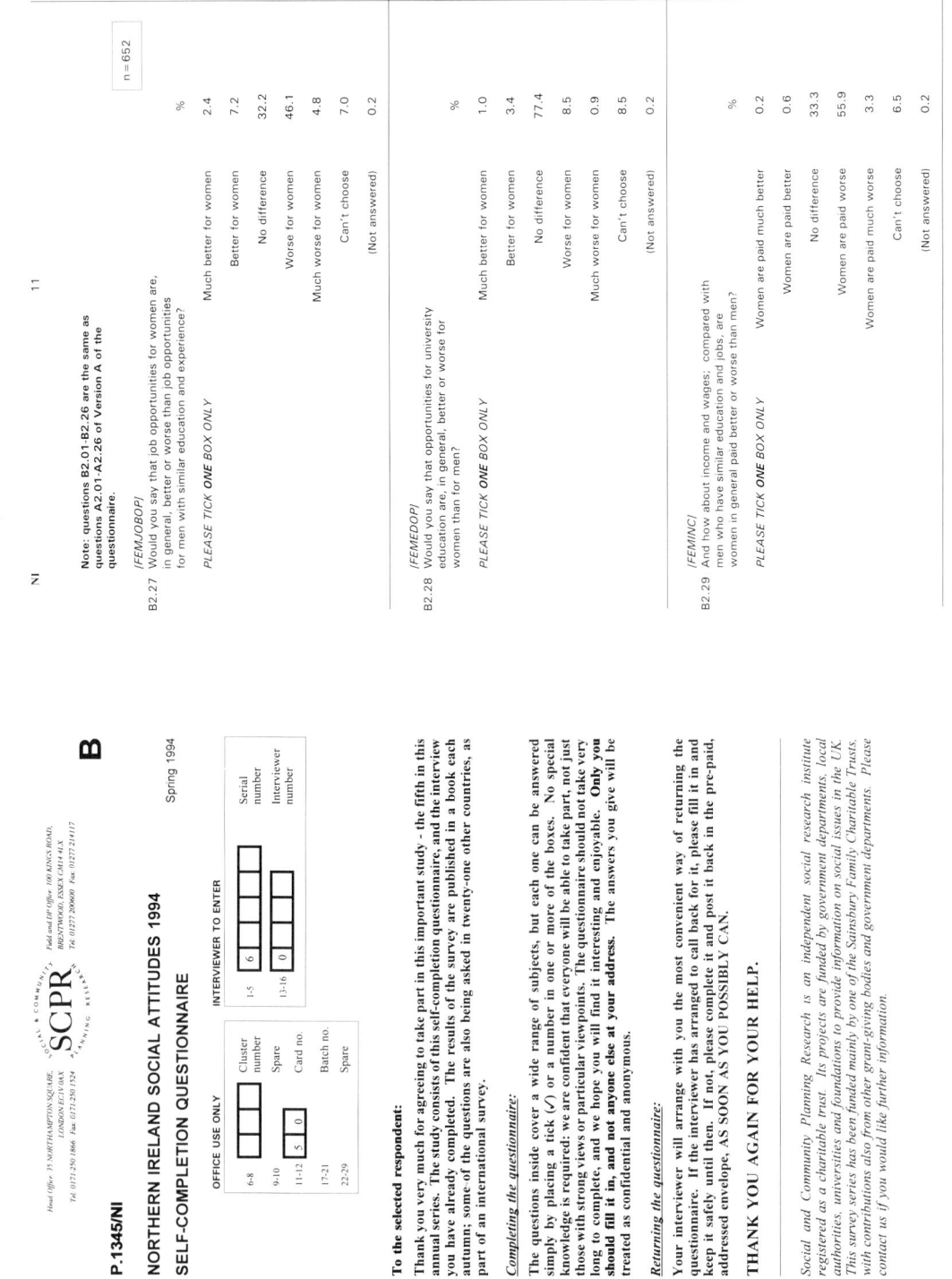

OFFICE USE ONLY

| 6-8 | Cluster number |
| 9-10 | Spare |
| 11-12 | Card no. |
| 17-21 | Batch no. |
| 22-29 | Spare |

INTERVIEWER TO ENTER

| 1-5 | Serial number |
| 13-16 | Interviewer number |

**To the selected respondent:**

Thank you very much for agreeing to take part in this important study - the fifth in this annual series. The study consists of this self-completion questionnaire, and the interview you have already completed. The results of the survey are published in a book each autumn; some of the questions are also being asked in twenty-one other countries, as part of an international survey.

*Completing the questionnaire:*

The questions inside cover a wide range of subjects, but each one can be answered simply by placing a tick (✓) or a number in one or more of the boxes. No special knowledge is required: we are confident that everyone will be able to take part, not just those with strong views or particular viewpoints. The questionnaire should not take very long to complete, and we hope you will find it interesting and enjoyable. **Only you should fill it in, and not anyone else at your address.** The answers you give will be treated as confidential and anonymous.

*Returning the questionnaire:*

Your interviewer will arrange with you the most convenient way of returning the questionnaire. If the interviewer has arranged to call back for it, please fill it in and keep it safely until then. If not, please complete it and post it back in the pre-paid, addressed envelope, **AS SOON AS YOU POSSIBLY CAN.**

### THANK YOU AGAIN FOR YOUR HELP.

*Social and Community Planning Research is an independent social research institute registered as a charitable trust. Its projects are funded by government departments, local authorities, universities and foundations to provide information on social issues in the UK. This survey series has been funded mainly by one of the Sainsbury Family Charitable Trusts, with contributions also from other grant-giving bodies and government departments. Please contact us if you would like further information.*

---

NI

11

Note: questions B2.01-B2.26 are the same as questions A2.01-A2.26 of Version A of the questionnaire.

n = 652

[FEM/JOBOP]
B2.27 Would you say that job opportunities for women are, in general, better or worse than job opportunities for men with similar education and experience?

PLEASE TICK **ONE BOX ONLY**

|  | % |
|---|---|
| Much better for women | 2.4 |
| Better for women | 7.2 |
| No difference | 32.2 |
| Worse for women | 46.1 |
| Much worse for women | 4.8 |
| Can't choose | 7.0 |
| (Not answered) | 0.2 |

[FEMEDOP]
B2.28 Would you say that opportunities for university education are, in general, better or worse for women than for men?

PLEASE TICK **ONE BOX ONLY**

|  | % |
|---|---|
| Much better for women | 1.0 |
| Better for women | 3.4 |
| No difference | 77.4 |
| Worse for women | 8.5 |
| Much worse for women | 0.9 |
| Can't choose | 8.5 |
| (Not answered) | 0.2 |

[FEMINC]
B2.29 And how about income and wages; compared with men who have similar education and jobs, are women in general paid better or worse than men?

PLEASE TICK **ONE BOX ONLY**

|  | % |
|---|---|
| Women are paid much better | 0.2 |
| Women are paid better | 0.6 |
| No difference | 33.3 |
| Women are paid worse | 55.9 |
| Women are paid much worse | 3.3 |
| Can't choose | 6.5 |
| (Not answered) | 0.2 |

NI

## 12

**B2.30** *[FEMPROM]*
And would you say that promotion opportunities for women are, in general, better or worse than promotion opportunities for men with similar education and experience?

n=652

PLEASE TICK **ONE BOX** ONLY

| | % |
|---|---|
| Much better for women | 0.6 |
| Better for women | 3.1 |
| No difference | 30.3 |
| Worse for women | 52.2 |
| Much worse for women | 7.0 |
| Can't choose | 6.6 |
| (Not answered) | 0.2 |

**B2.31** Please tick one box for each statement below to show how much you agree or disagree with it.

PLEASE TICK **ONE BOX** ON EACH LINE

| | | Strongly agree | Agree | Neither agree nor disagree | Disagree | Strongly disagree | Can't choose | (Not answered) |
|---|---|---|---|---|---|---|---|---|
| a. | *[WWHAPPI]* A woman and her family will all be happier if she goes out to work | % 1.4 | 14.4 | 39.4 | 35.8 | 4.0 | 4.2 | 0.9 |
| b. | *[WOMWKKID]* Women shouldn't try to combine a career and children | % 2.4 | 18.6 | 20.7 | 46.8 | 7.8 | 3.6 | 0.2 |
| c. | *[FEMHOME]* In times of high unemployment, married women should stay at home | % 4.3 | 17.1 | 18.1 | 43.7 | 13.8 | 2.7 | 0.3 |
| d. | *[WOMWKGD]* If the children are well looked after, it's good for women to work | % 12.8 | 62.4 | 14.3 | 7.8 | 0.7 | 1.6 | 0.4 |
| e. | *[MWEXTRAS]* Most married women work only to earn money for extras, rather than because they need the money | % 3.9 | 28.7 | 13.1 | 41.4 | 10.9 | 1.9 | 0.2 |
| f. | *[WOMSUFFR]* If a woman takes several years off to look after her children, it's only fair her career should suffer | % 2.9 | 16.8 | 19.7 | 46.9 | 9.7 | 3.7 | 0.3 |
| g. | *[WOMRIGHT]* Married women have a right to work if they want to, whatever their family situation | % 23.3 | 54.9 | 10.9 | 6.8 | 0.6 | 3.2 | 0.2 |

NI

## 13

**B2.32** For each of the jobs below, please tick a box to show whether you think the job is particularly suitable for men only, particularly suitable for women only, or suitable for both men and women equally.

n=652

PLEASE TICK **ONE BOX** ON EACH LINE

| | | Particularly suitable for men % | Particularly suitable for women % | Suitable for both equally % | (Not answered) % |
|---|---|---|---|---|---|
| a. | *[JOBMF1]* Social worker | 0.4 | 20.4 | 78.4 | 0.9 |
| b. | *[JOBMF2]* Police officer | 39.7 | 0.1 | 59.6 | 0.6 |
| c. | *[JOBM73]* Secretary | 1.4 | 56.9 | 41.0 | 0.6 |
| d. | *[JOBM74]* Car mechanic | 69.5 | 0.9 | 28.6 | 0.9 |
| e. | *[JOBM75]* Nurse | 0.2 | 37.3 | 61.8 | 0.7 |
| f. | *[JOBM76]* Bank manager | 23.0 | 0.5 | 75.9 | 0.6 |
| g. | *[JOBM79]* Family doctor/GP | 5.6 | 1.2 | 92.8 | 0.4 |
| h. | *[JOBM7111]* Member of Parliament | 12.2 | 0.4 | 86.9 | 0.6 |
| i. | *[JOBM712]* Director of an international company | 26.5 | 0.2 | 72.7 | 0.6 |
| j. | *[JOBM713]* Airline pilot | 54.8 | - | 44.4 | 0.8 |
| k. | *[JOBM714]* Local councillor | 9.7 | 0.6 | 88.9 | 0.8 |

**B2.33** Listed below are various areas of government spending. Please show whether you would like to see more or less government spending in each area.

Remember that if you say "much more", it might require a tax increase to pay for it.

PLEASE TICK **ONE BOX** ON EACH LINE

| | | Spend much more | Spend more | Spend the same as now | Spend less | Spend much less | Can't choose | (Not answered) |
|---|---|---|---|---|---|---|---|---|
| a. | *[GUSPEND1]* The environment | % 9.7 | 39.3 | 41.2 | 4.6 | 0.2 | 2.0 | 2.8 |
| b. | *[GUSPEND2]* Health | % 44.9 | 47.1 | 7.1 | 0.6 | - | 0.2 | 0.2 |
| c. | *[GUSPEND3]* The police and law enforcement | % 16.3 | 34.0 | 39.6 | 7.0 | 1.1 | 0.8 | 1.3 |
| d. | *[GUSPEND4]* Education | % 30.9 | 50.6 | 16.0 | 0.9 | 0.1 | 0.4 | 1.1 |
| e. | *[GUSPEND5]* The military and defence | % 6.4 | 15.3 | 41.5 | 24.0 | 9.4 | 2.0 | 1.3 |
| f. | *[GUSPEND6]* Old age pensions | % 42.8 | 47.2 | 9.1 | 0.2 | - | 0.2 | 0.4 |
| g. | *[GUSPEND7]* Unemployment benefits | % 18.1 | 36.1 | 32.7 | 9.0 | 1.4 | 1.8 | 0.9 |
| h. | *[GUSPEND8]* Culture and the arts | % 1.5 | 8.1 | 44.8 | 27.4 | 13.4 | 3.8 | 1.0 |

## 14

**B2.34a** *|POWER1|* Which of these three possible solutions to the U.K.'s electricity needs would you favour most?

n = 652

*PLEASE TICK ONE BOX ONLY*

| | % |
|---|---|
| We should make do with the power stations we have already | 63.7 |
| We should build more gas, oil or coal power stations | 28.7 |
| We should build more nuclear power stations | 6.5 |
| (Not answered) | 0.6 |

b. *|POWER2|* If we did make do with the power stations we have already, do you think ….

*PLEASE TICK ONE BOX*

| | % |
|---|---|
| … they would produce enough electricity for the U.K.'s future needs, **OR** | 41.9 |
| … that homes, businesses and industry would be forced to cut down on how much electricity they use? | 29.3 |
| Can't choose | 27.8 |
| (Not answered) | 0.9 |

c. *|NUCPOWER|* As far as nuclear power stations are concerned, which of these statements comes closest to your own feelings?

*PLEASE TICK ONE BOX ONLY*

| | % |
|---|---|
| They create very serious risks for the future | 53.3 |
| They create quite serious risks for the future | 30.0 |
| They create only slight risks for the future | 11.3 |
| They create hardly any risks for the future | 3.8 |
| (Not answered) | 0.7 |

## 15

**B2.35a** *|DAMAGE|* Which one of these two statements comes closest to your own views?

n = 652

*PLEASE TICK ONE BOX*

| | % |
|---|---|
| Industry should be prevented from causing damage to the countryside, even if this sometimes leads to higher prices **OR** | 81.9 |
| Industry should keep prices down, even if this sometimes causes damage to the countryside | 16.4 |
| (Not answered) | 1.3 |

b. *|CTRYJOBS|* And which of these two statements comes closest to your own views?

*PLEASE TICK ONE BOX*

| | % |
|---|---|
| The countryside should be protected from development, even if this sometimes leads to fewer new jobs **OR** | 61.0 |
| New jobs should be created, even if this sometimes causes damage to the countryside | 36.9 |
| (Not answered) | 1.3 |

**B2.36** Please tick one box for each statement below to show how much you agree or disagree with it.
*PLEASE TICK ONE BOX ON EACH LINE*

| | Agree strongly | Agree | Neither agree nor disagree | Disagree | Disagree strongly | (Not answered) |
|---|---|---|---|---|---|---|
| a. *|GOVENVIR|* The government should do more to protect the environment, even if it leads to higher taxes | % 7.8 | 39.3 | 33.4 | 16.1 | 1.0 | 2.3 |
| b. *|INDENVIR|* Industry should do more to protect the environment, even if it leads to lower profits and fewer jobs | % 10.8 | 41.3 | 29.8 | 14.9 | 0.5 | 2.7 |
| c. *|PPLENVIR|* Ordinary people should do more to protect the environment, even if it means paying higher prices | % 9.6 | 47.5 | 27.4 | 10.8 | 1.8 | 2.9 |

**B2.37a** *|TOWNTRAN|* Thinking first about towns and cities. If the government had to choose …

*PLEASE TICK ONE BOX*

| | % |
|---|---|
| It should improve roads | 50.4 |
| It should improve public transport | 49.1 |
| (Not answered) | 0.4 |

b. *|CTRYTRAN|* And in country areas, if the government had to choose …

*PLEASE TICK ONE BOX*

| | % |
|---|---|
| It should improve roads | 52.5 |
| It should improve public transport | 46.9 |
| (Not answered) | 0.6 |

NI  16

n = 652

B2.38 Please tick one box on each line to show how much you agree or disagree with each of the following statements.

PLEASE TICK ONE BOX ON EACH LINE

| | Agree strongly | Agree | Neither agree nor disagree | Disagree | Disagree strongly | (Not answered) |
|---|---|---|---|---|---|---|
| a. [HOUSBUIL] New housing should be built in cities, towns and villages rather than in the countryside | % 15.4 | 48.2 | 21.4 | 13.4 | 0.9 | 0.6 |
| b. [KEEPBELT] It is more important to keep green-belt areas than to build new homes there | % 17.1 | 45.5 | 20.5 | 15.5 | 0.5 | 0.9 |
| c. [PLANLAWS] Planning laws should be relaxed so that people who want to live in the countryside may do so | % 8.9 | 40.2 | 21.5 | 23.5 | 4.9 | 1.0 |
| d. [FARMRSAY] Compared with other users of the countryside, farmers have too much say | % 5.0 | 25.7 | 35.9 | 29.0 | 3.3 | 0.9 |
| e. [LESSVIST] The beauty of the countryside depends on stopping too many people from visiting it | % 1.4 | 19.9 | 27.2 | 47.7 | 2.8 | 0.9 |
| f. [CNTRPED] People should worry less about protecting the countryside, and more about those who have to make their living there | % 2.8 | 23.0 | 32.2 | 38.0 | 3.0 | 1.0 |
| g. [CBTROJO] Some parts of the countryside are now so popular that it's no longer a pleasure to visit them | % 3.7 | 43.1 | 25.8 | 24.9 | 1.2 | 1.2 |
| h. [CARALLOW] People should be allowed to use their cars as much as they like, even if it causes damage to the environment | % 3.1 | 20.0 | 30.8 | 36.6 | 8.3 | 1.1 |

B2.39 Here are some statements about the countryside. Please tick one box for each to show whether you agree or disagree with it.

PLEASE TICK ONE BOX ON EACH LINE

| | Agree strongly | Agree | Neither agree nor disagree | Disagree | Disagree strongly | (Not answered) |
|---|---|---|---|---|---|---|
| a. [COUNTRY1] Modern methods of farming have caused damage to the countryside | % 12.9 | 54.6 | 29.3 | 1.2 | | 1.3 |
| b. [COUNTRY2] If farmers have to choose between producing more food and looking after the countryside, they should produce more food | % 2.8 | 43.1 | 48.3 | 3.8 | | 1.5 |
| c. [COUNTRY3] All things considered, farmers do a good job in looking after the countryside | % 5.1 | 73.6 | 18.1 | 1.7 | | 1.3 |
| d. [COUNTRY4] Government should withhold some subsidies from farmers and use them to protect the countryside, even if this leads to higher prices | % 4.7 | 39.8 | 49.2 | 3.9 | | 1.7 |

NI  17

n = 652

B2.40 [FARMERS] Which of these two statements comes closest to your own views?

PLEASE TICK ONE BOX

| | % |
|---|---|
| Looking after the countryside is too important to be left to farmers - government authorities should have more control over what's done and built on farms | 40.4 |
| OR | |
| Farmers know how important it is to look after the countryside - there are enough controls, and farmers should be left to decide what's done on farms | 40.5 |
| Can't choose | 18.3 |
| (Not answered) | 0.8 |

B2.41 [MEMBENV] Are you a member of any group whose main aim is to preserve or protect the environment?

PLEASE TICK ONE BOX

| | % |
|---|---|
| Yes | 3.7 |
| No | 95.4 |
| (Not answered) | 0.9 |

B2.42 In the last five years, have you …

PLEASE TICK ONE BOX ON EACH LINE

| | Yes, I have % | No, I have not % | (Not answered) % |
|---|---|---|---|
| a. [PETITENV] … signed a petition about an environmental issue, | 31.1 | 65.0 | 3.9 |
| b. [MONEYENV] … given money to an environmental group, | 20.3 | 71.1 | 8.6 |
| c. [DEMOENV] … taken part in a protest or demonstration about an environmental issue? | 3.2 | 86.9 | 9.9 |

B2.43a [SINGMUM1] Thinking about a single mother with a child under school age. Which one of these statements comes closest to your own view?

PLEASE TICK ONE BOX ONLY

| | % |
|---|---|
| She has a special duty to go out to work to support her child | 10.1 |
| She has a special duty to stay at home to look after her child | 20.0 |
| She should do as she chooses, like everyone else | 60.7 |
| Can't choose | 9.0 |
| (Not answered) | 0.2 |

b. [SINGMUM2] Suppose this single mother did get a part-time job. How much do you agree or disagree that the government should provide money to help with child-care?

PLEASE TICK ONE BOX ONLY

| | % |
|---|---|
| Agree strongly | 27.0 |
| Agree | 45.7 |
| Neither agree nor disagree | 12.0 |
| Disagree | 8.5 |
| Disagree strongly | 1.2 |
| Can't choose | 5.4 |
| (Not answered) | 0.2 |

NI

**B2.44** *[SMUMSCH1]*
And what about when the child reaches school age? Which one of these statements comes closest to your view about what the single mother should do?

PLEASE TICK **ONE** BOX ONLY

n=652
%
She has a special duty to go out to work to support her child  21.5
She has a special duty to stay at home to look after her child  9.4
She should do as she chooses, like everyone else  60.5
Can't choose  8.5
(Not answered)  0.2

**B2.45** *[SMUMSCH2]*
Suppose this single mother did go out to work. How much do you agree or disagree that the government should provide money to help with child-care outside school?

PLEASE TICK **ONE** BOX ONLY

%
Agree strongly  15.2
Agree  46.1
Neither agree nor disagree  16.1
Disagree  13.6
Disagree strongly  1.3
Can't choose  7.6
(Not answered)  0.1

**B2.46** Please say how much you agree or disagree that …

PLEASE TICK **ONE** BOX ON EACH LINE

| | Agree strongly | Agree | Neither agree nor disagree | Disagree | Disagree strongly | Can't choose | (Not answered) |
|---|---|---|---|---|---|---|---|
| a. … unmarried mothers who find it hard to cope have only themselves to blame  % | 6.0 | 20.3 | 19.6 | 34.5 | 13.6 | 3.3 | 2.8 |
| b. … unmarried mothers get too little sympathy from society  % | 6.8 | 27.8 | 26.7 | 27.2 | 4.0 | 4.1 | 3.5 |

**B2.47a** *[INMARBABY]*
Imagine an unmarried couple who decide to have a child, but do not marry. What would your general opinion be?

PLEASE TICK **ONE** BOX ONLY

%
It would always be morally wrong  39.9
It would sometimes be wrong  12.2
It would rarely be wrong  3.1
Their decision would have nothing at all to do with morals  33.5
Can't choose  11.1
(Not answered)  0.2

NI

**B2.47b** *[SMUMBABY]*
What if a 30-year-old single woman who does not have a permanent relationship decides to have a child. What would your general opinion be?

PLEASE TICK **ONE** BOX ONLY

n=652
%
It would always be morally wrong  41.2
It would sometimes be wrong  14.2
It would rarely be wrong  3.3
Her decision would have nothing at all to do with morals  29.0
Can't choose  12.0
(Not answered)  0.2

Note questions B2.48-B2.51 are the same as questions A2.51-A2.53 of Version A of the questionnaire.

278

# Subject Index

age-group
  of carers, 53-4, 57-8
  and optimism, 190, 191
Alliance Party, 25, 27, 145, 147, 190
  supporters' constitutional preferences, 38-9, 41
Anglo-Irish Agreement (1985), 25, 151
apathy, 19-20
Asians, 96-7, 98, 100, 101-3, 187
Australia, 105

blacks, 96-7
Britain
  attitudes to EU, 145-7
  attitudes to immigration, 100-1
  childcare, 82-3, 86
  ethnic discrimination, 95, 96-7, 102-5, 108
  gender discrimination, 154, 156-60
    estimation and results, 160-5
  informal care, 51, 56
  perceptions of prejudice, 97-100
  women and work, 70, 74, 77-8, 87
British army, 25, 26, 44, 180
British Social Attitudes (BSA) survey, 70, 193

care *see* informal care
career breaks, 87
Catholics *see also* national identity
  attitudes to equality, 181-7
  constitutional preferences, 26-7, 33-47
  democratic values, 21, 22-3, 29
  and ethnic discrimination, 106-9, 185-7, 191
  labour market equality, 182-5, 190-1
  majority predicted, 46-7
  perceptions of disadvantage, 43-5
  and political efficacy, 17-18
  and political trust, 17-19, 180-1
  satisfaction with health services, 124-5
  support for Union, 26, 41, 45-6
ceasefires, 178, 181, 187-8
ceasefires (1994), 35
censorship, 186

Census of Population (1991), 74
Central Community Relations Unit (CCRU), 193
Central Survey Unit (CSU), 195, 198-9
childcare, 78, 80, 82-6, 90, 154
Chinese, 96-7, 100, 101-3, 187
class differences
  national identity, 143
colonialism
  and ethnic discrimination, 105-9
community background
  and constitutional preferences, 36
community relations, 178-91
  attitudes to equality, 181-7
  future of NI, 180-1
  optimism and pessimism, 187-91
confederation, 24
Constitutional Convention (1975), 13
constitutional options
  Catholic/Protestant preferences, 33-47
  and democratic values, 24-8
  preferences
    change over time, 34-5
    community background, 36
    national and constitutional identity, 36-8, 40-1
    party support, 38-41
    perceptions of disadvantage, 43-5
    socio-economic and demographic influences, 41-3
  views on future of NI, 180-1
Continuous Household Survey (CHS), 51, 53, 70
cultural identity, 151

Democratic Unionist Party (DUP), 25, 27, 145
  supporters' constitutional preferences, 38-9, 46
democratic values
  constitutional options and party support, 24-8
  and democratic process, 14-15
  democratic types, 19-22
  identifying democratic citizens, 22-4

public support for, 13-29
  religious and national differences, 15-19
demography, 41-3, 46-7
direct rule, 13, 28
disability, 49, 58, 125
disadvantage, perceptions of
  and constitutional preferences, 43-5
Downing Street Declaration (1993), 35, 151, 181, 187

Eastern Europe, 28
Eastern Health and Social Services Board, 116, 125
education, 153, 158-9, 162, 163-4
  and constitutional preferences, 43
  and democratic values, 24
employment
  attitudes to, 76-9
  of carers, 54-5
  equality in, 182-5, 189-91
  gender discrimination, 153-68
  occupation and industrial segregation, 72-6
  of women see women, employment of
  working arrangements, 86-8
England, 16, 18, 19
  democratic types, 20-2
Equal Opportunities Commission, 71
equality of opportunity, 80-2
  attitudes to, 178, 181-7
ethnic discrimination, 185-7, 191
  anti-immigration feeling, 100-1
  attitudes to integration, 101-3
  colonial relationships, 105-9
  against Irish, 95-7
  legislation, 103-5
  in NI, 97
  perceptions of, 97-100
European Union
  attitudes to, 145-7, 149

Fair Employment Act (1989), 179, 182, 185
Fair Employment Commission (FEC), 182

gender
  of carers, 53-4, 57, 61
  and constitutional preferences, 42-3
  and employment discrimination, 153-68
  equality, 81-2
  and labour market, 72

gender discrimination
  data and choice of variables, 156-60
  estimation and results, 160-5
  model, 155-6
General Household Survey (GHS), 51, 56
Goldthorpe schema, 41-2
*Growing Older* (White Paper), 50

health
  of carers, 54
health services *see also* informal care
  satisfaction with, 112-31
    data used, 116-18
    dentists, 129
    discussion, 119-23
    GP services, 125-6
    inpatient services, 126-7
    level of satisfaction, 114-16
    multivariate analysis, 116
    outpatient services, 127-8
    overall services, 123-5
    policy implications, 129-31
    results, 118-19
homophobia, 81-2, 186
housing, 125

identity *see* national identity
independence, 24
infant mortality, 112
informal care, 49-68
  attitudes to, 61-5
  direction and nature of, 59-60
  future of, 65-7
  means testing, 65, 67
  need for, 58-9
  sources of support, 60-1
  variations in responsibilities, 56-8
  volume of, 52-5
integration, attitudes to, 101-3
International Social Survey Programme (ISSP), 154
Italy, 28

job-sharing, 87

Labour Force Survey (LFS), 70, 72
labour market
  equality in, 182-5, 189-90
  'flexible workforce', 71, 87, 90
  gender discrimination, 153-68

occupation and industrial segregation, 72-6
reasons for work, 76-8
relative pay, 79-80
women in, 71, 72
legislation
  equality, 185
  ethnic minorities, 103-5, 179, 185-7
  gender discrimination, 153
long-term illness, 125

marital status
  of carers, 54
modernisation, 16

National Health Service (NHS), 51, 65 *see also* health services
  in NI, 112-14
national identity, 45-6, 140-51, 178, 179
  and attitudes to EU, 145-7, 149
  characteristics of those choosing, 143, 146-7
  and constitutional preferences, 36-8, 40-1
  democratic values, 15-19
  and ethnic discrimination, 106-9
  pattern of stability, 150-1
  and political allegiance, 143-5
  and religion, 141-3
nationalism
  and national identity, 143-5, 147
  Protestant/Catholic support, 39
Nationalist Party, 25
Northern Health and Social Services Board, 116, 125
Northern Ireland Assembly (1973), 13, 24
Northern Ireland Assembly (1982), 13
Northern Ireland Executive (1974), 24, 28, 29
Northern Ireland Labour Party (NILP), 25
Northern Ireland (NI)
  constitutional options, 24-8
  democratic types, 20-2
  ethnic minorities in, 97
  future of, 180-1, 187-91
  group with 'no religion', 149-50
Northern Ireland Parliament, 29
Northern Ireland Social Attitudes (NISA) survey, 16, 33, 43
  analysis variables, 201-2
  background to, 193-4
  change over time, 34-5

content of questionnaire, 194-5
data processing and coding, 201
fieldwork, 198-200
format of, 9-11
representativeness of sample, 203
sample, 195-6
sample design and selection, 196-7
sampling errors, 202-3
self-completion questionnaire, 200-1
technical details, 193-208
using of data, 208-9
weighting of sample, 197-8
Nuffield Foundation, 193

occupation
  and democratic values, 24
Official Unionist Party (OUP), 25, 27-8, 145
  supporters' constitutional preferences, 38-9, 41, 46
Operation 2000, 70

Paisley, Ian, 25
party allegiance, 25-8
  and constitutional preferences, 38-41
  and democratic values, 24-8
  and national identity, 143-5
  and optimism, 190
Patient's Charter, 116, 118, 129-30
pay, levels of, 153, 157-8, 162
Peace People, 141
Policy Planning and Research Unit (PPRU), 193, 198
political efficacy, 14-15
  democratic citizens, 22-4
  and democratic values, 25-6
  support for, 16-18
political parties *see* party allegiance
political socialisation, 16
political trust, 15, 180-1
  democratic citizens, 22-4
  and democratic values, 26-7
  support for, 18-19
Postcode Address File, 195
Protestants *see also* national identity
  attitudes to equality, 181-7
  and constitutional options, 25-7
  constitutional preferences, 33-47
  democratic citizens, 22-3
  democratic types, 21
  ethnic discrimination, 106-9, 185-7, 191

281

labour market equality, 182-5, 190-1
perceptions of disadvantage, 43-5
and political efficacy, 17-18
and political trust, 17-19, 180-1
Provisional IRA, 25

racial prejudice *see* ethnic discrimination
Rates Collection Agency, 195
religion
and constitutional preferences, 33-47
and democratic types, 21
and democratic values, 13-14, 15-19
and employment, 184-5
and national identity, 141-3
'race relations', 96-7
respondents with 'no religion', 149-50
repartition, 24
Republic of Ireland, 16, 25, 157, 166
Russia, 28, 29

Scotland, 16, 18, 19, 20-2
sectarianism, 13, 96-7, 140, 147, 150
security forces, impartiality of, 44
Sinn Fein, 25, 27, 145
supporters' constitutional preferences, 38-9, 41
Social and Community Planning Research (SCPR), 193, 198
social class
of carers, 54
Social Democratic and Labour Party (SDLP), 25, 27, 29, 145
supporters' constitutional preferences, 38-9, 41, 46
social mobility, 44-5
socio-economic influences
and constitutional preferences, 41-3
South Africa, 95
Southern Health and Social Services Board, 116, 123, 125
Stormont, 29

trade unions, 80, 159, 162, 163
women in, 88-9
travellers, 97, 105, 108-9, 186, 187

Ulster Defence Association (UDA), 141
Ulster Volunteer Force (UVF), 141
unemployment, 80, 125
unionism
Catholic support, 26, 41, 45-6
and national identity, 143-5, 147
united Ireland, 24, 149, 180
Catholic/Protestant preferences, 33-47
Catholic support for, 46-7
Protestant support for, 25-6, 41
United Kingdom, 33
democratic types, 20-2
democratic values, 14, 28
national differences, 15-19
United States, 15, 95, 105

Vanguard Unionist Party, 25

Wales, 16, 18, 19
democratic types, 20-2
Western Health and Social Services Board, 116, 125
women *see also* informal care
employment of, 70-90
attitudes to work, 76-9
childcare, 82-6
equality of opportunity, 80-2
gender discrimination, 153-68
part-time, 71, 72, 75, 77-8
pay, 79-80
reasons for working, 76-8
segregation of, 74-6
and trade unions, 88-9
views of future, 80
working arrangements, 86-8
Women's Working Lives Survey, 74, 82